IN
PURSUIT OF
RELEVANCE

IN
PURSUIT OF
RELEVANCE

Herbert J. Muller

INDIANA UNIVERSITY PRESS

Bloomington / London

Published in Canada by Fitzhenry & Whiteside Limited, Don Mills, Ontario

Library of Congress catalog card number: 70-163517

ISBN: 0-253-14190-7

Manufactured in the United States of America

To the memory of James A. Work

CONTENTS

P R E F A C E

AMONG THE CONVENIENT DEVICES OF PROFESSIONAL WRITERS is an excuse for reprinting a collection of miscellaneous essays, commonly under a title that suggests a central theme. As commonly the alleged theme seems too much like an excuse even when it gives the collection a measure of unity, for it is too patently an afterthought. This book may suggest the popular device because its chapters amount to separate essays that could be published independently. It differs from most collections, however, because none of the essays have been previously published as they stand, but in particular because it grew out of a quest for a theme. Long accustomed to being absorbed in big projects, I was for some time at a loss for one—toying with ideas that didn't work out, starting articles that I dropped after a few pages, completing several that I was no more satisfied with. At length it dawned on me that underlying the scatter of my abortive efforts there was indeed a common theme, an idea for a project big enough to keep me going for a long time. This was the question of "relevance."

I put the word in quotation marks because the student unrest that has made it a catchword on the campus, then a cliché in intellectual circles, has hardly given it a definite meaning that even students can agree upon. It points to their dissatisfaction with their education, but not at all to a clear, consistent, or uniform idea of just what kind of education they would consider "relevant." It also points to the reasons why I am offering a series of exploratory essays instead of a formal treatise with a beginning, a middle, and an end. The revolt of the students was what got me seriously concerned about the question of the relevance of their education to their interests and their needs, but then it made me more aware of how fluid, complicated, deeply troublesome a question it is in our extraordinary age.

Thus with the commonplace that we live in a rapidly changing society, and the corollary that our curriculum and educational policies need to be drastically overhauled in order to prepare students for life in such a society. Granted the need of change, we of course cannot simply scrap our traditional subject matter, nor can we aim to prepare students just for life "today," an evanescent present that came out of the past and in a moment will recede into it. Our fast changing society remains a product of the past, much of life will go on in much the same way, students at large still have the same basic interests and needs as the last generation of students, and the traditional pursuit of truth, beauty, and goodness is as relevant as ever. Fundamentals become more important just because the claims of the present have become so insistent, for the changes involve much that is questionable, as well as much superficial or ephemeral fashion. No effort is more relevant today than the effort to maintain standards of excellence and principles of order—intellectual, moral, esthetic.

Yet the basic demand of the dissatisfied students is quite legitimate. Change indeed remains the essential key to life today—continuous change on a scale and at a pace strictly unprecedented. It culminated in the 'sixties, by common consent the most revolutionary decade in our history as a nation. To me no change was more significant than the student revolt, which very few if any observers anticipated at the beginning of the decade, any more than I did. While its immediate cause was the war in Vietnam, it soon began to center on the role of the universities, which are providing much more direct service for society than ever before—a service clearly relevant to the interests of business and government, but much less so to either the personal needs of students or the needs of America as they saw them. As the decade ended, all the speculation about what the 'seventies would be like only underscored the fundamental problem. We cannot be sure what they will be like, needless to say, any more than can all the thinkers who are attempting something like scientific forecasts about what our society will be like in the year 2000. Because of the terrific drive of science and technology the future is at once more predictable and more unpredictable than ever before: predictable in that we can confidently anticipate many technological innovations, unpredictable in that we cannot anticipate their social and cultural consequences, not to mention what will be done about the many serious problems now on our hands. Quite deliberately we have to prepare students for life in a future about which the only certainty is that if there is an indefinite future—something we can no longer take for granted—it will be still more different from the past than life now is.

In this uncertainty we might take a clue from science. Here all the current theoretical answers are due to be modified when not superseded; the important thing is to keep asking the right questions, and also to keep in mind that the current questions may not be the right ones. Henceforth, at any rate, I shall speak of relevance without quotation marks, but with the understanding that it is a questionable term, and in the hope of asking the right kind of questions about it. And I shall deal with education in the broadest sense, as not merely the formal training of students but a process that all thoughtful people are engaged in throughout their lives, especially in our revolutionary age, when the idea that an education is "completed" by the award of a college degree is simply foolish. All major interests and activities involve traditional beliefs and practices, and so raise questions about how relevant these still are to the needs of today and tomorrow. It is easy to point out obsolete ideas in much popular thought, for example the slogans about free private enterprise, the virtues of competition, and the sacred rights of private property, which give a hopelessly inadequate idea of an economy now dominated by giant corporations, many of them working for and with the government. But it is not so easy for intellectuals or would-be educators to reconsider thoroughly their own cherished interests, practices, and beliefs. They too share in the great need of today, which is not merely education but re-education.

Accordingly I began by trying to ask searching questions about my own basic attitudes: specifically as a teacher of the humanities, an erstwhile literary critic, a non-professional historian, and a student of modern science and technology; more broadly as a naturalist, a pragmatist, a democrat, and a liberal, or a representative of a characteristic American faith. In so doing I have reconsidered several of my works, since I have been given to ranging widely and focusing on what I thought was the relevance of my subject to contemporary life, and I have also reconsidered a few works that influenced the education of my generation—works that I long considered "modern," but that young people today may relegate to an academic past as of merely historical interest. I have kept an eye on these young people, who are too often patronized as "the kids" when not attacked as "bums," if only because they got me started on this reappraisal, but primarily because of the American crisis. It is the most dangerous one in our history in that it is not a single crisis, like the Civil War or the Great Depression, but a whole set of crises—the revulsion against the war in Indochina, the frightening power of the Pentagon, the danger of a catastrophic thermonuclear war, the grave problems of the environment, the bankruptcy of the metropolis, the revolt of the Negroes, the revolt on the campus, the intense public hostility to the students—which have deeply split the country, undermined faith in its institutions, and badly shaken too the traditional faith in the promise of American life. For the first time in our history the youth in particular see no such promise. As George Wald remarked, "What we are up against is a generation that is by no means sure it has a future."

I would like to think that I am writing to as well as for the aroused youth, but about this have some doubts. They might feel like Thoreau: "If I knew for a certainty that a man was coming to my house with the conscious design of doing me good, I should run for my life." Simply using the phrase "young people" makes it difficult not to sound patronizing. (A possible substitute, "young adults," strike me as awkward.) Anyway they have reason to feel weary of all the advice they are getting these days, however well-meaning. So all I should say is that we are engaged in a common enterprise. My concern here is the *pursuit* of relevance, which is comparable to their quest of new values and life-styles more satisfying modes of self-realization and self-expression. For all their apparent certainties, especially about what they object to, they are asking questions and looking for answers, no less because they do not expect—or even want—fixed, final answers. Immediately many of them too might ask themselves more searching questions about their needs, their ends and means, or their quest for the good life.

The first chapter is an amplification of an article, "The 'Relevance' of the 'Humanities'," that appeared in the Winter 1970 issue of *The American Scholar.*

IN

PURSUIT OF

RELEVANCE

I

THE RELEVANCE OF

THE HUMANITIES

1 / The Basic Questions

IN THE UPROAR over the student revolt, conservatives at first insisted
that the militants were only a small minority, most college students were good loyal Americans. Now that demonstrations on the
campus have become more common, and the public has grown more
hostile to students in general as troublemakers, those who sympathize
with the revolt might assure conservatives that the radicals are still a
small minority. Most students are not rebelling against the whole Establishment, political or educational. In particular those headed for
some profession or for the business world—the large majority in America today—still have only incidental complaints about their education.
Thus technical or vocational schools, such as engineering and business
administration, have been little troubled by demands for relevance,
since no subjects are more highly valued than theirs in our kind of
society. Their students, mostly quite content with their prospects, seem
as content with their "practical" training. Many if not most of them can
be counted on to take their place in the great silent majorities of the
future.

Yet the vocal minority of activists have stirred up a much larger and
growing number of students who have become increasingly concerned

3

over the state of both America and its universities. While most concerned over the war in Vietnam, or now Indochina, many are unhappy
about their education too. And one reason is precisely the national emphasis on professional or practical training. They don't want to be mere
trainees, specialists, "one-dimensional" men well-adjusted to a technological society, able and willing to perform the services wanted by
business and government. If often uncertain about what they want to
become, they are thinking more about their personal development as
human beings. Hence their demands for relevance are especially pertinent for teachers of the so-called humanities, which are supposed to
turn out "whole" men, educate them for the full life or the good life.
There has in fact been much soul-searching in the profession, enough to
stir up talk about a "crisis" in the humanities—the most fashionable
state in our revolutionary age.

Now, I should say at once that their condition is not grave enough
to constitute a crisis, and indeed seems to me healthier than it was in
my youth, in part because of all the soul-searching. The humanities
curriculum has been uncommonly flexible over the last generation.
Many more courses have been offered in modern literature, art, philosophy, and history, while studies of non-Western cultures have also
proliferated. The modern has been stressed so much, in fact, that it
has entailed some sacrifice of traditional courses that may be richer,
more helpful in efforts to achieve "wholeness," or to maintain simple
sanity—the sanity badly needed at a time of widespread disorder and
malaise in art and thought. Students who would like to be turned
loose in contemporary culture, allowed to concentrate on doing whatever they think is their thing, only accentuate the need of some
professional discipline if we are to preserve any notions of quality,
coherence, or even basic relevance in the curriculum. The chief business of a university is properly *learning,* in the humanities ideally
learning what is important or essential for a liberal education, but in
any case always with an eye to intellectual development, not merely
to personal interests. Just because I consider the demands for more
relevance essentially legitimate, I would first make some reservations.

Discontented students are typically vague, inconsistent, and sometimes unrealistic about the kind of education universities should offer.
Given their many diverse interests, it would be impossible to design
a curriculum that would satisfy all of them, not to mention all the
rest of the students who want professional training; I take for granted
that there can be no one ideal curriculum. Most unrealistic is the
loudest demand—immediacy, or relevance to burning contemporary

issues. Obviously the whole curriculum cannot be geared to the war in Vietnam, the problems of the black ghettoes, or any other political issues. Efforts to keep it up to date might call for as radical revision in the 'seventies as they would have in the revolutionary 'sixties, and at that might not meet the shifting demands of students. In a society changing so rapidly it now takes only a few years to produce another "generation" of students, with a sufficient "gap" between them and their predecessors. Before the student revolt there was much talk about the "silent generation," and though the revolt inaugurated some changes on the campus that seem certain to last, and may well lead to more troubles, conceivably another silent generation might emerge from weariness with all the turmoil, or from cynicism.

In any case the humanities must continue to discharge their primary responsibility of transmitting our cultural heritage. This traditional role will surely remain relevant, not only because of the richness of this heritage, but because of the need of a basic common culture, for want of which it is no longer possible to be at all certain what a supposedly educated person knows. As surely there is still room in our universities for the many scholars who may be detached from the problems of our day, or the particular interests of aroused students, but who manage to instill the excitements of learning for its own sake, together with an appreciation of the great works of the past. All of us who have had the good fortune of sitting under teachers who communicated their enthusiasm for their subject know that the direct bearing of this subject on contemporary problems mattered little. And the traditional emphasis upon a knowledge of the past is especially pertinent at a time when too many people lack historical sense, in the conceit of modernity fail to appreciate all that we owe to the past, or in effect equate relevance with provinciality. Impatient students may need to ponder the old saying that one who knows only his own time and place cannot hope really to know them. Just because they have a vivid sense of a fluid world they may have a greater need of getting some bearings, dropping an anchor now and then. Altogether, a major aim of a liberal education is to help students to discover what *is* most relevant for the purposes of a lifetime.

Yet the primary point remains that the revolutionary change has given them a lively sense of *dis*continuity, the too frequent irrelevance of traditional beliefs, attitudes, and policies. I have made these reservations only in order to clear the ground for a consideration of their legitimate demands, and then of the troublesome questions they force. For in general it is the best students who are making these demands—the most mature, sensitive, imaginative, and creative; conventional or mediocre students remain content. The demands are also linked with a serious concern about national problems that clearly do deserve the name of crisis. In confronting the fundamental problems of our affluent, commercialized, regimented, technocratic society, the dissident students have at least been asking the right questions about this kind of society. My own experience over forty years confirms the observation of the Cox Commission on the disorders at Columbia, that the present generation of university students is "the best informed, the most intelligent, and the most idealistic this country has ever known." In view of the sorry state of America, and their growing passion to do something about it, the burden of proof is on their teachers.

And so, at last, to begin at the beginning, with fundamental questions about our own concerns. What are these humanities, and why are they supposed to be more humanistic than other subjects? Usually we take for granted that we are responsible teachers, but just what is our responsibility? We are confident too that our subject is relevant to the purposes of a higher education, but what are these purposes? What is the social usefulness of whatever we teach? In a world radically different from the placid academic world in which our subjects grew up? I think we might be grateful to our aroused students for the realization that we don't at all know for sure the answers to these questions. Or at least the many who think they know surely do not agree, on anything but sonorous generalities that are usually remote from what they actually do in their teaching and their research, and that are likely to sound hollow these days.

In the first place, we have no clear definition of the humanities. We might say that we too are suffering from an "identity crisis," but in plainer words we too often don't really know what we're talking about. In effect the humanities are what is left in the curriculum when the sciences and technical or vocational studies are set apart. Presumably they include English, the classics, foreign languages, history, philosophy, now departments of religion, and perhaps the fine arts; but if so they have no common core, such as a classical education once had. Neither do they have any common objective, beyond the vague generalities about the promotion of humanity, wholeness, freedom, vision, wisdom, etc. that are paraded on ceremonial occasions. It has been said, for example, that their basic aim is "the understanding of the nature of man"; but if so it is not at all clear that the study of middle English or the history of the Middle West is necessarily more humanistic than the study of biology, psychology, sociology, and anthropology. What most clearly unites the humanities in practice is the common aim they share with the sciences—mastery of a specialized body of knowledge, with techniques to match.

This may obscure the lofty humanistic aims they profess, but anyway it forces other basic questions. What subjects should be emphasized, and why? Which are most important, if any? Why should a course in literature commonly be required, but not one in philosophy? Why is it desirable for students to get all the "book learning" required in our courses? To students who question the value of these courses the honest answer must first be a disagreeable admission. Choice of subject matter is largely determined by old academic habits, coupled with the traditional assumption that teachers always know better than students what they ought to know. It is buttressed by scholarly research, which has now produced a "knowledge explosion" in the humanities too. But this only forces the questions of relevance, relative importance, and reasoned choices in requirements.

At any rate, we are pretty sure to go on talking about the humanities, for want of a better name or any possibility of a precise name for the miscellaneous subjects now so labeled; so let us consider an approach to them that might be more relevant—the problem of values. Their concerns sometimes include the perennial question not answered by science: "How shall we live, and what shall we do?" In the traditional conception of high culture as the pursuit of truth, beauty, and goodness, they are like all other subjects in the curriculum as modes of knowledge or truth, but they are distinguished by their concern with beauty and goodness too. Specifically, they are concerned with human values other than wealth and power, technical efficiency, practical utility: to wit, with civilized values—esthetic, moral, intellectual, or broadly spiritual— that are notoriously neglected and often abused in our industrial society, whose main concern is a very gross national product. They might accordingly make it their business to educate students in the value-judgments that natural scientists are not trained to make, and that social scientists commonly taboo on principle. In effect the student revolt was a demand for the application of such judgments, especially moral judgments.

Only this approach won't do either as a means of defining or uniting the humanities. In practice their teachers have diverse concerns, generally narrower and less philosophical, and sometimes inimical to a primary concern with value-judgments. In philosophy logical positivists have ruled out ethics on principle; historians, seeking to be impartial or objective, may tell us that their business is only to understand, not to judge the past; English teachers have grown wary of the traditional stress on the social, moral values of literature because this has tended to obscure its formal, esthetic values; and in all fields scholars keep publishing learned articles that assume the value of their specialty, often attack the judgments of other scholars, but have little connection with the basic problems of value-judgments or value systems. All these teachers have good reasons for sticking to their specialized concerns. But in so far as they maintain that their subject is humanistic, their students have as legitimate reason to ask: What is it good for? What use has it for non-specialists today? In a world in crisis?

Briefly, teachers of the alleged humanities need to reconsider their stock in trade. Or since our actual objective generally comes down to making students more like us, we need to think harder about our own designs for living and learning. The traditional assumption has been that these designs incorporated universal, timeless values, which would enable students to make the best of any world; but this will no longer do. We now have to prepare students for life in a fluid world in which all such complacent assumptions are questioned, the eternal verities may appear to be only outmoded cultural prejudices, and nothing is fixed, nobody can say what will happen the day after tomorrow. It will not do either merely to maintain that more of the past ought to be alive than it is, for however convinced we may be that our own interests are as meaningful as ever, we now have to *make* them meaningful to the many thoughtful students who really care about the state of America. As they see it, teachers of the humanities are too often saying in effect: Let us carry on reverently our great tradition, which failed to prevent us from landing in a God-awful mess, and which suggests no way of getting out of it.

Let us accordingly take a closer look at this humanistic tradition. An immediate difficulty is that from the Renaissance on it has been an essentially aristocratic tradition, in not merely an intellectual but a social or class sense: it provided an education for a privileged few. Its elitism was plainest in the classical education of yore, which in Oxbridge prepared young gentlemen for secure upperclass berths and seemed relevant because it reflected the accepted values of the ruling class. Even so it became increasingly sterile; while it failed to awaken any real passion for the classics in most of the young gentlemen, it failed more conspicuously to give them an understanding of their revolutionary industrial society. At best, humanistic culture in Matthew Arnold's sense, a knowledge of the best that has been thought and said, did not prepare students to *do* much about social and political problems. In the more democratic, less cloistered universities of America the miscellaneous humanities that replaced the classics, and had to contend against a growing emphasis on technical or vocational training, were less remote from public concerns, but they remained pretty academic as the possession of campus mandarins. Henry Adams complained that Harvard had prepared him for life in the eighteenth century; so he spent the rest of his life trying to catch up with the nineteenth century, anticipate the twentieth. Down to recent years many other students of the humanities might have echoed his complaints, but few did so loudly or effectively if only because of the social prestige conferred by their degree. They would in any event pass for "educated" men, still an uncommon distinction.

By now elitism has taken a new form, the rise of a professional elite engaged in what a technological society dignifies as the "knowledge industry." This has involved not only the manufacture of vastly more knowledge but more stress on the transmission of knowledge to students, who may be kept too busy mastering subject matter to do much inquiring or pursuing of truth on their own; in what is now called the "educational process" learning may in effect be less an active verb than a noun meaning memory. In the humanities such elitism is exemplified by the Ph.D. industry, which in the last ten years has processed more misnamed doctors of philosophy than American universities produced in their entire previous history. This has accentuated the most obvious curse on the humanities and their alleged ideal of "wholeness"—the increasingly intensive specialization. The close studies required for dissertations, like as not on trivial subjects because they are supposed to be contributions to knowledge, are seldom calculated to make budding scholars any broader, wiser, or more humane than specialists in the sciences, or to give them a philosophical view of their subject in relation to other subjects, much less to make them better teachers.[1] The indus-

1. As an example of literary studies I cite a superior dissertation of its kind, a study of Stephen Crane by an obviously intelligent, sensitive man. In developing his thesis about Crane's central concerns he did a thorough job of covering the various interpretations buried in a number of major studies and some eight hundred scholarly and critical articles, representative of the flood of literary scholarship in our day. He brought out no quality of particular distinction, however, in the thought, the insights, or the style of Crane—no reason why a minor writer, even if one of some intrinsic interest as well as historical importance, should get so much solemn attention, including the usual disagreements over his intentions, and now portentous studies of his "symbolism." To me he made it plainer that American literature is simply not rich enough to sustain the horde of scholars who have been cropping or mining it in the last generation. As for

try accordingly turns out men who, as the saying goes, are good "in their field," but who may recall Stravinsky's description of linguists as men who know everything about language except how to use it. For humanistic purposes the chief value of a Ph.D. may be that its possessor can sneer at it in good conscience, from a professional berth in which he can cultivate broader interests. But as it is, the rule of "publish or perish," or production for academic profit, makes it more practical to go on with narrow, specialized research, the results of which may then be inflicted on hapless students. When we talk of educating *Homo sapiens*—a possibly conceited name for man, but still indicating his real potentialities—honest-to-God humanists might recall an old proverb: May God deliver us from the lies of honest men.

They might also question the related addiction to "objective" analysis, due primarily to the influence of science. This is by no means the mere "myth of objective consciousness" that Theodore Roszak has tried to explode. The effort at detachment, a dispassionate view, a transcendence of merely personal preferences, or a spirit that can be called either philosophical or scientific remains a triumph of human thought; and it is an absolutely essential effort if a university is to remain a center of civil, reasonable, profitable discourse. Yet it has encouraged self-deception in scholars who are not in fact wholly objective, and can never hope to be in humanistic concerns. In particular the fashion of objective analysis has clouded the lofty aims habitually ascribed to the humanities. It repels many students as academic because it too often fails to make knowledge meaningful in terms either of their felt experience, their personal interests, or relevance to contemporary life; for while scholars always plug their own judgments in their field, they may deliberately shy away from broader commitments on social, political, and moral issues. They have also made much of new methods of formal criticism, especially in literature and philosophy—so much that our age has been fondly called the greatest age of criticism; but this has too often become another oppressive form of professionalism or expertise, which may distract attention from broader humanistic concerns. (As Bertrand Russell remarked of modern philosophy, its main concern was no longer "with the world and our relation to it, but only with the different ways in which silly people can say silly things.") And again specialists in it may maintain

---

relevance, the writer suggested no convincing answer to questions mature students might ask a teacher: Why should we read Crane so closely? What does he have to say to us that we don't know and ought to know? In what sense is he important for the general reader today?

the illusion of objectivity by refraining from the social and political criticism that was common enough in the great writers and thinkers we study, that flows naturally from any serious concern with human values, and that so many of our best students feel is a crying need.

Such independent criticism, I should say, has become a major function of the universities, more important than ever before because they have become so deeply involved in our society by providing all the services it wants. I should therefore take pains to make clear at once that I do not mean the university should be "politicized." No one can properly speak for the university as a whole—neither the trustees nor the administration nor the faculty. The administration may reasonably make a point of maintaining neutrality, partly out of prudence, so as not to antagonize state legislatures, alumni, and other sources of necessary financial support, but also for the sake of academic freedom, the maintenance of an open forum for all kinds of views. Radicals who argue that the university must be politicized if it is to be responsible usually imply that it should be run by and for radicals—certainly not conservatives, who have meanwhile profited less than they from an a-political academic freedom. As for the faculty, I take for granted their right to speak out freely as individuals, on or off campus, or even to take a stand as a body on what they consider vital issues, as in some institutions they did by denouncing our invasion of Cambodia; for in so doing they are only announcing a majority opinion that in no way imposes orthodoxy, is binding on dissenters, or restricts their academic freedom. But it seems to me as clear that they cannot be expected to take a stand on all important political issues, else they would be forever meeting and debating national policy. They have their own work to do as teachers and scholars, which for most of them may have little if any direct bearing on politics. Similarly I do not mean that teachers of the humanities should make social criticism their main business. It might be quite irrelevant in some of their courses, such as archaeology, musicology, and foreign languages, and in any case there is always need of some detachment from contemporary issues.

Yet the development of a critical spirit is very much their business. It is in keeping with a liberal education, which is ostensibly an education for freedom, inasmuch as no man can be really free unless he has some power of independent critical judgment, or is to some extent philosophical. It is in keeping too with the often declared aim of inculcating wisdom. If this might lead to complete detachment from temporal social issues, as it did historically with the wise and holy men of the East, they nevertheless had positive commitments that might support Edward Shoben's definition of wisdom as "no more than knowledge tempered by judgment—that is, knowledge shot through with bias, passion, and commitment." Certainly there can be no hope of wisdom or even humanity in America today without a highly critical spirit, a readiness to entertain unpopular ideas, and to recognize a particular need of such ideas. And in various connections, without sacrifice of academic dignity or the values of disinterestedness, teachers of the humanities can at least raise pointed, fundamental questions: immediately about an affluent society dedicated to mere affluence, or a mindless way of life; a democratic society that not only falls short of its avowed ideals of equality and social justice but forgets that democratic principles are essentially moral principles, entailing moral obligations; a technological society that is concerned primarily with efficient means rather than humane, civilized ends, dedicated to a mechanical, now seemingly irresistible kind of "progress," without regard to human costs; and altogether a "national purpose" of which Clark Kerr tells us the multiversity has become the "prime instrument."

Such questions arise quite naturally for another obvious reason why criticism may be considered a major function of the university today—the challenge of radical change in the conditions of life, natural, social, and cultural. As naturally it would therefore lead to criticism as well of the cultural heritage we are transmitting. Such criticism of course need not mean what the word connotes to most Americans, merely finding fault, tearing things down, knocking instead of boosting, etc. Perhaps a better word for it might be "evaluation": a more systematic effort to single out what is questionable in our heritage, and also what is most valuable, worthy of preservation, or even essential to survival. Similarly social criticism should involve a clearer recognition of the values of science and technology, not merely the common abuses of them. So considered, a deliberate focus on criticism could provide a means of integrating the curriculum, uniting the liberal arts and the sciences in a common enterprise, and emphasizing that learning—the distinctive business of a university—involves not only knowledge and the uses of reason but feeling, sensitivity, and taste, and on all counts is a means to more conscious, intelligent commitments. Most obviously, it could largely dispose of the problem of relevance, or of giving more point to the business of learning.

As it is, too much of the professional stock in trade of the humanities is of primarily historical interest, inert knowledge that has little point except for some enthusiasts or prospective specialists. For the living purposes of students today it may be as dead and done with as the "influences" on past writers or thinkers that scholars love to track down, or the topical references in many works that have to be explained in footnotes. We forget that most students, even the brightest of them, don't want to become scholars. Or let us say simply that we are all likely to get into a professional or academic rut. Life in a rut is comfortable and secure, since we still have enough students willing to settle down with us there as transients. It helps to explain why the humanities remain fairly respectable in a society that values science and technology much more highly, and why we are in general much better paid than we used to be. There are "radicals" among us, to be sure, and a widespread popular suspicion that there are too many of them; periodically the word gets around that we are corrupting the youth of America.[2] For the most part, however, we are tolerated as harmless fellows. How could students be corrupted by a study of the classics, archaeology, the Renaissance, Shakespeare, Gothic art, baroque music, or foreign languages? Such interests are considered impractical, of course, not really essential, in effect irrelevant to the serious business of life; but still a kind of luxury our indulgent society can afford.

But all this is too easy. Trouble begins with any serious effort to spell out concretely what our purposes ought to be and how to achieve them. Then we may realize that we cannot be sure of the answers—all we can be sure of is that we can never hope to agree on what are the right or the best things to do. Still, there is no need of absolute agreement, no reason to think that it would be any more desirable than the placid agreements of the past. All I am saying is that we need to ask searching questions about our subjects and our aims. And since I cannot speak for my fellows, knowing only that they are doing all kinds of things, and that it is always too easy to be critical of the other fellow's aims, I shall now speak only for myself—and begin with my own troubles.

---

2. We are perforce included in the recent indictment of the "whole academic society" by Martha Mitchell, wife of the Attorney General of the U.S., who said it is responsible for "all of our troubles in this country," including "the sins of our children." We can only hope that she was not parroting the attitude of her husband toward civil liberties when she added that academicians "don't know what's going on" and so "don't have any right to talk"—a right she herself exercises rather freely.

2 / Some Personal Doubts

Needless to say, I am sure I am a good humanist. Having long specialized in breadth, courses combining literature, history, and philosophy, which I focused on the basic issues of modern life, I took for
granted that they were clearly relevant. The question never occurred to
me until a few years ago when, in a seminar in political philosophy
centered on the issues of democracy, I started with some study of freedom in the ancient world for the sake of historical perspective—a major
item in my own professional stock in trade. One day an impatient student suddenly launched a harangue on the terrific problems looming
up, such as the population explosion, the prospects that millions of people are going to starve to death; and here we were way back in ancient
Greece, reading Plato's *Republic.* Patiently I explained that while I
shared his concern over these problems we could not tailor the whole
curriculum to the present emergency, we had to try to get down to basic
principles, and we needed some perspective in order to size up both our
current crises and our traditions and living beliefs, or simply as a means
of keeping our heads. For the long run it was indispensable to any
hopes of wisdow.

Yet even as I made the sensible answer I felt pretty academic. I
stick to this kind of wisdom, or am stuck with it; but is it the best
wisdom for aroused students at this time? Specifically, are the perspectives got from the political thought coming out of the little Greek
polis really of much help in understanding our massive technological
society? As for the *Republic,* it is relevant because of Plato's concern
with fundamental issues, such as justice, rule by an elite, and his
pointed critique of democracy; but even apart from his dubious model
of a just society—serviceable neither for ancient Athens nor for us—
the terms of his argument are hardly applicable to the political problems of America, a radically different experiment in democracy on
an immensely larger scale. So too with the "tragic sense" of history I
have long dwelt on, with much stress on basic incongruities, ambiguities, ironies, paradoxes. It seems to me clearly essential to a proper
understanding of not only the past but our situation today, and as
essential to hopes of wisdom. But this can become too easy a habit, or
lead to an aloof, tired kind of wisdom; and again I cannot be confi-

dent that it is the best kind for students much concerned about the state of America, wanting to be "involved" or "committed." It is not enough to tell them that the human condition has always been tragic, for they see evils that are quite unnecessary, clearly remediable, and moral failures lacking in tragic dignity.

Or "wisdom" may be too highfalutin' a word. While we naturally tend to be too confident that we both possess it and impart it, we cannot in any case hope to turn out a generation of wise men. Enough if we meet the simple need for more intelligence: an informed, critical intelligence, guided by a proper concern for human values, which can then be brought to bear on our social and political problems. This, however, is substantially what students have been demanding of us. Repelled by the ruling values of our society, especially by all the counterfeit idealism and hypocrisy that go with them, they are questioning the relevance of our own values to the "real" world—a world of flux in which the clearest constant is the urgency of many problems, and the prospect of a future still fuller of problems. Hence I have had second thoughts too about other traditional objectives I have been pleased to share.

One has been to turn out "cultivated" men, "well-rounded," with broad interests. These are clearly admirable types, especially needed in a technological society, and we must hope that it still finds enough professional room for them. Then we must acknowledge that we have not been doing too well by this objective because of all the specialization, but we must also wonder whether our society does find enough room and use for them. If students preparing to follow us into the academic profession may expect to find a suitable niche (though now with increasing difficulty because of an overproduction of Ph.D.'s), what about the many more students who are going out into the world? What kind of "culture" do they need? Not being a career counselor, I cannot be sure, but I have some doubts about the usefulness of the traditional kind, our staple product. While corporation and government executives often talk as if they valued this product, in practice it appears to be of little service except perhaps for conversational purposes over luncheon martinis—and then with reservations. The interests and tastes that marked the cultivated man in the past may seem merely genteel in an age of discontinuity in which young people have been developing a culture of their own, a "counter culture" involving new styles in art and thought as in dress, speech, and behavior. Breadth of interest, or whatever qualities mark what executives call "broad-gauged" men, may serve students no better in their professional life unless such interest is concentrated on contemporary problems. And let us grant too the plain value of concentration on a particular subject if a student is wholly engrossed in it, all his faculties are engaged by it, for he may then display more imagination and sensibility than students roaming over the liberal arts.

Similarly with a related objective, going back to Aristotle, that has become popular of late—education for a wise use of leisure. This might seem eminently relevant in a society that promises increasing abundance and leisure. It is most obviously needed, however, by technical or vocational students, who are least likely to get it or even want it. It can also look like a tacit admission that the humanities have little other real use today. In any case, the aroused students are not concerned about the uses of leisure, which for them is usually no problem—they have plenty to read, think, and talk about. They want challenging work, opportunities to be of use to their society, or to do something about the abuses of its wealth and power. The most ardent of them are likely to be the most uncertain about their careers, and for good reason. As John Gardner has said, "One of the most difficult problems we face is to make it possible for young people to participate in the great tasks of their time." The immediate question remains: Can the humanities do more to prepare them for such participation?

Among the possible answers is a course I have ventured on the impact of modern technology on society and culture. No subject is more important today; it is the locus of all problems of human values, a means of making value-judgments more concrete and directly relevant; and it gives students an opportunity to explore independently whatever problem they are especially interested in. But for the purposes of a humanities curriculum it raises obvious practical difficulties, apart from all the traditional boundaries it cuts across: it calls for more knowledge of science and technology than most teachers of the humanities have. However desirable it be that they have such knowledge, it cannot reasonably be expected of them, any more than I can be expected to master linguistics, mathematics, or symbolic logic. And the course also brings me back to the reservations I expressed at the outset. My growing concern over the abuses of our fabulous, fearful technology makes me suspect I am becoming obsessed by them. Thereby it makes me appreciate more the conventional values of detachment, "idle" curiosity, or even a *right* to irrelevance amid the clamor of our day. Just because students are so much concerned about contemporary problems, they might be better off for some respite from them, some contemplation of matters of perennial significance, and more opportunity to know better the deep, lasting satisfaction of an intimate acquaintance with the great works of the past.

In this belief I am also inclined to reassert the traditional rights of teachers. Since I encouraged the students to participate in the conduct of the seminar, they had many lively discussions, talking to one another instead of merely back to me, often threshing out fundamental issues; but sometimes they went off on tangents, got engrossed in incidental matters of intense interest to them, and then might look bored when I turned off the discussion to introduce matters I thought more important. If relevance is essentially subjective, in a university it cannot be determined solely by the personal interests of students. Teachers still need to speak with something like our traditional authority about what they need to think about, and need to know in order to think well. With all due respect for thoughtful students, we cannot treat them wholly as equals. Even those who are demanding equality generally share our assumption that they need teachers. Only this leaves us with the need of drawing some fine but firm lines, as between authoritativeness and authoritarianism.

A related problem is suggested by my references to elitism, which reflected the current attitudes that have made "elite" a bad word, not the honorable word it used to be. This usage derives from a belief in democratic values, ideals of equality, respect for the dignity of all men —the humanity that is supposed to be a major end in the study of the so-called humanities. As democrats we accordingly object to Plato's ideal republic because he shows no respect for the common people, no real concern about them except to keep them in their lowly place, never permit their vulgar desires to breed pernicious ideals of freedom and equality. Today the objections to elitism are strengthened by the growing complaints about the "meritocracy" the universities have done most to establish—complaints chiefly from the public, which regards it as undemocratic, but also from superior students who resent the pressure on them to become grinds. So we may forget the long historic struggle to institute standards of merit in place of arbitrary aristocratic privilege. We may forget too other commonplaces, that democracy of course needs some kind of elite to provide its leaders, that as intellectuals professors constitute an elite, and that so do the bright students—especially the radicals—who are rebelling against a system acceptable to the majority. We all resent efforts of voters or tax-payers to dictate academic policy, or any interference by the government that supports us. As democrats we all face the perennial difficulty of reconciling the claims of equality with the need of maintaining standards of excellence.

Teachers of the humanities in particular might be more troubled by their standards of merit, which in technical studies can be more easily determined by testable knowledge and proficiency. In my own natural preference for independent, gifted students I may not be doing full justice to the claims of conventional or ordinary ones. At that these may have abilities not sufficiently recognized in the academic scheme, just as may black students with relatively low IQ's.

In short, I am still up in the air. While I may get a better view from there, it is hardly reassuring. My belief that almost any subject can be made relevant enough not only leaves unanswered the question of how best to do so but might suggest that any old program will do, whereas a humanities curriculum whose traditional aim has been described as a quest for order and meaning is already cluttered with all kinds of miscellaneous courses. The most obviously relevant of them may also support the traditional tendency to exaggerate the importance of subject matter, *what* is taught rather than *how* it is taught, or the knowledge that teachers impart rather than the attitudes they induce. Knowing of no ideal curriculum, I conclude by amplifying some of the questions I have raised—and again some of the complications they involve.

3 / Some Reconsiderations

WHAT WE NEED, President Theodore Hesburgh of Notre Dame has said apropos of the student unrest, is "a rebirth of academic, civic, and political leadership—a sharing of those youthful ideals and dreams, whether they are impossible or not." Why a *re*birth? It follows that the universities have not been providing such leadership or nourishing such idealism. As for the humanities, I suppose they cannot be expected to provide leadership in our technological society, or perhaps either (alas) in the multiversities it has spawned, but what about idealism? Although we of course can't simply "teach" it, and need to be wary of mere exhortation, we might wonder how much our practice has tended to nourish any but academic ideals not vitally related to our students' quest of freedom, justice, and significance in a society that once upon a time was dedicated to ideal propositions. At least we must question the traditional assumption of a "transfer of learning"—the assumption that exposure to humanistic learning necessarily induced humane, civilized attitudes. Apart from some difficulty in detecting such attitudes in many a learned article, we must remember that the many Doctors of Letters in Germany who supported Hitler included Dr. Goebbels.

Accordingly we might reconsider the common assumption that political interests are not our business. Such interests were accepted as a matter of course in the old classical education, whose avowed aims included the education of man as a political animal, a responsible citizen, fit to become a leader in his society. While in America political leaders now come chiefly out of business, law, and machine politics, and are served by specialists trained in the social sciences, it is still habitually said that one aim of a liberal education is to turn out good citizens. What, then, does it take to be a good citizen today? To my mind it need not mean dedication to political activity, or constant readiness to march in demonstrations, and it cannot mean a lot of desirable things, such as a full comprehension of economic problems. But surely it should at least mean a live sense of the responsibilities of freedom, coupled with the responsibilities of America as a world leader; as live a concern with human values, an awareness that political issues come down to moral issues; and some ability to size up leaders, distinguish honest thought from campaign rhetoric or blah-blah—matters that are very much our business. As it is, among the fundamentals commonly neglected because of all the specialization is the study of semantics, or specifically the analysis of propaganda, the systematic, high-powered abuses of language in both business and government. In an age that is making so much of "communication skills" we could likewise do with more stress on the ethics of communication, honest and dishonest uses of language short of the flagrant abuses.

Such objectives would not necessarily swell the common complaints of students that they are neglected as individuals. Except for dedicated vocationalists, they have rightly grown more concerned about their personal development, but to almost all of them this includes their development as social beings, necessary to becoming full-fledged individuals. And so we must ask persistently the most relevant but most difficult question: What are the basic needs of our students today, other than their immediate professional needs?

In view of all the fashionable talk about the virtues of "dialogue," we might first try to have more of it with them, listen more to what they think they need. So in fact we have begun to do, as a result of the student revolt; in many of our departments they are being given some voice in the determination of academic policy. Only then the troubles begin again.[3] Students naturally have many different ideas about their needs, some of them still conventional, others hazy; they are no more likely to agree than their mentors. The more sober ones also realize a major difficulty in efforts to provide for more independent study, that many students are not prepared for such study because of their schooling; these still want their grades, credits, all the trappings of conventional academic "performance." At the root of both the student revolt and our routine academic problems are the failures of our school system—which by middle-class standards is a success because it maintains class privilege, inculcates conformity to the accepted values, and discourages unconventional styles of learning and living. But most troublesome are the issues raised by the most conspicuous rebels against the whole system, the young radicals on the New Left and the devotees of the "counter culture."

These issues seem to me significant enough to be considered at some length, as I shall do in later chapters. Here I shall merely indicate the tightrope that I think teachers of the humanities have to walk. On the one hand, we ought to acknowledge our debt to the radicals whose tactics we are likely to deplore; by their "confrontations" they generated the pressures among many more students that made us reconsider our responsibilities, realize the need of reforms. On the other hand, the extremists among them have confused the issues because they are not really interested in improving the humanities curriculum, much more interested in starting a revolution—an "impossible dream" that we cannot share with them even if we feel the need of radical change, since they have no mass support, least of all from the workers. More difficult for us, however, are the problems raised by the generation gap in culture. Our students came to maturity in a culture quite different from that we grew up in, the world of rock music, the Beatles, Allen Ginsberg, pop art,

3. An incidental administrative one was illustrated by the complaint of graduate students who sat with faculty members on a committee in my department. They wanted to get down to bedrock, thresh out all the basic issues of ends and means in the teaching of English, but the professors cut the meeting short. Although quite possibly these professors were too set in their ways, I confess to sharing their feeling about the prospect of many committee meetings, lasting long hours. In our Age of Committees—the bureaucratic way of tackling or evading problems—I shudder to think how many man-years have been wasted in long-winded talk, beating about the bush, repeated distraction by trifling questions or irrelevancies, with decisions (if any) referred to executive committees or larger meetings that repeat the process. Experience of this process is perhaps a basic need of students, as a kind of *rite de passage*, but I prefer to evade this responsibility whenever possible.

camp, psychedelic experience, Happenings, the theatre of the absurd, now reflected in films too—all of which we may "understand" as a revolt against a technological society, perhaps take some pleasure in, but cannot as intimately know and appreciate as they can. Hence we should humbly acknowledge that our maturity does not guarantee sensitive taste or sound judgment any more than full understanding, yet not affect up-to-date interests and attitudes or ever surrender the values of maturity, which among other things assures us that the bulk of this youth culture is ephemeral, new fashions will come, the latest word is never the last or the best word. In teaching we at least need not feel stuffy if we still prefer Chaucer to Ginsberg, Rembrandt to Andy Warhol, Tragedy to Happenings, or even the Victorian John Stuart Mill to Herbert Marcuse.

Still, most of the discontented students have reasonable ideas about their needs. They take seriously our clichés about education for freedom. In general they want more freedom to inquire, to criticize, and to dissent, and with it less stress upon book knowledge, what is tested in too many examinations. At the same time, they are not simply rebelling against the past; they can and do share many of our interests in it. Neither are they rebelling against all authority, but rather making heavier demands on their teachers. Basically they are seeking authority in what amounts to no mere revolt but a quest for satisfying designs for living and learning. Certainly they welcomed the authorities who alerted them to the gravity of the problems of the environment; whereupon they helped to organize teach-ins all over the land. As for teachers of the humanities, they are in effect asking us to earn our traditional authority by making our values more meaningful in the "real" world. And on this score in particular we need to listen to them, for in some ways they know this world better than we do.

Thus "the quality of American life" is no tiresome cliché to them. They grew up in the affluent society, most likely in suburbia, and know more intimately the common hollowness of its living values that we generalize about from an academic distance. Liable to the draft, often exposed to the brutalities of the police, they have more first-hand experience of the moral failures of the nation that seldom directly affect us. Likewise they may suffer more from the feelings of randomness, aimlessness, and meaninglessness of modern life that we take judicious note of in lectures, comfortably sustained by our conviction that we ourselves have high aims. They may really feel that life in America is a tale told by an idiot, full of sound and fury, signifying nothing. On all counts they may have a keener sense of crisis than we, who talk so freely about crisis, even to an academic one in the humanities. They are on the frontiers, where universities presumably ought to be.

In any case, they will inherit all the messes created by their elders in a technological society; so they force another question that has become more pressing than ever before. How well is their education preparing them for the future? I have read that the humanities encourage dreaming about the future, but if they used to, on the recent record I doubt it. Dreaming is now most popular among naive celebrants of science and technology, who keep offering visions of all kinds of new wonders. Serious efforts at forecasting, such as those by the Commission on the Year 2000, make plainer that we cannot educate students for a known future, just because it is safe to predict that the fantastic pace of technological development will continue, with incalculable social and cultural consequences (just as no one foresaw the far-reaching effects of computers). What do teachers of the humanities have to contribute to such enterprises? They are scarcely qualified as forecasters, of course, and as dreamers they are now disposed to visions of the future as nightmare, such as *Nineteen Eighty-Four* and *Brave New World*. But even so I assume they have a positive contribution to make.

The uncertainties of the future make all the more essential the development of a critical, inquiring spirit, with more stress on questions than on answers, which in theory the humanities are devoted to. Now teachers might encourage more the adventurous, experimental spirit displayed by many students. The possible excesses in their experiments in life-styles may be offset by the flexibility and open-mindedness so plainly needed in a fast changing society; and at least they are not just the foolish, irresponsible youngsters that academic reactionaries (like Jacques Barzun) make out. Above all, however, teachers of the humanities have something to say about the most important consideration—the question what America *ought* to do with its fabulous technology. In their ideal role as defenders of human values, they can promote criticism of the actual uses of this technology, the trends toward something like Brave New World. And here again they might give more heed to students' notions about their needs. "The best informed, the most intelligent, and the most idealistic" younger generation in our history not only constitute our best hope for the future but will have to bear the brunt of it. I would give them more freedom to design experimental courses on their own, as some are doing in "free universities."

In this spirit I consider, lastly, the question Roger Shattuck asked of teachers of the humanities: "Are we the Establishment or the Underground?" The answer as I see it is that we are both: an Establishment because of common scholarly and pedagogical tendencies, a vested interest in hanging on to our professional privileges; and an Underground in an ambiguous sense, as a haven for molelike research but also a source of subversive ideas by conventional standards. There is plenty of potential dynamite in our curriculum. While most apparent in courses on the modern world, it can be found too in many other courses, such as American literature and history, political philosophy, and even religion. In particular it is implicit in the sonorous generalities about the aims of the humanities. Taken seriously, these aims can constitute a devastating indictment of a society that does not welcome criticism of the American way of life.

Thus if the humanities indeed make people more "humane," our students might be more repelled by the barbarous inhumanity of our war in Indochina. If they further our understanding "of such enduring values as justice, freedom, virtue, beauty, and truth" (to cite one of the generalities), students might grow more indignant over all the injustice, hypocrisy, and falsity accepted in the American way. If they "help men to live more fully and creatively and to expand their dignity, self-direction, and freedom," students might grow still more aware of all the obstacles to full, free personal development in our society, including its universities. Or if we simply awaken them to the values of beauty, and to the importance of esthetic judgments in any consideration of the quality of American life, they might be appalled by the national insensitivity to ugliness, the commercial blight on the landscape of what used to be called God's own country.

Having dwelt conscientiously on the limitations of the humanities, I feel free to conclude by emphasizing that a great many teachers do take seriously their avowed objectives, and do achieve them to an extent no less real and important because it cannot be measured at all precisely. It may be enough that they simply stimulate students to think, about fundamental issues. They have surely contributed to the emancipation of mind without which there could have been no student revolt. (And it is easy to forget how many good students have survived the "system" all along.) Years ago Whitehead said of the mediocrity of the learned world, "It is tame because it has never been scared by facts," but now enough of us have at least been scared. The trend, especially among the younger members of the profession, is clearly away from the conventional routines. Apart from all the soul-searching, one positive sign was the recent revolts at the annual meetings of the

Modern Language Association, the American Historical Association, and other such academic trade conventions, which have long been so distinguished by the tameness of their proceedings that hardly anybody outside the profession paid any attention to them. (I can imagine no crueler punishment in the academic world than sentencing a person to read all the papers delivered at any one of these conventions.) The rebels were substantially supporting the student demands for more relevance.

But then we must realize that we are headed for more trouble. Insofar as we satisfy our aroused students we will incur more of the growing public hostility to the universities; we cannot satisfy both them and all the Americans who resent them. Whatever our choice, we cannot hope to play it safe as either an Establishment or an Underground. However good or bad the good old days, they are almost surely gone forever.

II

THE USES AND ABUSES

OF HISTORY

1 / The Seamy Side of American History

"THE TRADITIONAL EUROPE—the Europe of our history books, the Europe of Louis XIV and Napoleon and Bismarck—is dead and beyond resurrection," wrote Goeffrey Barraclough, a distinguished medieval historian, as long ago as 1955, "and we may disabuse our minds of the illusion that there is any special relevance, from the point of view of contemporary affairs, in studying those neolithic figures." Today more historians are saying that the subject of history is on trial. They are wondering out loud whether it has a future, or whether the past can be made vitally relevant to contemporary needs.

Offhand, their worries seem odd at a time when their subject is apparently flourishing as never before. Whereas a century ago there were only a handful of history professors in America, the catalogue of a large university today may list well over fifty courses offered by its history department, many more than are offered by European universities. Besides the traditional fields of ancient, European, and American history they cover Russia, East Europe, the Near East, the Far East, Latin America, Africa—every region under the sun. Other departments offer many more courses in history: of economic theory, literature, language, art, philosophy, religion, science, etc. In all fields of thought there is much stress on growth or development, a key idea that requires historical study. The whole past of mankind is being scoured—an enterprise especially important, it would seem, now that all men have been brought together in One World. So it has often been said (by me, among others) that our age is more historically minded than any previous age.

Nevertheless our age is also being described as "anti-historical," for obvious enough reasons. Except for introductory courses, most of the offerings of history departments are designed primarily by and for specialists, most of whom write scholarly articles or treatises that nobody reads except other specialists. Most college graduates, especially those from technical or vocational schools, know little but the history they were taught in high school. Students flock to the increasing number of courses about the contemporary world. More specifically anti-historical is the vogue of the social sciences, which typically concentrate on contemporary society, with little reference to any but recent change, and with as little historical sense. The relativism they have helped to propagate has made the study of past societies seem more irrelevant to the needs of our own, with its very different climate of opinion. Americans in particular plainly have no such deep sense of the past as men did when much less was known about it. And as plainly they have an excuse for their relative indifference to it in the conditions of life today, beginning as always with the extraordinary pace of change that makes the past recede so fast and so far. In private life this appears in the mobility of most Americans, the impermanence of surroundings, the scattering of kinship groups, the disappearance of old homesteads and family traditions, the rootless ways of life—altogether, the loss of the means by which people used to form deep attachments or reverence for old ways. The many people who enjoy history in the form of novels or movies, typically glamorized versions of the past, enjoy it chiefly as mere entertainment, an escape from reality rather than an illumination of it. Hence J.H. Plumb has lamented "the death of the past."

Now, even so I should say first and last that the study of history can be made vitally relevant to contemporary interests and needs. From my own experience I know that it can be vital in the profoundest sense —engrossing for its own sake, a source of much richer, deeper, more lasting pleasure than is afforded by the endless entertainment in our society. If people are growing incapable of appreciating the drama of human history, the wonders, the terrors, and the mysteries of the past, I am tempted to say simply so much the worse for them. Yet this will not do. The bulk of history, as written and taught, is prosaic.

Even apart from all the names and dates that bored students too often have to memorize, it seldom gives a stirring sense of the drama of human history. Scholarly books have been growing less readable because of a professional suspicion of a lively style, a kind of premium on dullness that swells the flood of trivial monographs by which the profession—like all learned professions today—maintains itself, gives young specialists the means of acquiring status. And from my own experience I have also learned some misgivings, in particular about my own works, immediately *The Children of Frankenstein.*

Obviously relevant as a study of modern technology and its impact on society and culture, this includes a long historical introduction that I thought important for the sake of perspective. It throws light on the continuities in the history of technology, the power that man has sought over his environment ever since he began chipping flints, and the deep cultural roots of technology in Western civilization, which from the outset displayed a genius for practical arts and skills, and with their aid developed modern science. It emphasizes the profound changes that technology brought about in man's way of life as early as the discovery of agriculture, when he moved from the cave to the village, and then again with the rise of civilization, when he took to city life—changes that complicate the question of just what is the "natural" life for man. At the same time it makes clearer that the Industrial Revolution marked another turning point in history, the rise of a radically different kind of society, and of ways of life that might legitimately be called "unnatural." When I reviewed this introduction with my students, however, they asked almost no questions, partly because most likely they knew too little history to question or quarrel with my account, but also I felt because they found the detail much less interesting than it seemed to me; no doubt I could have dispensed with some of this detail. In particular the students were impatient to get at the contemporary problems that concerned them, such as the crisis of the environment. And this raised the critical question.

A historical survey could show that man has been abusing the environment over the ages—deforesting, exhausting soil, creating dust-bowls. It could also give a more vivid idea that man has never shown less respect for the natural world than do Americans today, who are forever exploiting, bulldozing, littering, and polluting it. But chiefly it would serve to demonstrate that our situation today is strictly unprecedented. The ecological crisis created by the immense increase in population, coupled in America with the still more rapid increase in industrial production, wastage, and pollution of air, water, and soil, looks like the most dangerous crisis the human race has faced in its entire history. For the first time it is conceivable that the earth may become uninhabitable. Accordingly the most apparent lesson of the past is that it can teach us nothing about how to deal with the ecological crisis, simply because no nation has ever faced one of this kind. So the impatient students might ask: Why waste time on a historical survey that finally shows only how America blindly led the way in creating the crisis? Why not get down at once to the desperately urgent problems, and what we will have to do if we hope to solve them?

Yet the answer is easy enough. Students need to be fully aware of how novel the whole set of problems is, and why fresh thinking is therefore called for. As it is, we are for the most part confronting the problems with business as usual, politics as usual. We are committing a common kind of historical fallacy, today the most dangerous kind —adhering to traditional ways, "safe-and-sane" policies, "tried-and-true" methods, which might once have been appropriate, but have become clearly inadequate. As students hope, agitate, or take to action, they need to know considerably more about American history—and get a considerably different idea of it from what they were taught in the schools—in order to realize what they are up against, see more clearly what is relevant or irrelevant. The primary obstacle to efforts to deal with the ecological crisis is the American way of life, which in its affluence is novel, in other respects a century or so old. It is not only the ways of business and government but the attitudes of the American people, who are no less products of the past because they have little sense of it, or worse, a false sense that confirms their tendency to self-righteousness.

So too with other issues that first aroused the students, the war in Vietnam and the treatment of the Negroes. To size them up properly also calls for some elementary historical sense, of a too uncommon kind. For we are not dealing with a great country, a great people, that suddenly went sour. We are dealing with prejudices, stupidities, hypocrisies, and injustices that come out of a long tradition. They are linked with sentiments and beliefs, habits of thought and behavior, that are deeply embedded in the American consciousness. They are aggravated by popular notions of the national greatness, which has become a curse because our immense wealth and power have created the delusion that we are both able and fit to lead whatever we call the "free world." A clearer, fuller awareness of all this may dishearten young people, possibly kill the hopeful spirit they must retain if there is to be any hope for the country. But it is clearly relevant, finally essential to intelligent efforts to realize their hopes.

In *The Children of Frankenstein* I concluded on a sombre note, the real possibility that America might go down as the greatest failure in history, or that it might be spared this ignominy only because history will have come to an end. If so, it would be a tragic failure because of all that America has represented at its best, what led the Frenchman Turgot to say early in the American Revolution, "This people is the hope of the human race." Perhaps aroused students need to realize more fully that their own idealism comes out of a long tradition—ideals of freedom, equality, and social justice, government of, by, and for the people, and opportunities for common men, which have been repeatedly affirmed by our greater leaders and writers, and have always been a real factor in our history. Only some knowledge of human history can make one appreciate that the "truths" proclaimed by Thomas Jefferson about the inalienable rights of all men are more remarkable because they are not at all self-evident, inasmuch as the overwhelming majority of people through the ages never enjoyed these rights. Almost as novel was the national mission as conceived by Abraham Lincoln and others, which was not to lead the world but to set it a shining example, show it that popular government could work. Hence America remained until recent times a world symbol of idealism. Even the materialism for which it was also known all over had an ideal quality for common people, signifying their hopes for a better living. Students might be reminded too of the extraordinary historical novelty they represent, since never before and nowhere else have so many young people from the middling ranks of society—millions of them—enjoyed the opportunity of a college education.

Today, however, America is hardly an inspiring symbol of democratic idealism, least of all for university students all over the world. It is the prime symbol of capitalistic conservatism, hostility to all popular revolutionary movements. As an avowed defender of the cause of freedom it is notorious for its self-righteous abuse of its power. Americans have always been a self-righteous people, of course, perhaps no more so than the British in the heyday of their empire, or the Germans under Bismarck and Hitler, but today more conspicuously than any other people because their nation is the greatest power on earth, and more naively because of their provincial ignorance of the rest of the world. "No people in the annals of time," President Nixon characteristically told them about the frightful war in Vietnam, "have made greater sacrifices in a more selfless cause than the American people"; so he assured them that we were at last on the way to "a just and lasting peace in the Pacific and the world." And this rhetorical nonsense is more depressing for a reason probably unknown to him. His statement would not hold true for any of the many wars we have fought in our history, beginning with the American Revolution. Always there have been high-minded idealists among us, and brave soldiers; but in no period were Americans united in a selfless cause that demanded great sacrifices. Nor has their society ever been a great society by humane, civilized standards.

For the sake of toughening the idealism that is still alive, it may therefore be well to say the worst about American history. Let us begin by considering a possible measure of truth in the stereotypes of Communist propaganda, that we are "capitalist-imperialists." Because of the fears of Communist aggression and expansion, Americans forget that since the World War we have been by far the most expansionist power. We have managed to get all over the world, setting up several thousand military bases. We had military adventures in Cuba, the Dominican Republic, and Laos before we attacked North Vietnam. Our CIA agents have instigated revolts against regimes we didn't like, as in Iran and Guatemala. In our alleged role as defenders of the free world we have everywhere supported dictators, requiring only that they be anti-Communist, or on our side. Foreign aid programs have likewise been designed primarily to protect or promote our own interests. By now there are signs of a possible reversion to our tradition of isolationism, because of the heavy costs of maintaining our power, but this isolationism has typically been the reverse of the coin, another expression of provincial ignorance and conceit. Meanwhile we continue to assert our right to defend whatever we call our "vital interests," whether in Southeast Asia or in Latin America. John F. Kennedy, the most civilized of our recent Presidents, himself laid it down that we would not permit the establishment of another Communist government in the Western Hemisphere, in effect denying the right of Latin American peoples to choose their own form of government.

Such tendencies may not seem imperialistic to Americans because they marked our history from the outset, under different names. The early colonists began pushing back the Indians, slaughtering them when they resisted invasion of their land, on the assumption that the newcomers had a God-given right to this land. Hence the vaunted conquest of a continent entailed a long series of wars with the hapless Indians, called "savages," whose treatment by Americans remains a disgrace to this day. When the Mexicans got in the way of our expansion, they too had to be fought, then forced to cede large territories. Once we had made good our right to a continent, we took to the European style of imperialism—adventures abroad—after the Spanish-American War. Then it became our manifest destiny to be a Pacific power, even though no other power as yet menaced our security. Capitalism became a plain factor as marines were sent into Central American and Caribbean countries to protect our business interests.[1] Today capitalism does not seem to me clearly the driving force in our expansion all over the world, except as it contributes to the fear of Communism and the obsession with the Cold War, but at least business interests are among the vital interests we are supposedly defending. For American business too has spread all over the world. It is another form of the expansion that has been a key to our history from the outset, that to most Americans has always seemed our manifest destiny, and that to the rest of the world may now look like imperialism.

Next let us consider the favorite topic of our history in the schools, the Civil War. Our historians, who typically have given far more attention to American history than European countries give to their national history, have dwelt especially on this Civil War, which has inspired some hundred thousand books. It was a parochial affair, of little interest to European historians; and what is its relevance today? In our schools the chief interest is in its battles and heroic legends, not its causes and consequences; it is a major reason why our youngsters learn more romance than significant history. For the rest of us the war is important because it preserved the Union, while in Abraham Lincoln it produced the most beloved of our national heroes, who even when cut down to life size remains an inspiring symbol of the democratic faith. But otherwise the Civil War is relevant chiefly as a national disgrace, a lesson in moral failure that most Americans have

---

1. Patriots might ponder the testimony of Marine Corps General Smedley D. Butler: "I spent thirty-three years and four months in active service as a member of our country's most agile military force—the Marine Corps. . . . I helped make Mexico and especially Tampico safe for American oil interests in 1914. I helped make Haiti and Cuba a decent place for the National City Bank boys to collect revenues in. . . . I helped purify Nicaragua for the international banking house of Brown Brothers in 1909-1912. I brought light to the Dominican Republic for American sugar interests in 1916. I helped make Honduras "right" for American fruit companies in 1903. In China in 1927 I helped see to it that Standard Oil went its way unmolested.

"During those years I had, as the boys in the back room would say, a swell racket. I was rewarded with honors, medals, promotions. Looking back on it, I feel I might have given Al Capone a few hints. The best he could do was to operate his racket in three city districts. We Marines operated on three continents."

yet to learn, including a staggering moral debt on which they are still defaulting.

Here we need not rehearse the story of the extravagant inefficiency, blunder, and corruption that prolonged the war, making it the bloodiest of the century, and helping to excuse the countless desertions on both sides. As for the causes of the war, our historians are still debating them, but among them was certainly the issue of chattel slavery. The South was fervently defending an ugly institution that had been abolished in the rest of Christendom, including "backward" Latin America. The Emancipation Proclamation that nominally put an end to it remains the least inspiring of the revered national documents. Issued by Lincoln as a "military necessity," it freed slaves only in Confederate territory, excluding loyal slave states; so as a British newspaper pointed out, it proclaimed that only loyal citizens of the United States could own a human being. In his debates with Stephen Douglas, Lincoln had expressed the sentiment that prevailed in the North too: "I am not, nor ever have been, in favor of bringing about in any way the social and political equality of the white and black races."

Hence the South was able after the war to nullify the Constitutional Amendments that granted equal rights to all citizens. By Jim Crow laws it restored complete white supremacy, and thereafter Southerners would continue to this day celebrating the Confederacy, or refighting a war that they stubbornly refuse to admit was a civil war. (While Northern schools teach that America has never lost a war, Southern ones still worry over the problem of how or why their glorious Confederacy lost this one.) In the North black people were in time allowed to vote but were still denied social equality; racism segregated most of them in slums. Today, a century after the Civil War, Northerners are paying the heaviest price for its failure to assure elementary social justice, a victory for either democratic or Christian principles. The racism that was preserved with the Union remains the sentiment of most Americans. To one who knows American history the violence of the revolt of the blacks is less surprising than its belated eruption, the suddenness with which resentment of their degradation flared up after smoldering for a hundred years.

Studied as a failure, the Civil War might also acquire much more than the merely parochial, dramatic, or romantic interest it has had for too many historians. It is relevant especially to the basic questions about the bonds that hold a nation together, the dissensions that may tear it apart. Lee Benson has suggested that it could be studied in ways that would be profitable for French Canadians, Czechs, Yugoslavs, Indians, Nigerians, and many other peoples in the new nations that embrace sharp tribal, racial, regional, or cultural differences. For Americans today it could be as profitable as a study in political failure because of the growing dissension and revolt. The years preceding its outbreak exposed the abiding weaknesses of the American political system in the separation of powers that blurs responsibility, the common lack of principle in politicians, and the habit of evading the main issues, as the new Republican Party did in electing Abraham Lincoln President while he himself remained silent during the campaign. The sorry aftermath of the war looks worse because of the greatness that Lincoln rose to under awful responsibility and the tragedy of his assassination, comparable to the tragedy in our time of Martin Luther King, which so far has appeared to sober or inspire white Americans little more than the magnanimous spirit of Lincoln did in the years following his death.

The treatment of the black people brings up the treatment of other racial minorities in a country that would eventually be pleased to call itself a melting pot. This was no mere myth, inasmuch as most of the millions of immigrants were in time assimilated, many of their descendants rose to positions of eminence; but it takes on a mythical air in the popular versions of our history.[2] As it was, "niggers" were joined in the copious national vocabulary of contempt by many other peoples—kikes, wops, micks, chinks, greasers, krauts, polacks, etc. These were all suspect as "aliens" too, out of whom came "radicals" and "foreign agitators." That they actually produced few radicals is more surprising because most of the immigrants were segregated in slums, exploited by industry, and condemned to poverty. While many eventually came up in the world, millions remained poor. And America was harder on the poor because of the higher expectations due to the rising national prosperity, which was producing millionaires by the thousands. In a country that fancied itself as a land of opportunity, and that increasingly identified its idealism with material prosperity, most middle class people believed—as they still do today—that like the niggers the poor were naturally lazy, shiftless, and improvident. Michael Harrington's discovery of the "other America," at a time when talk

---

2. Daniel Boorstin, for instance, has written that America was the first nation "to enlist the *vast* majority of its citizens in a *strenuous* quest for justice for *all* races and ages and religions" (my italics)—a statement that seems incredibly naive for a reputable historian.

was all about the "affluent society," helped to start a "war" on poverty that remains a skirmish if only because the national tradition has fortified indifference to the lot of the poor. In the richest nation on earth many millions therefore live in poverty of a degree unknown in Holland and the Scandinavian countries, which have also done away with the slums that disgrace American cities.

Still another reason why America was hard on the poor was that it lagged behind European industrial countries in social welfare legislation, including protection of workers against the abuses of unregulated private enterprise and the failures of capitalism to provide security. Early in our century the Progressive movement finally pushed through some elementary reforms, against bitter opposition from business interests, but not until Franklin Roosevelt's New Deal did America begin to catch up with what Bismarck had done for Germany fifty years before. Then the reforms it initiated benefited the middle class much more than the poor. Now those who rejoice over "welfare capitalism," because big business has at last come around to accepting the welfare state, forget that America still lags behind Europe in welfare legislation, and that the federal government spends more in subsidizing business interests than it does on aiding the poor. Likewise the affluence that came as the nation more than quadrupled its gross national product in a generation was largely concentrated in the upper middle class. Another by-product of the affluent society was a deterioration in public services, except for highway programs. Today one might expect public indignation over the economizing in health, housing, and other neglected domestic needs—except that this neglect is an old story.

Hence those who call for drastic changes in policy and attitude cannot count on wide public support. The more radical among them cannot draw inspiration from a study of the American past, since it will show that a basically conservative country has never developed a strong radical tradition; efforts to do so have repeatedly petered out, succeeding only in maintaining a tradition of excessive fear of radicalism that conservatives have always exploited. Rebellious young people should know too that America never produced significant youth movements or student revolts either, as European countries have. This helps to explain why they are taken so seriously, a thought that might excite them by making them feel more like pioneers or modern frontiersmen; but they should also realize that the public hostility they have aroused is not due merely to complacence. It is a deep-rooted aversion to nonconformists or trouble-makers, now intensified by the frustrations and resentments of a lower middle class that has enjoyed a meager share of the national affluence, but is as far as ever from being a revolutionary class.

Finally a study of the American past may sharpen a realization of new dangers. In spite of its expansionism and the many wars it fought, America never developed a professional military class with great political power. Now it has a military-industrial complex with frightening power, greater even than the German military had before the World Wars. All domestic programs, including the popular "war" on pollution, are menaced by the exorbitant demands of the Pentagon, the more insatiable because of its highly organized inefficiency and waste. The young people who organized the first significant protest against the war in Vietnam, and did much to make it unpopular, might accordingly have expected popular support for their attacks on the Pentagon. But if they did they overlooked other lessons of the past that help to explain its new power. The traditional fear of radicals intensified the fear of Communism that made the Cold War the overriding national concern. Although President Kennedy learned to mistrust the advice of the military after they led him into the Bay of Pigs fiasco, in Lyndon Johnson and Richard Nixon they had Presidents who trusted their judgment, even though on the record of the last ten years it has been remarkably poor; all the Commanders in Chief agreed that Communist expansion had to be contained at any cost. Always the Pentagon can count on other traditional sources of support: venal Congressmen, politicians thinking first of getting defense business into their districts; the interests of big corporations, always a political power in the land; now the no less selfish interests of labor unions, which have a big stake in the weapons industry; and in Americans from top to bottom the national conceit that assumes we ought to be first in everything, including weapons, and ought to have our own way, by force if necessary, no matter what the rest of the world thinks.

Altogether, the lessons of American history are in this view pretty sad, emphasizing the real possibility that just because of the advantages we enjoyed in a new land of immense resources we might go down as the greatest failure in history. The youth might not be comforted either by the thought that we would then join eminent company. A study of the whole recorded history of man is finally always a study of failure, the failure of societies, kingdoms, empires, whole civilizations; and the greater the society or people, the more conspicuous is the story of rise and fall, come and go—the common fate of mortality.

Yet it is much more than this, of course. It is also a study of great achievement that survives the failures and the deaths, and that may still inspire. So we may hope that America too will be remembered for its dreams and its ideal achievements, not merely its failures. And so I am led to the possible values of a long and wide view of history, means of transcending notions of relevance that too often come down to provincialism.

Such a view I ventured to take in my first effort to write history, *The Uses of the Past*. Published some twenty years ago, the book has had a considerable sale to this day in paperbacks, suggesting that my effort to create a usable past for our own living purposes has been helpful. In all modesty, I had some clear advantages as a non-professional historian who felt free to wander all over world history, as few professionals dare to do, but in particular brought to my survey the interests of the general reader, in effect was looking for relevance in the various societies I drew "profiles" of. Still, my enterprise was a bold one, perhaps presumptuous. In dwelling on what seems significant to us today, one is likely to do some injustice to past societies, whose people did not toil and suffer just for our sake, and to cloud the humane objective of sympathetic understanding, of effort to convey what it felt like to be an ancient Athenian, Roman, or Chinese. In particular one is likely to have dubious parochial notions about "significance"; all-important though this idea is, historians cannot agree on criteria for it. Moreover, a great deal has happened in the twenty years since I wrote. History is constantly being rewritten, and not merely to provide a job for the possibly too many historians; the past takes on new or different meanings in keeping with the accumulation of more knowledge, but especially with changes in contemporary interests.[3] Accordingly I have reconsidered my work, with an eye to all the history that has been made in the last generation, and especially to the question raised by the youth who have been shaped by that history: To what extent is the past as I saw it still usable for their living purposes?

3. As an example I cite the Crusades, which conventional historians still consider a supreme expression of medieval piety. In my own brief account of them, in a chapter emphasizing the basic contradictions of the Middle Ages, I noted the typical blend of piety, rapacity, and ferocity. Today some historians are downgrading the religious zeal still more, emphasizing the worldly ambitions of the popes and the Norman chieftains. One sums up the Crusades as a "long chronicle of greed, stupidity, duplicity, and incompetence"; another as a "singular monument of human folly." To them the chronicle is significant chiefly as the beginning of Western imperialism. I would add that it was also a striking example of the long Western tradition, still very much alive, of addiction to brutal violence in the name of idealism. So one may understand the otherwise incredible remark of the late Cardinal Spellman, who told our G.I.'s in Vietnam that they were "soldiers of Christ."

2 / A Long View of World History

As I have already indicated, I hold to my basic premise of the vital importance of history. Only through such study can we hope to get a clear idea of who we are, where we are, and how we got this way, and only with such an idea can we judge what is most relevant for our purposes and our best interests; we have to look back before we can look ahead with any hope of reasonable assurance. Though people may no longer realize it, the past is always alive as a major source of our basic interests and needs, our rights and duties, our hopes and fears. As a people we can no more get along without some knowledge of it than an individual could without memory. The serious danger is not simple ignorance of the past, which is never complete. It is oversimplified, distorted, or false notions about it, such as are commonly engrained by the nationalistic history taught in our schools. This accentuates the measure of truth in Hegel's oft-quoted remark, that all we learn from history is that men have never learned from it. But it is also a challenge to historians, who have grown more sophisticated about the uses of the past, above all more critical of its conventional use to sanction current authority, the old ideas of old leaders—a use now especially resented by the young, and a reason why a generation gap may be a hopeful sign. Chiefly I would qualify my comment on the description of history as a series of messes, that only by a historical analysis can we determine how we got into the latest mess, and how we might get out of it. Except as a reminder of the perennial dangers of selfishness, arrogance, and greed, an analysis of the failures of past societies will not help much in determining how to get out of the extraordinary messes we have got into because of our science and technology.

And so with my opening chapter on the cathedral of Hagia Sophia, or the "Holy Wisdom," as a symbol of the Byzantine Empire. Having made this empire survive and fall in two more books, I found in each effort something more to say in its behalf. Besides the glories of its art, it had a heroic aspect in its conscious role as defender of civilization and Christendom, always menaced and repeatedly beleaguered by barbarians or neighboring empires; the ungrateful West was especially indebted to it for holding at Constantinople in 717 A.D. against the all-conquering Arabs, throwing them back when they might otherwise have overrun Europe and made its history incalculably different—including the history of its still more ungrateful offshoot America, most of whose people have had only the vaguest notions about the Byzantine Empire if they ever heard of it at all. But after each later effort I confessed to the same conclusion: I still find the empire unattractive, the Byzantines hard to love or even to like very much. Certainly their history offers little but their art to inspire us, still less to teach us about the messes we have got into. Fascinated though I was by the mystery of its survival for a thousand years after the fall of Rome, I would not urge any student but lovers of history to study it.

Yet I used the Byzantine Empire chiefly as a springboard, from which to plunge directly into the complexities, ambiguities, incongruities, and paradoxes of human history, and then go on to an exposition of my "tragic view" of history, an effort to write it in the spirit of the great tragic poets—with compassion, irony, and reverence. Today this effort raises difficulties that I acknowledged earlier, and that call for some personal confessions. It may not be appropriate for the history of America in the last generation. At least it is now harder to view our follies and our moral failures with compassion or reverence, and though irony still comes easily enough, it may not do for indignant young people. I shared the indignation of the college students that exploded all over the land when President Nixon announced his decision to invade Cambodia, with a fanfare of his usual cheap rhetoric. Wryly I read the calm conclusion of my Preface, that it might be helpful to try viewing our world with both pride and alarm, both tempered by historical sense. Now I find it harder to take pride in our achievements, even such awesome feats as putting men on the moon, for they have been primarily technological, and such idealism as inspired the space program was clouded by the characteristic insistence on planting the American flag on the moon. And I view our prospects with much more alarm than I did twenty years ago.

Still, students might appreciate more the observation of Whitehead I cited, that the present is holy ground because it is all there is—the past is summed up in it, the future implicit in it. Their ardor and their indignation make it holier, while making America worthier of a compassionate, reverent view such as they too find it hard to take. And if the world or the present is too much with them, few will be forever ardent or indignant. They will have more need of thought and feeling tempered by historical sense as they settle down and go their various ways. In any case, I still believe that a tragic sense of history can be the most inclusive, embracing both the most awful and the most splendid possibilities of man's life, as Shakespeare did in magnificent poetry. Lacking it, radicals are always likely to be inhuman, and reformers shallow.

Similarly with what I called "the method of tragedy"— a deliberate, resolute complication of all issues by an insistence on tension, uncertainty, ambiguity, and paradox as the essential conditions of civilization, and by ironic qualifications of all the great achievements, reverent qualifications of all the great failures. Perhaps I should now say more emphatically that this way of viewing history may not be precise, rigorous, or decisive enough to be dignified as anything like a scientific method, or least of all to serve the purposes of historians trying to answer specific questions, doing the indispensable spade work. But in view of the current rage for methodology, with an illusion of scientific exactitude, I repeat that this approach can be not only inclusive but consistent, disciplined, and at least roughly systematic. In particular it seems to me a sound approach for the purposes of the general reader, or the seeker of relevance. Psychiatrists have remarked that history so viewed has a therapeutic value, in that high tragedy takes us all the way through the worst in order to earn a peace without victory, an acceptance of the human condition, or a realization of the possible dignity of failure. Today a stress on the therapeutic values of the past may seem a mode of escapism from the responsibilities of the present; yet it might hearten as well as sober the many Americans who are facing up to these responsibilities.

For the rest, I would not bore readers with a detailed account of the revisions I would now make, amplifying here, condensing there, modifying some observations, acknowledging that even Muller can nod. But I think it worth while to review at some length the philosophy of history I operated on—a fundamental subject that is unknown to most students, including too many majors in American history. This was summed up in a set of propositions that seemed fairly obvious to me as a non-professional or an outsider, but that are far from being universally accepted, in practice still less than in theory, that are of course all debatable, and that raise the basic issues of the uses and abuses of history. The propositions were listed methodically as follows:

1. That the ideal of history, in the words of Morris Cohen, is "an imaginative reconstruction of the past which is scientific in its determinations and artistic in its formulations";

2. That history is more genuinely scientific in spirit as it takes into account the reasons why it cannot be utterly objective or strictly scientific in method;

3. That among these reasons is the necessity of dealing with a complex of factors—physical, biological, psychological, cultural—that cannot be measured, isolated in controlled experiments, or reduced to a single cause;

4. That among these factors is the force of human will—of mind and character, ideas and ideals;

5. That this force makes it neecssary to pass ethical judgments in history, and that such judgments are in fact implicit in the works of the most resolutely amoral historians;

6. That our scientific, esthetic, and moral interests alike call for a world view, a kind of anthropological study of civilizations as a perspective on our own civilization;

7. That in this perspective we can make out universals or underlying uniformities but cannot claim possession of the absolute truth about man and the universe, cannot hope for complete certainty about beginnings and ends; and

8. That this is not simply a depressing conclusion.

To review something of what I wrote in developing these propositions, the interest of most general readers in history is more humanistic or literary than practical or scientific. Beginning as an interest in the obvious drama, for youngsters in the battles, it matures as a deepening sense of the abiding mysteries of man's life that evoke pity, fear, and awe—to me a tragic sense, but in any case a sense of the wondrously varied possibilities of the human spirit. It is this that the imaginative historians convey, and that is wanting in too many specialized studies or pedestrian texts that bore students. Nevertheless the poetry of history resides in its truth—the truth historians must of course always aim at. It is the drama of actual men who once strutted and fretted even as we do, in a bygone era that can be made as real as the ever fleeting present. I should now emphasize still more the impressive advance in historical understanding over the last century, through not only the accumulation of an enormous body of factual knowledge, by roughly scientific methods of gathering and assessing the data, but a widening of horizons, an exploration of new approaches, a supplementing of political and military by economic, social, cultural, and intellectual history. This I appreciated more when I ventured to attempt a History of Freedom—a history that could never have been written in any past society. Whatever their chief interest, students may now find history more pertinent to it.

Another gain is the wider, fuller awareness that this impressive advance is not an advance toward the final, absolute truth about the past, and that history is not and cannot be a strict science, as some of its practitioners dreamed of making it in the past century. Historians naturally aspire to objectivity and exactitude, and many lesser ones may cling to the illusion that they are wholly objective; often history is now classified among the social sciences instead of the humanities (a supposed honor that incidentally does not impress philosophers of science); but to my knowledge few important historians would deny that they are giving as well as finding meanings, offering interpretations that are personal, partial, and subject to revision or supplement. The most apparent exception is the still common professional habit of declaring that the "real" cause or the "essential" truth about something or other is "not this, but that"—a habit natural to men enthusiastic over their own interpretations, but objectionable because such assertions can never be conclusively demonstrated. No doubt some students will be irked when absolute authority is denied Marxist, Marcusian, or other radical interpretations of history that they wish to take as gospel. They may not welcome either a pretty safe rule I suggested elsewhere, that whenever they read *"not* this *but* that"* they should substitute *"both* this *and* that,"* and then some. But if not, they should at least have some sense of the common danger of oversimplified versions of the past, which they can easily recognize in 100 percent Americans. It points to one of the most practical reasons for studying history.

More debatable, or at least more often obscured in practice, is my proposition that among the complex of factors that cannot be isolated, measured, or graphed, and so make it impossible to generalize about history with scientific precision and certainty, is the force of human will, of sentiments, ideas, and ideals, and of the influence of great leaders.[4] This proposition should appeal to young people who are

---

4. I am bypassing here the problem of causation in history, as I did when I spoke of "factors" instead of "causes"—a concept that has come into some disrepute in science because it has been employed too crudely. Historians use various other substitutes or euphemisms, such as "conditions," "influences," "elements," and "roots." Although I think we cannot escape the idea that historical events have causes, it seems to me enough if students recognize that we can never strictly verify a presumed set of causes, much less the "real" or the "basic" cause that appears in historical loose talk.

For those interested in looking into this problem I recommend David Hackett Fischer's lively book *Historical Fallacies,* in which causation provides some of the hundred-odd fallacies he makes out. Apparently I am myself guilty of what he calls the fallacy of indiscriminate pluralism, "causal explanations where the number of causal components is not defined, or their relative weight is not determined, or commonly both." I remain an unabashed pluralist, however, for while I try to discriminate among causes, I see no way of exactly defining their number or determining their relative weight. Fischer's ideals of accuracy and

rebelling against our economic, social, and political order, and who are seeking leadership no less because they are critical of authority; but it is countered by the strong positivistic, behavioristic, and deterministic trends in our intellectual climate, as well as by the low conception of human nature that American society operates on, the assumption that economic motives are all-important. More specifically, the influence of Marx and Freud has led to much emphasis on the unconscious, non-rational causes underlying ostensibly rational beliefs and decisions. Likewise there has been much talk about the "vast impersonal forces" that govern history. These have become more conspicuous since an Industrial Revolution that nobody planned, now the terrific, seemingly automatic drive of our technology that is clearly irreversible if not irresistible. Nevertheless the impersonal forces resulted from a vast deal of conscious, rational effort, the volitions of many enterprising persons, and the terrific drive works through the ideas and beliefs of men, a culture that has fostered science and technology much more than did any non-Western culture. Our only hope of controlling the drive, directing it to saner purposes, lies in a fuller consciousness of what we have been up to (such as Marx himself achieved by a rational analysis), and a clearer devotion to human values other than efficiency, wealth, and power. In any case it is ideas and ideals that have enabled man alone of all animals to make history, and that alone give it significance.

In view of the immense power now at his disposal, especially a power for destruction, enlightened leadership has become more important than ever; so I would repeat more insistently that great men have made a significant difference in history. Granted all the discounts made familiar by the revulsion against the Hero theory of history—that they may be unconscious agents of larger forces or products of their age, the times must be ripe for them, their achievement may be determined by accident, it is rarely if ever what they hoped for, and so on—I find it impossible to believe that history would have been just the same had there never lived a Buddha, Confucius, Jesus, or Mohammed, an Alexander the Great, Jenghiz Khan, Napoleon, or Bismarck. In our own time Marx and Lenin, who played down the influence of great men in the name of historical materialism, make plainest how much difference they may make. Everywhere men have responded to the mere ideal of greatness, enshrining it in their

---

precision are useful for professional historians who set themselves a specific problem, but they tend to narrow the range of historical inquiry more than I care to.

national heroes, who may then continue to influence history as legendary or even mythical figures. Add that many other great men had a negligible influence, if any, on the course of events—such men as Socrates, St. Francis, Shakespeare, Michaelangelo, and Beethoven —history would nevertheless have been infinitely poorer without them.

An insistence on all this is by no means pure idealism. The inspired and inspiring leader may be Winston Churchill, or he may be Adolf Hitler. Hence my insistence on the necessity of passing ethical judgments on history. True, such judgments appear too often in a crude, obtrusive moralizing; they are passed too freely in popular or nationalistic history, confirming the inveterate tendency to self-righteousness; they may also bolster the conceit of modernity, that our ways are better than the ways of the benighted past; while young people may judge the past too harshly because it is often used as well to sanction conventional ideas about right and wrong, proper behavior that includes a respect for elders who may not deserve it. Many historians, however, have long tended to shy away from ethical judgments because of their aspirations to objectivity or impartiality. They have learned to be admirably fair, often even kind to the past, condoning such barbarities as slavery, torture, and the burning of heretics and witches as products of their times. I think we cannot afford to be so kind in judging our own history, especially the history made in our century. After our best efforts at sympathetic understanding of the past, we need to keep history relevant by maintaining moral standards, saying plainly (in the spirit of the old-fashioned Lord Acton) that deceit is always deceit, corruption is corruption, cruelty is cruelty. And in simple honesty, or in fairness to our students or our readers, we ought to disavow plainly all pretense of complete neutrality. Historians are always judging policies and men, as indicated by all the loaded adjectives they habitually use in their factual narratives (unscrupulous, just, brutal, gentle, etc.), and they are always operating on assumptions about what is natural, normal, important, and good for man. They can be more nearly objective if they make their judgments explicit, try to lay their basic assumptions on the table face up.

My proposition of the need of a world view has become a commonplace (though hardly an incentive to most professional historians), but it has gained more point since the rise of the whole non-Western world, which was only beginning when I wrote, and lately the awareness that the ecological crisis is worldwide, our "little spaceship" is becoming overcrowded and its resources are limited. Likewise the relevance of a study of other civilizations and cultures is more clearly not only a better understanding of the rest of a One World that is far from being one in common thought and feeling, but a perspective on our own civilization, for Americans a better understanding of themselves and the possible degree of unnaturalness or even inhumanity in their way of life.[5] Although students are now more disposed to recognize such relevance, and many are attracted by exotic or "alien" ways, they might still profit from more reading about world history. Otherwise what I had to say about the obvious barriers to sympathetic understanding—racial, religious, national, and cultural prejudice—calls for some supplement and revision in the light of recent history.

Racial prejudice, always ugly, has of course grown more dangerous since the revolt of the black people. Inasmuch as the aroused students sympathize with their cause, there is only to add that they might look into some recent historical studies, in which more attention has been given to the effects of slavery and segregation on black people, their mentality and their culture. All who believe in equal rights need to realize clearly that the Negro is not just a white man under a black skin, in America any more than in Africa, even if he is one of the many who aspire to no more than the status of a middle-class white man. They might also reconsider the ideal of the melting pot. This is not homogenization, but a respect for cultural differences and for the values of diversity.

Christianity, on the other hand, has grown distinctly more tolerant, more respectful of other religions, in the last twenty years. Like most people, I never dreamed of the startling changes in the Roman Catholic Church initiated by the beloved Pope John, which have survived in a ferment among the laity and priesthood that embarrasses Pope Paul. Protestant churchmen too have played a conspicuous enough part in the movement for world peace, the protest against the war in Vietnam, and the struggle for civil rights to earn the honor of denunciation by our Right-wingers. Although bigotry is still common, especially in the Fundamentalist South, Christian prejudice

5. How simply absurd the state of America can look was suggested by the solemn advice a medical authority in Los Angeles offered about its smog. On the worse days, he said, people should put off housecleaning, shopping, and cooking if possible, and also avoid drinks and stimulating foods, anything that might increase their pulse. In other words, our phenomenal industrial progress has gone so far as to make normal domestic life dangerous. To young people who ask how then they should pass their time at home, since all exercise or excitement should be avoided too, one might suggest that they keep singing "God Bless America."

no longer seems to me a major obstacle to better understanding, or one that students need to worry over.[6]

Nationalism, however, has weakened little if any despite the general acceptance of the United Nations. It does not help that this is not just an expression of "human nature" but a development of recent centuries, first in European countries, then in the colonial peoples they treated as inferiors. Hence it has become rabid in many of the new nations, if only as a means of bolstering their self-respect. The growing self-consciousness has also intensified tribal or regional differences, since most of these nations do not have a national language, society, or culture. Sticklers for definitions may therefore ask just what nationalism means in the world today; but however defined, it has clearly split the supposedly "monolithic" Communist world—a development that Americans might welcome except that the hostilities between the Soviet Union and China constitute another threat to world order and peace. Meanwhile national self-righteousness remains most dangerous in America because of its great power and its self-defined role as defender of the "free world." Americans might profit most from a long view of the past, including imperial history.

As for cultural prejudice, the story since I wrote has been confused. There have been some gains in understanding and respect for other peoples and their different ways because of vastly increased travel and communication, foreign aid programs, and the spreading awareness of One World. Eager young people in particular have perhaps learned more from their travel than from books. In other respects cultural conceit has become more marked just because the whole non-Western world has taken to modernizing or Westernizing. While Europeans still tend to some resentment of colonial peoples who demanded and

---

6. I would also make less of my quarrels with Arnold Toynbee, who when I wrote was accorded more respect than he now appears to be. At the time he was still maintaining that the One True God who was our only hope of salvation was the Christian God, a view that struck me as surprisingly parochial for a world historian, but in the concluding volumes of his *Study of History* he changed his mind, putting other higher religions on a par with Christianity (though without bothering to revise the first six volumes accordingly). He then continued to irritate me by maintaining that the only justification of the ordeals of a civilization was giving birth to a higher religion, therefore dismissing out of hand the first "litter" of civilizations—to my mind an inhuman way of describing millions of human beings—and expressing as low an opinion of Western civilization; but he has since mellowed on this score too. At any rate, I believe few historians take seriously his religious interpretation of history, which I doubt would impress many students either. Although I was stimulated by his *Study,* I am reminded of Thomas Huxley's saying: "Few literary dishes are less appetizing than cold controversy."

won their independence, Americans are prone to such conceit because of their much superior technology and the pride of their technicians in their know-how. Non-Western peoples are prone to ambivalent attitudes, welcoming the assistance they need from foreigners, yet resenting it too because no people loves to go to school under foreigners. The new African nations introduce a particular complication due to their crying need of education. What kind of higher education should it be? What they have been getting is an essentially Western education, in a foreign rather than their native language because the books they need or think they need are in foreign languages; and I gather that they are not doing well in adapting this to their own cultural tradition, or to the peculiar needs of their people. Hence I would now add a word on behalf of cultural prejudice, at least in the form of a decent respect for native tradition or pride in the best of it, as a means to preserving the values of cultural diversity and resisting the trend to a drab uniformity. Conceivably Africans might have something to teach us in their efforts to modernize if they strive to retain something of their traditional values of community, kinship with the good earth, and natural, human rhythms of living, or freedom from the tyranny of the mechanical clock.[7]

It was not Western conceit, however, that led me to ignore the history of Africa in my book. The simple reason was that I knew virtually nothing about it, if only because little had been written about it. Since then studies have revealed some fairly impressive kingdoms with a higher level of civilization than had been generally assumed, and in America the revolt of the Negroes has naturally focused more interest in it. Even so I doubt that it would illuminate or enrich the basic uses of the past. Except for ancient Egypt, and later as a source of slaves, African peoples have had little influence on world history and little more to teach the rest of mankind. To my knowledge

7. I have often wondered about an Oxford-trained Nigerian sociologist whom I had as a graduate student. Although intelligent and thoughtful, he never responded to my assignments of papers expressing personal opinions about issues under discussion; invariably he handed in scholarly research papers, with the usual footnote references to the authorities he had consulted. Upon getting his Ph.D., he returned to Nigeria to become a professor in its university; and what kind of sociology is he teaching? My hunch is that it is some Western brand, including authorities who might not be at all authoritative on the needs of Nigerians formed by their different tribal cultures. In fairness I should add that some African educators who came to a summer conference in America for advice about how to teach the humanities and social studies got little help, for the American professors soon realized how poorly these subjects are taught in our own schools.

they produced no great writers or thinkers, political or spiritual leaders, and offered no new perspectives beyond those anthropologists have got from studies of their primitive cultures. They did produce too many chieftains who contributed to the evils of the slave trade by their willingness to sell human chattels. No doubt black students will find more of value in their history, especially their art; but at the risk of offending them I meanwhile think it fair to say that black has not been simply beautiful in Africa, past or present. Then I can add emphatically that neither has white, anywhere, at any time. Among the plain lessons of world history is that color has never been the key to it, and that the feelings of white Americans about it are a vulgar prejudice, engrained by the worst in their own history, but not embedded in "human nature."

Offhand, there is little need today of defending my proposition that in this long and wide perspective we cannot claim possession of the absolute truth about man and his world, and that history itself is the deadliest enemy of the Eternal and Absolute. Although the man on the street may still think and feel like an absolutist in his unreasoned convictions about the rightness of his beliefs and sentiments, including vague notions about a God who blesses America, the great majority of students disclaim absolute standards of right and wrong, absolute certainty in the high matters of God and his relations to man, and most of their mentors in the universities are conscientious relativists. Aside from conventional sermons, the eternal verities resound chiefly in patriotic, Rotary, and other routine forms of oratory or blah-blah that evoke easy feelings of uplift without deep or firm conviction. Yet just because of the general acceptance of relativism by the thoughtful I would now shift my emphasis and dwell more on the uniformities and continuities in history, the universals of culture, and the absolute goods —good for their own sake, requiring no religious or scientific sanction —that make life worthwhile for all who accept the undemonstrable assumption that it is worth being a human being. These include the elementary goods of health and physical well being, comradeliness and love, but also such cultural goods as the satisfaction of natural curiosity, the esthetic sense, and the craftsman or creative impulse, which all civilizations have made much of. Granted that there is too much loose talk about a human nature that is everywhere the same, and can't be changed, we cannot speak of the "dehumanizing" tendencies of modern technology, as its critics (including me) do so freely, without some assumptions about our common humanity, a bedrock human nature, and basic needs higher than the material well-being that most Americans can now enjoy. Thus our systematic fouling of our environment has not only had some harmful physiological effects—it is an exasperating, ugly business, bad for mental health.

Then I can repeat my final proposition, that the admission of a principle of relativity and ultimate uncertainty need not be simply depressing. If it is to many people, the possession of absolute truth is not clearly a need of human nature on the basis of the historical record and the experience of many other people in our time, especially young people. In any case the principle has sprung from a more comprehensive knowledge of history, it is a means to fuller understanding of both past and present, and it is relevant especially because it fosters the positive values of humility, liberality, openness of mind, or the tolerance indispensable for social harmony and simple humanity as well as the pursuit of truth. So I repeat too my conclusion. We doubtless suffer from too much doubt, with the attendant dangers of half-heartedness and demoralization; but we are likely to suffer much more—as people have all through history—because too many men are too sure of themselves.

My subsequent discussion of the question what, then, is the meaning of man's history has both lost and gained some point. Although logical positivists still maintain that the question is meaningless, because we cannot possibly give it a precise, positive answer, we have to consider it because men have persistently asked it, and the answers they gave have influenced the history they made. These have involved an image of the future that might lead to resignation, as in the last centuries of ancient Egypt, or that might sustain and inspire people, as the Jews were inspired by their hopes of a Messiah, but in any case made a real difference. And above all in the recent centuries of Western history, when men took to the novel theory of progress, set about making good their belief that the future would be better than the past. Today few writers hold to a clear faith in progress; it remains at best a hope. Fewer are attracted either by the ancient theory of cycles revived by Spengler and Toynbee, since it has become plainer that our end would almost surely be different from that of the civilizations of the past, and might put an end to history. Yet the belief in progress remains a vital factor, possibly a decisive one, because it is still held by many scientists, engineers, and other technicians who are busier than ever in making our future, promising new wonders. And indirectly they force the basic question by the revulsion they have stirred.

The many young people who are oppressed by a sense of the emptiness or meaninglessness of American life may try to make it more meaningful by taking to political action or the various manifestations of their counter culture. Some may be led to the larger question of the meaning of man's whole history on earth. They are taking a more serious interest in religion, which historically has offered answers to the question. Then they might be attracted by Buddha's wisdom of non-attachment or renunciation, on the assumption that earthly life is unworthy of serious concern. Or they might be more attracted to Paul Tillich, who urged Christians to take history with complete seriousness, an "existential concern," and who assured them that it did have some transcendent, ultimate, eternal meaning, which he did not pretend to know but for him was best symbolized by Jesus as the Christ. Some such belief is at least what William James called a "vital option." For modern technology has forced the issue by making the end of the world—anticipated by early Christians and periodically by odd sects thereafter—a real possibility. And what then would be the point of all man's arduous effort over the long bloody ages? While an unbeliever myself, I can appreciate why many people find intolerable the idea that it would have no enduring significance. They might not be comforted either by the probability now recognized that there are some forms of life on millions of other planets, unimaginably different from the forms we know, but some of them conceivably "higher" than we.[8]

At any rate, I again still hold to my answer: History has no certain meaning, but it is not simply meaningless either because man is free to give it various possible meanings. So historians do with the societies or ages they study, and so people do with their own lives. As with our lives, we can also ask what history has meant at its best, what it can mean or ideally ought to mean. And among the actual pertinent meanings for me is a progress: never pure and steady, never predetermined or guaranteed, with today no assurance whatever of indefinite continuation, but still a real progress, most obviously in mastery of the environment, most fundamentally in the growth of consciousness, the seat of all human values, and so the realization of richer, finer possibilities of life, as represented by the great works of art and thought, the lofty ideals that have come down through all the failures—the most important kind of history, too little of which gets into most texts. Sub-

8. I am ignoring existentialism, the popularity of which reflected the anxieties of our age, because I have found in it no clear attitude toward history or the values man has created in its course. Acute students may find Heidegger, for example, less obscure than I do when he expounds the nature of "Being," but they may also come out like one of his students who was alleged to have declared solemnly, "I am resolved—only I don't know to what." My impression is that existentialism is no longer popular with the young.

stantially it is the meaning Hegel saw, "the progress of the consciousness of freedom." It is the growth of a power of self-determination or freedom to make history, and beginning in ancient Greece the growth of conscious ideals of freedom and the life of reason, in time the ideal of the free, responsible person with a mind of his own.

Hence I still hold as well to my faith in the free, open society as the kind most conducive to the growth of such persons. Then one can dwell, as I proceeded to do and have been doing ever since, on the inescapable costs of consciousness and self-determination, the constant possibility of foolish or even fatal choices, and the new problems invariably raised by every major creative achievement, the hardest problems that begin with freedom, alike for the society and for the individual. Today I would add a reservation chiefly to my concluding statement that the future of the open society was wide open, to triumphs or to disasters of a magnitude hitherto undreamed of; for there is some question about how open our technological society is, and whether its automatic drive to material or technical progress gives us any real choice in futures. But I still think, as young people must hope, that the future remains open.

Of the ancient societies that I went on to survey, some acquaintance with Israel, Greece, and Rome is clearly essential to an understanding of our Western heritage, which is as essential to a truly liberal education. It is no less desirable today when an understanding of our technological society is more imperative, for from our cultural heritage come the human values that have been so notoriously slighted. Now that "the quality of American life" has become a cliché, students may have no clear idea of what the phrase means or of the standards of excellence it implies, moral, esthetic, intellectual, or broadly spiritual. Granted that we will never agree on the good life, and in my view never need to agree, a study of our heritage can both clarify and enrich possibilities, suggest standards of judgment. For such purposes the art and thought of ancient Greece are especially pertinent. Among other things, its culture might make Americans realize the importance of esthetic values in judgments of the quality of a society, since they don't seem to mind much all the ugliness around them, or maybe even to notice it.

My survey of "Holy Russia," Byzantine and Marxist, which was more obviously relevant, calls for some modifications to keep it so because of the changes in the Communist world. When I wrote, my account of Stalin's tyranny would have been denounced by Moscow as vicious falsehood had any Russians thought the book worth attention (none ever have so far as I know), but it has since been vindicated by Khrushchev and documented by some Soviet writers. The liberalizing trends in the Soviet Union, which had not yet begun, remain uncertain but have made a significant difference, and I should guess are irreversible. Philosophers in the satellite countries and especially Yugoslavia have been stressing much more the liberal, democratic, humanistic elements in the inconsistent thought of Marx, including an early concern for the individual that led him to declare that the ruling principle of the ideal classless society he predicted would be "the full and free development of every individual." Americans might ask themselves: Is there a better guiding principle for an affluent democracy? Needless to add, the Soviet Union does not operate on this principle, but in practice America hardly does either. A demand for something like it was at the heart of the student revolt.

In the Soviets there has been no such revolt, only some evidence of latent rebelliousness among the young. The plainest reason is that the government would certainly not tolerate large or widespread demonstrations. Anyway there is now much less revolutionary fervor in the Soviets than I assumed. The distinct improvement in the standard of living has brought the result that Engels in his last years feared in Europe: the "proletarians" look much more bourgeois and have the same material goals. Both the government and the people are even more devoted than Americans to the goal of steady economic growth, since they still have a long way to go to reach American standards. Hence I now see no possibility at all of my conjecture at the end of my chapter, drawn from Silone, that the final battle might be between Communists and ex-Communists. In America both have at most a slight influence, far from enough to touch off a final battle. The growth of technocracy, and with it the growing gap between rulers and ruled, make it more likely that America and the Soviet Union might converge toward an approximation of Aldous Huxley's Brave New World. Meanwhile the life-and-death decisions made by a few men at the top in both countries, on the basis of secret information, make any confident prediction impossible.

In China, however, the situation is quite different. Here there is still plenty of revolutionary fervor, which lately produced the excesses of the "cultural revolution" of Maoism as well as wild talk about a world revolution. I could boast of my suggestion, offered well before the event, that national pride might lead China to defy the Soviet Union (an idea that our State Department was slow to catch on to even after the event—it continued to justify our aggression by the ogre of "monolithic" Communism). But chiefly I would stress a basic element of Mao-ism that is much more relevant than the hopes of world revolution that attract some of our young radicals. In its ideal theory it promises not only economic growth but above all the growth of people, and *all* the people. It falls far short of the ideal of the full and free development of every individual in that it denies freedom of fundamental criticism or dissent, demands acceptance of the gospel according to Mao; but at least it downgrades material or economic incentives and exalts the in-terests of human beings above the ideal of efficiency. Hence its opposi-tion to specialization and professionalism, bureaucracy and technocracy, or rule by experts. While maintaining that in the long run it will in-crease productivity by the energy, enthusiasm, and creativity it enlists, it is meanwhile willing to sacrifice efficiency for the sake of human de-velopment, for example by locating an industry in a rural instead of an appropriate urban area in order to educate the peasantry. Altogether, it is a much more remarkable social experiment than that of the Soviet Union, with its huge bureaucracy.[9]

How successful the experiment has been is hard to say, inasmuch as reliable statistics are not available and anyway would not measure the kind of progress it is seeking. It seems clear, however, that China has succeeded much better in feeding, housing, educating, and keeping healthy the bulk of its vast populace, now nearing 800,000,000, than have any of the other undeveloped countries in the last generation, the bene-fits of whose economic growth have been largely confined to a small urban middle class. Waiving for the moment the obvious possibility that the technocrats may take charge before this goes to press, I should say that the real test will come if or when China approaches the level of industrialism and affluence attained in the Soviet Union.

How much, if anything, this experiment owes to the Confucian tradition of historic China that I surveyed I do not know. Mao of course claims the authority of Marx and Lenin, not of Confucius. Yet the experiment is in any case in keeping with the naturalism and humanism of Confucius, the historic concern of the Chinese with ideals of har-monious relations, more specifically with values rather than facts, quan-tities, or mechanisms—the idols of our technocracy. As an educator I would like to prescribe a course in Confucianism for all engineers,

---

9. For a fuller account of it, see an article in the *Center Magazine* of May 1970, "The New Man in the New China," by John W. Gurley. An economist, he is much more sympathetic to this unorthodox experiment than are the great majority of his fellows, who take for granted that economic growth requires proper economic incentives and a lot of experts like themselves.

economists, and other technical experts—that is, if one could catch them young enough, before they had become thoroughly infected by American notions about what is practical. Other students would find too little room for freedom and individualism in the thought of Confucius, but they too might profit by his kind of wisdom and natural piety. It would at least illustrate the most important kind of history, the development of civilized values and spiritual ideals.

This would lead naturally to the subject of my concluding chapter, the uses of the future—a subject about which much more now needs to be said.

3 / *The Uses of the Future*

ONCE WHEN I WAS INVITED to talk to a class of engineering students, I began by remarking that engineers had done much to develop the fabulous technology that enabled us to achieve almost anything we wanted, and I then asked them what seemed to me the obvious question: *What* did we want? What *ought* we to want? What did *they* think? The class went blank: nobody had an answer. By prodding I finally managed to stir up a timid, tentative suggestion or so, but it appeared that these builders of the future had never even thought of such questions. Like other technicians, they were prepared to go on building it in whatever ways their employers prescribed, presumably confident that all would be for the best. So the automatic drive of technology will continue.

For this reason, however, the uses of the future have acquired much more than academic interest. They have been filling volumes because the future has become more insistently with us than ever before, or in the current jargon, our technology has made us "future-oriented." In recent years many specialists have been busy at systematic efforts to forecast it, up to the year 2000. Others dwell on the alarming or even fatal possibilities if present trends continue, and explore strategies for dealing with the urgent problems so as to give us a choice in futures, or some say about what our history *ought* to mean. To this enterprise historians might contribute more by studies of deep trends. Having made no efforts at prophecy myself, I should repeat that none of these specialists can forecast the future with any certainty if only because there is no telling what we will do about all our problems, but then add that their efforts are nevertheless indispensable to the education on which we must bet in the race with catastrophe. Although here I cannot go into this large subject, which is now technically dignified as "futurology," it is most relevant for young people—they will be in their prime in that year 2000. I conclude by supplementing a few remarks I made at about the time they were born, an age ago.

We had a possible advantage, I noted, in our very awareness of crisis, such as past societies lacked at what we can see were decisive turning points in their history. Today we have a much keener sense of crisis, but its advantages may be offset by its oppressiveness. Whereas I suggested that we did not really know how great were the destructive possibilities that scientists had developed, we now know that we and the Russians alike have much more than enough power to blast the entire earth; it has made pointless my speculation about the possibility of a single power dominating the world, for only some benighted generals believe that either side could win a thermonuclear war. In but a paragraph I touched on technology as the source of our immediate problem, both the possibility and the need of some kind of world order—the only specific problem I considered. We have since created or grown aware of such other grave problems as the environmental crisis, the population explosion, and the increasing gap between the few affluent nations and the many more poor ones, in a world even more revolutionary than I then realized. While our government faces more problems than ever before, the one certainty that the specialists in "futurology" agree on is that it will have to deal with still more in the years ahead. Meanwhile it faces —or fails to face up to—the most dangerous internal dissension since the Civil War. The danger may be exaggerated by the disposition to blow up all serious problems into crises, but unquestionably there are more explosive possibilities than a generation ago.

For such reasons the traditional uses of history in terms of analogy have grown more dubious. Analogy is indeed as indispensable to thought as is metaphor, which it resembles, but it is therefore necessary to keep in mind the dictum of James Bryce: "The chief practical use of history is to deliver us from plausible historical analogies." Today an example is the common defense of our war in Vietnam by the argument that we must prevent another Munich—a superficially plausible argument that ignores the significant differences in the two situations, such as the differences between Czechoslovakia and South Vietnam in both government and strategic importance, and the far greater military power of America than the power of China, supposedly playing the role of Hitler. In a long view another example is the fall of Rome, on the implications of which I dwelt because it was then fashionable to draw analogies between the Roman Empire and America. Perhaps it is still salutary to consider some rough analogies, such as the symptoms of "schism in the soul" analyzed by Toynbee (now better known as "alienation"), the pride in engineering, the disease of gigantism, the rule of business and the money spirit, and again efforts at world leadership that to other countries look like imperialism. Yet the fundamental differences between Rome and America have become still more conspicuous. At the time I found it hard to understand how Spengler and Toynbee could overlook these differences as they went about fitting our civilization into their neat invariable cycles, but by now our science and technology have made it simply impossible to find in analogy with the declining centuries of Rome the key to the history we have been making. Whereas for various reasons—economic, political, social, cultural—the Romans lost the power to maintain their empire, our distinctive problems arise from the immense power we go on acquiring.

Hence one may question the possible analogy suggested by Andrew Hacker's bleak view of our prospects, *The End of the American Era.* The many signs of our unfitness either to lead the world or to offer it a shining example, including the unwillingness to make the sacrifices necessary for adequate efforts to deal with our domestic problems, lead Hacker to conclude: "We have arrived at a plateau in our history, the years of middle age and incipient decline." If so, we would resemble other middle-aged societies of the past that went into a decline, or more lately Britain and its lost empire. Yet the quite possible end of the American era raises questions for which the declining societies of the past suggest no answer. What would become of our most powerful military establishment? Our immense industrial establishment? What nation, if any, would take our place as a world leader? Would Americans consent to retire and decline quietly? Would they be permitted to? In any case the common fate of stagnation in ancient Egypt, Rome, India, Islam, China, and many lesser societies would appear to be not for us; for if Americans have lost much of their traditional confidence and buoyance, and may even be in a mood for decent stagnation, I make out no sign of lessening in the dynamism of their technology, or of halt to its headlong drive, which will prevent them from sitting tight or pretty.

Even so, what Americans perhaps most need to realize is that despite all the uncertainties, magnified by the historically unprecedented state of the world, the plainest lessons of history are still relevant. In our pride we have been rehearsing ancient follies and evils. We have no reason whatever for our traditional belief in a manifest, unique destiny to escape the fate of all other peoples, the old story of rise and fall, come and go. History is big enough to swallow us too, in ways quite imaginable if not predictable. Then Americans might appreciate more the piety of history. It can deepen and widen a sustaining sense of continuity and community, or of the story of all mankind. It can teach the meaning that Jacob Burckhardt wrested from a deeply pessimistic view of modern history, a reverence for the permanent values created by man. As I concluded, it might free us from the vanity of grandiose hopes, as of petty concerns. It might teach us that "ripeness is all," and that it is enough.

Twenty years ago I wrote that I was not optimistic about our immediate prospects. Now that I feel distinctly less optimistic, I nevertheless adhere to the credo I defended: a liberal, democratic, humanistic faith, grounded on the claims of reason and empirical knowledge, toughened by a tragic sense of history that most liberals have lacked. With this I linked the need of an adventurous spirit, a call for bolder, more creative thought that might now seem superfluous in view of all the bold adventure in science and technology, but that has become still more necessary because of all the problems they have created, and the archaic ideas on which our leaders continue to operate. To these themes, however, I shall be returning in later chapters. On my immediate subject of the uses of the future, I would now add chiefly a note on the idea of progress.

For two centuries this idea has been central in Western thought, an index to the intellectual climate, or specifically to hopes and fears of the future. In our so-called Age of Anxiety the revulsion against it has been among the most conspicuous tendencies in the world of thought. Due less I think to anxiety than to disillusionment, this has involved a kind of romantic despair that dismisses even the hope of a better future as naive. It is not actually an utter despair, which would mean the death of the spirit, logically an end to all effort to improve our state; for there is still a pervasive, live sense of possibility, and not merely the possibility of the worst. So it is important for students to realize that the idea of progress is by no means as dead in serious thought as many literary intellectuals suggest. Apart from all the scientists who cling to optimistic visions of what science can accomplish, it may be found in such reputable thinkers as Bertrand Russell, Alfred North Whitehead, Albert Schweitzer, Karl Jaspers, Lewis Mumford, Erich Fromm, and assorted semi-Marxists. It is no less heartening because it survives more as a hope than an absolute faith. Any conviction that the future is bound to be better may rightly be called naive; and the history of America over the last hundred years, down to this day, is the clearest proof of how dangerous an easy, unthinking optimism can be. As it is, the hopeful belief in the possibility of a better future continues to animate a vast deal of effort, including the efforts to forecast the future so as to anticipate problems, avert the worst dangers, and give us a real choice in futures.

Although inclined to rejoice in the knowledge that I will not live to see that year 2000, I can therefore conclude, not merely in compassion for young people, that their naturally more hopeful spirit is not necessarily naive either. They have the best reason to complain that the time is out of joint, and to curse the fate that they were born to set it right; but few are simply cursing. While many are dropping out of society, going their own ways, many more are actively combatting evils and striving for betterment of their society. In effect they are regarding a time out of joint as a challenge. For this spirit, which was rare in the youth during the crises or the decline of past societies, they may thank the distinctive Western idea of progress.

III

A HARD LOOK AT ETHICS

1 / The Moral Dilemma

LTHOUGH THE NATIONAL SHOCK over the atrocities charged against some G.I.s in Vietnam was a heartening sign that Americans are still capable of moral indignation, it was pretty depressing too. Many people were shocked because they believed the myth, fondly cultivated by the military, that "our boys" are cleancut, wholesome lads, very different from the merciless Vietcong. Had they followed the war at all closely they would have known that all along our military men were condoning when not committing atrocities. More than once they could have seen on their television sets South Vietnamese soldiers killing in cold blood captured or wounded Vietcong. And though President Nixon dutifully announced that all Americans found the atrocities abhorrent, the plain truth was that many didn't. On public opinion polls most made excuses for our boys: after all, war is war, you have to do a lot of killing, you can't be gentle with the enemy, etc. They should know, for they have been bred to a tradition of violence that has often condoned brutality, sometimes outright atrocity. Noam Chomsky has quoted from his daughter's fourth-grade reader on social studies, which told how Captain John Mason exterminated the Pequot Indians:

> His little army attacked in the morning before it was light and took the Pequots by surprise. The soldiers broke down the stockade with their axes, rushed inside, and set fire to the wigwams. They killed nearly all the braves, squaws, and children, and burned their corn and other food. There were no Pequots left to make more trouble. When the other Indian tribes saw what good fighters the white men were, they kept the peace for many years.

The text gave no hint of moral indignation. It added only the thought of the little boy who was told the story: "I wish I were a man and had been there."

Few grown-up Americans wished they were in Vietnam with our good fighters there. But in their weariness with a war that we no longer had hopes of winning, most still missed the point of our failure by civilized standards, or elementary moral standards. They were sick of the war because of its costliness and apparent futility, not its barbarity, the frightful tactics of our military—the many more thousands of Vietnamese peasants who were killed or mutilated by dropping bombs and napalm on their villages. So the routine butchery went on for years, always to the fatuous refrain of our generals that we were winning the war, with daily boasts about how many Vietcong we had killed, boasts supported by a pretense of an exact body count that would be ludicrous if it were not so utterly callous. And our inveterate self-righteousness obscured the lasting significance of these "victories"—the new, frightening kind of inhumanity that has entered history.

Now, up to a point this is an old story, only the latest version of the inhumanity of man to man through the ages. Atrocities have always been commonplace. The Mongols who swept through the Near East and Europe set something of a record for them even by modern standards, slaughtering in cold blood countless civilians, perhaps a larger proportion of the population than was slaughtered in World War II. Yet their bloodthirstiness emphasizes that we are dealing with something really new. It is a highly organized, systematic kind of atrocity that is not simple bloodthirstiness, is not called atrocity, and is not felt as such by the men who commit it under orders instead of by cruel impulse. It has been variously described, for example by Erich Kahler as "a-humanity," a culmination of the dehumanizing tendencies of modern technology, or by Gunther Anders as a "truly infernal innocence." However described, it is a product of modern technology, not a mere regression to barbarism. "Technologically," said General Westmoreland, "the Vietnam war has been a great success"; and as a good soldier, or trained innocent, he could not see that morally it was a disaster.

So the innocence poses a moral dilemma. As the systematic atrocity went on, more and more Americans were repelled by it. But just *who* were responsible for it? How could they be *held* morally responsible? Is it possible to punish anybody except the relatively few who regress to old-fashioned atrocity?

These would not include our airmen. Granted that some of them are doubtless capable of cruelty, they kill peasants, women, and children

only when put in bombers and given orders. Observers on the scene
have reported that some feel troubled now and then but most carry on
in good conscience, if only because they never come face to face with
their victims. Similarly with their immediate superiors who give them
their orders: they too are members of an organization, acting in the line
of patriotic duty, passing down orders from higher up. As we go up the
scale we come to such types as General Curtis LeMay, who as one of the
Chiefs of Staff kept urging his policy for ending the war in Vietnam,
"Bomb them back into the Stone Age"; but primitive as his own mentality seems, bombing was his assigned business, and he was only urging
the kind of policy that became official in World War II—the massive,
indiscriminate fire-raids on the cities of Germany and Japan that has-
tened the defeat of the enemy, or "saved American lives," by taking the
lives of many more thousands of civilians than were exterminated at Hiroshima. Finally we come to Lyndon Johnson, who made the decision to
step up the war and extend it to North Vietnam. In a real sense it was
his war, inasmuch as he did not consult the people beforehand or dare
to ask Congress to declare war; so the blood is on his hands. Yet he has
given no public sign of a guilty conscience, presumably for the same
reason as all the others down the line: as Chief Executive he was only
doing his duty as he saw it. Add that he inherited a policy of intervention initiated by President Eisenhower, carried much further by President Kennedy, and it appears that nobody can be charged with guilt.

We have a contrary precedent, to be sure, in the punishment of the
"war criminals" who carried out Hitler's policy of systematic bestiality.
Directly responsible for the extermination of I forget how many thousands or hundreds of thousands of Jews, Adolf Eichmann was tried
and legally executed, like some of his superiors after the Nuremberg
trials. Most of us felt this was quite proper. For all our sophistication
about punishment as an irrational way of dealing with crime, our blood
still cries out for it when we are faced with such terrible crimes; *somebody* had to be punished. Still, many of us felt uneasy. Eichmann was
pronounced quite sane by psychiatrists; he was seemingly emotionless,
untroubled by remorse; and he had good reason for his calm demeanor
—he had merely carried out orders in a cause he believed just. In short,
he was a "sincere" man, a good patriot, in this view not at all insane.
It was only the monstrous policy he was dutifully executing that was
insane.

Hence the less monstrous but still barbarous policies of leaders in a
democracy are even more troublesome. The crimes of Eichmann could

be written off as a kind of aberration, specifically of Hitler's mania; but the moral disaster of our war in Vietnam cannot be so dismissed. Again an outraged moral sense may cry out that *somebody* ought to be punished. As it is, we jail young men who burn their draft cards as conscientious objectors to an immoral war—who practice, in other words, a disobedience that the German "war criminals" were punished for *not* practicing. Why should we not jail instead the generals who urged the war and still order the frightful tactics? Or even ex-President Johnson?

Well, of course we can't. The law of the land cannot permit the punishment of political leaders for even terrible mistakes, else we would soon run out of leaders. Neither can they be readily turned over to an international tribunal, as the Nazi leaders were, even if Americans would ever put up with such a thing; the world would be in constant turmoil if national leaders were kept liable to punishment. And in view of our inherited moral code it is not at all clear that they *ought* to be punished. In simple humanity we must continue to take motives into consideration, make allowances for sincerity or mistakes made in good conscience. There is no question, I suppose, that Lyndon Johnson decided to escalate the war out of patriotic motives, just as Harry Truman did in authorizing the dropping of the atomic bomb on Hiroshima— another ghastly mistake. Moreover, Johnson was following the typically American moralistic line that came down through Eisenhower, Dulles, and Kennedy. However self-righteous, it involved a sincere belief that we had a moral obligation to defend the "free world" against Communist aggression, or to "liberate" the South Vietnamese from Communist domination.

In short, the moral dilemma is like all real dilemmas, not at all simple or easy of solution. I can see no possible way of holding either American or other world leaders to strict moral account. The Nuremberg trials offer no help, for none of the states that held them have followed the precedent they established there, granted their own soldiery the moral right to disobedience, and no strong state would allow an international court to punish its leaders, any more than the United States would. (Remembering Adolf Eichmann, let us note that psychiatrists pronounced Lieutenant Calley "normal in every respect": in murdering peasants, women, and children at My Lai, he was just one of our boys obeying orders.) At the same time, the need of efforts at a solution is more pressing because of the terrific power at man's disposal. We now have to live with the ultimate in monstrous folly, the constant possibility of a catastrophic thermonuclear war. Whether Russian, Chinese, or American, the leader who touched off such a war would almost certainly still think of himself as a true patriot. The last word in "infernal innocence" might be the last word in the history of the human race.

What, then, can we do about it? We might at least begin with a systematic effort to call things by their right name. We might say that the infernal innocence of our leaders is truly infernal but can no longer be regarded as wholly innocent, as for certain our war in Vietnam cannot be—a war that President Johnson escalated under false pretences, that has long been defended by blatant misrepresentations, and that has cost some million Vietnamese lives. In connection with the atrocities committed by our soldiers, we might consider the precedent we ourselves set in the hanging of General Tomoyuki Yamashita, who was in command of the Japanese troops in the Philippines during the last year of the war. His troops brutally killed peasants for much the same reason our soldiers have in Vietnam: they were fighting guerrillas who mingled with the peasants and made it impossible to be sure who were or were not aiding them. Yamashita was charged with responsibility for the indiscriminate murder of unarmed civilians despite the fact that there was no evidence, no charge even, that he ordered the atrocities, condoned them, or in his remote mountain headquarters knew anything about them. Nevertheless he was sentenced to death by our military commission, and the sentence was affirmed by the U.S. Supreme Court.[1] In ordering his execution, General Douglas MacArthur said loftily that he had utterly failed "his soldier's faith," his duty to mankind. "The soldier, be he friend or foe, is charged with the protection of the weak and unarmed. . . . When he violates this sacred trust he not only profanes his entire cult but threatens the very fabric of international society." Accordingly it follows that General Westmoreland should be executed—he was in command when the atrocities were committed in Vietnam. Needless to add, he will not be; but Americans might ask themselves why he should not be in view of the principles of justice pronounced by both our military and our judicial leaders.

This is only a beginning, however, and it will not get very far with conventional patriots. We need to reconsider our whole moral code, including the traditional virtue of patriotism, and judge how relevant it is to the radically changed conditions of man's life in One World. Let us

1. This story is told in detail by A. Frank Reel in *The Progressive* of March 1970, under the title "Must We Hang Nixon Too?" Reel was a member of the defense counsel assigned to Yamashita.

therefore now begin at the logical beginning, the fundamental question of what is right and what is wrong, and by what standards we can judge.

2 / *The Need of a New Code*

NO QUESTION is more important than the question of right and wrong, since every one of us has to answer it in daily conduct; and about none is there more skepticism today. As the popular saying goes, Who is to say? Who is to judge? Then it follows that nobody has a right to judge others. The obvious reason for such skepticism is the decay of belief in absolute standards of right and wrong, a relativism due to an awareness of the different codes in other societies, past and present, but also to the plain disagreements in our own society, today especially between old and young, and to the questioning of all traditional beliefs. As plain to the thoughtful are the complications of the moral judgment, the necessity of qualifying all commandments, making allowances for circumstances, and the impossibility of laying down specific rules for the common moral dilemma of conflicting loyalties or feelings of obligation. "Thou shalt not kill"—unless murder is organized in war, made a patriotic duty. Nor is this a cynical observation, for even highminded people may agree that war is sometimes justified, as most of us felt it was in combatting the dangerous evil of Hitlerism.

Yet we all go on judging, as we must; and we can avoid much confusion by hanging on to a few elementary truths, beginning with the reality of a moral law within that forces us to judge even our own behavior. No matter how selfish, all people who are at all normal have some conscience, some sense of duty, some notion of ought and ought not. No serious thinker, or no known society, has even maintained that people have a right to reject all duties, consider only their own sweet pleasure, declare that right is whatever they say it is. The reason is quite simple: as far back as we can see him, man has always been a social animal, living in groups, which is impossible without some kind of moral code. And the necessities of social life have also led to broad agreements underlying all the diverse codes. We cannot logically derive *ought* from *is*, thinkers are now fond of telling us; so we may forget that in fact we do so anyway, if only because fellow feeling is a reality.

Almost all of us can agree that people *ought* to be fair, honest, responsible, decent, even kindly. Likewise we can agree that as a general rule they *ought not* to murder, steal, cheat, deceive, rape, or needlessly injure other people. The "general rule" brings up all the complications of the moral judgment, such as mercy killings, white lies, and the questions of just what fairness and decency require; but at least we do have some guides in making such judgments. Who would flatly reject the Golden Rule? Or in making exceptions, the proposition that one ought to be willing to generalize the principle leading to the exception? Without ever insisting on the rightness of all my own judgments, I would insist that opinions about right and wrong are not "merely" subjective or "merely" emotive, as positivists tell us, for man has clearly become capable of forming rational judgments, based on knowledge and experience.

Hence the changes in beliefs about right and wrong over the centuries, and especially in modern times, are not just a further reason for skepticism. They reflect among other things wider experience, fuller knowledge, fuller awareness of the power of unreasoned custom and convention, and the growth of a critical spirit—means to forming more enlightened and humane judgments. Let us again hang on to an elementary truth, that almost all of us agree that people *ought not* to be enslaved or tortured, even though such practices were legal in many societies, and Christian churchmen themselves long accepted slavery, in the Middle Ages deliberately practiced torture. Then I would insist that our changed views on these matters are not "merely" cultural prejudices, any more than they are "merely" personal opinions. The Charter of the United Nations demonstrates that thoughtful people all over the world can agree, in theory if not in practice, on once revolutionary ideas about human rights. We can and must go on trying to form rational judgments, adjusted to both new knowledge and changing conditions of life—the enterprise I am now engaged in. And immediately I should stress that in so massive a society the changes force much closer attention to social and political ethics—not merely to ethics in private life or personal relations—including the uses of the great power now exercised by both big business and government. About these matters neither Sunday school ethics nor philosophical texts have had much to say.

Returning to the issue I began with, the frightening inhumanity that has entered history, it most obviously calls for a reconsideration of the old principle that the end justifies the means. Despite the evil reputation this has acquired, all of us except the purest idealists accept it up to some point, as we must if we approve of any forcible resistance to tyranny, crime, or other evils, any fighting or killing in self-defense, or for that matter the eating of meat, which requires the slaughter of animals who have never harmed us.[2] Yet the Machiavellian principle of course deserves its evil reputation, since it can be and has been used to justify all kinds of inhuman policies; under it anything can go, and the ruthless go best. Today we need to be especially wary of it because of the awful means provided by modern technology, and so need to be constantly aware of the obvious objections to it. In so far as we operate on the principle, as individuals or as a people, we must be certain of both the rightness of our ends and the necessity of our violent or otherwise deplorable means; we must know that we can never absolutely separate means and ends, since they are always interacting, shifting as they influence one another; we must realize in particular that ideal ends have repeatedly been not only obscured but corrupted by inhuman means, or specifically that war can never assure "the just and lasting peace" that President Nixon promises in the Pacific; and we must be warier because of the growth of nationalism, which has made great nations much too sure of the rightness of their ends and therefore of whatever means they see fit to employ.

Hence the virtue of patriotism plainly needs to be downgraded. We can no longer afford such crude sentiments as "My country, right or wrong," nor in saving American lives the crude conceit that they are any more sacred than the lives of other human beings. We must question even such seemingly noble appeals as President Kennedy's: "Ask not what your country can do for you; ask what you can do for your country." Today such patriotism is inspiring only if it is granted that the best thing you can do for your country may be unsparing criticism of its moral failures, even flat refusal to support an immoral war. Likewise the virtue of sincerity needs to be qualified. In one aspect it is more necessary than ever because of all the routine, high-powered hypocrisy in business and government; but in our day it needs more urgently to

2. I make a point of beginning with this reservation because I have found that when I introduce the question in the classroom, most students at once declare that they reject the principle. My reason is not merely that it is important to be clear-eyed and intellectually honest, and aware of the inescapable complexities. Precisely the better students today are likely to be floored by the fundamental questions—the elementary ones—because these are seldom introduced in their advanced courses, or may embarrass sophisticates. In discussing basic issues of human values, for example, I have had classes look blank when I asked them: "What is it that makes life worth while to you?" Freshmen would of course come up with stock responses, but students grown properly wary of such responses may need to be told that no questions are more relevant than these obvious ones.

be informed, enlightened, civilized. Mere good intentions can pave the
way to disaster, or to hell on earth. In daily life much ugly feeling and
behavior can spring from beliefs sincerely held, such as racial prejudices.

To come to the possible need of a new ethic, perhaps the clearest
example is the issue of birth control. By now the moral right to practice
it is accepted by a large majority of educated people, including American Catholics. Instead, opposition to it may be considered immoral in
view of the population explosion and the threats of mass starvation. One
who knows anything about the ignorant, poverty-stricken masses of
Latin America may feel that Pope Paul's condemnation of it is truly
inhuman. (Let His Holiness ponder a recent item in a Mexico City
newspaper: a man who had long been unemployed hanged himself
when he finally did manage to find a job, because he could no longer
live with the thought that six of his ten children had died of hunger
within the past year.) But now a new issue has arisen—the spreading
argument for compulsory birth control. This would mean a denial of
poeple's age-old right to have as many children as they please, a right
that may seem more sacred in view of God's bidding at the outset that
they should multiply. The argument for it is none the less humane, in
terms of the rights of children to hopes of a decent life—hopes that
too many millions of them are already denied in the poor countries,
where the population is increasing most rapidly. Similarly with the
spread of legalized abortion. Although theologians do not agree at
what stage the human embryo acquires an immortal soul, the rights
of the unborn in any case now seem less compelling than the right of
women not to bear an unwanted child.

In America, which authorities agree could readily feed well enough
twice its present population, there is less apparent need of compulsory
birth control, and I should say no foreseeable prospect of it. Nevertheless many young people today believe that it is a moral imperative not
to have more than two children—an attitude quite different from that
of their parents, who limited themselves to two for the sake of their
own pleasure or convenience. The honorable reasons for their belief include an awareness of the environmental crisis at home. Unlimited
breeding would mean still more congestion and pollution, still more
waste of the world's natural resources. And the problems of the environment—the pressures toward an ever higher standard of intolerable
living—bring up another set of reasons for taking a hard look at our
moral code. Biologists tell us that almost everything we now do to the
natural environment is harmful to the race and works against its
survival.

René Dubos has accordingly said that "it is a moral obligation for the scientific community to devote itself in earnest to the study of ecological systems, both those of nature and those created by man." To my mind it is a much clearer moral obligation for both business and government to reconsider what they have been doing to the environment. Whatever the legal rights of businessmen to pollute air, soil, and water, established by long practice in the name of free private enterprise and with the compliance of government, they have no moral right whatever to profits at the expense of the public welfare. They no longer have any clear right either to invoke the traditional sanctity of property rights, least of all in the name of corporations, which legally are still regarded as "persons" entitled to life, liberty, and the pursuit of happiness. Property rights may seem sacred when they come down to one's own home and land, something almost all of us cherish; but even these we need to reconsider. There is surely nothing sacred about the rights of real estate interests to their kind of land development for private profit, without regard for civic or national interests, exemplified by the realtors in Florida who pushed a big new development that would have menaced what is left of the Everglades. ("People are more important than alligators," they argued; but I for one would take alligators in preference to these predatory people.) Private persons too no longer have a clear right to use their land in whatever way they see fit, for example by spraying it with DDT or other pesticides that may destroy wild life. In general, a respect for the good earth, as not a commodity to be exploited but the mother of man, or the only home he has, may now be considered a matter of social ethics as well as prudence.

Another of the traditional sanctities that has become more questionable is the gospel of work—work, that is, in the Puritan sense of a moral obligation, with the corollary that idleness or sloth is a deadly sin. This made good moral sense through the long ages when scarcity was the rule (even though it was seldom applied to the aristocracy), and it is still not simply archaic in our age of abundance, since it is a means to personal responsibility and self-respect. Yet as a Puritan gospel it soon became inhuman, a too easy means of disclaiming responsibility for the plight of the poor, on the bourgeois assumption that they didn't work hard enough and were always inclined to shirk their duties. Today it is a major obstacle to efforts to deal humanely with the problems of poverty. Most Americans consider immoral such proposals as a guaranteed minimum income for all people whether or not they work, disregarding the plain truth that a great many of the poor and their dependents are unemployed or unemployable for no fault of their own.

Meanwhile the regulations of welfare programs, administered by middle-class people, never allow the poor to forget that they are receiving charity and their integrity is therefore suspect. And today the gospel makes less moral sense because it blesses a great deal of socially useless work. That the manufacture, advertising, and sale of eyewash helps to keep our economy "healthy" is a sorry comment on the American way of life.

For such reasons it is not merely young radicals who are calling for revolutionary changes in attitudes and values. I shall keep returning to issues that suggest the need of drastic revision in our traditional morality, especially in social ethics. At present, however, I see no immediate prospect of a social any more than a political revolution in America; so I should first say that familiar old principles, including simple Christian ones, might do well enough if they are reinterpreted, adapted to new conditions, and above all strictly and consistently applied. Thus birth control is a defiance of God's will only as this is interpreted by some Christians; it is quite consistent with the Christian principle of respect for the person, and Christ's own concern for the poor. (As a simple mammy observed, the good Lord sends rain too, but people put on raincoats or put up umbrellas.) The immediate need, in any case, is to quicken a moral sense that has been numbed. It is to enlighten this sense by insisting on the relevance of the moral judgment to all our basic problems, economic, social, and political. It is again to call things persistently by their right names, say plainly that many accepted practices in business and politics come down to greed, sham, fraud, simple dishonesty. We might then go on with efforts to develop more moral imagination, about such accepted national goals as steady economic growth. All this amounts to education, as always a slow, uncertain business, never a quick solution, at best no more than a hope for the long run, and then in the knowledge that there has never been a way of holding nominally Christian nations up to Christian principles of behavior; but I can see no better hope. And at least it is a real one in view of the student revolt, which began with an insistence on not only the relevance but the necessity of moral judgments in national affairs.

In what follows I am accordingly playing the old-fashioned role of moralist, taking a hard moral line. This too can be inhuman, of course, for all too familiar reasons. Simple realism requires a recognition of the practical necessities of expediency and compromise, which make it impossible for leaders in the world of affairs to operate on pure idealism; the strict moral judgment is always likely to be too narrow, harsh, and intrusive, as in our Puritan tradition; it recalls the abiding dangers of self-righteousness that beset moralists of all schools; and always the primary need is no doubt humility, together with a spirit of charity, in a constant awareness of human fallibility and frailty. Yet we can count on ample realism in our political and business leaders, too often benighted when not serving selfish interests, and typically glossed over with platitudes or moral pretenses. We need not worry over an excess of pure idealism, like pacifism, or of too strict moral judgment in public life. We have more than enough professional realists—in political "science" too—who forget or even deny that the basic principles of democracy are moral ends, such as justice and a respect for human rights, not merely more expedient means of running government. In humility I would add chiefly that any effort to apply moral judgments consistently to the national life will involve considerable beating of dead horses. My excuse is that they are not really dead, a lot of them are alive and kicking, and on the American scene they can be expected to survive a lot more beating.

At any rate, I now begin with a hard look at our political life.

3 / *Ethics in Politics*

THE BASIC POLITICAL CRISIS of our day, it is commonly said, centers in the legitimacy and the authority of our political institutions. The reasons for the crisis are as usual complex, but they plainly involve moral issues. Negroes, peace demonstrators, draft resisters, and many other young people are most obviously questioning when not defying the authority of the government on moral grounds. Its vulnerability is now typified by John Mitchell, whose chief concern as head of the Department of Justice (aside from winning votes for Richard Nixon) appears to be the maintenance of law and order, not justice in terms of either constitutional or human rights. On the other hand, Right-wingers, Southern segregationists, and other nominal defenders of law and order have attacked the Supreme Court, whose decrees George Wallace was proud to defy. The great majority of Americans who lie somewhere in the middle do not seriously question the legitimacy of our institutions, if only because most of them are little concerned about social justice or civil liberties; yet they do not wholeheartedly believe in the virtues of American government. As taxpayers—the political role that most concerns them—they have been growing resentful of the scandalous income tax favors granted the rich. In particular they usually have a low opinion of Congress, assuming that it is made up chiefly of politicians out for their own good. Thus postmen, who are conservative enough types, defied the law by going on strike when a Congress that had inaugurated the Nixon administration by voting itself a salary raise of over 40 per cent dawdled for more than a year over a proposed raise of only some 5 per cent for these poorly paid employees of the government.

At that most Americans are not sufficiently aware of all the specific shortcomings of Congress by ethical standards. It persistently refuses to hold itself up to the standards it now and then demands of men appointed to the Cabinet or the Supreme Court. Its archaic structure, including a seniority system that gives excessive power to the chairmen of committees, becomes disgraceful when such power is exercised by men as shameless as Senator Eastland and the late Mendel Rivers. It is no less shameless in all the favors it does for business lobbies and big campaign contributors. It shows only a fitful concern over the federal agencies set up to regulate business, which are commonly loaded with men more interested in protecting business interests than public interests. Like many congressmen, these men may sincerely believe that whatever is good for business is good for America, but anyway they put first the interests of private profit, betray a pretty low conception of the public good. And so on, through all the obvious reasons why citizens who are well informed about the workings of our political institutions are most likely to feel that their legal authority is jeopardized by their want of moral authority. Hence the political crisis dramatized by angry protests, demonstrations, and civil disobedience cannot be resolved merely by sanctimonious insistence on the necessity of Law and Order, nor by tough new crime bills either—the now popular solution. It is a moral crisis, and it will remain dangerous until political leaders clearly recognize that it was brought on by the moral failings of American government.

This is not the place to tick off in detail all these failings, or to go into all the new menaces looming up, such as the invasion of privacy.[3]

---

3. I will mention, however, one especially disgraceful example—the treatment of Martin Luther King by the F.B.I. under the orders of J. Edgar Hoover. They kept him under surveillance by tapping telephones and bugging rooms on the excuse of his possible connections with Communists, and though they discovered no such connections, the news was leaked that they had evidence of irregular sexual activities. Mrs. King indignantly denied the truth of the report, which may well be only another effort to smear a black leader, but the rest of us might be as shocked by the knowledge that our government stores away in its

Instead I propose to consider at some length our Presidents in recent times. Because of their office they normally command more respect from the American people than does Congress or any other of our political institutions. (Although one might be dismayed by a Gallup poll early in 1970 revealing that the living men in the world most admired by Americans were Richard Nixon, Billy Graham, and Spiro Agnew, the poll was not significant so far as Nixon was concerned: Americans almost automatically select their President to head such lists.) Always in the spotlight, Presidents also do more to set not only national policy but the tone of our political life. And because of their great responsibilities, as the most powerful men in the world today, they best illustrate both the necessity and the complications of the moral judgment in our most dangerous age.

Given the long tradition of irresponsibility in American government, the unsavory connotations of our word "politician," and the popular assumption that politics is necessarily a rough and dirty game, only the naive can expect unswerving devotion to high principle in our leaders. Yet these leaders still include, as they always have, some genuinely high-minded men. In our time I take as an exemplar Adlai Stevenson. Like his hero Abraham Lincoln, he of course made concessions to expediency during his political career, as any man must if he hopes to make good and do good in high office. In his last years as Ambassador to the United Nations he was under a cloud because he was continuing to support President Johnson's foreign policy, refusing to resign as a group of intellectuals begged him to do, but their disappointment in him was itself a tribute to his reputation for integrity and high-mindedness; and he himself was deeply troubled because he was uncertain what patriotic duty demanded of him, whether to resign or to remain in office where he might influence foreign policy. For he was still loyal to the principle with which he had started out on his career, the effort to make the word "politician" respectable by giving it the meaning it should have—a professional public servant. He was still dedicated as well to the challenge he sounded in his speech of acceptance in the presidential campaign of 1952: "Let's face it. Let's talk sense to the American people. Let's tell them the truth"—the truth about the ordeal of the twentieth century, in which no great decisions could be easy or painless decisions. He grew troubled by "the quality of American life," a phrase he used before it became a cliché, especially because of its moral slackness. And

---

files countless reports or rumors about the private lives of American citizens. Ardent believers in the rights of Americans might regard J. Edgar Hoover as Public Enemy No. 1.

though he twice suffered crushing defeats by General Eisenhower, he won so large and devoted a following that he cannot be considered a mere failure, another proof that high principles won't do in American politics. His fame in his day, his popularity all over the world, were due wholly to the best in him, and to the belief that he represented the best in American tradition.

Stevenson's other rare qualities—his wit and humor, his grace and civility, his capacity for ironic detachment and self-criticism—stand out more when he is set beside his victorious rival, President Eisenhower. Of most popular "Ike" it should be said first and last that by ordinary standards he was clearly a "good" man. He owed his popularity immediately to his engaging grin, but also to the best in him—his basic decency, his unquestionable good will, his earnest desire for peace, his humility as a military hero who was never so vain and arrogant as General Douglas MacArthur. For such reasons voters could share his own illusion that he was "above politics." Nevertheless it was an illusion, made easier for him because in political campaigns Richard Nixon did the dirty work in the interests of the Republican Party. That he as sincerely believed all the platitudes he expressed so freely, in particular about moral and spiritual values, brings up immediately the complications of the moral judgment of national leaders today.

In the White House Eisenhower was not a bold or vigorous leader, but a bumbling President who made plainest that good intentions are not enough for leaders these days. He set the tone for a humorless, complacent, intellectually and spiritually torpid era. Having made a mediocre record, he gave himself away in his Memoirs, in which it appears that he never did anything seriously wrong, his political opponents were always at fault. The memoirs betrayed not so much vanity as his intellectual limitations, beginning with the rudimentary notions about economics that had led him to define the supreme challenge facing the nation as balancing its budget. Lacking the humor and the style of Adlai Stevenson, his Memoirs betrayed as well his shallow culture. Civilized in his intentions, he displayed little concern over the quality of American life if only because this called for esthetic, ethical, and philosophical judgments beyond his ken. Another reason why most Americans responded to the campaign slogan "I like Ike" was that he was as insensitive as they, sometimes as coarse in his judgments. Thus he believed that the egregiously self-righteous John Foster Dulles was a great Secretary of State, handing foreign policy over to him, and as self-righteously he himself condemned Communism for its "materialism" while standing in awe of big businessmen, whose success hardly exemplified a high order of the moral and spiritual values he was fond of parading.[4] Unable to appreciate a truly civilized man like Stevenson, he could not see either that his opponent was more devoted to truly spiritual values.

As striking a contrast to Eisenhower was the far more complex John F. Kennedy. The youthful author of *Profiles in Courage* rose to power as a ruthless politician, quite unlike Stevenson too, undistinguished for either honesty or the political courage he had described as the "most admirable of human virtues"; among other things, his long silence over the viciousness of the popular Joe McCarthy, whom Stevenson was the first national leader to attack, earned him widespread distrust. From the outset of his career, however, he also had a high resolve to do good in the Presidency to which he aspired, and was always quite conscious of the compromises with principle that seemed to him necessary for success in politics, as "the art of the possible." Never so naive as Eisenhower, he had much more ironic self-awareness, capacity to be really honest with himself. With this he had as much more interest in ideas, necessary to make effective his high resolve. In his successful campaign for the Presidency it became more apparent that he was an urbane man of much charm. Like Stevenson he had style—style not merely as a literary attainment, still less a means of creating a good "public image," but as an expression of genuine qualities of mind and character. And as President he won his remarkable popularity the world over by not only his youth and charm, but his humanity and good will. At home he won over many young people too because beneath his coolness he was really concerned about the quality of American life; upon his assassination, they perhaps realized most keenly how much it had meant to have a really civilized man in the White House. As grief and shame then made him a national hero and martyr, all the best in him became more radiant.

Yet his virtues were then magnified, his failings minimized too much. Morally considered, he remains an ambiguous figure. As President he

4. His own naive materialism is one reason why he got us involved in Vietnam. In 1953, when the French were still fighting there, he explained at a press conference why we were aiding them: "Now let us assume we lost Indochina. If Indochina goes, the tin and tungsten we so greatly value would cease coming. We are after the cheapest way to prevent the occurrence of something terrible —the loss of our ability to get what we want from the riches of the Indochinese territory and from Southeast Asia." This might seem clear proof that capitalism was the driving force that got us into the war, but I think Eisenhower was only rationalizing our policy by what seemed to him a practical motive. At least his consistent interest in cheap ways of doing things strengthened his resistance to proposals that we send in American troops.

was still disposed to betray both his intelligence and his idealism for political reasons, or want of courage to take unpopular stands, and never distinguished himself as a gallant fighter. Having attacked the Eisenhower administration for doing nothing about Castro, and called for intervention, he sanctioned the incredibly stupid Bay of Pigs invasion, under a cloak of hypocrisy. He paved the way for Lyndon Johnson by getting us much more deeply involved in the war in Vietnam, supporting what he knew was a corrupt, dictatorial Saigon government that made a farce of our alleged defense of "freedom." Having also made much of a "missile gap" in his campaign, he at first denied the truth when his Secretary of Defense McNamara discovered there was no such gap, in fact we were far ahead of the Russians, and he then rejected McNamara's sensible proposal of a principle of nuclear parity— we had to maintain "superiority"; so at a cost of many more billions he got us much more deeply involved too in the mad folly of the nuclear arms race, in which superiority was meaningless because it could no longer give security. Although he had a political excuse in that the Republicans, led by Richard Nixon, would surely have accused him of risking the national security had he accepted the principle of parity, my guess is that "history" will not forgive President Kennedy so much or so easily as most Americans still do. To young people he lives on as a kind of legend, but a paling one because he left them no fighting cause.

Or "history" may preserve the legend of the tragic hero because of his youth, in a deeper sense. As Adlai Stevenson said after his death, and Arthur Schlesinger amplified in *A Thousand Days,* Kennedy was the "contemporary man." Born during World War I, and still a young man when he fought in World War II, he represented a new generation that grew up amid accelerating, often turbulent change, and he responded in ways that may still appeal to young people today. He was "cool," with a style of his own; he was idealistic but tough-minded, scornful of conventional rhetoric or platitude; he was open to experiment and adventure. "What was forbidden," concludes Schlesinger, "were poses, histrionics, the heart on the sleeve and the tongue on the cliché." At least Kennedy still has more to say to our youth than do Lyndon Johnson or Richard Nixon, who presided over the revolutionary 'sixties.

To Johnson it is hard to be fair because it is chiefly the worst in him that has lived after him, in a nation still torn by the grievous consequences of his failings. The best in him—both his exceptional abilities and his democratic virtues as a simple Populist—came out in the Great Society programs he succeeded in pushing through Congress, a legislative achievement unmatched by any President before him. Now it might be forgotten because he sacrificed these programs to his growing obsession with the war in Vietnam he plunged us into. When he stepped down from the Presidency, his many critics in the press took pity on him, stressing his achievements, dwelling on the tragedy of a remarkable career ruined by one fatal blunder; and I suppose this is the decent way to treat ex-Presidents, especially because political controversy in America is often brutally unfair. Yet I think judgment of Lyndon Johnson is properly harsh because his fatal blunder was due to moral failings, not merely to faulty judgment. Beginning with his misrepresentation of the Tonkin Gulf affair, he was never honest about the war with the American people, he was vindictive in his treatment of its critics (especially Senator Fulbright and Walter Lippmann), he showed no decent respect for world opinion either, he stubbornly refused to modify his policy until it became obvious that he was highly unpopular, and thereafter he gave no sign that he had either the honesty to recognize or the courage to admit that his war was a terrible blunder, a moral disaster too. Then his performance in his televised interviews with Walter Cronkite made it still harder to forgive him. It was a thoroughly undignified performance, almost incredible because of its misrepresentations as he posed for posterity, tried to rewrite history to suit his overweening vanity.

Thus in his first interview, "Why I Chose Not to Run Again," a life-long politician who had thoroughly earned his reputation as about the most power-hungry man ever in the White House insisted that he never really wanted to be President. The "credibility gap," which became notorious because his lack of candor is written all over the record, he blamed wholly on the news media. In an orgy of self-pity he complained that he had never been really understood, never for any fault of his own. He affected to scorn public opinion polls, which he had boastfully waved at reporters until they began showing his unmistakable unpopularity. Even so he insisted that he could surely have been re-elected in 1968, and that Hubert Humphrey was defeated because of a speech in which he had departed from the administration's policy. There had been nothing wrong with this policy. And so on, through the second interview on why he had halted the bombing of North Vietnam, in which he denied credit to the few men, notably Clark Clifford, who had been honest enough to realize and admit their mistake in supporting the war.

Now, in all this I think Lyndon Johnson was in his way "sincere." When he stated that he had never wanted to be President, I did not

doubt that he had had misgivings, even before some newsmen confirmed that he had expressed them. To me the main point was that
these were occasional moods, for his interview the only moods he chose
to remember; on the public record he more often had quite different
moods, ambitious or conceited ones on which he habitually acted. By
now, I suspect, he really believes his other falsifications of the record,
and could not tell the truth about his Presidency if he wanted to. In
view of his unquestioned intelligence and ability, the common report is
accordingly what a "complex" man he is, how "intriguing and para-
doxical" (in the words of James Reston) his performance was in these
interviews. To me he seems basically naive in his vanity, which accounts for both his sensitivity and his insensitivity—a thin skin over a
thick hide of conceit. A self-righteousness that made it easy for him to
be dishonest with the American people now comes out as an egregious
self-pity that makes it impossible for him to be honest with himself.
And it is quite different from the self-righteousness, linked with high
principle, that made Woodrow Wilson a tragic figure in his defeat.
Such patriotism as inspired the foreign policy of Johnson was not so
much a lofty idealism as a vulgar national conceit, an arrogance that
frightens our allies more than it does our enemies—and that is a particular reason for judging him harshly.

Hence I cannot see him as a tragic figure. In his interviews he was
at best pathetic as he revealed another source of his self-pity, a painful
consciousness of his heritage as a poor Southern boy from the back-
woods. He suffered from his unpopularity with intellectuals and newsmen, his inability ever to win the kind of prestige President Kennedy
enjoyed; he resented all the Kennedys because of these feelings of in-
feriority that wounded his vanity. I suppose he might be pitied too
because he is doomed to failure in his fervent efforts to go down in
history as he sees himself, for historians are sure to point out the un-
trustworthiness of his memoirs of his Presidency. Yet all this only
accentuates his lack of heroic quality, or greatness of soul. As a leader
he had the will and the force of a tragic hero, but not the gallantry or
the dignity, the grandeur in defeat. He still seems quite unable either to
understand or to accept his fate. Not to mention his addiction to "corn
pone," the antithesis of a grand style: whatever tragic quality his career
may have is harder to feel when he speaks for himself.

As for Richard Nixon, finally, judgment is initially complicated by
the series of "new" Nixons over the years. Their emergence was a tacit
admission that the old Nixon of the 'fifties was an unprincipled politician, rightly known as Tricky Dick or even Dirty Dick; as a cam-

paigner his tactics were less slimy than Joe McCarthy's, but still led him only to the "middle of the gutter." When he set out on his own in the Presidential campaign of 1960 he began behaving with more dignity, or maybe just more political prudence. In *Six Crises* he wrote that experience had taught him to try to create a new public image by being "sincere," being "himself." But this only raised the critical question that would be forced by the coming of more Nixons: What is the "real" Nixon like? Presumably he is the man now in the White House. Always an ambitious man, he has at last achieved his highest ambition; no longer rather pathetically insecure and lonely as he was as Vice President under Eisenhower, who patronized him as "my boy," he is now master in his own house; and the responsibilities of high office might be expected to bring out the best in him, as they did with Harry Truman. At the outset of his administration he indeed began talking and acting more like a statesman, as he has done periodically since. Yet even before the nasty election campaign of 1970, when he put aside his avocation of statesmanship to devote himself wholly to his chief interest, politics, he continued to suggest the qualities of the old Nixon, the antithesis of Adlai Stevenson: an unscrupulous politician, now able to maintain a dignified appearance because he turned Spiro Agnew loose to do his hatchet work, but still incapable of firm devotion to any principles higher than the interests of business, the Republican Party, and Richard M. Nixon. Whoever the "real" person is, he still seems to me dubious enough to justify plain speaking about the man on the public record.

"The study of Richard Nixon," writes John Osborn, who has made perhaps the most patient effort at sympathetic understanding in *The Nixon Watch,* "requires a steadfast clinging to the fact that he is human." But he adds: "That is not easy." Nixon made it harder in his Presidential campaign of 1968. Beneath some improvement in his manners it was an essentially irresponsible campaign because of his alliance with the likes of Strom Thurmond, his vicious attacks on Ramsey Clark, his many hollow promises, his failure to tell the American people anything like the hard truth—in general, his politicking without either clear program or clear principle. It seemed more disgusting when Joe McGinniss published *The Selling of the President,* a revelation of the high-powered, cold-blooded, cynical merchandising methods that now magnify the worst in traditional American politics, lower still more the tone of our political life. Among other things his campaign managers set about creating his "public image" as a warm, compassionate man—what they knew he most conspicuously is not. Nixon played along willingly, apparently forgetting his former resolve to be "sincere." Perhaps the kindest thing to say for him was that the phoniness was in keeping with his habitual style, and so might be his way of being "himself."

Among his cheap campaign promises was an unspecified plan for ending the war in Vietnam, which may now serve as a test of his moral sense and his integrity. In referring to the war as a problem he inherited from the Johnson administration, he has not been at all candid about his own record. A pure hawk from as far back as the early days of the Eisenhower administration, when he proposed sending in American troops to aid the French in Indochina, he vigorously supported Johnson's war until it became obviously unpopular; then it became politically expedient to make some show of efforts to get us out of it. He has never intimated the moral objections to the war that made it unpopular over the rest of the world, but has gone so far as to call it "our finest hour." In extending the war to Cambodia, he boasted of our military success without intimating either the least compunctions about our bombing of its villages too, adding to the toll in peasant lives. Or let us take him at his own admirable word on the basic requirement of foreign policy in a democracy: "The American people cannot, and should not, be asked to support a policy which involves the overriding issues of war and peace unless they know the truth about that policy." As President, Nixon has yet to tell them that truth. After a year in office, under pressure from the Senate, he finally told them only part of the truth about our secret war in Laos; among the significant facts he refused to let the taxpayers know is how many billions this war has cost them. And he remained basically dishonest about the main issue, the war in Vietnam.

The disingenuous or false statements that give a lofty air to his television addresses to the American people have included the old chestnut about how North Vietnam had launched its aggression against South Vietnam in 1954, with the support of Red China and the Soviet Union. The truth is that a civil war began in 1956, without outside aggressors, after President Diem of South Vietnam, with American support, refused to hold the "free general elections" called for by the Geneva Agreements we signed; President Eisenhower later explained our repudiation of these Agreements by admitting that Ho Chi Minh would have won the elections by a big majority. So began our policy of supporting corrupt, dictatorial, unpopular governments in Saigon. To put it bluntly, either Nixon is remarkably uninformed about the war that started when he was Vice President, or he was lying to the American people. Though he no doubt has some capacity for self-deception, he was more plainly lying when he repeatedly said that we had made "every possible effort to end this war through negotiations at the conference table," insisting only on an "honorable peace" that would assure the right of the Vietnamese people freely to choose their own form of government. In fact we had refused to negotiate over a primary matter, our support of another corrupt, unpopular regime in Saigon that was jailing its political opponents, muzzling the press, and doing its best to deny the people a free choice in their government. His notion of an "honorable peace" remains unclear, but it looked more like the old vain hopes of a military victory when he kept boasting—just as Lyndon Johnson had—of the steady progress we and our allies were making in defeating the enemy, and threatening them with severe retaliation if they went on trying to defeat us. We will never be humiliated, he said with his jaw set, adding—like Johnson too—that he did not intend going down in history as the first American President to lose a war.

On the home front Nixon has similarly displayed in practice most concern for the interests of the military. While he cut a few billions from the huge appropriations for the Pentagon, he supported most vigorously an ABM program that would eventually cost many more billions, and he economized most conspicuously on education, housing, health, and other domestic programs. He also supported the dangerous nuisance of supersonic planes, as a matter of "national pride." Granted that their cost is piddling by Pentagon standards, his sense of the nation's pride raises a fundamental issue that because of the exorbitant demands of the military has been getting belated attention—the question of national priorities. It is of course impossible to determine these priorities by any purely rational method, much less a scientific one; the many public needs can never be precisely weighed or placed in a definite scale. It is none the less clear that priorities involve moral judgments about the public welfare, and I should say flatly that it is not only foolish but immoral to squander a billion or so on supersonic planes while economizing on the plain needs of human beings. Apparently our President does not think our national pride has suffered because housing in the wealthiest nation on earth has been getting steadily worse, health standards have fallen well below those of western Europe, and we have much more poverty than it does, much worse slums.

And so his "public image," now assiduously cultivated by his White House staff, forces another fundamental question: Does Richard Nixon really *care* about all the hungry, the poor, the jobless, the black people, the slum-dwellers in America? On his record to date I see no evidence that he does care at all deeply, or at least that he cares as much as he does about the support of his great not-so-silent majority, who resent the "trouble-makers" concerned about these problems. He won his loudest acclaim for his proposal to guarantee every family of four a minimum income of $1,600, which was indeed bold for a Republican; yet no family in America could live decently on such a pittance, which might seem another disgrace in the richest country on earth, especially if the guarantee institutionalized this level of poverty as tolerable. The black people he has alienated by his notorious shiftiness on desegregation and civil rights, in keeping with the "Southern strategy" of his most trusted adviser, John Mitchell. On no issue has he betrayed a passion for social justice. Or if he is to some extent growing as earnest as he habitually sounds, he does not yet manage to sound like a humane man. Here he suffers more by contrast with his prospective opponent Robert Kennedy: another morally ambiguous figure, like his brother John, who earned widespread distrust as an ambitious, unscrupulous politician, but who also won a devoted following by his humanity as well as his charm, his genuine concern over the many millions of unfortunates in America. The majority who (as I write) support Nixon are scarcely a devoted following, or at most are devoted because in appealing to their fears he has called for no sacrifice of their prejudices or their selfish interests. The "hard-hats" who warmed his heart by their aggressive display of patriotism have been most successful in keeping Negroes out of their unions, and in winning fat wage increases in defiance of his alleged war on inflation.

Hence Nixon has failed dismally in his declared intention of uniting the country, bringing Americans together. To be sure, no man could unite them today, given the deep and bitter dissensions. He has a further excuse in his knowledge that Americans are weary of crusades, not at all in a mood for sacrifice or heroic action. Yet he is clearly incapable of inspiring a great national effort, bringing out the best in the people. So far from providing the moral leadership requested by his Commission on Campus Unrest (whose report Spiro Agnew at once furiously denounced), he leaves coldest precisely the most idealistic Americans, especially the young. His best excuse for disdaining the hundreds of thousands of peace demonstrators who came to Washington was perhaps the worst that can be said about him: he has nothing to say to the aroused young people. They were either contemptuous or amused when later he told them that he wanted just what they did.

In all this I may be doing him some injustice. It is harder to be cer-

tain what the "real" Nixon is like because he lacks a style ¢
except for banalities easy to parody. ("Now let me make th
clear"—usually a sign that he is about to fuzz up some issue.,
natural desire to go down in history as a good President, I think it ¹⋅
quite possible that he is basically sincere according to his lights. So
perhaps the fairest thing to say about him is that his lights are dim.
He has given no sign of philosophical humor, capacity for ironic detachment or self-knowledge. His vanity in the White House became
ludicrous when he put its guards into Balkanish costumes and had
Marine bands make more noise to emphasize the dignity of his high
office. He appears to be a coarse-grained, shallow man, intellectually,
morally, spiritually. He was bound to sound hollow when he at last
took up the common refrain about the quality of American life, for he
had never expressed in word or deed any real concern over the esthetic,
moral, and spiritual failings of America. He gave away his own standards of quality when he explained the popularity of Hollywood West-
erns by the wholesome moral they taught—the good guys always beat
the bad guys. (He neglected to mention that in John Wayne's
"Chisum," which he was pleased to see twice, the good guys won by
taking the law into their own hands.) The nature of the "spiritual
values" he habitually rang in as a campaigner in the Eisenhower era
was uncertain, but grew clearer when the Rev. Norman Vincent Peale
presided over the wedding of his daughter, Billy Graham was called
in to bless his inauguration. Even so he failed to demonstrate the power
of Christian thinking when he called the week in which the American
flag was planted on the moon the greatest week in human history since
the Creation, and had to be reminded by his spiritual mentor Billy of
the week in which his Lord died to redeem mankind.

Altogether, these moral judgments of our Presidents may well seem
too harsh by the standards of ordinary times. They are perhaps too
harsh even for our own time, inasmuch as our leaders not only have
to play politics at home, with an eye to a great unheroic majority, but
have to deal with international affairs still governed by *Realpolitik*
when not by fanaticism; there is no easy righteous way of dealing with
the Russians, the Chinese, the North Vietnamese, the Arabs, and all
the other troublesome peoples. Yet our times are so dangerous, and so
often barbarous, that moral judgments of leaders are more imperative
than ever before. We can no longer afford as much sham, irresponsibility, and dishonesty as Americans have traditionally put up with in
politics. And if my own judgments are unfair, I should at least insist
on the relevance of the kind of questions I have raised in sizing up our

leaders and candidates for leadership. Does this man have enough political courage to take an honest stand even if it is unpopular? Does he
really care about all the victims of the American way of life? Is he a
civilized man, really concerned about the quality of our life? Is he
sensitive enough to the routine barbarities of our time? Humble enough
to be aware of the dangers of the national self-righteousness? On all
counts, what does he have to say to the earnest, thoughtful, idealistic
young people of America?

Their discontents bring us back to the failings of their elders, the
majority of Americans who elect our leaders and make it too easy for
them to be dishonest, hard to be candid, courageous, humane, civilized,
consistently ethical, or truly Christian. The dearth of great men, inspiring men, on the political scene today is hardly surprising when the
American people appear to be in no mood for greatness, for great
leaders today would surely have to tell them hard truths, call on them
to make sacrifices of their selfish interests. Most of them do not want
to know the truth about our war in Vietnam, or more precisely, would
refuse to accept it. Yet it is too easy to blame everything on the obvious
shortcomings of the American people. First we must consider their
privileged leaders, including the many more they do not elect—in business, technology, the media, education, the world of thought—who help
to mold public opinion and public taste. With them too it is important
to apply an insistently moral judgment.

4 / Ethics in Business and Technology

IT HAS LONG BEEN CUSTOMARY to distinguish problems as political, economic, and social, with specialists to study each. This is of course a
convenient distinction for practical purposes. It has become increasingly
artificial, however, with the growth of a technological society in which
big organizations or power establishments directly affect the lives of all
of us. The policies of General Motors alone, for example, affect millions
of people, ranging from its employees, suppliers, and retailers to its
customers, not to mention the state of America as a whole. More clearly
than ever before all these problems are social, in that none can be divorced from considerations of the public welfare. And all are therefore
moral, especially in a democracy. The trouble with too many of the
specialists is that in the name of realism, objectivity, or science they

have slighted when not ignored ethics in their field of study. However unwittingly, they have supported another of the double standards in American morality, one for private life and another for business or economic life. I have been saying that we can no longer afford to divorce politics from ethics to the extent that they have been in traditional American practice. Still following a hard moral line, I now say emphatically that American business needs to be judged by much higher standards than it usually is. As emphatically I repeat what I remarked years ago, that it is doubtful whether dishonesty has ever before been so pervasive, systematic, dynamic, and respectable as it is in America today.

Nominally, all respectable businessmen subscribe to a professional ethic that condemns fraud or dishonesty and parades the responsibilities of service to the public, in Rotary speeches even the ideal of Christian service. In common practice, however, it is a distinctly lax ethic, which permits deceitful advertising and packaging, manufacture of shoddy or worthless products under fancy names, collusion to milk consumers, indifference to public health and safety, and other abuses of power over a mostly uninformed, gullible public. To cite but one scandalous example, the drug industry was at last report exploiting the health needs of the American people to make the highest profits of any major industry, running close to 20 per cent, and much of it through misleading or strictly false claims for pills or placebos, promoted by some $900 million a year spent on advertising—incidentally about three times what the nation spends on medical education. Hence the great economic, political, and social power exercised by big business poses the basic question that concerns me here: How can it be kept morally responsible? Since it has little to fear from the law at present, and ethics cannot be simply legislated anyway, I again see no way except education, as best exemplified by Ralph Nader—the development of an enlightened public opinion that might bring pressure to bear on it.

Immediately this points to another failure in responsibility in big business, the mass media that most directly influence public opinion and mold public taste. Television, the most popular of the media, has been the most venal in its devotion to the business of selling commercials, and its subservience to the Madison Avenue sponsors of its program.[5]

---

5. Spiro Agnew confused this issue when he frightened the news media by his attacks on what he called their irresponsible criticism of the Nixon administration. While many newsmen unquestionably have a low opinion of Richard Nixon, they are seldom so outspoken as are ultra-conservative commentators and editors (not to mention Spiro himself) in their attacks on liberals. The

Since the big networks have made immense profits from franchises
granting free use of the public air waves, and television has become
such a political power that Richard Nixon spent a record $20 million
on it in his campaign for the Presidency, they might be expected in
patriotic return to grant free time to major contenders in elections, but
they resist such proposals; they regard their franchises as private property, not a public gift. And so they bring us to the root of the whole
problem, the free private enterprise system. Still celebrated as the heart
of the American Way, the source of our distinctive virtues, this was
long ago effectually divorced from the Christian ethic as business sought
and won economic autonomy, and today it is more obviously the main
source of the abuses of business, in the interests of private profit rather
than the public welfare. Granted its real virtues in stimulating enterprise, the many honorable exceptions to its shady practices, and to my
mind a trend toward more responsibility to the public interest, it is
nevertheless shielded from the moral judgments applied to ordinary
human relations by the attitudes expressed in such common sayings as
"Business is business," "Business and sentiment don't mix," and "We're
not in business for our health."

   Let us go beneath the many too familiar complaints, even though to
most Americans they are not familiar enough. The objection to advertising, for instance, is not merely that so much of it is deceptive or
strictly dishonest. Basically it fails to show a decent respect for people.
In exploiting their ignorance, gullibility, or irrationality, it commonly
preys on their vanity, their selfish desires, their meaner aspirations to
status, their pathetic fears of being unsuccessful, unpopular, sexually
unattractive, etc. If the products it glamorizes give them what they want
or make them feel better—the standard defense of advertising—it does
so more often than not by debasing the public taste, just as it debases
the common language, makes a whore of our "mother tongue." And
now that it has become at least a $15 billion industry, indispensable to
our kind of economy, it accentuates the basic failure of this economy
to take adequate care of public needs. The many grave domestic problems confronting the nation, such as the ruin of its big cities, can be
met only by a mighty, costly national effort that would require sacrifices

---

great bulk of the American press has long been conservative, supporting the
Republican Party; and anyway it has made its main business less to inform than
to entertain the American people. The big television networks, which provide
chiefly show business for their many millions of customers, have also been most
notorious for their timidity, shying away from controversial programs that might
upset their audience, lower popularity ratings.

by taxpayers and consumers. Meanwhile the advertising industry does its gaudy, expensive best not only to persuade people to gratify all their private, selfish wants, but daily to create artificial new wants. "It is now or never," President Nixon rang out when he at last woke up to the problem of pollution. If American business goes on having its way, it will be never.

Inasmuch as industry has been the primary source of pollution, it might fairly be expected to assume a primary responsibility for cleaning up the foul environment, or at least to submit gracefully to regulation. As it is, a typical news item begins: "Industry spokesmen told federal officials yesterday that they are all for water pollution abatement, but . . . ." There is always a but, in this case that such abatement "shouldn't be overdone to the point of trying to make waterways too clean too soon, or at too great a drain of company profits." Spokesmen for industries polluting the air are at best as lukewarm in their cooperation for the public good. They all have a point, of course, since their business is first and last to make profits. Still, even one following a soft moral line might ask: Why should they not sacrifice some of their profits to pay for some of the harm they have done to the environment in which all of us have to live? In practice they appear to resent just the inconvenience of altering their customary irresponsible ways of doing business. All the signs are that industry will make no real financial sacrifice—the costs of whatever "abatement" it submits to will be passed on to the public in higher prices. If by any chance President Nixon did insist on "now," he would have still more inflation to combat, with no more whole-hearted cooperation from business, except perhaps support for economies in public welfare programs.

A somewhat subtler but still fundamental issue is raised by another standard refrain of manufacturers of products that appear to have unexpected harmful effects: there is "no conclusive evidence" of serious effects. With the tobacco industry the moral issue is not at all subtle: for purely commercial reasons it is still trying to discredit the very strong evidence that cigarettes may cause lung cancer. (If ever marijuana is legalized, it can be counted on to rush into production without bothering to weigh the evidence about its effects.) But there is more to think about in all the chemicals now in daily use—food additives, detergents, pesticides, wonder drugs, contraceptive pills, etc.—which may have bad side- or after-effects, such as were dramatized by DDT. Somebody has remarked that at least Americans don't have to worry about cannibals any more because we're all inedible—we have more DDT in us than the U.S. Food and Drug administration permits in meat; but then the question is, just how much DDT can we stand in us? The answer is that we don't know. I assume that only long-range studies will yield "conclusive evidence." Meanwhile we do know that it has killed many birds and fish, got into vegetable and animal life all over the world, and that there is every reason to believe that it is not good for any form of life, including us—enough evidence to persuade some countries to ban its use. Meanwhile, too, the odds in doubtful cases in America usually favor industry, the interests of private profit, which have most influence in government. My point is simply that in such cases the burden of proof should rest on industry, not on the interests defending the natural environment and the public good. Now that unforeseen side- and after-effects have been widely publicized, it is plainly un-ethical for manufacturers of new chemicals and drugs to rush them into the market without first doing a thorough job of research on such effects.

That all but the most flagrant abuses of private enterprise are usually tolerated by the government brings up another plain shortcoming in its ethic, the political uses of its wealth and power. The outright cor-ruption that has been traditional in American politics for more than a century, dating from the wholesale bribery of legislators in the railway era, remains common in state and municipal government, but when now and then a particularly scandalous example is exposed the public forgets that it is businessmen who do the corrupting. More insidious on the national scene is the accepted practice of indirectly bribing politi-cians by big campaign contributions. Although it may be said that businessmen are only protecting their own interests, perhaps in the sincere belief that these are in the national interest on the horse-and-sparrow theory ("The way to feed the sparrows is to feed the horses"), the result is obvious inequities. They have wangled special favors for the wealthy in income tax regulation, of which only the most notorious example is the pampered oil industry. In the growing "grants econ-omy" they also get far bigger subsidies from the government than do the poor. The chief beneficiaries from agricultural subsidies, for in-stance, are big wealthy farmers (like Senator Eastland), not the many poor ones for whom they were ostensibly designed. In various ways businessmen support a system that has been described as "socialism for the rich and free private enterprise for the poor." And now that big business has become more closely allied with government, above all in the military-industrial complex, it is freer to identify its interests with the national interest. Corporations engaged in the weapons industry, normally on contracts that protect them from risk, naturally support the exorbitant demands of the Pentagon to which domestic programs have been sacrificed. They have no compunctions either about manufacturing the most frightful weapons requested by the military. The Dow Company publicly disclaimed all moral responsibility for its napalm—it was only fulfilling government orders. By these standards it would presumably be willing to serve the interests of a Hitler, as Alfred Krupp did.[6]

Here we are brought to an issue of wider import, the compulsions of modern technology. It has now been acknowledged that the military decision to bomb North Vietnam was made because that was what we were best at; ethical considerations did not enter, except for the usual flimsy pretense of hitting only military targets. (One might incidentally observe that moral obtuseness is a common sign of stupidity: our generals have yet to learn that our best isn't good enough for combatting guerrillas in underdeveloped countries full of jungles instead of industrial targets.) Napalm was no doubt introduced for the same purely technical reasons—it was "effective." At home the drive to do whatever is technically feasible, without regard to human costs, may now be symbolized by supersonic planes. They are so far from being even clearly profitable that the big airplane companies refuse to make them unless the government pays for their cost, but despite their threats to the environment the program went on because they represented "progress," in which America must be first. If or when the men responsible for this kind of technical progress think of the public interest, it is not typically in terms of basic human values.

Among them perhaps the most faithful, uncritical servants of business are the engineering profession. Elsewhere I have cited a consulting engineer who was much troubled by the common disregard of his fellows for their professional oath "to serve the public interest above all others," and an editor of *The Institute of Electrical and Electronics Engineers* who agreed in deploring their habitual silence about obvious violations of their ethical code:

> It was not engineers who mounted the assault on pollution, but surely it was engineers who first knew what was happening to our water and to our air. It was not engineers who forced the program of safety in automobile design; but who was more aware of the problem? Who

6. It might be noted that at the Nuremberg trials Krupp was not given a death sentence, only jailed for some time, even though he contributed more than the generals to the rise of Hitler, and as an employer of "slave labor" during the war was aware of his atrocities. By American standards he was not a full-fledged "war criminal," just a smart businessman who unfortunately worked for the wrong side.

better than the engineers involved knew of the dangers in the Apollo spacecraft design and could have issued more effective warnings? Who can better police extravagant proposals for government contracts than the engineers, and indeed, who can better tell us of the deficiencies and dangers in atomic power plants than the engineers who design them?

Those working for the government are presumably more devoted to the public interest, but may still take as narrow, short-sighted a view of it as the Army Corps of Engineers—dedicated to keep on building dams all over the land at whatever cost to the natural environment.

More complex issues are raised by another kind of "progress," the accepted national goal of steady economic growth. It has been endorsed by almost all economists, who typically avoid value-judgments for the sake of objective description and analysis, but nevertheless assume that such growth is a good thing. (Kenneth Galbraith is a conspicuous exception.) It is indeed a reasonable goal for the many poor, undeveloped countries. At home it makes clear sense up to the point of taking care of the needs of a growing population. Yet it has been by no means simply a good thing, and by now the acceptance of it as a national goal may be regarded as a bad thing, especially on moral grounds. The immense growth in the gross national product has meant nothing like a comparable gain in the public welfare. While the GNP includes the huge production for the Pentagon, the many billions squandered in obsolete weapons, it has been swollen in the private sector by the production, advertising, and fancy packaging of all kinds of trivial goods, good for little but to keep up with the Joneses—paltry or false values that economists ignore in their apparent assumption that all that matters is the quantity of goods. They have shown little interest either in the problems of the distribution of the national wealth, the poverty amidst increasing plenty, the glaring inequities. The devotion to steady economic growth could make good moral sense if the annual increases in the GNP were devoted to relieving and reducing poverty, cleaning up the rural slums and the black ghettoes, but in fact much more of it goes to the prosperous in the form of still more automobiles, color TV sets, speed boats, new gadgets, new models of everything under the American sun—in effect therefore guaranteed to be obsolescent within a few years, so as to create a market for newer models.

Still other objections ignored by most economists center in the environmental crisis. Steady economic growth will mean immediately more polluting and fouling of the environment, increased production of garbage, trash, all the solid waste that litters it. The waste in turn accentuates another glaring inequity, that Americans, constituting 6 per cent of the world's population, already squander some 40 per cent of its natural resources, while most of the rest of mankind live in poverty, do not even get enough to eat. Thinking of the world's needs, Robert McNamara—once head of the Ford Motor Corporation—has said that we do not need and cannot afford still more automobiles every year. Thinking of the world ecological crisis, some scientists say more plainly that the chief national need is austerity, less production of material goods, or a lower standard of living for the prosperous. A moralist might add that without some practice of austerity, instead of forever spending, consuming, and wasting while the quality of our life deteriorates, we have no right to preach to the world the virtues of free private enterprise, democracy, Christianity, or any of our national idols. As it is, we set the world a bad example, for the many poor countries aspire to something like our affluent way of life instead of concentrating on the abolition of abject poverty and misery; and while they face the prospect of falling ever further behind America, we contribute to their aid a small, dwindling fraction of one per cent of our gross national product. If in this respect we are no worse than most other countries, including the Communist ones, we might at least give up the indecent conceit that we are a great people, much less a Christian one.

As realists who in their professional work ignore such moral or idealistic considerations, economists are only typical of most technical specialists in our "advanced" society. The vast assortment of new technicians —systems analysts, system engineers or designers, data processing specialists, operations researchers, computer programmers, social engineers, model-builders, etc.—have generated the belief that we now have a "new breed" of man, commonly called technological man. Beneath their devotion to ultra-modern techniques, however, most of them are essentially old-fashioned bourgeois types. Their values are the familiar bourgeois economic values, only improved means to the goals of efficiency and economy, wealth and power. They accept the economic and political *status quo,* perhaps recognizing the need of new policies or reforms, but not of radical changes in attitudes, a concern first and last with basic human values, the quality of life, the ends of the good life. Always granted many honorable exceptions, they are not deeply troubled by the economic, political, social, and cultural failures of our technological society, which in view of our immense resources may now rightly be called moral failures. They lack a world view adequate to the challenges of modern technology, either the new opportunities or the new menaces it has created. I venture to say that their ruling professional attitudes, which on the surface are eminently relevant, are therefore now essentially archaic, irrelevant to the fundamental needs of America and of the world.

Of the many social and political scientists among our specialists I shall say more in a later chapter. Here I should add that I am now talking about intellectuals, including educators—not merely businessmen and their servants. In the past most intellectuals were literary or humanistic types, commonly much concerned about human values, and therefore addicted to social criticism; among Spiro Agnew's names for their impudent survivors (who include me) is "effete snobs." But Zbigniew Brzezinski has welcomed a "profound change" in the community: these old types are rapidly being displaced by "organization-oriented, application-minded intellectuals," under whose leadership America has become *the* creative society" (and who, I might add, are much less likely to offend Spiro). Today they are leading America into a new era that he has christened "technetronic," because one of its sires is electronics. This will be another revolutionary era, so much so that America is suffering grievously from its birth pangs, but Brzezinski rejoices in our mission to lead mankind into it. If so, a moralist might remark that despite his own role as prophet he is at heart no more a new breed of man than are electronic engineers, or than other "futurologists" who accept basic trends without close attention to the possibility or the desirability of resisting them. Thus he dismisses attacks on American "imperialism" as irrelevant: they only distract intellectuals and statesmen from our inescapable revolutionary mission. "For better or worse," he declares, "the rest of the world learns what is in store for it by observing what happens in America." It would be easier to share his optimistic belief that the changes will be for the better if so many of his "organization-oriented" fellows were not oriented in favor of amoral judgments, or in effect of the establishments that control—or fail to control—our terrific technology.

Among them is Henry Kissinger, now an influential figure in the White House. As a professor at Harvard, he was a realist whose course on foreign policy centered on a discussion of strategies by which America might achieve its objectives or fulfill its own needs. He had an easy way of disposing of students who raised moral objections to our policy: they were "instant moralists." At the same time, however, he sounded a plaintive note in a Harvard-Oxford television debate on our policies in Vietnam: he said he was most disturbed because others were questioning not merely our judgment but our motives. Now as an architect of our foreign policy he no doubt feels free to question the motives of the Soviet Union, Red China, North Vietnam, and other countries that give us trouble, but on the record our own motives remain immune to moral judgment—they are always pure, as President Nixon says over and over. So, like other realists, Kissinger can have it both ways. Students and other doves who want to put an end to the killing in Vietnam, Laos, and Cambodia are "instant moralists," while he can concentrate on devising effective strategies for securing whatever he considers our national interest because this is above criticism.

But I will not read the roster of hard-headed specialists or experts, in government and out, who have refrained from moral judgment of our national policy.[7] Let us again get down to the fundamental issue, the authority and the influence of experts. In a technological society these types are so obviously indispensable that it is idle merely to scorn expertise or attack the "cult" of the expert. Among them are of course modest men who have learned the elementary lesson of exhaustive study, that the more one knows about economic, political, and social problems, the more fully one realizes that there are no simple or certain solutions. As acknowledged authorities, however, they are prone to arrogance, excessive confidence that their judgments are necessarily better than those of non-specialists who take a broader or more philosophical view of problems. In a society that puts a premium on know-how, they are not typically distinguished for large-mindedness, imaginativeness, vision, wisdom, or know-what. Outside their specialized field, or sometimes in it, they can be remarkably shallow, even naive. In their common addiction to technical jargon they may be blind to the ethics of such jargon, which is too often a pretentious way of expressing commonplace ideas— in effect a fraudulent way of boosting their self-esteem—or worse, a way of neutralizing or concealing moral issues, as it was when our military undertook the "pacification" of regions in Vietnam. (A recent example was the extension of our bombing raids to Cambodia, for the purposes of what Secretary of Defense Laird called "interdiction.") Experts are seldom distinguished for moral sensitivity either. And so they too force the hard question: When they are in positions of au-

7. Those who wish further examples might consult Noam Chomsky's article "The Responsibility of Intellectuals" in the *New York Review of Books,* February 23, 1967. Chomsky is perhaps too rigorously moralistic in his judgments, but at least he thoroughly documents them. Among his hair-raising examples was Professor David N. Rowe, Director of Graduate Studies in International Relations at Yale University, who proposed to the House Committee on Foreign Affairs that the United States buy all surplus Canadian and Australian wheat so as to weaken the government of China by bringing about mass starvation in the country.

thority, how can they be held to moral account for the policies they authorize?

Emmanuel Mesthene, a leading authority in the study of modern technology and its social consequences, has addressed this whole issue in characteristic terms. The technical process of government, he writes, "is clearly a job for experts and for all the sophisticated information-handling and management techniques that can be brought to bear on it." Once more the magic word is "techniques." If it doubtless befits what is now called the "science" of public administration, those of us who still cherish breadth of view, know-what, and moral imagination may be reminded of ex-Secretary of Defense McNamara: an exceptionally able, up-to-date administrator and expert in cost-analysis, who on periodic visits to Vietnam was so unsophisticated as to be taken in by our generals, every year returning to announce that we were winning the war. When Mesthene goes on to say that a democratic system must also provide "effective mechanisms for monitoring and evaluating actual performance" by the experts, we may shudder a bit at the "mechanisms," but anyway wonder to what extent the unspecified standards of performance would involve values other than technical efficiency. (How well has Henry Kissinger performed as Nixon's chief adviser on foreign affairs?) Mesthene also notes with regret that "our social and moral sciences are as yet far from being equipped, conceptually or methodologically," to deal with problems of value-judgment concretely and rigorously. Although I do not know what he means by the "moral sciences," and doubt that there are any worthy of the name of science, I am pleased to think that there are no technical experts in them. In any case I again conclude that our only hope of holding our experts to strict moral account is not any "scientific" standard of performance, but a more sensitive, enlightened public opinion.

This brings us back to the American people. The most apparent reason for their limitations as voters is that the great majority of them are poorly informed about the basic issues, often woefully ignorant. But a related reason is that their moral sense is pretty blunt, their moral judgments are as coarse. This too explains why they are taken in by unscrupulous politicians, advertisers, and publicity men—and why they are not making an earnest effort to become better informed. They remain devoted to a way of life involving attitudes that in a time of crisis can be considered highly immoral, particularly in the light of the Christian principles they profess to believe in. Again I propose so to consider them.

5 / *The American People*

WE MUST ALWAYS KEEP IN MIND what absent-minded literary intellectuals and single-minded radicals may appear to forget: there are millions of decent, friendly, kindly Americans. To a considerable extent most middle-class people live up to their image of themselves as hard-working, law-abiding, home-loving, self-respecting people. Critics of American society may also forget that it produces not only many persons like themselves but the many more they are appealing to. Beneath the conspicuous materialism there is still a large reservoir of simple good will, potential idealism. As a great many people responded to the best in Adlai Stevenson and John F. Kennedy, so they might respond again to a high-minded leader. Between the World Wars Ortega y Gasset argued that one reason why America was not fit to lead the world was that its people had not suffered enough, as had all the major European peoples. Now they are beginning to suffer more, immediately because of the costly, futile war in Vietnam, then because of all the grievous, apparently insoluble problems at home. They are at last entering the history known to all other peoples, in which national frustration and defeat are normal episodes. When President Nixon assures them that we will never accept humiliation in Vietnam, they might even begin to realize that we have long since been humiliated in world opinion.

Yet the suffering has scarcely brought out the best in the American people. In their sense of frustration, most feel only resentful, angry, bitter, the more so because they have no clear idea of what has gone wrong and why. All they know is that taxes are high, the cost of living keeps going up, their cities are often buried under smog, their streets are no longer safe at night, the youth are taking to drugs, Negroes and students have been getting violent—there are all kinds of trouble and trouble-makers. Lower middle-class people have reason for resentment in that the government has been paying them much less attention than either the poor or the rich, but they have been taking out their resentment chiefly on students, peace demonstrators, and especially Negroes. Surveys reveal that a large majority of them believe that black people have just as good a chance as they do for good jobs, housing, and education, and some 40 percent even complain that the blacks have a better chance. Such seeming ignorance is unpardonable obtuseness because they don't have to read statistics or scholarly studies to know better—all they have to do is to look around in their cities and suburbs, or in their labor unions. The harsh truth is that most of them are as indifferent to social justice for any but themselves as they are to civil liberties.

At most they have some excuse for not realizing how well off they are by the world's standards, inasmuch as the needs of people are not determined by mere subsistence, but by the standards of their society, the accepted way of life; television commercials daily drill into them reminders of all they need to keep up with the Joneses, not to mention the latest models and gadgets they do not own. Nevertheless they take for granted their automobiles, television sets, and all the other material goods that do give them a much higher standard of living than the vast majority of the world's population. They are largely indifferent too to the plight of the millions of poor whites who do not enjoy their own privileges, still regarding them as lazy, shiftless, or naturally immoral; they have no idea why poverty today, though less common than in the past, is more of a problem for the same reason that they feel bitter about their own relatively low status. And as one moves up the income scale one finds only a little more sensitivity, enlightenment, or moral imagination. Americans as a whole are forever whining about the taxes they have to pay for the privilege of consuming far more than their share of the world's natural resources. Briefly, they are the most spoiled, self-indulgent people on earth. They look more like a sick people because their frustrations, resentments, and anxieties spring from no high purpose, no vision of the good life beyond status, ease, comfort, and pleasure.

So we return to the crucial questions. Are the American people ready and willing to support the mighty national effort necessary to effect even elementary improvements in the quality of American life? Certainly they are not prepared to spend the many billions it would take to clean up the black ghettoes, but what about problems directly affecting whites too? On polls most of them indicate a belief that the government ought to spend more money on a few domestic programs, in particular for combatting pollution and organized crime. There is nothing like a majority, however, in favor of increased spending on medical care, better housing, better schools, or attacks on the basic causes of crime in the street. Even on pollution their response is far from certain. They clearly do not realize how many billions it would take, in both tax money and higher prices for industrial products, to restore a decent environment, or simply to prevent it from becoming more uninhabitable. As for the world ecological crisis, and the increasing gulf between affluent America and all the poor peoples of the world, I assume there is no question: the American people are not at all prepared for austerity, any sacrifice in their standard of living. No government programs are less popular than foreign aid programs, known to Americans as "give-aways," not as modes of either national prudence or Christian charity.

In view of the reservoir of decency and good will, I suppose some further excuses for them may be in order. It is perhaps unreasonable to expect any people to make such sacrifices except in such plain emergencies as war, and even in war Americans have never had to endure the ordeals common in Europe. At home they prospered during World War II, made more money than ever before, while making no sacrifices more grievous than getting along with gasoline rationing and fewer automobiles; and during the costly war in Vietnam their standard of living continued to go up, while their fighting was done for them chiefly by the sons of the poor. As a people they have never been put to a really severe test. Now they can hardly be expected to face up resolutely to crises they have only begun to realize dimly are crises, with little help from their Presidents. (Nixon followed up his ringing now-or-never declaration of war on pollution by proposing a pitifully inadequate program.) Meanwhile we have to grasp at straws, the beginnings of public realization of what the country is up against. Americans may at least be aroused by such obvious nuisances as smog, oil slicks, and sonic booms. Although long accustomed to noise, congestion, filth, and ugliness, and always averse to paying higher taxes, a normal concern for the welfare of their children might at last make them think soberly about the kind of environment these children will have to grow up in. Then they might be stirred by moral indignation, perhaps enough to make them support efforts to curb traditional practices that threaten the public welfare so plainly and seriously that they must be called evils. If it is too much to expect that all such awareness will induce them to get along with fewer automobiles, they might possibly begin to question the need of annual new models and other fixtures of the American way of life.

In any case the effort at education must go on. Let us consider again the possibility of a new moral code, a "transvaluation of values" such as Nietzsche proposed. His thought might serve admirably as both an antidote and a tonic. In his attacks on what he called the prevailing "slave morality," he offered the most devastating critique of the mediocrity of modern mass society, for which America might now be considered preeminent because of its affluence: the shallow complacence, the slavish conformism, the slavish materialism, the rule of money values, the lack of real style, the devotion to a paltry kind of happiness, and withal the hypocrisy of a society that calls itself Christian. For all his extravagances, and such misleading banners as "beyond good and evil," he always put morality first. It was an aristocratic morality that exalted the virtues of courage, an independent spirit, a lofty sense of personal honor, the will to surpass oneself—together a "religion of the freest, gayest, noblest souls." Young people today might be stimulated in particular by his primary concern with individuality, full self-realization, and by his insistence on the necessity of involvement and personal commitment. In time they might learn to appreciate as well qualities rare in philosophers—a keen sense of the difficulty of complete intellectual honesty, or of inescapable ambiguity in any commitment, a "radical irony," and a tragic sense of life. In his view a truly free, independent spirit must reject any easy faith, any hope of sure solutions, any promise of lasting salvation—any effort to escape the hard conditions of man's life.

But Nietzsche is of course strong medicine, much too strong for ordinary mortals. No people as a whole has ever been capable of his aristocratic morality, still less of his radical irony. He himself confessed as much: "Hatred of mediocrity is unworthy of a philosopher. . . . Just because he is the exception, he must protect the rule, and he must encourage self-confidence in all the mediocre." At that Nietzsche is pretty heady for young people too. In exalting his "master morality" he praised war and cruelty, attacked both Christian and democratic principles, freely indulged in a hatred of common people that he declared unworthy, and in his often nasty or violent moods branded as slavish such qualities as modesty, sympathy, kindliness, public spirit, and brotherly love—qualities that the young must respect if they are concerned with social justice or simple humanity. And otherwise Nietzsche's basic ethic is not really new. His aristocratic virtues are incorporated in Western tradition, from Homer on down through the Renaissance. The individuality he prized is enshrined in Emerson's gospel of self-reliance. At his best, Nietzsche can toughen this American gospel by an irony and a tragic sense of life that are lacking in Emerson and most other typically American writers and thinkers (not to mention the nation's leaders today), but that are not alien to Western tradition.

So I repeat that familiar old ethical principles might serve well enough if they are readapted to contemporary conditions and consistently applied. Let us consider Kant's categorical imperative: "So act as to treat humanity, whether in thine own person or in the person of another, as an end withal, never as a means only." It is of course strictly impossible never to treat people as a means to some end. Still, they should at least never be treated *only* as means, but always with respect for their humanity, their dignity as persons. The moral short-comings of American society—in politics, business, technology, education, or the thought of our technical intelligentsia—might be summed up in the statement that too often people are regarded only as means, to either selfish or technical ends. They are reduced to voters, consumers, labor or manpower, role-players, statistical samples or symptoms, instruments of the "national purpose," holes in a punchcard, means of "feedback"—anything but as full-fledged persons with minds and lives of their own. The trouble with too many Americans (as Emerson complained more than a century ago) is that they are not interested enough in becoming such persons, do not sufficiently respect their own humanity.

I V

A NEW LOOK AT FREEDOM

1 / The Basic Issues

LTHOUGH SOME THINKERS still speak of "true freedom," by which they usually mean being virtuous and wise by their own standards, or in the Communist world obedience to a state that supposedly governs in the best interests of the people, there is no real question that the issues of freedom are extremely complex. In experience the term means concretely freedoms of various kinds, political, economic, social, academic, intellectual, spiritual. When we speak of "personal freedom," to the youth the most precious kind, it involves all these other kinds, and then some. Freedom is always relative too, a matter of shifting degree, for of course no man ever is or can be wholly free. Man is always subject to the constraints of physical necessities or natural laws, so much so that some thinkers deny that he is actually free; to social constraints, since from the days of the cavemen he has always lived in groups or tribes; and in great societies or nations to legal or political constraints. He is also subject to internal or self-imposed restraints, ranging from obedience to the dictates of God through fears and anxieties to the compulsions of neurosis. A further complication is "subjective" freedom, or the state of feeling free, even though objectively considered the person might appear quite unfree. (As a loyal Nazi said when told he no longer enjoyed freedom of speech, "Who wants to make a speech?") And such ambiguities have grown more pronounced in the so-called free societies, especially because of modern technology.

Let us look at the American people today. They are still pleased to think of themselves as a "free people," and they certainly enjoy political rights unknown to the vast majority of mankind through the ages until our time. They also enjoy far more freedom in the sense of opportunity than did the poor, illiterate peasant masses, or than still do the great majority of people in the rest of the world. Among their historically novel advantages are free public schools for all, means of widening their opportunities. Yet a common word for Americans today is "slavish." Over and over again we hear that they are fettered by compulsions to keep up with the Joneses, to conform, above all to consume. "Theirs not to question why, theirs but to go and buy." That for the most part they appear to be willing slaves only accentuates a deeper, unconscious bondage to modern technology. While this has blessed most of them by freedom from want, it harries them by creating artificial wants, a need for ever more material goods to maintain their status, or their illusion of personal freedom. Many writers substantially concur with Herbert Marcuse: "A comfortable, smooth, reasonable, democratic unfreedom prevails in advanced industrial civilization." And the increasing signs of anxiety beneath the superficial complacence of Americans suggest another popular theme, the "escape from freedom." This may recall Dostoyevsky's now celebrated parable of the Grand Inquisitor, who maintained that for the masses of men freedom is an intolerable burden. I doubt that this is literally true of most Americans, doubt still more that they yearn for the Inquisitor's prescription of "miracle, mystery, and authority"; but at least he points to another complication, the responsibilities of freedom, and the real question whether Americans are up to these responsibilities or fit for freedom.

No less ambiguous is the state of the youth of America. Demands for freedom have been among the rallying cries of the student revolt: more freedom in their social life, freedom to dissent, freedom from academic regulations and routines they consider irrelevant to their needs, and the right to participate in the formation of academic policy affecting them. They have also been rebelling against the conformity of their elders. At the same time, teenagers have been enjoying more freedom than ever before in all history—freedom from the adult responsibilities of working that youngsters used to begin assuming at an early age, and opportunities to enjoy an unprecedented wealth of entertainment and of material goods. Their conspicuous self-indulgence raises some question about whether they too are fit for such freedom. As students in college millions of them—up to half of those of college age—likewise enjoy opportunities once restricted to a very small minority. Never before have young people had such a wide range of choice in vocation, habitat, and the uses of leisure, and now such a freedom of choice in values and life-styles. They may be considered the most pampered college students on earth. And certainly they have been able to express their dissent, more freely and forcibly than American students ever did in the past.

Yet once more I think their complaints are basically legitimate. In the schools their education was not only free but compulsory, no matter how inferior their school, in an authoritarian system in which they were treated like children even as they matured. As they went through the prescribed routines that seemed carefully calculated to discourage personal independence, initiative, imaginativeness, spontaneity, and creativity, and that are nevertheless still approved by most parents as a necessary discipline and a preparation for respectable status, they were given no say about the means or the ends of their education. In the universities, where they have much more freedom of choice in courses and potential careers, many feel oppressed by a professionalism that restricts their personal development, especially because they do not aspire to conventional status in American society. They begin to realize that the notorious permissiveness that gave them so much freedom as teenagers is due primarily to slackness, not to any positive faith in the values of personal freedom, least of all to any belief in the possible values of nonconformity. As they try to express or assert themselves they grow more aware of public hostility, and the menace of violent repression. Altogether, I think students do not appreciate enough their privileges, the freedoms and the opportunities they enjoy; but I also think they have good reason for not simply enjoying them, or not feeling so free as objectively they appear to be. They are seeking personal fulfillment in a society that is not at all dedicated to the ideal of "the full and free development of every individual."

So let us get down to the basic issues of freedom. Since everybody uses the word, we have to begin at the logical beginning, the old question of what we mean by it. Given the various kinds of freedom and the many different concepts of it offered by philosophers, nobody can say what it really and truly means. We cannot possibly give it a precise meaning either, one that would satisfy rigorous semanticists; for purposes of analysis thinkers may narrow its meaning to a particular kind, but only a broad concept can embrace its various meanings in common usage as in common experience. In my own attempt to write a History of Freedom, I operated on a definition that still seems to me useful because it is both broad and relatively objective or neutral:

"the condition of being able to choose and to carry out purposes."
involves the most common idea of freedom *from* external constra.
linked with the idea of rights; freedom *to* do what one wants, or
portunity, positive ability with available means; and the vaguer b
no less important idea of freedom *of* choice, a conscious power of mind
that distinguishes man from other animals. All correspond to the
popular assumption that freedom is a good thing, but by no means imply
that it is always or necessarily good; man is obviously able to choose
and carry out foolish or evil choices. My definition is neutral in that
it leaves open the question of freedom *for* what. This has become more
important since Americans have acquired a wealth of means, or possibilities of making asses of themselves, but first let us stick to a fairly
objective meaning on which we can hope to agree, as we cannot on
the proper uses of freedom. It is a condition in which a man is able
to answer this question for himself.[1]

Then to begin at the historical beginning, we immediately run into
the basic ambiguities that persist beneath the major developments in
modern times. Culture, in the sense of all learned belief and behavior,
was the primary means to the development of the distinctive powers
of man, the effective freedom he achieved through a measure of control over his environment; and it also enslaved him, imprisoned him
as it still does most people today. The rise of civilization, a much more
complex, highly organized society than the prehistoric village, greatly
extended his powers and his range of choice, enabled him to cultivate
interests beyond the basic needs of subsistence; and it also restricted
freedom in various new ways, especially for the many poor who now

1. I am waiving here the issue of free will vs. determinism, an old controversy
that is still going on. Through science we have indeed learned a vast deal about
the natural, social, and cultural determinants of human behavior, and it is never
clear just how man can be free in a presumably lawful universe. Nevertheless
I am content to stick to the empirical fact that man does have distinctive powers
of mind that have enabled him to carry out all manner of purposes, to acquire
an extraordinary power over nature, and incidentally to debate freely and self-
consciously whether he has done all this of his own volition. It seems to me as
clear that whatever people profess to believe in this matter (as in the past about
an omnipotent, omniscient God who predetermined everything), they continue
to think, feel, and behave as if they were to some extent free agents, responsible
for their decisions, and especially for whatever personal achievements they are
proud of. B. F. Skinner, an eminent behaviorist who denies that man is free,
is also pre-eminent for his confidence in his own ability to condition people to
suit himself. At any rate, the issue does not appear to be a live one for the
youth who are asserting their freedom or demanding more. Among the evi-
dences of human freedom are qualities they especially prize—personal independence, nonconformity, imaginativeness, and creativity.

emerged as a distinct class, while it supplemented prehistoric taboos by inhibitions that led Freud to view civilization as essentially a restriction of individual liberty, a source of discontents. The early civilizations, which were all ruled by autocratic gods and god-kings, or in effect by "miracle, mystery, and authority," set up no conscious ideals of freedom. These first appeared in ancient Greece, where they centered on political freedom, and they were inherited by Western civilization, along with the problems they created that the Greeks and Romans failed to solve. But in our most dynamic of civilizations "freedom" took on changing meanings or contents that enriched, endeared, complicated, and confused the concept. Since I shall dwell on the complications, including new menaces to individual liberty in the "free societies," we might first recall in piety the major battles that have been fought and substantially won—among others the battles for religious freedom, universal suffrage, the abolition of chattel slavery, the rights of workers to organize, the emancipation of women, and the abolition of child labor. We owe an immense debt to the past, which entails an obligation to carry on the endless battle.

Now to reconsider some specific issues, with an eye in particular to the individual or the personal freedom in which the youth are most interested.

2 / *The State and the Individual*

FOR ALL THE "ADVANCES" of Western civilization, and lately the revolutionizing of man's life, we still have to deal with the most conspicuous historical source of constraints on freedom—the state. In *Man vs The State* Milton Mayer has reviewed the failure of the wise men, beginning with Socrates, ever to define clearly and unequivocally people's rights against the state, and above all the rights of the *person*—not merely "the people." In the *Apology* Socrates asserted most memorably the rights of individual conscience, telling the men of Athens that he would obey God rather than them, die rather than alter his ways; but after he was sentenced to death—by "the people," be it noted—he not only accepted their verdict but argued in the *Crito* that citizens must obey the laws, do whatever their country bids. Similarly John Stuart Mill faltered in *On Liberty,* the classic argument for the fullest possible personal freedom. The only liberty worth the name, he maintained, is that of pursuing one's own good in one's own way, so long as one does not clearly harm others or restrict their liberty to do likewise; the state has no right to constrain the individual for his own good, only to prevent harm to others or to protect itself. The trouble remains that almost anything one says or does, or fails to do, may have harmful effects on others; while failing to draw a clear line, Mill even went so far as to argue that the state had a right to compel "certain acts of individual benevolence." And so with liberal jurists and philosophers to this day: always they hedge their ringing declarations of rights. The state must never restrict constitutional liberties, for example, such as freedom of speech—unless there is "clear and present danger." How clear and how serious? Danger to whom?

For lovers of liberty the problem remains that it is always the state that answers such questions, draws and enforces the lines. Today, as Mayer points out, the problem is more acute because whereas law in the Anglo-Saxon world has traditionally been regarded as the bulwark of liberty, it is now widely regarded as its enemy. To many Americans it is the bulwark of social injustice, not to mention the common brutalities of its enforcement. More and more of them regard civil disobedience as not only a moral right but a duty.

Now, as an admirer of John Stuart Mill I should first say that the problem he tackled is strictly insoluble. While he rightly emphasized that there was "no recognized principle" by which the propriety or impropriety of government interference was judged, I know of none that would make it possible to draw a hard-and-fast line between the rights of the individual and the necessary constraints upon his freedom —a line that the state nevertheless *has* to draw. It is no more possible to give a precise, invariable answer to the question Abraham Lincoln asked of Congress: "Must a government of necessity be too *strong* for the liberties of its people, or too *weak* to maintain its own existence?" Perhaps he was wrong in deciding that maintaining the existence of the Union justified a Civil War, during which he restricted the liberties of the people in the North too; but certainly he was no tyrant bent on oppressing them. As for the individual, the principle of Aristotle still holds: "No man is a judge in his own cause." He who defies the state or the law may be a highminded idealist, a self-righteous egotist, a neurotic, or a fanatic, whether on the Left or the Right. In any case no state can ever afford to give its people the right freely to disobey any law they consider unjust. And in our time the problem has been further complicated because the state has done much more to promote the effective freedom of its citizens by social welfare legislation. In so doing it has intruded on individual liberties in many ways unknown to the Founding Fathers, making compulsory not only education but vaccination, sanitation, the payment of social security taxes, medicare taxes, minimum wages, and so on—compulsions that almost all liberals approve. Today we all must depend on it to combat social evils, such as pollution, by drastic regulations. The traditional idea that every gain in the power of the state means simply a loss in the freedom of its citizens was never realistic, but it is now clearly obsolete. In a democracy it is as hopelessly unrealistic to regard the state as simply the enemy, always *versus* man.

Yet all of us but anarchists have to go on trying somehow to draw lines. It is easy to criticize Mill's principle, but what are the alternatives? Who can suggest a precise or infallible way of drawing the lines? Knowing of no such way, I still see no better guiding principle than Mill's, when applied in his own humane, reasonable, liberal, flexible spirit, always with an eye to changing conditions.[2] It is not an exciting way of looking at our problems, least of all for young people filled with indignation. Nevertheless the issues remain complex, the anger on all sides today makes it more important to try to keep one's head. And the youth might at least welcome Mill's sober belief that the greater danger is not too much freedom and individuality, but the inveterate tendencies to coerce and to conform.

So I believe it clearly is even in these turbulent days. The increasing violence, capped by the recent wave of bombings, is indeed unquestionably dangerous. Civil disobedience may be condoned, or even upheld as a moral right, when it remains civil, but smashing, burning, and bombing cannot be regarded as rights or tolerated by any state. Many of us who deplore the violence may still condone it too readily out of sympathy with the indignation of its perpetrators, especially the blacks, or out of a guilty conscience such as George Orwell confessed to: "I had reduced everything to a simple theory that the oppressed are always right and the oppressors are always wrong: a mistaken theory, but the natural result of being one of the oppressors." Yet I cannot believe there is any real danger of the government's becoming "too weak to maintain

2. The glaring sin of the "saint of Victorian rationalism" was his argument that despotism was "a legitimate mode of government in dealing with barbarians," people not yet "capable of being improved by free and equal discussion"; and by barbarians he meant non-Western peoples, the subjects of the British Empire. But a disciple of Mill should have no trouble rising above this Victorian prejudice, which he himself might have been trusted to outgrow had he lived later. Thus he began as a champion of *laissez faire* but veered toward socialism as the growth of industrialism made plain the abuses of unregulated private enterprise, the harm it was doing to workers.

its own existence," or too lenient with law-breakers (unless they are businessmen). Much more apparent are the dangers of the trends to a police state, fortified by oversimplified choices—either security or liberty, either Law and Order or anarchy. If need be, said Spiro Agnew, "the American people would choose the policeman's truncheon over the anarchist's bomb." As yet we are of course not reduced to any such choice; but conceivably we might be by such tough attitudes, which are only provoking more violence.

Meanwhile the fear of riots and crime has led to plain encroachments on ordinary rights. The anti-conspiracy and riot-control law passed by Congress has produced some convictions even though conspiracy was not at all clearly proved; all leaders in demonstrations are liable to the charge that they crossed state lines to incite a riot, especially since Attorney General John Mitchell announced his belief that disorders on the campus were due to "hard-core nihilists" moving from state to state to destroy our institutions. For Washington, D.C., Congress has approved the no-knock provision that enables the police to break into private homes without warrants, and "preventive detention," which enables a judge to keep accused persons in jail before their trial because he believes that if free on bail they might commit more crimes; although the laws are probably unconstitutional, John Mitchell believes they will set a good example for the rest of the country. And in a nation now ridden by fear such laws are clearly popular, so much so that even many liberal Senators are afraid to oppose them. On polls most Americans reveal not only their usual ignorance of the Bill of Rights but their approval of tougher anti-crime measures, just as a large majority believed that the murder of the four students at Kent State was the fault primarily of the students. Most unpopular are the defenders of constitutional rights, such as Ramsey Clark, whom Richard Nixon singled out for attack. ("We're going to have a new Attorney General!" he promised during his campaign—and this was one promise he kept.) Again "the people" don't care about the rights of the person.

Another fast growing menace is the invasion of privacy, made possible in particular by computers and electronic super-snooping devices. The government is compiling an ever larger dossier on all citizens through census, income tax, social security, and other records, all of which the computer makes instantly available. Such data is clearly necessary for administrative purposes, and as yet constitutes only a potential threat; it might even remind us of all that the government is doing for people by contrast with what Edward Shils called "the golden age of privacy," Victorian times when people were free to be poor, hungry, sick, or dying in complete privacy. But the data is all there, and not merely in the form of statistics—it is under individual names. In the meantime some plain abuses are flourishing. Both the U.S. Army and the F.B.I. have files on suspected "subversives," including much unproved rumor and hearsay, to which the suspects are denied access. For years the F.B.I. has also kept an ear on these suspects by wiretapping and bugging, in violation of the law, and now the Justice Department has announced the right to do so in the interests of whatever it conceives to be "national security"—a right that is being exercised much more freely under John Mitchell, since he sees conspiracies everywhere. The individual has no more protection against state and local police, who likewise bug many phones—nobody knows how many. And Congress has only begun to consider protecting citizens from invasions of their privacy by business interests too. Super-snooping devices are freely advertised and sold. Credit bureaus, one of which alone has an inventory of 70 million names, have been unregulated even though their records include hearsay and nobody knows how much misinformation, since the public was denied access to them. The American Security Council, supported by large firms, boasts a file of 6 million "peaceniks," "pseudo-intellectuals," and other subversives, useful for blacklisting purposes; it too is unregulated, and tax exempt to boot. And so on—into the nightmare of all that Big Brother might find out and do about anyone at a moment's notice long before 1984.

All such disrespect for rights has not only obviously failed to achieve any real security, but strengthened the case for civil disobedience. Now as I see it, there can never be either a legal right to civil disobedience or a hard-and-fast rule for defining a moral right; the issue is always complicated by the motives of those who defy the law, the question of the justice of their cause, their willingness to accept both the legal consequences and the moral responsibilities of their acts, the extent to which they are merely asserting their own conscience or trying to persuade others to disobey, perhaps to instigate a popular revolt— complications that were largely ignored by Thoreau in his classic essay on the subject, written after spending but one night in jail. (At what point of injustice would he have sanctioned violent resistance to the government?) Yet all history indicates that there can be no blanket condemnation of civil disobedience either, least of all in a nation proud of its Revolution. From Socrates and Jesus down through the centuries to the Germans who refused to obey Hitler, mankind has honored many martyrs to the law who obeyed their conscience. History rather lends positive support to Thoreau's contention that an undue respect for law may be the greater danger, above all in the eyes of those who value freedom and justice. Granted the obvious need of law, and of enforcement of it by the state, we cannot reasonably demand that all citizens respect it unless it commands respect—and by a just administration as well.

At least there is surely no sanctity in the law as it is actually administered, by police, prosecutors, judges, and attorney generals, or today as it is enforced by Mayor Daley, Judge Hoffman, Governor Reagan, and John Mitchell. There is no moral authority either in a legal system that metes out vindictive punishment for civil disobedience to such obviously high-minded men as Fathers Daniel and Philip Berrigan, treating them as common criminals, while it coddles Southern segregationists who for years have refused to obey the law of the land on no moral grounds higher than their right to go on treating Negroes as inferiors. Whatever one thinks of the tactics of the Berrigans, Benjamin Spock, and other such "conspirators" against the draft, they are not self-serving men but patriots trying to awaken Americans to a vitally important issue, a war they consider both immoral and unconstitutional. Again I can see no real danger that America will ever have too many of such conscientious objectors, much more reason to believe that the sanctimonious when not hysterical insistence on Law and Order is a more serious menace to democracy. What troubles me is not that so many young men are resisting the draft, but that they are forced to make so cruel a decision, often to pay so heavy a price for obeying their conscience.

And then again that "the people" are against them. In a democracy "the people" necessarily means in effect a majority, which in America is indifferent to the constitutional checks upon the possible tyranny of the majority. Most Americans do not realize either that the democratic principle of government by the consent of the governed clearly implies a right to *dissent,* or as both Jefferson and Lincoln explicitly said, even a right to revolution. While they dissent freely enough as Republicans or Democrats when the wrong party is in power, and feel as free to disobey traffic laws and others that interfere with their own sweet pleasure, they are hostile to anything like radical dissent. And their hostility extends beyond the political activities of the youth to other quite legal expressions of unconventionality, such as long hair. Accordingly they bring up a still larger subject, the unlegislated constraints on freedom. In the history of America political repression, in defiance of constitutional rights, has periodically been flagrant enough to be frightening, as it was in the Joe McCarthy era; but it has troubled only

the minority concerned about these rights, directly affected only those
who were branded as radicals or pinkos. More pervasive and persistent,
always directly affecting almost all Americans, have been social constraints. While these have naturally been reflected in laws regulating
social behavior, they operate as powerfully in private life without any
legal enforcement.

3 / Society and the Individual

To BEGIN WITH, we are of course dealing with another old story, dating
from the rise of culture—the power of custom and convention in all
societies through the ages. Obvious as it now seems, it is a power that
until recent times was largely unrecognized, resented only now and
then or here and there, because most people have always accepted un-
thinkingly as natural and necessary the way of life in which they were
brought up. Today young people rebelling against their elders' way of
life perhaps need to realize more fully how old and universal the
story of conformity is. Nevertheless we are again dealing with something new in the history of freedom. Society, Mill complained, was
becoming the main enemy of personal freedom. Like de Tocqueville
before him, he recognized that democracy, which in theory prized it,
in practice generated pressures against individuality. It fostered the
tyranny of public opinion, which was the opinion of the common man,
and at that seldom really his own—it was common to all the Joneses.
Thus in social life Americans have long been hounded by the fear of
being thought queer, "different" in any but superficial respects. And
with the growth of an immense industrial society the pressures against
the individual have notoriously grown massive. Regimentation in factory and office, standardization of all kinds of goods, the increasing
uniformity in the vast suburban sprawl, mass culture providing standard
entertainment, incessant bombardment by admen pounding in the
need of buying what everybody else is buying—all such driving tendencies have made it harder for people to pursue their own good in their
own way. They have transformed natural conformity into conform*ism*,
a more compulsive kind that makes people more fearful of nonconformity, and today more hostile to the youth.

Now, these complaints are so familiar, and so often stereotyped, that
I pause to consider some of the confusions and complications that may

be as often overlooked. In the chaos of laws regulating social life, reflecting the tyranny of public opinion, some are relics of Christian tradition, not products of democracy or a mass society. Sunday blue laws, for instance, are clearly inconsistent with the principle of religious freedom and the separation of church and state, but for most people are only an incidental nuisance; they are free to drink all they want in their homes, dash off in their cars, entertain themselves in many ways not approved by the old-time Puritan God. Legislation against suicide, though rarely enforced, is a plainer anachronism; in a free, secular society a person surely ought to have the right to put an end to his own life if he finds it intolerable. More troublesome are laws regulating sexual behavior. Most of these too are seldom enforced, otherwise (as Kinsey pointed out years ago) up to 90 percent of American males would be in jail; but by the same token those who happen to be picked up by the police have a right to complain of injustice, which makes nonsense of the mystique of the sanctity of "the law." The many laws, varying from state to state, also contribute to a hopeless confusion, with no clear principle at all about what kind of sexual behavior is harmful, to whom, and why. Injustice is aggravated and confusion compounded by shifting *mores* in a period of increasing sexual freedom, which still shocks so many people that legislators seldom dare to repeal or alter the laws on the books, but which is enjoyed —or abused—even by many conformists in suburbia.

Offhand the clearest test of Mill's guiding principle is the laws against homosexuality. On his grounds the punishment of homosexuals who make public advances to young boys may be justified, as an offense against the youngsters; but what of the many more—numbering into the millions—who make love in their own way in privacy? What harm are they doing to others? As it is, they have been liable to not only legal punishment but much personal suffering, in a society that has developed a peculiar horror of them, branded them as "perverts," and so has afflicted many of them with feelings of guilt. Still, the horror raises another difficulty. Lord Devlin, a broad-minded jurist, has maintained against Mill that society has a right to prohibit kinds of behavior that outrage the prevailing moral sense, even if they do not clearly harm others, for to permit them would weaken the moral bonds indispensable for holding a society together. The basic needs of society must come first even if its accepted beliefs are prejudices, as he grants they commonly are. I suppose his argument might seem especially reasonable in America today, given its deep divisions, the tendencies to slackness, and the disrespect for authority. And it may be argued that the individual too is likely to suffer if he outrages the accepted moral sense, unless he is an uncommonly independent person. At least Mill is vulnerable on this source, for in arguing the supreme importance of individuality, the need of going one's own way, he slighted not only the values of community but the deeper human need of a feeling of belonging, for lack of which many people today suffer from a feeling of meaninglessness.

Yet I substantially adhere to Mill's principle, on the grounds that he was emphasizing what most needs to be said, today even more than in his own day. Lord Devlin may be no less embarrassed by the need of drawing lines, for his argument could be used to justify the long historic record of intolerance, bigotry, oppression, persecution. Thus Catholics used to persecute Protestants, and vice versa, because they felt outraged on lofty religious grounds; they were convinced that correct belief was necessary for the salvation of their immortal soul, and that tolerating heretical beliefs—the most terrible of social infections—might jeopardize the salvation of their children; but who would justify such discrimination today, much less persecution, even though millions of Fundamentalists still feel this way and dominate many communities? Granted that there is always some danger in tolerating unconventional behavior that deeply offends most people, on behalf of their children too, I again see no real danger of too much individuality in America today, and always a greater danger in the common impulse to coerce. Similarly the greater need is continued effort to enlighten public opinion, especially because many Americans have grown more tolerant, more sophisticated about sex, more aware that the horror of homosexuals is peculiar to our culture. As for the many young people who in trying to pursue their own good in their own way are outraging their elders, I shall keep returning to the confusions and the excesses they are naturally liable to, but also to my belief that the basic impulse of most of them is healthy.

Philosophically considered, Lord Devlin speaks out of a long tradition going back to Plato, naturally dear to conservatives in particular, that the principal need or the proper goal of the good society is harmony. With the rise of industrialism a literary offshoot of this tradition was the idealization of the "organic society" of the past, supposedly typified by the Middle Ages, in which every man knew his place. Naturally we are all for social harmony in the abstract; or at least few would set up disharmony as a natural goal. Even revolutionaries dream of a classless society that would at last achieve permanent harmony. So I venture a few elementary observations. No civilized society can hope for the harmony of any beehive or anthill, least of all if it is a free, open society. Throughout history all important innovation has always meant some disharmony, conflict with traditional ways. All the great creative ages, such as ancient Greece, the Renaissance, or for that matter the Middle Ages, have been marked by much discord and conflict if only because they were creative. Many great men, from the prophets of Israel, Socrates, and Jesus on, have been conspicuous trouble-makers, resented especially by the conservatives of their day. In particular the long struggle for freedom has always been just that, a struggle against powerful conservative interests, often a violent conflict. Discord remains no ideal, good for its own sake; but it has its uses, and it is not only normal but necessary for any effort to approximate the good state or the good society. Today the rhetoric about national unity will remain empty rhetoric so long as that effort goes on.

Or unless it is superseded by a new offshoot of the old tradition, sprung from modern technology. Various technicians who might all be called social engineers dream of achieving social harmony through new techniques, improved communication, and efficient organization that would eliminate all friction, in effect realize the ideal of mechanism. Some writers fear that this is not an idle dream: the "new utopians" may succeed in eliminating the nuisance of individuality, producing the smooth, comfortable unfreedom of Brave New World. To me this still seems only a remote possibility; for a long time to come we can count on plenty of friction, discord, conflict. But meanwhile our technology is the locus of another large set of problems.

For all the popular complacence it has induced by its triumphs, it is a basic source of social disharmony. More and more serious thinkers are concluding that the crises it has created demand a fundamental re-organization of both government and society, a new politics, a new legal code, a new social ethic, or a new religion. Inevitably they differ when they begin to spell out these terms in concrete proposals. About how to keep a technological society democratic, for example, some call for much more government control over private enterprise and the uses of private property; others, fearful of centralized technocratic government and the growing gap between rulers and ruled, call for more "participatory democracy," especially in local communities; still others call for a new political philosophy, to replace an eighteenth-century theory about the limited powers and responsibilities of government which Americans still appeal to while government has been steadily extending both, and to define more clearly what it should and should not do today to realize the democratic ideals of equality and freedom. But since they generally agree that all such proposals should be effected by democratic means, and that any "new" ethic, social religion, or value system would require changes in basic attitudes, all in effect agree on the need of basic efforts to educate the public.

On this score I should once more say first that the too familiar story of the mechanizing, dehumanizing, depersonalizing, alienating tendencies of modern technology call for considerable qualification, in the light of an elementary historical sense. So far from being fatal to individuality, our technological society provides far more opportunity for self-determination, self-expression, and self-realization than was enjoyed by the masses of men who throughout history toiled in ignorance, poverty, and frequent misery. With few exceptions, the societies of the past were authoritarian societies, in not only their government but their unquestioned traditions, their gods or superstitions, their social customs, their family life, and such education as they offered. Our society is freer too in that it provides what Mill regarded as the necessary conditions for the realization of individuality, "variety of situations" and above all opportunities for making choices. All people except the very poor have a much wider range of choices in their manner of life than did the illiterate peasant masses who in pre-industrial societies always made up the great majority. Add that millions of people now have to work in factories or offices, where the story goes that they are dwarfed by big organizations, reduced to cogs in an impersonal mechanism, made slaves to mechanical or bureaucratic routines, but then ask: Are they really littler, less human, less free than the peasant masses who year in and year out were compelled to go through the same routines, with very little if any opportunity to change their occupation or their habitat, embark on anything like a career?[3] It is the very real gains in effective freedom, for both society and the individual, that make people more aware of the compulsions, the abuses of power, the opportunities missed, the wrong choices, the failure of most people really to make their own choices, and all the other standard complaints.

---

3. Students—and intellectuals too—might get a more vivid sense of what life used to be like for the vast majority of people from F.M. Esfandiary's *Optimism One*. It is a consistently extravagant, one-sided book from its opening sentence: "Today optimism is the only rational philosophical outlook for modern individuals. . . . Ours is the Age of Success." But as an Iranian by birth, brought up in the Old World, Esfandiary knows better the common life in pre-industrial societies and can appreciate more all the advantages we take for granted. At least he can serve as a healthy antidote to a too easy, merely fashionable pessimism or cynicism about modern man.

Still, the complaints are legitimate just because we have developed a relatively free society, with an unprecedented wealth and power that we could obviously make far better use of. While we of course have to pay a price for our new goods, our whole new way of life, it need not by any means be so heavy a price as it has been made by the failures of our political, business, and educational leaders. It will not do either to say that our complaints are rooted in very novel expectations, exorbitant by the standards of the past, for we are entitled to our rising expectations by our awareness of richer, finer, or simply more humane possibilities of life that now could be realized. That most men have always put up with poverty is no reason at all for not insisting that the extent of poverty in most affluent America today is both unnecessary and unjust, especially since we could afford to spend $25 billion to land an American on the moon. It has been said that "privacy" is another modern concept, unknown to all the people in the Old World who used to live in big families, rarely had a room of their own, and were under the constant surveillance of spirits, gods, and demons; but this gives not the slightest reason either to discount a desire for privacy or to condone the growing invasions of it. Our basic needs are no less real and important because some of them have become needs only in modern times.

And so with the values of individuality and personal freedom, which we have come to prize more than did any past society. True, we need to discount the often excessive alarm over the "identity crisis," the atomized masses, the feelings of alienation and impotence, and so on, in an awareness that the great majority of people in the authoritarian societies of the past were not treated as individuals, their stable or fixed identity in the village was not a truly *personal* identity, they rarely felt lost because there was little social mobility, they were sharply separated from the ruling classes, and if resigned to their lot, not consciously alienated, they were nevertheless in a real sense outsiders. But we also need to take quite seriously the worries over the pressures against the individual, the problems of personal identity, and the possibilities of alienation because they reflect a real growth of individualism, more concern for the person or the self, more potential power of self-determination, and more reason for feeling alienated from a society in which Americans like to say "Be yourself," but are mostly hostile to young people who are really trying to find or to be themselves.

Here I pause to consider a further ambiguity. With this growing concern for the individual has come a strong tendency in the social sciences to minimize his importance or even his reality, to treat him as a mere product of his society and culture, a cell in the "social organism," or even as a "discredited hypothesis," a "fiction." Hence I repeat the assumptions on which I operated in my efforts to write a History of Freedom: "that society is not in fact a biological organism, least of all when it becomes so highly organized as civilized societies are; that the individual is never a mere cell but has some independent existence, behaving or misbehaving in some ways of his own choosing; that as a product of his society or culture he is still strictly an individual, unlike all the other products; that the creative individual is the most apparent agent of social and cultural change; and that whatever value the social sciences have in promoting understanding and social well-being can be realized only in the lives of individuals." Though I state this as a personal conviction, not a scientific truth, I have found no reason to modify it. And since few young people doubt that they have a power of independent choice, many are insisting on the right to be themselves, I shall also repeat that my conviction is not so idealistic as it may sound in our behavioristic, deterministic climate. The historically rare privilege of a wide range of choice open to young people is also their problem. They *have* to make critical choices about their vocations, social roles, life-styles, the kind of company they want to keep, the kind of self they want to be—choices that leave them wide open to more discontent than the youth of the pre-industrial past who followed almost automatically the ways of their fathers. And their problem is aggravated because in their preparation for adult life they are constantly rated, from the early years of grade school all the way through graduate school, and as they exercise more freedom of choice are liable to penalty.

The competitiveness encouraged when not compelled by all this rating is intensified by another abiding source of confusion, the gospel of individualism as it has been preached in America. This has been an economic individualism, later dignified as "rugged"—a gospel that today might be called obsolete except that in the glorification of free private enterprise it remains a powerful tradition. While it inspired many little businessmen, with the growth of industrialism it soon came to mean chiefly economic freedom for the men at the top—freedom to make millions, like as not at the public expense. It meant little to the mass of underlings they employed, workers whose efforts to win more economic freedom for themselves by forming labor unions and going on strike were bitterly fought by businessmen down to our time. Otherwise the gospel served chiefly to confirm a kind of individualism in

America that de Tocqueville was struck by more than a century ago: a calm, settled policy—beyond simple selfishness—of every man for himself. Today it serves to confuse the issues of an economy dominated by giant corporations, in which there are still some rugged individualists at the top, but many more conservative young "organization men" who want first of all security, not opportunities to get more rugged. For my purposes here the gospel of individualism remains relevant because it was quite different from the ideal of individuality upheld by John Stuart Mill, the fullest and most harmonious possible development of a person's capacities for the pursuit of truth, beauty, and goodness. Above all, it tended positively to impoverish individuality, restrict or warp such personal development, by confining interests to economic activities, the practical business of making money. As a class the business leaders of America have hardly stood out as either great personalities or cultivated men.

The many students headed for the business world remain generally indifferent to Mill's ideal, the more so because of the growing vocationalism and specialization that narrow their studies. With the many dissident young people, however, the traditional gospel of individualism is clearly passé. They are not demanding freedom to make a lot of money, nor seeking either a good secure berth in the business world. Rather they appear to be seeking what Herbert Marcuse called freedom *from* the economy and its imperious demands. Hence they recall us to the question of freedom *for* what. Many say they just want "to do their own thing," but what is their thing, and why or to what extent is it worth doing? Many also want freedom to take "trips" whenever they please, but what do they bring back from their trips? They may recall the traditional distinction between liberty and "license," which usually led to the conclusion that a man was "really" free only when he was doing what is right and good—by the writer's standards; yet there is such a thing as license, irresponsibility, or simple self-indulgence. It is plain enough in the behavior of many teenagers. Even the many more dissidents who seem to me basically earnest might think harder about the question of what is right and good, and about the responsibilities of freedom, including a respect for the claims of society as well as for the rights of others.

Nevertheless they can claim the support of quite honorable tradition for their basic demands—tradition they might also look into more closely. As Benjamin Constant pointed out in the past century, freedom for the ancient Greeks meant the right to participate actively in public affairs, not the right to privacy, an independent life of their own, or freedom from the state; their rights as citizens entailed public interests and duties that required considerable sacrifice of their private life. By contrast Mill's definition of personal freedom represented a distinctively modern ideal, the more so because he insisted that "whatever crushes individuality is despotism." Today student rebels want both these kinds of freedom. The ideal of participatory democracy that the Greeks realized in their little *polis* cannot possibly be realized as fully in our massive society, with its big government and many other big organizations, including universities; but it has grown more relevant as a means of resisting impersonal rule by bureaucracy or technocracy, assuring more government "of, by, and for the people." Mill's ideal of personal freedom is obviously relevant, no less because of the difficulties of defining, defending, and realizing it.

In both political and social life the youth have returned, if not always consciously, to the traditional association of Liberty, Equality, and Fraternity. Since de Tocqueville many thinkers have remarked that the democratic ideal of equality is by no means inseparable from the ideal of liberty, but more or less antithetical; some have gone so far as to argue that the more equality there is, the less freedom, and vice versa. Athenian democracy is a plain proof that the principles are in fact by no means inseparable, since it was founded on slavery. As for American democracy, de Tocqueville, and after him Mill, made it plain that the principle of equality could lead to the tyranny of the majority, or especially of public opinion. Yet these ideals are by no means simply antithetical either, but intimately connected, both historically and logically. Granted that the citizens of Athens were a small minority, they did not and could not achieve the measure of freedom they enjoyed until they were granted equal rights. In Western civilization the struggle for freedom was again a struggle for more equality in rights, or in Christian terms, more recognition in legal and political practice of the spiritual equality of men, their common dignity as beings endowed with an immortal soul. America became the first full-fledged democracy because it was the first nation to grant equal suffrage, which gave all citizens a say in their government and a means of standing up for their rights, and also the first to grant a measure of equality of opportunity through free public education. Then the emancipation of women became the clearest proof of the necessity of a principle of equality to secure their freedom. Today young people have become concerned about equality primarily through their sympathy with the blacks, whose nominal freedom has been severely limited because they were denied social equality. Similarly the related ideal of fraternity, which has been obscured by the American gospel of individualism but has grown more meaningful to the youth, can be realized only by men who feel in some sense equals.

Hence the youth have also grown more concerned about social justice as a primary end of democracy. Justice too cannot be equated with freedom, nor with equality either, since throughout history all civilized societies had codes of justice but few proclaimed ideals of freedom and equality, many legalized slavery. But justice too cannot be sharply separated from these ideals. Some connection was apparent as early as the Code of Hammurabi, who expressed a concern for the weak and the poor that might promote their effective freedom by protecting them against arbitrary treatment by the wealthy and powerful. The very idea of law implies equity, or something like equal treatment, which in legal practice has never been realized to this day, when the rich enjoy obvious advantages in court over the poor, but which in time was erected into a principle of equality before the law. In any case, it is not fortuitous that democratic principles of justice came to include both freedom and equality. In our time they also include concepts of freedom that have grown more meaningful to students: freedom as not merely the absence of arbitrary constraint or coercion but positive opportunity, available means to choose and carry out one's purposes.

This leads back to the kind of personal freedom that clearly seems to be their main concern—freedom to express and to fulfill themselves in ways of their own choosing. Here again they might appeal to much reputable authority, beginning with Socrates: "The unexamined life is not worth living." They should find congenial an underlying agreement on the idea of freedom that Mortimer Adler made out after he and a team of scholars had surveyed twenty-five centuries of thought on the subject: "A man is free who has in himself the ability or power whereby he can make what he does his own action and what he achieves his own property." With the help of Mill (who does not appear to be one of their gods. I suppose because of his old-fashioned prose) they might more effectively defend themselves against charges of eccentricity or egotism: he maintained not only that really independent persons are better persons, but that society is better for having a rich variety of such persons. John Dewey too may already seem old-fashioned to most students today, but they are committed to something like his conception of freedom as personal growth through experiment and adventure, and might welcome his stress on not only man's distinctive capacity for growth but the necessity of constant growth for full self-realization: "Except as the outcome of arrested development, there is no such thing as a fixed, ready-made, finished self." Most of them clearly do welcome the spontaneous activity that Erich Fromm has stressed as an essential sign of positive freedom.[4] No less pertinent is what Christian Bay calls "potential" freedom, "the relative absence of *unperceived* external restraints of individual behavior" (my italics)— the kind of restraints that we are all liable to because of all we accept as a matter of course in our society and culture, but that have become more insidious because of the kind of voluntary servitude induced by an affluent, technological society, and more specifically because they weaken the ability of people to resist manipulation by advertisers and other propagandists serving special interests. Bay remarked that the literature on "potential" freedom is scanty, but it seems to me plentiful enough in recent times. At least most of the dissident youth have come to perceive some commonly unperceived restraints in the American way of life.

More dubious is the traditional notion of "spiritual freedom." As exemplified by the Christian teaching "In God's service is perfect freedom," this now means little to most Americans, young or old. In my own histories I made little of such freedom because it is essentially subjective, a feeling that might more precisely be called peace of mind, and in particular because historically it distracted attention from the common garden varieties of objective freedom that were my main concern. In the Eastern religions, which have been preeminent in the cultivation of spiritual freedom, it led to a holy indifference to the wretched earthly lot of the masses, or to any effort at social or political reform. In the West Martin Luther, who preached most eloquently the "spiritual liberty" of Christians, was positively hostile to religious, intellectual, and political freedom, as were all the major churches until modern times. Yet more broadly considered, not restricted to either the service of God or communion with a World Soul, the notion of spiritual freedom has become more relevant. Defined as relative freedom from anxiety, neurotic insecurity, neurotic compulsion, or whatever the causes of the millions of crack-ups in America, as well as all the signs of mental or spiritual disorder short of technical mental illness, it is clearly essential to self-determination, personal growth, healthy spontaneous activity, and greater "potential" freedom. As for the rest-

4. I should add that the "purposes" in my own definition need not be deliberate or planned, but may include impulsive, spontaneous ones. Thinking of the ex-slave who said he liked this here freedom because "there's a kind of looseness about it," I want some looseness on principle.

less youth, I do not think they are seeking primarily peace of mind, but many are much concerned with subjective freedom or the psyche. One reason for the growing interest in Zen Buddhism, for example, is that among other things it proclaims that spiritually we are indeed born free and equal, and promises means of realizing some kind of spiritual freedom.

In other respects the youth are supplementing or qualifying traditional concepts of individualism, aside from the gospel of every man for himself. They are much concerned about the values of community that Mill slighted, just because he took them for granted. Aware of the common lack of real community in American society, which is accentuated by the compulsive groupism or togetherness, they are seeking community with their fellows in various ways, by organizing demonstrations, living together in separate groups, flocking to rock festivals, or simply getting together to enjoy a culture of their own. Hence they are not loners like Thoreau, who went off to live by himself at Walden's Pond and in his essay on civil disobedience spoke only for himself. Many are more attracted, and confused, by the romantic kind of individualism that in the past century produced the cults of the rebel, the nonconformist, the esthete, the bohemian—the superior individual as one necessarily set apart from ordinary humanity, "not like other men." Ralph Waldo Emerson appeared to support such individualism when for the sake of epigram he wrote: "Whoso would be a man must be a nonconformist." Taken literally, this may encourage the compulsive noncomformity of the beatnik, the necessity of wearing long hair to assert personal independence, all the pressures on teenagers by peer groups. But this is to repeat that the youth are naturally liable to confusion and excess as they try to be themselves. Most of them, I think, are learning to be more truly independent, deciding for themselves when and whether or not to conform, and feel no more obligation to lead unconventional lives than Emerson himself did.

At the end we might well return to history and take a new look at still another kind of freedom—the freedom of whole peoples to determine their own destiny as independent nations. Before World War I this had a clearly ideal aspect because so many peoples were ruled by other peoples, as North Americans had been by England, Latin Americans by Spain, and European peoples by Czarist Russia, the Austro-Hungarian Empire, and the Ottoman Empire. As a freedom-lover Woodrow Wilson accordingly made the right to self-determination one of his Fourteen Points when he led America into the World War, and at the treaty of Versailles helped to break up the empires in Europe. Following World War II liberals again sympathized with the revolt of non-Western peoples against their European masters. But the upshot of all this, needless to add, has been disappointing. The European peoples that became independent nations soon took to the sins of the old nations, quarreling over disputed territory, setting up tariff barriers, and oppressing minorities within their own borders, while few of them took to democratic ideals. The new Asiatic and African nations are still wrestling with the grievous problems of governing their people, mostly poor and illiterate, with no tradition of self-government, still less of democratic government. Split by tribal, linguistic, cultural, and other differences, few of these nations are really a "people."

Today the right of self-determination for all peoples still has an ideal aspect, which was plain to Americans when the Soviet Union crushed the Hungarian Revolution and invaded Czechoslovakia. It has not been so plain to them in our own hostility to popular Leftist movements, as in Castro's Cuba, or in our attack on North Vietnam. And now that some kind of world order has become imperative, the right of self-determination is a manifest anachronism when it takes the form of a claim to complete national sovereignty, a right by powerful nations to do whatever they determine is in their own interests. At stake was at first hopes of peace, but now the avoidance of catastrophe for another reason too—the ecological crisis. America has no right to dump poison gases into the ocean, to pollute the upper atmosphere by supersonic planes, or to take whatever liberties it wants with the rest of the environment on our space-ship. National sovereignty no longer gives it a right either to squander so much more than its share of the world's resources. Young people are being not only idealistic but realistic when they call for a Declaration of Interdependence.

V

THE USES OF SCIENCE

*1 / The Essential Values and Limitations
of Science*

FOR MOST PEOPLE the relevance of science derives from its practical
utility, all the power it gives us. For most pure scientists this is only
a by-product, even irrelevant to their basic motive, which is simply a
passion for getting at the truth, or in homelier terms the satisfaction
of natural curiosity. On both counts, however, science has had a
phenomenal success in our time. Allied with technology, it has produced the endless stream of new wonders that people now take for
granted. On their own Einstein and Planck launched physicists on
extraordinary adventures of thought that have revolutionized our
conception of the universe. Out of theoretical physics came atomic
power, which awakened our government to the importance of science;
it began pouring vast sums of money into "research and development,"
rising to as much as $17 billion a year. Science has become an Establish-
ment, no less prestigious because it has little political power. Yet its
immense success has not been crowned by universal esteem. Among
ordinary people awe of its wonder-working powers is mingled
with a growing mistrust of it, verging on hostility. With many literary
or humanistic intellectuals such hostility is pronounced. The aroused
students have mixed or confused attitudes, since many of them have
scientific interests, but there is a strong undercurrent of hostility because
of what passes for rationality in the social or behavioral sciences.
Certainly science is not their god.

Now, these attitudes are quite understandable. From its beginnings in the seventeenth century modern science has been a profoundly unsettling force, undermining ancient certitudes, repeatedly conflicting with popular belief. In our time the fear of science goes back to the beginning of the phenomenal success story—the atomic bomb. Although scientists did not make the decision to drop the bomb on Hiroshima, they did give us this dreadful power; and then they proceeded to make H-bombs, ever more appalling weapons that we have to live with. Among the incidental contributions of others was napalm, which for students became a prime symbol of frightfulness. Humanists resented as well the prestige of the scientific or technical intelligentsia, who in ruling the roost have not been conspicuous for their devotion to the traditional values of culture. The many positivists bred by science keep insisting that it alone gives us valid knowledge or truth; so literature is reduced to a pastime, a source of merely formal or emotional pleasure. Scientists are often arrogant, if typically in naive ways. And too many of them have been willing to devote their knowledge and skill to dubious purposes. One may forgive the physicists who gave us the atomic bomb because they feared that German physicists were devising one for Hitler, but it is hard to forgive the scientists who have been working for the Pentagon on chemical and biological warfare. If they too are patriots, they have nevertheless been engaged in a frightful business, and the biologists among them who received medals from the generals should have known what even President Nixon finally learned, that biological warfare would not pay, it cannot be controlled.

Still, it was another biologist who managed to teach Nixon this, persuade him to reject the advice of the military. Previously the Federation of American Scientists had protested against the production of chemical and biological weapons. For the atomic bomb that gave science an evil reputation also brought many scientists to their social senses, made them realize their public responsibilities more keenly than they ever had before. Immediately they responded by putting out the *Bulletin of the Atomic Scientists,* on its cover a clock with its hands pointing to seven minutes to midnight; it remains among the best of our journals (and one that I could wish was read more by students demanding relevance). Eminent scientists took the lead in calling for a treaty banning further testing of bombs, warning against the dangers of radioactive fallout, appealing for disarmament, and lately attacking the Pentagon's dedication to the extravagant follies of the nuclear arms race. They have not been too happy either about the eminence of science as an Establishment, for its lavish support has entailed much unwanted secrecy in research, bureaucratic controls, loss of spontaneity and freedom, and threats to the integrity of science in its pursuit of truth. There remain plenty of abuses of the power it has given us, as well as abuses of science itself; and to these I shall return. But since it so plainly has valuable uses too, for both practical and intellectual purposes, I shall first try to clear the ground of some common sources of confusion and misunderstanding.

To begin with, science is now usually paired with technology, especially by the many critics of modern society; we often hear that the villain in our piece is science-and-technology. Their alliance was indeed anticipated as early as Francis Bacon, who in trumpeting that knowledge was "power" foresaw the many wonders that would be wrought by applied science, and they have become ever more closely allied over the last hundred years, above all since science became an organized establishment. Some of its enlightened champions, such as Jacob Bronowski, themselves refuse to draw an invidious line between pure and applied science. No doubt men engaged in both may work in much the same spirit as they try to solve their problems, often in collaboration. And there is such a thing as "pure" technology too—delight in applying knowledge and exercising skills with little or no thought of practical utility. It goes back as far as the builders of the great pyramids in Egypt, residence-tombs for the immortal pharaohs that were much vaster than they needed to be even for royal purposes; my guess is that proud builders first sold the idea to Pharaoh. Similarly the builders of the Gothic cathedrals often competed in the height of their spires, for no religious, artistic, or practical purposes, only to demonstrate their mastery. Today technicians may work in the same impractical spirit on grandiose projects, such as supersonic planes.

Yet I think it essential to distinguish between pure science and technology, as Francis Bacon also did at the outset: "The contemplation of things, as they are, without superstition or imposture, error or confusion, is in itself more worthy than all the fruit of inventions." Scientists themselves are likely to insist on the distinction just because of the close alliance in government-sponsored research and development, with invariable emphasis on "development." Whereas technology used to be a by-product of basic research, which was conducted by men who just wanted to find out whatever they were interested in looking for, it has now become a primary source of such research, often dictating its aims, as it has most obviously in the nuclear energy and space programs. Scientists are naturally irked by constant demands for practical utility, instead of the discovery of more things to contemplate, and by restrictions on their freedom to follow their hunches wherever these may lead them. Today they worry more over threats to the integrity of science because the social or political decisions about aims are often made without sufficient scientific interest or authority, and in particular because technological applications are rushed in before sufficient scientific inquiry into their possible effects on nature and people.

Among the many examples are the operations of the powerful Atomic Energy Commission, sired by the atomic bomb. Ever since the outset, when the A.E.C. ignored the dangers of radioactive fallout until scientists sounded a loud alarm, it has remained consistently lax in setting standards to protect public health. Now that it is promoting the "peaceful uses" of the atom, by way of improving its public image, it continues to minimize the risks of radioactivity produced by nuclear reactors and the problem of disposing of radioactive waste. When scientists produce evidence of serious hazards, such as cancer, its standard answer is always that the benefits outweigh the risks.[1] The basic complaint of scientists is that the Commission's judgment of what are "acceptable" risks is a social judgment, not a scientific conclusion. They might add that its social judgment too was questionable when the alleged benefits accrued chiefly to the military, but remains so now that it is minimizing the danger of accidents or explosions in industrial nuclear power plants, which might take a terrific toll in lives and property over a large area. Though slight, the danger is real enough so that insurance companies have refused to insure the corporations building the plants. (Taxpayers may not be pleased to learn that the federal government solved this problem by paying the companies some hundreds of millions for insurance; though at that this would cover only a fraction of the billions in claims that might be expected.)

In simpler human terms, the important difference between science

1. I cite a chilling report in the *Center Magazine* (May 1970) by Dr. John W. Gofman, who studied the effects of radioactivity in a biochemical laboratory belatedly set up by the A.E.C., after above-ground bomb testing in 1962 became a scandal because the state of Utah was hard hit by radiation. "No one in the A.E.C.," he writes, "ever asked the question: If we do this weapons test, what will it mean? How will it affect health? If we use nuclear explosives for making harbors or canals or getting at underground resources, what will be the cost to society?" Among other things, he and his co-workers discovered that the standards set by the Federal Radiation Council, defining how much exposure to radiation is allowable, were useless. Much disturbed when these findings were aired, the A.E.C. merely stood by its old arguments: there was no real risk, or at least not enough to outweigh the benefits—which the Council also evaluates, not without an eye to the interests of industry.

and technology may be made clearer by another look at major representatives of the latter—engineers. Although natural scientists, like all of us, are wont to talk grandiloquently about their profession, typically they do regard the disinterested pursuit of truth as an end in itself, pure science as one of the noblest interests of humanity. Engineers naturally have a high regard for their profession and talk too of its service to humanity, but as typically they conceive this service more narrowly in terms of immediate practical utility, to their own society. In practice they have been much more willing to serve uncritically the interests of business and government, they have issued no journal comparable to the *Bulletin of the Atomic Scientists,* and they have raised no strong protests against the mad folly of the nuclear arms race or the operations of the A.E.C. Unlike many scientists, they have not been calling for national austerity either, less production of material goods. They lend some support to Herbert Read's sweeping indictment of industrial technology: "The technological revolution lacks any moral or aesthetic foundation." This is too sweeping, unfair to the engineering profession; but at least they have displayed less professional concern with basic human values than scientists have.

Hence I would question another conventional distinction. Science, it is said, deals with the world of facts, or what *is*; the humanities with the world of values, or what *ought* to be. The distinction is roughly useful or even essential, since there are in fact "two cultures," based on different ways of looking at man and the world; yet it needs to be kept rough. Positivists have made it too sharp by concluding that values are merely subjective, secondary, of a low order of reality if real at all, while too many humanists have been confirmed in an old tendency to put values—especially those labeled "spiritual"—in a high or holy realm where they cannot be contaminated by the supposedly vulgar materialism of science. Actually all scientists are of course committed to values, even apart from their conviction that their own work is valuable. They have added an Eleventh Commandment, Thou shalt seek the truth, which is no more a factual or scientific truth than are the other ten. Their discipline requires a simple truthfulness that is scarcely demanded in business, politics, or diplomacy, and for that matter is not stressed in the Ten Commandments either. Their discipline supports as well the value of intellectual freedom, a right to inquire, criticize, and dissent, and a rare intellectual honesty, a scrupulous avoidance of wishful thinking together with a constant respect both for fact and for mystery, what is not or cannot be positively known. As Jacob Bronowski adds, it therefore implies a sense of human dignity, respect for a being who is able to formulate and maintain such high standards. Needless to add, the individual scientist as a human being may be as fallible, stubborn, and vain as the rest of us; I am speaking of the ideals developed by the scientific community as an international cooperative enterprise. But these ideals explain why the rise of modern science led to the Age of Enlightenment, with its struggle for freedom of thought, speech, and press, and had much to do with the rise of democracy. Today rebellious students might respect the scientific community as the one community that on principle not only permits but puts a premium on dissent—so long, that is, as it is based on a respect for evidence and the standards of truth-seeking that have given science its authority.

In any case the findings of science cannot be divorced from the world of values. Even when scientists conscientiously confine themselves to the world of fact, on the grounds that here alone they can attain strictly verifiable knowledge deserving the name of "truth," they contribute to a body of knowledge about the universe and man, the natural and the social conditions of his life, that is not only relevant but essential to any effort at intelligent value-judgment. Hence science has had a profound influence on ethics in particular. Beginning with the ethical value of the scientific spirit itself, a critical spirit that refuses to accept any belief merely on the basis of traditional authority, convention, or what passes for common sense, it has led to many specific influences. Among the conspicuous examples are Darwin's theory of evolution, with its implications about the nature of man, the conditions of his development, and now the possibilities of guiding his evolution; the anthropological study of morals as *mores*, and of the fantastic diversity of cultures that made clear the relativity of values; and Freudian theory, with its implications about sexual behavior and the ethical problems created by the drives of the unconscious. The conclusions that have been drawn from such knowledge are not themselves strictly scientific, and often have been dubious, as in the loose talk about the survival of the fittest, the evil of any inhibitions, and a sloppy relativism implying that any opinion is as good as any other. But this brings up another elementary question that too few students of either the humanities or the sciences have sufficiently pondered.

Since we cannot possibly escape the influence of science, we might try to get clearer ideas about what it can and cannot tell us. It can tell us much about the human condition in the natural world that may help us to form better judgments and make wiser choices, but it cannot itself teach wisdom, any more than reverence, brotherhood, or love.

By no scientific method can it ever answer the perennial questions about how to live and what to live for. It cannot teach us simply to *accept* the human condition, the terms of which may seem just as hard today as ever in spite of all the power it has given us. While it has done much to alleviate physical suffering, men will surely continue to suffer, and science cannot make suffering *meaningful,* as religion has tried to do. And beyond such obvious limitations lie other basic ones even in its pronouncements about the natural world. Too few students comprehend that the revolution in modern physics revolutionized conceptions not only of the universe but of the nature of science and scientific "truth." As Einstein said of his theory of relativity, anybody could disprove it tomorrow, by bringing in new evidence, but nobody could ever prove he was right; all comprehensive theories about the universe are necessarily hypothetical, tentative, approximate, subject to revision because new evidence keeps coming in. Since this is not the place to go into the technical, abstruse subject of epistemology or the philosophy of modern science, suffice it that physicists realize that their most exact of sciences can never tell us the final truth, the whole truth, and nothing but the truth about the physical universe. As it is, much talk about science—whether praising it or attacking it—is based on archaic or crudely simplified concepts of it. Least sophisticated are many specialists in applied science.

Then it may be repeated that no more can the humanities guarantee wisdom, or tell us the final truth about the human condition. Because the common hostilities seem to me especially unfortunate in a society devoted chiefly to the values of power and affluence, too little concerned about the values of either science or the humanities, I would stress the esthetic, imaginative, broadly spiritual values of science, approached as a humanistic study—and then the problems this raises.

Students of the humanities usually rub their eyes when they read J.W.N. Sullivan's statement that for natural scientists the chief value of science is probably that "it provides the contemplative imagination with objects of great esthetic charm"—a statement borne out by the esthetic terms, such as harmony, symmetry, and elegance, commonly found in the writings of the greater scientists. "Why should an esthetic criterion be so successful so often?" asked the physicist Murray Gell-Mann; and he answered: "I think there is only one answer—nature is inherently beautiful." But most students of the sciences might be no less surprised by Sullivan's statement.[2] The immediate reason is

2. When I asked a geologist friend whether it made sense to him, he was at first simply mystified. Then his eyes lighted up. "By God, that's right! That's

that science is rarely taught as a humanistic study, most often as a highly technical, specialized subject. At that it is not "science" but a large, loose collection of sciences, now embracing some 900 fields, each with its own technical vocabulary and specialized methods. Hence the basic problem of communication today. Typically there is as little communication between specialists in the various sciences as between them and specialists in the humanities. The problem is aggravated by not only the knowledge explosion but the rapid pace of important discovery, which makes it almost impossible for non-specialists to keep abreast. By now the frontiers of science—the scene of revolutionary goings-on —are remote from the knowledge even of most educated people. Science is no longer public property.

Since I could not hope to survey here the whole field of science, I now propose to focus on the life sciences. The scene of the latest scientific "revolution," they also bear most directly on issues of human values, my main concern. And specialists in them have been most insistently sounding the alarm over what technology has been doing to the whole biosphere, our environment and us.

2 / *The Biological Revolution*

As a layman, I should first say emphatically that I must speak diffidently about the exciting work in biophysics, biochemistry, and genetics that has produced the so-called biological revolution. Although I have read around, I cannot pretend to a real grasp of the subject. With its highly technical vocabulary, it points again to the basic problem of communication in a world of specialists who in effect speak foreign languages that the rest of us cannot hope to master. Likewise I cannot judge with any assurance between the various authorities who differ about how fast and how far this revolution is going, just what possibilities of control it will give man. Anyway, it is enough for a layman that while biologists do differ about these possibilities, and some may therefore be too confident in their predictions, all seem agreed that we are dealing with very real and important possibilities, and that the

---

why I spend so many afternoons in the laboratory, and why I stay in the university instead of going out into business and making a lot more money!" Once more I am pointing to a valuable kind of relevance likely to be overlooked these days.

drive to realize them will go on. When I read some time ago that the gene had been isolated, I also read that nobody was surprised. In biology "break-throughs" appear to be the normal mode of advance these days.

The possibility most discussed is the guidance or control of human evolution. The means include not only parental selection and artificial insemination, which has been practiced for years, but in time also genetic surgery and engineering, even genes made to order. Another means is cloning, the production of a genetically identical individual from the cells of a living organism; this has already been done with frogs, and biologists predict that within ten or twenty years it will be possible with human beings. Such other imminent possibilities as the control of sex in foetuses seem merely incidental. But other fields of the life sciences are no less astir. Still another imminent possibility that excites some biologists is the creation of life, once the province of God alone. Biochemistry promises not only more understanding of the nervous system and how it produces memory, language, and logic, but means of manipulating it to increase its efficiency. Medicine promises an extensive prolongation of life by organ transplants, organ regeneration, and maybe spells of hibernation; one conference of biologists and medical men took seriously the possibility that people may live to be hundreds of years old, and nobody dismissed even the idea of a thousand-year-old man. "No end is in sight!" exclaimed one geneticist, surveying his own field. Except possible extinction, on an earth made uninhabitable, ecologists might add. They represent the most obviously relevant of the life sciences to a world in crisis.

Otherwise the possibilities looming up appear offhand to be cheering. John Doe will doubtless welcome the chance to live to be a hundred or so years old, to choose the sex of his children, to give them superior genes, or maybe even to reproduce a couple more identical John Does. Yet the biological revolution will create all kinds of social and political problems. Even the apparent blessing of the prolongation of life will mean that a world that bids fair to be overpopulated would be still more crowded; and what would our society do about all those old people—people whom right now it finds less use for than did any past society? Worse, the new powers that biology will give man may look alarming when one asks: Who will exercise these powers? For what purposes? Under what control? Conceivably they might be exercised by another Hitler. (And scientists cannot afford to forget that some of their German fellows were willing to perform experiments, including fiendish ones, on Hitler's victims in the concentration camps.) Or say that they will be exercised only by scientists, without compulsion, can we trust to their knowledge of people and their wisdom? When an eminent psychologist writes that before long we can hope "to change man's emotions, desires, and thoughts by biochemical means"—to transform personality itself—who are "we"? Who wants to put psychologists in charge of his personality? Or if one is properly transformed, presumably made well-adjusted (like the creatures in Huxley's Brave New World), who then would be the "real" person, if any?

Meanwhile I for one shudder as I keep hearing about biological engineering, genetic engineering, euphenics or the "engineering of human development," just as in my studies of modern technology I kept running into social engineering and human engineering. Everywhere it is engineering, which once had to do with engines or machines rather than the manipulation of human beings, or what are now too often referred to as "human resources." I have been most comforted when biologists point out that a human being has about half a million genes (as I recall the latest figure), and then stress the staggering complexity of man's genetic base, how much more they need to know before they can hope to launch a sound, comprehensive eugenic program.

Still, in time they do expect to know enough. Biological technology will then saddle them with new responsibilities; they will *have* to be concerned with human values. While many workaday laboratory men want to go on with their habitual inquiries, saying that social and political problems are sticky questions and none of their business, many other biologists already have a keen sense of public responsibility; they seem more concerned than any other body of scientists, even to proposals of drawing up a Biological Bill of Rights. They have an advantage over the nuclear physicists in that when these suddenly gave us atomic power we had a bomb before we knew it, or had thought about what to do with it; so we knew nothing better to do than drop it on Japan, and then with the Cold War to set about making bigger and better bombs. The biological revolution is still in its infancy, giving us some time to try to get set for what is coming. Let us therefore take a look at the biological profession as a whole, beginning with a consideration of two contrasting extremes in attitude.

One is represented by James Watson's *The Double Helix*. His very lively, exciting account of how he and Francis Crick discovered the structure of DNA has more suspense because of its candor. As he tells it, their driving motive was simply ambition—to get there first, win a Nobel Prize, beat Linus Pauling to it. He incidentally remarks that their discovery would benefit Biology (with a capital B), but he has nothing to say here about its possible benefits to humanity. Even so his book is a refreshing antidote to the mystique of science—the professional image of the scientist as a selfless man dedicated solely to the cause of truth, a kind of intellectual saint, or eunuch. In fairness let us add that scholars in the humanities are animated by no more passion for the service of mankind; they have their share of personal ambition, seek the normal goals of status, prestige, fame. But since Watson is not an altogether humble man, it is also fair to add that he did not impress me as a genius, at all comparable to an Einstein; he and Crick were just very bright, ingenious young men who succeeded in solving a puzzle, one that required no extraordinary intellectual powers and that somebody was sure to solve before long. Except for its possible applications, the biological revolution is in this respect distinctly less revolutionary than that in modern physics, which defied axiomatic assumptions, required radically new ways of looking at the universe. When Francis Crick later wrote in *Of Molecules and Men* that in time physics and chemistry will be able to explain everything, I recognized wearily a pretty old idea, and one that Einstein would have considered naive.

At the opposite extreme was another geneticist, the late Herman J. Muller (whom I knew well because he was my cousin). An ardent idealist, he was always concerned with human values, believed that science should be committed to them, insisted that it was the duty of scientists to see to it that their discoveries were used to benefit mankind. As a young man he resolved to devote himself to basic genetic research in order to prepare himself for his main effort, to help enable man in time to control his evolution. Like Watson, he enjoyed his victory in a race for discovery about mutations and X-rays that won him a Nobel Prize, and as naturally he enjoyed his fame; yet there was no question of his dedication to his high cause, or what he called the "rights of posterity." In his later years he was always full of alarm about the dangers besetting us, especially from radiation, but he remained basically optimistic, confident that man would make rational, beneficent use of the new knowledge and power he was destined to acquire. To the end he retained something like the hope expressed in his first book, *Out of the Night*: a vision of man's power "to invent *new characteristics, organs,* and *biological systems* that will work out to further the interests, the happiness, the glory of the godlike beings whose meager foreshadowings we present ailing creatures are."

As a crusader he could look somewhat naive in his optimism (not to mention impatient with fellow geneticists who disagreed with him). As an ailing creature myself, I should confess that I find it hard to rejoice in the glory of those godlike beings to come, or even to believe they will come. Right now there appears to be a better chance of our world's becoming uninhabitable long before we could start inventing new "biological systems." Yet just because pessimism is now perhaps too easy I appreciated more both Muller's idealism and his optimism. It is heartening that scientists in general tend to be distinctly more optimistic than humanists, even though they know more fully the reasons for alarm. The typically American faith that something can and should be done about all our problems often looks naive; but if scientists are to be saddled with new responsibilities, we all must hope that they retain something of this faith, else again there is no hope for any of us.

Still, they can be trusted to remain optimistic enough, if only because they will go on making exciting discoveries by their proved methods. From now on I accordingly propose to dwell chiefly on the excesses of their faith, and then on the complications of their responsibilities, the troublesome questions that should concern all of us—scientists and humanists alike—as we try to discharge our common responsibilities. And to emphasize that I am not writing in an invidious spirit, not looking down on scientists as a race of Calibans, I am making a point of citing eminent biologists as authorities for some of my disagreeable remarks.

As Loren Eisley among others has complained, some scientists are crudely naive in their optimism. In popular journals they still offer us dazzling visions of a future teeming with new wonders, new powers, without regard for civilized values or obvious human problems. (Among the visions they get enthusiastic about is that of babies in bottles.) Others can be as naive in their arrogant assumption that science alone can give us the answers. Even the distinguished George Gaylord Simpson, who wrote that the question "What is man?" is probably the most profound that can be asked, added that all attempts to answer it before Darwin are worthless, we had better completely ignore them; so it appears that wisdom entered the world in 1859, and all the great writers, including Shakespeare, go down the drain with Plato, Aristotle, and the prophets of Israel. Peter Medawar, who in a review of Simpson's book deplored this foolishness, then endorsed another form of naive faith. In a basically sensible article attacking the excessive gloom of many writers, the too acute sense of human failure, he said we should remember that human history "is only just beginning," only in our own civilization have human beings "begun to be, in the biological sense, a success"; and as for the deterioration of the environment that threatens this success, he said it is "a technological problem for which technology has found, is finding, and will continue to find solutions." So it becomes necessary to repeat that technology alone will never do. It cannot repair all the havoc we have wrought on our earth, its solutions are always likely to involve new forms of ravage or pollution, and faith in it only obscures the abiding source of ravage, which is the ruling values of our society, in particular the sovereignty of the profit motive. Conservationists are still battling against odds because our politics and our laws have always favored business interests that seek to exploit the environment.

Among ecologists I find very little naive optimism. They know that technology cannot solve all the problems it has created, but chiefly creates a need for still more technology. So far as I know, they do not call themselves environmental engineers either. If often dazzled by hopes of new techniques, such as systems analysis, they are more aware of their handicaps in dealing with not only extremely complex but always strictly unique ecological systems, on which they cannot readily perform controlled experiments. Unable to provide the "conclusive evidence" demanded by business interests, while knowing that there is very good reason to believe that most of what we do to our natural environment is harmful, they have made clearest the dangers of what Americans call progress. To them especially students are indebted for their sudden concern over the environmental crisis. For they have been assuming most fully a primary responsibility of biologists today—educating the public.

This can never be an easy task, or a simple responsibility. Biologists cannot be asked just to take to the stump, or turn their lecture platforms into soap boxes. Since so much of their knowledge is highly technical, they cannot be expected either always to talk effectively to a lay audience. At most the rest of us can hope only that they keep in mind both the necessity and the difficulty of properly educating us. Then they would have a right to expect humanists to take a proper interest in biology, and cooperate in the task of education. But they might also reconsider some basic articles in their faith as scientists.

The sociologist Philip Rieff has told of a physicist who was asked whether he would continue work on his experiment if he knew that its successful completion might result in the destruction of the world: his answer was Yes. As I have reported elsewhere, I got the same answer from a geneticist about the researches in his field, whose alarming possibilities he freely admitted. He had a clear excuse in that he was interested in their beneficent possibilities too, but anyway he was fired by the passion to get at the truth at any cost—what has always been the soul of pure science. It is of course an honorable passion, shared by inquirers in all fields. In any case the drive of science to find out whatever can be found out is sure to go on—it is as irresistible as the drive of technology. Yet in our time it has plainly had very dangerous consequences that scientists can no longer afford to ignore, as they traditionally did on the placid assumption that any advance in knowledge was simply a progress, always good for man. It brings up an aspect of the extraordinary growth of knowledge in our time that is especially pertinent for biologists: a growth that is in a way quite natural, yet unnatural too, like cancer, in that it is not a harmonious or controlled growth as it is in living organisms.

Nor has it been determined by scientific priorities. I take it that scientists will never agree upon such priorities, any more than humanists can in their own interests, for there is no scientific method for determining them. By the same token, however, scientists might give more thought to the ethics of priorities, the question of what we *ought* to know or most *need* to know. As it is, we now have as plain an overproduction of knowledge as of material goods, much more than we can digest, and a great deal of it relatively trivial, especially in view of our critical needs. In so far as scientists have any say in decisions about priorities, or allocations of funds for research, they might reconsider even such exciting possibilities as the creation of life. It would be a very rudimentary form of life, vastly inferior to the billions of forms that nature has produced; and what urgent human purpose would it serve?

Another questionable article in the traditional faith of science is linked with the ruling faith of our own civilization, above all America. This is the belief that man has not only a natural passion to master nature but a kind of moral obligation to do so. Thus at the turn of our century Bishop Lawrence of Massachusetts stated as a first principle that man, when strong, "will conquer Nature, open up her resources, and harness them to his service," and he added that this was man's "divine mission"; so he was able to edify his wealthy parishioners with a sound American conclusion: "Godliness is in league with riches." By now God is usually left out (except on our coins and dollar bills, which may not give Americans a vivid idea of him), and the inspiration of a divine mission runs a poor last among the inspirations of businessmen, technicians, and scientists alike; yet it is still taken for granted that the conquest of nature is man's natural mission. This too is up to a point an honorable passion; or at least I certainly welcome many of the goods that have come out of our conquests, and do not at all want to be a slave to nature, which is hardly a noble master. Nevertheless the drive to acquire ever more power over it looks much less honorable when one recalls the plain objections to the goals of American society.

In economic activity it is the drive to "maximize" production, whether or not the goods are really useful or good for much. It suggests what has been called the "pig philosophy," the popular assumption on which advertising flourishes, that if anything is good, more is always better. It is more piggish because Americans already consume many times their share of the world's natural resources. It is absurd too, for it has led to not only a huge wastefulness but the systematic fouling of the natural environment. And the headlong drive looks blinder because man now looks somewhat less like a "biological success," in any but a superficial sense. It is not merely literary people but sociologists and psychologists who speak of man's alienation from nature, and from himself.

Hence René Dubos has suggested that we need a new social ethic, "almost a new social religion," based on the idea of living in harmony with nature instead of forever conquering or exploiting it, and of recovering the sense of kinship with the rest of creation that was so beautifully exemplified by St. Francis of Assisi. Substantially he agrees with Lewis Mumford, who points out that "conquest" is an obsolete military term, suggesting a kind of imperialism in the drive to realize the prophecy of Descartes that men would become "the lords and possessors of nature," and who argues that we should substitute for it the "cultivation" of nature—an age-old practice that now has more civilized connotations. As one who happens to like the only earth we have, I do not suppose that to formulate and try to inculcate a new social ethic is a strictly scientific task, or a primary responsibility of biologists. But they might tell Americans—as Dubos and others are trying to—that their way of life is as unwholesome on biological as humanistic grounds; for people can live in harmony with much of their man-made environment only by virtue of deadened sensibilities, with the help of alchohol, tranquillizers, sleeping pills, and such other drugs as TV shows. The life sciences might also contribute to a clearer conception of "human nature"—a term that we must all use, despite all the loose talk about it, if we are going to speak of "mankind," the "human condition," or especially the "dehumanizing" tendencies of modern technology. Specifically, it is in the nature of man that his so-called higher needs have become basic needs. They are the needs, once more, of a creature who in the course of biological evolution developed brain-power, potential capacities for the pursuit of truth, beauty, and goodness, or for the realization that he couldn't live on bread alone (not to mention the savorless kind manufactured in America).

If this kind of talk seems highfalutin' or alien to scientists, one reason is a basic ambiguity of the biological sciences. In one aspect biologists are naturally disposed to humanistic interests because their subject includes a study of man, his relations to nature, his development through the long ages, his potentialities today; so they may take an organic, holistic view of him, even have a pious sense of his immense debt to the countless generations, who helped to establish his position in nature and to develop his potentialities.[3] In a plainer aspect, however, they are not so disposed because of tendencies they share with all scientists—tendencies to specialize, narrow the field of study, concentrate on small segments, and reduce to basic elements, like cells, genes, atoms, electrons, or in physics now something called quarks. Needless to say, these tendencies are largely responsible for the triumphs of science, and in biology explain why the molecular biologists are now riding high. But they also encourage the old fallacies of reductionism, the identification of the physical basis of something as its essence or the "real" truth about it, and then the "is nothing but" fallacy, such statements as that man is nothing but a collection of chemicals, a machine, or an animal with motions in the brain called thought, on a par with the urine produced by kidneys. (In popular thought this comes out in such sayings as that love is nothing but a biological urge to reproduce the species—a statement, I have remarked, that is a strictly inaccurate description even of lust, inasmuch as a young man who has his eye on a pretty girl doesn't give a damn about the species, and the last thing he wants is reproduction.) For such reasons the "natural order" described by scientists is for our living purposes strictly unnatural, especially because it has been fragmented differently in the various sciences, making impossible, as the biochemist Erwin Chargaff has said, "a uni-

3. A striking example of the humanistic values that may be derived from a study of biology is Stanley Burnshaw's *The Seamless Web*. In this he develops his thesis that "poetry begins with the body and ends with the body"—the body, that is, studied as an organic whole, not separated from "mind" or "soul." Among many other things, he draws on Walter Cannon's classic studies of "the wisdom of the body," the wonderful ways in which it maintains its stability in its continuous interaction with a changing, often disturbing outside world, without conscious direction by the brain, and more swiftly and surely than the cleverest brain might manage.

fied and consistent vision of Nature"; for men still have some sense of an honest-to-God world—not a mere whirl of electrons, quarks, or what-nots—and a natural world, let us add, that men could find their way around in and understand well enough for their human purposes long before they had anything like our scientific knowledge of it. And in biology reductionism may be especially unfortunate because it induces a kind of innocent irresponsibility.

Again I cite René Dubos: "The most damning statement that can be made about the sciences of life is that they deliberately ignore the most important phenomena of human life." He suggests that one way they can help to provide a basis for a new social ethic is by studying the responses of the total organism to the total environment, as a means to developing a "science of humanity." Here again I must be humble. I would not think of damning the molecular biologists who have contributed so much to our understanding of genetics; I have no idea how biologists might go about studying the total organism in relation to the total environment, or how fruitful such studies might be; I have some doubts about the possibility of an adequate science of humanity; and I would repeat that science cannot answer the first and last questions about how to live and what to live for. (If Francis Crick is right in saying of people trained in the liberal arts that "tomorrow's science is going to knock their culture right out from under them," I still can't believe that even molecular biology can replace that culture.) All I would say is that in my readings about our environment I have been dismayed to learn how little study has been made of its effects upon people. As Dubos points out, "It is tragically symbolic of the distorted sociotechnological philosophy which now governs human life that immense efforts are being made to develop new coating and finishing techniques to protect automobile bodies against the corroding effects of air pollutants, whereas hardly anything is being done to study the effect of pollution on the human body!"

At least some biologists are exploring the whole problem, suggesting possible criteria of an "optimum environment" for man. In defining the optimum they are considering not only physical health but mental health and emotional stability, which on the face of it have suffered from the increasing noise, congestion, and pollution, even if to an extent unknown or for a long time unknowable because of cumulative, delayed effects. They have some positive evidence got from studies of animals, which has shown, for example, that their behavior may be seriously disturbed by crowding. At any rate, the criteria they suggest include a measure of quiet, privacy, open space, diversity of surroundings, greenery, and respect for wild life.[4] In short, they are concerned about the quality of the environment, which has much to do with the quality of American life. They realize that decisions made about an optimum environment and means of achieving it must finally rest on ethical and esthetic choices, not merely technical ones. In effect they are concerned with the response of the total organism, which forces consideration of the higher needs of man.

The possibilities of such study remain uncertain, not to mention the unlikelihood of our achieving anything like an optimum environment. Much more certain, however, are the new powers that biology will give us, for better or worse. These bring us back to the critical questions about who will exercise them. Biologists appear to be generally agreed that there should be no coercion—people ought not to be forced to adopt the new techniques. Remembering Hitler, we might all agree too that these powers should not be turned over to the state. In the democracies, then, the various possibilities of biological technology will presumably be left to "society," or in effect to the kind of people now in charge or aspiring to take charge. If so, we will need to reconsider our social ethic.

In America the new possibilities would mean considerable exploitation by commercial interests, just as the many new drugs have been exploited by the scandalously profitable drug industry. The rest of us must then hope that somehow we would manage to breed more Ralph Naders. Another consequence, I suppose, would be a field day for behavioral scientists, or the specialists in the various kinds of human "engineering"—types who do not much impress me by their humility or their wisdom. The psychologist who welcomed the prospect of changing man's "emotions, desires, and thoughts" by biochemical means neglected to consider the obvious question: Who will engineer the engineers, and for what purposes other than a mastery of the latest techniques? The trouble remains that a master of techniques is naturally tempted to employ them whenever possible, just as many surgeons love

4. Since there still are many nature-lovers, to whom the idea of living in harmony with nature may be meaningful, I add the comments of an Indian woman: "The white people never cared for the land or deer or bear. When we Indians kill meat, we eat it all up. When we dig roots, we make little holes. . . . We shake down acorns and pinenuts. We don't chop down the trees. We only use dead wood. But the white people plow up the ground, pull up the trees, kill everything. The trees says, 'Don't. I am sore. Don't hurt me.' But they chop it down and cut it up. The spirit of the land hates them." Not believing in a spirit of the land, Americans may compensate by hating themselves more than they realize. Now that DDT is threatening the bald eagle with extinction, one may wonder: How much is it worth to them to preserve their national symbol?

to operate, at the drop of a customer's hat.[5] Meanwhile these surgeons point to the serious problems that are already arising in medicine, in particular the distraction of sensational achievements like heart transplants.

These have benefited a very few people, selected at random, and at that have been a very slight benefit despite the "success" proclaimed in headlines, since most of the patients died soon. At a time when the country is short on doctors, nurses, and hospital space, they are a distraction from basic problems because they require whole teams of surgeons and nurses, and prolonged care. They confirm the tendency of the most ambitious medical students to go in for mastering the latest techniques, instead of the care of patients as whole persons who need to be known—a tendency especially deplorable in many poor countries, as in Latin America, where the masses get much too little medical care for the commonplace diseases they suffer from. And once organ transplants become standard procedure, more widely available, they will pose an ethical problem for public policy. They will be available for relatively few people, since there is no prospect whatever of there being enough surgeons to take care of all who could benefit from them. On what basis will these few be selected? As a heart transplant now costs about $45,000, in America a likely answer is that the wealthy will get first choice, while the many poor will continue to get inadequate medical care, perhaps grow resentful of still another inequity. Selection on the basis of need would involve difficult choices, but as it is the American Medical Association can hardly be expected to explore even the elementary problems of medical ethics. Its main concern has long been the professional interests of doctors, not the public welfare or the Hippocratic oath.

Similarly with organ regeneration and other means of prolonging life, which I assume would be expensive and not available to all who

5. I wonder, incidentally, about the possibilities of "programmed dreams" that are now being studied by the Hudson Institute, and that Herman Kahn—the best known operator in the think tanks—has predicted confidently will be realized before long. Although I know nothing about the program, I assume the object would be to give people soothing or heartening dreams, or whatever the dream engineers think is good for them. I should think it likely that they might include something like the "hypnopedia," or teaching during sleep, that Huxley predicted in *Brave New World*. If so, Americans might anticipate dreams interlarded with commercials. Or if we keep moving toward a police state, the specialists could presumably program nightmares to scare the hell out of recalcitrant people. All this is pure speculation as far as I go—but it is not idle speculation in view of the fantastic kinds of possibilities that Kahn assures us will become realities.

wanted them. But other questions are raised by the usual objective of
doctors, which is to prolong the life of their patients at almost any cost,
in keeping with the desire of most people to hang on to life as long
as possible. The questions concern the interests of society, for this
practice also fills our overcrowded hospitals with dying people, who
may spend their last weeks or even months there, and it involves the
doubtful blessing of preserving the lives of countless people who have
grown senile, helpless, useless to themselves too, many of them living
on only as vegetables. It will accordingly make better sense if scientists
succeed in postponing senility and achieving a limited degree of reju-
venation, as they seem confident they will. Even so, however, many
people may not welcome the prospect of a very long old age. As a matter of human dignity, they may assert the right to die. No doubt much
more important is the right to live with dignity, in a decent environment; but this too is obscured by all the to-do over the sensational
possibilities. Little thought is being given to their long-range social
consequences, again least of all by the American Medical Association.

And so, finally, with the possibilities of guiding or controlling human
evolution. They may seem academic because of the urgent, immediate
need of curbing the population explosion. At best it would take generations to make any significant change in the genetic constitution of the
human race, still more to achieve a scientist's dream of making man
"the absolute master of his own biological personality." Yet the whole
question is far from being academic, even apart from the virtual certainty that sooner or later man will have the power to alter his genetic
make-up. There is a practical need of thinking about it now because
in some ways our genetic stock has been deteriorating; man has long
been interfering with natural selection by scientific medicine, preserving the lives of people with inherited defects that would normally have
prevented their passing them along as they now do, assuring a steady
accumulation of such defects. And it is time to begin thinking too about
the ethical and philosophical questions that will be raised by efforts to
improve our stock, even if scientific breeding remains as voluntary as
geneticists usually assume it should be.

Thus biologists now talk of "purposeful evolution," the need of giving
evolution a "rational direction" to assure the "betterment" of mankind;
but what shall our purposes be? What is rational for man, who is not
simply a rational animal? Or necessarily a more useful member of
society when he has a high IQ? What constitutes betterment? About
genetic surgery, more specifically, Salvador Luria (among other geneticists) has asked the pertinent question: "Who decides what are good

genes and bad genes, what are good people and bad people?" It appears that some genes are unquestionably bad, such as those that cause feeble-mindedness and physiological defects; but there is considerable question about good genes, or more strictly good combinations of genes, and above all about good types of people. Animal breeders can and do breed for specific traits, but human beings have a wide range of diverse potentialities, such as intelligence, imaginativeness, creativity, sensitivity, and sociability or non-aggressiveness. Who would rank these on a scale?

Laymen may accordingly rejoice that geneticists are soberly discussing these questions, not rushing in with positive answers. More than one of them have remarked that biologists are no more competent than the man on the street to deal with the ethics or the philosophy of the problems they are raising. If only for this reason, however, I think they generally are more competent, even apart from the necessary job they do in clarifying the problems. They cannot claim scientific authority when they make value-judgments, but most have the humility to recognize this, and also to recognize the inescapable need of such judgments. And on the latter score the prospects are hopeful. Professors of biology report that in just the last few years their students have grown much more interested in social problems, or more broadly questions of human values. Knowing some of these students, I know they are more competent in these matters than the too often ignorant, gullible, prejudiced man on the street.

There remains a quite different breed of scientists to whom this whole discussion may seem irrelevant—the behaviorist psychologists. B.F. Skinner, the most eminent of them in America, is confident that he can take people just as they are born today, and by proper conditioning make them over into something like the godlike beings that Herman J. Muller dreamed of producing by a control of human evolution that would take generations. Skinner has boasted that he could produce "a world in which people are wise and good without trying, without 'having to be,' without 'choosing to be.'" By his "science of human behavior" he would have made all their basic choices for them while conditioning them in their early years. (In *Walden Two* he pictured this utopia in fictional form, but with complete scientific seriousness.) I cannot take his claims at all seriously—except as a symptom of the brashness to which American scientists are prone, in their passion for quick and sure results, and in particular as an example of the spreading tendency in the social and behavioral sciences to manipulate people, with few if any qualms about experimenting on human beings. These sciences call for some separate attention because their rapid growth and spreading uses in our time are especially characteristic of our technological society, and because what has made them relevant to the interests of the technical intelligentsia is now making them seem irrelevant to many students.

3 / *The Behavioral Sciences*

SINCE I CANNOT HOPE to cover adequately this large subject either, I shall again focus on the issue of human values and value-judgments. Professor Skinner, who is sure he knows what is "wise and good," points to a basic ambiguity, or finally a basic confusion, in the social and/or behavioral sciences. (The distinction between them is not too clear, inasmuch as all are dealing with some sort of behavior.) Like him, many psychologists, social and human engineers, and others who are trying to influence behavior seem confident that they know what is good for people. Throughout these sciences runs the common assumption that the judgments of specialists or experts on social problems are better than the judgments of laymen, and if they are primarily concerned with means rather than ends, they at least tacitly approve the ends, often help to set them. But many of these scientists—especially those who call themselves social or political scientists—taboo value-judgments on principle. They pride themselves on their objectivity, or their neutrality. They assert tacitly when not explicitly that their contributions to knowledge are more valuable because they keep their science value-free.

Now, this taboo can be considered an honorable admission of the limitations of their science. It goes back to Max Weber, one of the great pioneers, who recognized that sociologists could not by any properly scientific method verify their judgments of social good and evil. He was deeply troubled, however, by his injunction against such judgments because it in effect divorced science from the humanities, or from values and ideals he was much concerned about. Today social scientists pride themselves on a divorce that keeps their science pure. They differ from Weber too in that he was much troubled as well by' the irresistible growth of bureaucracy, the whole drive to efficiency and a merely technical rationality. They feel quite at ease in a technological society because they share its ruling values, put their faith in organization, technique, methodology, and especially statistical or quantitative methods, now with the help of computers.[6] And in particular Weber realized that the vital question of "significance" in the selection of subjects for scientific inquiry could not be answered by scientific methods. Today the word is that the formulation of a research problem "should be influenced primarily by the requirements of scientific procedure," and too few researchers have either the imagination or the philosophical sense that enabled him to choose clearly significant subjects.

The obvious trouble is that "the requirements of scientific procedure" as now conceived rule out the most fundamental problems, including the all-important questions about the good society, the good state, the good life. Researchers confine themselves to factual questions they can hope to answer by their methodology. Granted that they have contributed much useful knowledge, they have also ground out a great deal of trivial data, dressed up in a pretentious technical jargon that gives an illusion of significance. At best the approved methods lead them to concentrate on repetitive, mechanical activities, the predictable "reactions" of most people; they have had much less to say about free, spontaneous, imaginative, or creative activities—the kind of experience most of us value most. And the neglect is more unfortunate because the bureaucratization of the social or behavioral sciences, with the consequent specialization and fragmentation of knowledge, has led to various forms of reductionism. The most respectable "scientific" accounts of human behavior are of crowd behavior or conditioned behavior, in which people look least like purposeful, potentially responsible human beings. Man is not studied as a whole man, much less as an individual. Given the countless fragmentary accounts, we are left with the hopeless task of putting man together again.

All such tendencies are more unfortunate because of the taboo on value-judgments. This has led to the logically unnecessary conclusion that such judgments are "merely" personal preferences loaded with emotion, and so has buttressed the illusion of complete objectivity or neutrality that has made social scientists another species of technicians, too often willing servants of a technological society. Apart from their enthusiasm over their own "contributions," they too are of course committed to some values: at best the ideal values of the scientific spirit, which may make them critical of the repressive tendencies of our so-

6. As always, there are of course prominent exceptions to these generalizations. I am speaking of the prevailing tendencies in the professional establishment. Thus David Riesman, among the notable exceptions, I gather has not been highly esteemed by his establishment because in his acute studies of American society he has not depended on the approved methodology or refrained from value-judgments.

ciety, but also more questionable assumptions, usually silent, about what is good for society. They naturally like social "stability" and "harmony," for example, but not merely for the reasons of most political philosophers from Plato on; a relatively stable society is easier to study, assuring the regularities required by their methods. For the same reason they are mostly averse to radical change; though no social fact is more obviously significant than change in our time, they cannot readily handle it by their methods. Always with some important exceptions (such as the maverick C. Wright Mills), they in effect support the basic *status quo*. And since the kind of power their knowledge has yielded is mostly power over people, not by and for the common people, too many have been willing to devote their skills to ways of manipulating them in the interests of the managers of our society. The scandalous example is the well-paid experts in motivational research who help advertisers to exploit the gullibility of faithful American consumers, debauch the tastes of an affluent society. Although their practice is perhaps a logical use of a "value-free" science, it is a clear betrayal of the traditional scientific ideal of the pursuit of truth for the sake of truth, or for the sake of humanity.

All this I say a little wearily because I have been saying it for some years, perhaps somewhat obsessively and without enough attention to the important exceptions.[7] So I conclude, perhaps somewhat more freshly, with a closer look in particular at political science, or what was once known as the study of government—a study that has grown especially relevant since students have grown so critical of American democracy. For some years the ruling vogue has been behavioralism, which its practitioners have complacently called a "revolution," since it appears that no science today can be respectable without one. Though the systematic studies of political behavior they have turned out may strike laymen as innocuous, not at all revolutionary, the point is that they have created a "science." As W. Riker explained, the traditional studies of government produced at best "only wisdom and neither science nor knowledge"; and though he freely granted that wisdom is useful, the result was nevertheless "a failure to live up to the promise in the name of political *science*." Now the promise has been realized by a concentration on method. Beginning with fact-finding, polling, and tabulating, this has evolved methods of political analysis, lately in-

7. These may help to explain why a disproportionate number of student rebels have come out of the social sciences. My impression is that most of these students have been rebelling too against the irrelevance of their professional disciplines, but no doubt they have been influenced by the sociologists who are outspokenly critical of American society.

cluding such fashionable refinements as communications models, games theory, and systems theory. Needless to add, behavioralism is "value-free." Applicable to the study of any kind of government, it declares no political preferences, except perhaps in the choice of efficient means. It scrupulously avoids the main concerns of political philosophers from Plato and Aristotle down through Locke, Rousseau, Mill, and Marx to John Dewey and a few other survivors of an antique breed, who worried over the problems of justice and the good state.

Hence behavioralism has been contaminated by little if any wisdom. Some twenty years ago Harold Lasswell heralded the vogue by his highly regarded book *Politics: Who Gets What, When, How:* an empirical, analytical study of influence or power, stating conditions without preferences, or any philosophical efforts either to criticize or to justify conditions. Although it has to some extent been outmoded by the development of a much more elaborate methodology than he employed, he anticipated this in a Postscript added in 1958 in which he called for "a map of public affairs . . . that is carefully researched and systematically organized." His "contextual" approach to the "science of politics," involving reference to both history and society, was also more comprehensive than that of the ordinary behavioralist today, but at least he recognized the need of a great many specialists to fill out an adequate map. Otherwise he differed most obviously in his stress on the need of systematically projecting trends of conditions, "future lines of political change." In his Postscript he stated his belief that "a major responsibility of the specialist on politics is to re-edit maps of the future, and to improve the methods by which the job is done." To my knowledge the behavioralists have not assumed this responsibility; or if they have tried, they missed the boat on the striking changes since he wrote, as did he himself.

What, then, are the uses of this kind of political science? Like the social sciences in general, it has produced much pertinent knowledge, including studies of the behavior of voters that should be of particular interest to students organizing for political action. As naturally behavioralists have been engaged in much trivial research, of a mechanical kind on which graduate students can be turned loose to gather data for processing by computers. On the whole I think it fair to say that they have not distinguished themselves by their sense of "significance." Because of their preoccupation with method and factual description, and their distrust of philosophy or "mere" theory, they have contributed little to a basic understanding of American democracy, usually asking only superficial questions about how it operates. They have made much of the "decision-making process," for example, but without making close studies of the basic power structure that clearly influences the decisions of administrators, and has produced a military-industrial complex. Sheldon Wolin has remarked their failure to inquire into a potentially rich subject, the current structure of income taxes as an index to the power and powerlessness of social and economic groups, and to our system of values. They have not studied thoroughly either the familiar phenomenon of corruption, flagrant or routine. And such oversights are themselves significant, as any student of the sociology of knowledge could tell them. The "neutral" methods of the behavioralists predispose them to a basic conservativism, of which they may be unconscious because many think of themselves as liberals. Concerned with such problems as "system maintenance," they accept the American political system as it is, with allowances for the usual *ad hoc* efforts at reform, but without consideration of possibly radical defects that explain, as Wolin has pointed out, why office-holders may be "systematically mistaken." Although I do not know how useful their studies have been to office-holders, at least the powers that be have little reason to be disturbed by them, or to brand them as "effete snobs."

As one who is still concerned about the old-fashioned concepts of freedom and justice, and inclined to prefer "only wisdom" to this kind of political science, I am no doubt disposed to be unfair to it. But on the record there remains a positive reason for distrusting it. As David Easton confessed in a presidential address to the profession, political scientists failed to anticipate the revolutionary 'sixties. So did almost all the rest of us, we might confess; but they were specialists in political behavior, they supposedly had their finger on the public pulse, and they might at least have been expected to recognize symptoms of coming unrest. As it was, they gave little heed to the crises, including the crisis of political authority, even as these became plainer to the rest of us. In the decade from 1958 to 1968, when the *American Political Science Review* published hundreds of articles, Easton points out that it published only three on the urban crisis, four on racial conflicts, one on poverty, two on civil disobedience, and two on violence in America. I should add that the methods of the behavioralists are basically inadequate for an understanding of a revolutionary world. So one may expect that the great bulk of their ostensibly realistic studies will soon have only the historical interest that most behavioralists themselves lack, and will have nothing like the enduring, intrinsic interest of the political classics they have shunted aside. De Tocqueville's *Democracy in America,* written well over a century ago without benefit of methodology, remains not only a much richer work but a more acute, penetrating study than any I know of by contemporary political scientists who pride themselves on being scientists.

At any rate, I sympathize with students of political science I know who have wearied of the means and ends of behavioralism, or what Christian Bay has called "the cheerful science of dismal politics." They should therefore be heartened by a growing revulsion against it within the profession. All along more philosophical students of government (like Sheldon Wolin) have been critical of it, unhappy over the decline of political philosophy in the curriculum, but now there is a movement that David Easton dignifies as "the post-behavioral revolution." It is attacking the complacency of the behavioralists, typified by one who rejoiced that their discipline was enjoying "a new coherence, a pleasant sense of unity, and a self-confident identity that fits its rapid growth and healthy mien." It is giving the discipline an identity crisis by insisting on the public responsibilities of political scientists at a time of crisis, which require a direct, unabashed concern with human values. More specifically, it is demanding not only relevance but *action*.

This may make a layman wonder again. The attainment of more relevance should not, I think, be too difficult. Instead of considering primarily the requirements of scientific procedure, which in political matters does not yield scientific certainty anyway, political scientists have only to try to ask more significant, fundamental questions. If they may then be tempted to identify relevance with immediacy, any thorough study of the current crises would force fundamental questions; the crisis of political authority would appear to be an especially rich subject for inquiry—and good for the professional soul because it would require more attention to history. But the demand for commitment to political action is more troublesome. What, then, becomes of the "science" of politics? According to Easton, the post-behavioralists are uncertain about this, some of them willing simply to drop it as inadequate for contemporary needs, others hoping to give up their scientific research only temporarily as a matter of strategy in "abnormal" times. In either case, they could not speak with scientific authority once they are engaged in political action, yet they should feel some kind of professional responsibility for their commitments, in their role as teachers too. Then the question is, how well has their professional training prepared them to assume such ethical responsibilities?

As I see it, a commitment to political action in America today calls for more philosophy, not more science; more stress on the moral ends of democracy, not merely system or more efficient means; more thought about the good state in its service of the good life, including civilized values; less rejoicing over "the end of ideology" and less complacence over the pragmatic genius of the American political system, with more openness to the possible need of radical change; more attention to visions of the future, the real power of the dream (as demonstrated by Martin Luther King); a more comprehensive "map of public affairs," in which the political is distinguished but never sharply separated from the economic, social, moral, and intellectual; or again simply more respect for wisdom—an imprecise term, yet referring to a recognizable quality, so that most of us may agree that the term is applicable to depressingly few American statesmen in recent years. Altogether a large order—no doubt too large for a proper science. But if students of government have a perfect right to go on studying political behavior, with the aid of something like scientific methods, political science might profit from a clear recognition that it can never achieve the measure of precision, certainty, and predictability of the natural sciences. Then its practitioners might consider more deeply the inescapable philosophical question: As one of the sciences of man, what should a science of politics be like? They might even consider why Aristotle thought of it as the master science, because its end was to secure the highest goods attainable by action.

V I

THE USES OF TRAGEDY

1 / The Values of Literature

ALTHOUGH THE VALUES OF LITERATURE have been clouded or minimized by the triumphs of science and technology, I would still
maintain that they are not only as important as ever but more important
just because of these triumphs. Ideally, literature is the best corrective
for the deplorable tendencies of our technological society. It deals directly with the world of immediate sensations, the qualities of experience, the concrete realities that are most real to us, but are obscured by
the abstractions of business and science, when not discredited as merely
subjective. In fiction and drama it is perforce directly concerned with
the individual, who has been neglected in scientific study and subordinated to the needs of technique and organization. It is a universal
mode of communication, at a time when so many specialists do not
speak the common language, and in communicating so vividly and
richly as it can it may restore a respect for our "mother tongue," which
is constantly debased for commercial and political purposes, and in the
world of thought is sicklied o'er with the pale cast of technical jargon.
On all counts it can therefore enable people better to realize their humanity, appreciate what constitutes the dignity and worth of man. In
rendering the extraordinarily diverse possibilities of life it can likewise
help them to realize their individuality, fulfill themselves.

"Ideally," I began, literature can best serve these humane purposes.
Actually, of course, much contemporary literature conveys little idea
of rich possibility, still less of human dignity. So far from being a corrective of the dehumanizing tendencies in our society, it supports Ber-

nard Malamud's complaint of "the colossally deceitful devaluation of man in this day." And the study of literature is something else again. As a required subject in the schools, it is among the most routine studies, another form of the "knowledge" that the hapless students must acquire in order to pass tests and gain credits; too many teachers stir little sense of either the richness or the vital relevance of literature, and so fail to stimulate a love of reading, without which the knowledge has no real value except as a certificate that the student has been "educated." In the universities the study of literature is afflicted by the common tendencies in the so-called humanities that I noted at the outset. Too often literary works are reduced to objects for professional, impersonal study.

About the vast output of literary scholars in our time, I shall repeat only that the bulk of it is of primarily historical interest, or of interest only to other scholars or specialists. Though presumably born of a love of literature, it is not designed to stimulate such love in common readers, nor focused on the values that make literature especially important today. For such broader purposes literary criticism ought to be more helpful, but too much of it too has been highly professionalized, designed chiefly for specialists. The "new criticism" of a generation ago, and the newer criticisms since then (I am not up on the latest labels), have generally concentrated on formal analysis and classification, objective study of technique, structure, genre, paradigm, and other technical matters. Thereby critics have illumined the formal, esthetic values of literature that distinguish it from other major interests, and incidentally justify their role as professional specialists. But they have also tended to slight its relations to other vital interests and its social uses as a criticism of life, including the light it throws on moral issues and its value in developing moral imagination. In effect their disciples in the universities too often make their subject literary criticism rather than literature, whose creators through the ages have generally been interested in much more than its formal values or the present concerns of critics. And in particular they have tended to discourage when not to disparage the *personal* responses of students, who likewise typically have broader interests. They may obscure the immediate pleasures—and the pains—of readers, the plainest reasons why literature can offer valuable experiences.

Here I take for my text Walter J. Slatoff's *With Respect to Readers*. His thesis is that in the current stress on objective analysis the experience of individual readers is neglected—experience that needs to be respected because it is the source of the living values of literature. I should add at once that there are obvious reasons for not respecting much the experience of many ordinary readers, which involve stock responses, lazy, muddled, crude, or merely fashionable. But certainly the diverse experience of thoughtful, sensitive students ought to be given more attention than it is by teachers or critics who concentrate on a supposedly impersonal study of literature and tend to disparage "emotional" responses. In fiction that moves them they may appreciate better the simplicities in the credo of Joseph Conrad, who said that the task he set himself was not to amuse, edify, console, frighten, or shock, but "to make you hear, to make you feel . . . before all, to make you *see*." In the immediate experience of reading, vivid sensory images are likely to be more important—and more memorable too—than literary qualities defined after reflection or analysis.

In particular Slatoff questions the common emphasis on the values of esthetic distance or "detachment" in reading. Necessary as some measure of detachment is, to avoid the common confusion of literature with life, it can be too comfortable, having "affinities not only with certain kinds of truth and beauty but with indifference, complacency, callousness, and finally inhumanity"—the inhumanity, say, of German Doctors of Letters who became Nazis. Students who are deeply moved by their reading, as presumably their teachers would like them to be, are never so detached as critics may sound. Slatoff stresses rather that literature can be a disturbing experience. Today I should say that it may often be too disturbing, since the aim of some writers appears to be chiefly to shock; but unquestionably one common value of literature is as an unsettling experience. Much modern literature is most obviously relevant because it conflicts with conventional ways of seeing, feeling, and thinking. For that matter very little serious literature, past or present, supports the American way of life. Students need not be deeply disturbed by their reading to appreciate its possible values as a disruptive, subversive influence, even a means to stimulating anxiety rather than relieving it.

Similarly Slatoff questions the almost invariable traditional stress on literature as an ordering experience, giving form, coherence, and therefore significance to sensation, feeling, and thought that in daily experience are a jumble, or just one thing after another. He emphasizes that literature can be a movement not toward but away from order and coherence. Again I should say that the traditional view still needs to be stressed, given the esthetic disorders and the common indifference to form in our day, but then add that literature may clearly be valuable by breaking up conventional ways of ordering experience. It seems to me as clear that there is more tension, incoherence, inconsistency, or unresolved disorder in many of the greater works than traditional critics have been wont to find. Few great writers have been serene, utterly detached, in complete command of their soul, or of their thought and feeling.

And so I am led to my main concern in this chapter—tragedy. In my youth tragedy, in both drama and modern fiction, became my favorite form of literature because it gave me my most deeply moving experience. In writing about it I rationalized my pleasure in it by describing it, in the terms of I.A. Richards, as "perhaps the most general, all-accepting, all-ordering experience known." Today I would stress more that for many readers it is a disturbing, even harrowing experience because it does not so completely order and accept, but I still consider it one of the most valuable of experiences because it has embraced the most wonderful and terrible possibilities of the human spirit. Its values are not merely esthetic but ethical and philosophical, as a profound comment on the conditions of man's life. Now the immediate question is: How relevant is the comment of the greater tragic writers for the youth today?

2 / *The Relevance of High Tragedy*

AMONG THE REASONS for "the asphyxiating atmosphere in which we live," Antonin Artaud began an essay entitled "No More Masterpieces," was "our respect for what has been written, formulated, or painted, what has been given form." He defended the general public that lacked this respect, which was the insignia of a self-styled elite. "If the public does not frequent our literary masterpieces, it is because those masterpieces are literary, that is to say, fixed; and fixed in forms that no longer respond to the needs of the time." For his first example he chose *Edipus Rex*. "Sophocles speaks grandly perhaps, but in a style that is no longer timely"; it is "too refined" for our age, with its "rude and epileptic rhythm." Shakespeare will no longer do either because he was too much interested in psychology, and "both the theater and we ourselves have had enough psychology." Artaud went on to propose his idea of what we really needed, "a theater of cruelty."

He wrote this way back in 1958, before "relevance" had become a magic word. Today we are scarcely asphyxiated by a respect for the literary masterpieces, even in the universities. Although we still have an academic elite to embroider, annotate, and teach them, the problem now is to demonstrate that their "timeless" values may still be timely. In particular the great tragedies of the past may seem archaic in a day that produces little stirring tragedy in either drama or fiction, no tragic heroes of stature and force, but instead has typically created the "anti-hero," such as the futile protagonists of Samuel Beckett's *Waiting for Godot*. The grand style of both Sophocles and Shakespeare would ring hollow in a contemporary play. And what is Edipus to us? In an alien world of gods and oracles, by an extraordinary series of coincidences—a billion to one shot—he unwittingly murdered his father and married his mother, and so gave his name to a Freudian complex; but he did not himself suffer from this popular complex, of which Sophocles knew nothing. Although students can and do enjoy his strange drama, the question remains what it means to them, whether it means any more than the horror films many also enjoy, or whether it seems as relevant as the theater of cruelty, of absurdity, of negation, of "black comedy," or other characteristic expressions of the contemporary spirit. Certainly it has no direct bearing on the social and political problems they are more obviously concerned about.

To me the issue here is not merely academic or literary, nor a merely personal matter either—a defense of my own literary tastes. Although I would not maintain that a tragic sense of life is necessarily the profoundest, truest sense, or that it is a primary need of young people today, it is distinctly relevant to the state of America. The want of it in our mass culture is one clue to what's wrong with America. The popular insistence on wholesome morals and happy endings, drama in which the good guys always win out over the bad guys, reflects an engrained immaturity that in political life appears as an insistence that America should always have its own way, vainglorious boasts about its never having lost a war, a blind resentment of the troublemakers who are blamed for the frustrations of the hard-working good guys, and an inability to face up to either the complexity or the gravity of the nation's problems. No course in tragedy could assure maturity, much less an understanding of our problems; but if the masterpieces have any effect on people, they might help to induce more mature, responsible attitudes.

So let us take a closer look at *Edipus Rex,* and first of all face the difficulties it poses for modern readers, in the very different conditions of our life. The tragedy is indeed set in an alien world, for it is due directly to the gods, foretold by oracles. Although scholars disagree about the attitude of Sophocles toward these gods, he never questions their existence—their oracles are always right. Needless to say, nobody today can believe in the Greek gods, but their will or their whim cannot be translated into Christian terms either. If the will of the Christian God is no more comprehensible, the doctrine of predestination is dead too; no sophisticated reader today can imagine him decreeing the fate of Edipus. And difficulties remain even when these specific religious terms are translated into broader philosophical terms. Behind both Greek and Elizabethan tragedy, as behind most serious thought in the past, was a sense of some kind of order above man, divine or moral, in a universe somehow concerned about man. If many students still have some such belief or hope, usually vague, more are inclined to assume that the universe is indifferent to man; but all alike are interested primarily in the natural, social causes of human tragedy. In these realistic terms the fate of Edipus remains a fantastic accident, far removed from tragedy in common experience.

Like the heroes in all the great tragedy of the past, Edipus is also removed from common experience by birth and social status. He is King Edipus. Although concerned about the welfare of the citizens of Thebes, who are represented by a Chorus, he is set apart from them and is not representative of their ordinary aspirations, sorrows, and miseries. Little of the daily life, the common indignities of the sufferings of the many, got into Greek tragedy. Or say that King Edipus was representative as a father symbol, and it only emphasizes how different his tragic role was from the role of such symbols in America today—most popular Ike, for instance. For that matter he was not clearly a father symbol for democratic Athens; scholars disagree on the meaning his tragedy had for the Greeks. And this points to another elementary difficulty obscured by the scholarly commonplace that the tragic poets dealt with universal, timeless themes, not contemporary problems. Sophocles was not addressing mankind or posterity. He was an Athenian addressing his fellow Athenians on an annual civic festival, employing Greek myths and legends to express his thought and feeling about issues—moral, religious, and sometimes political (as in *Antigone*)—that were of vital interest to them as Greeks, not citizens of eternity. Whatever *Edipus Rex* meant to the Athenians, it has surely lost some of the timeliness it had for them.

Yet most of us who know it still find it an exceptionally powerful play—and for reasons not really difficult to understand. As a literary masterpiece it is not in fact "fixed." Its choral form is fixed, to be sure, but that need not bother us; we may appreciate the possible advantages of the Greek chorus more because we have grown more aware that all theater necessarily depends upon some conventions, and modern playwrights have felt much freer to experiment with new forms that violate traditional conventions. Above all, the *meaning* of a literary masterpiece is by no means fixed. By its nature as a great work of art it has no one definite, exclusive meaning, whatever the intention of its author, but is richly suggestive, has a wealth of possible meanings, including some its author did not consciously intend or his contemporary audience recognize. For this reason generations of readers are needed to make it an enduring masterpiece, as critics keep on finding meanings that make it more relevant to the interests of their own age. With *Edipus Rex* the plain proof is that scholars and critics—most of them quite confident that they know what the intention of Sophocles was—have come to disagree more widely than ever in their interpretations of it.

Hence students need to be warned against the constant tendency of scholars to pin down meanings, tell us what a masterpiece is "really" about. An example of a favorite kind of scholarly performance is John Jones's treatise *On Aristotle and Greek Tragedy,* a vigorous demonstration that almost all the scholars before him have misinterpreted a classic. Today, he argues, we misread Aristotle's *Poetics* because of our interest in character, especially the tragic hero, whereas Aristotle said plainly: "Tragedy is an imitation not of human beings but of action and life." Jones insists there is not a shred of evidence that he entertained the concept of the tragic hero; always he focused on action. In this view the action of *Edipus Rex* is the king's search for the truth, which finally vindicates the oracles. "Our experience is of something decisively accomplished"; since it is "an ultimately fortunate thing that the parricide and incest should be established," the play is no tragedy at all as most of us conceive the term; but Jones stoutly insists too that we have no right to force on Greek tragedy "the local and no doubt transient self of the modern West."

Although no Greek scholar myself, I think Jones makes out a plausible case for his version of Aristotle's *Poetics,* and just possibly for what he calls the "true" Sophoclean standpoint; but I insist that we have a perfect right to bring our own interests to Greek tragedy and find meanings relevant to our experience, so long as we do not simply force them on the work. If we are more interested in the tragic hero than Aristotle was, or maybe the Greeks were, the drama of Sophocles offers ample grounds for this interest. (Not to mention *Prometheus Bound:* what would it be without Prometheus, the archetypal rebel against tyranny?) It also rewards a concern for the philosophical implications of tragedy that Aristotle virtually ignored, beginning with the obvious question: Are the gods just? As for *Edipus Rex,* Jones's interpretation of it as a success story simply impoverishes it, deprives it of significance for modern readers. Since he concedes that "probably not much of the ancient tragic experience is recoverable by us," he makes plainest that we have no right to insist on any "true" standpoint, the "real" meaning of a great play.

As it is, we have a wide choice in interpretations of the tragedy of Sophocles, and reason to question the conventional ones. In keeping with his reputation among the Greeks for God-fearing piety, and the conventional piety often expressed by his choruses, most classical scholars have maintained that his tragic heroes are rightly punished for their *hubris* and so illustrate a wholesome moral, the wisdom of humble submission to the gods. C. M. Bowra, who admits that Sophocles does not explicitly answer the questions he raises, nevertheless comes to the traditional conclusion: "The gods are always right and should not be opposed. . . . Sometimes indeed they are hard to understand, but none the less men must assume that all is as it ought to be." So it is even with King Edipus, whose dreadful fate Bowra grants was not clearly deserved: having expressed skepticism about the oracles, or in effect the "divine governance" of the world, he too finally learns that the gods are always right, "man must humble himself before them and admit that he is nothing and that he knows nothing." It accordingly appears that Sophocles was saying substantially what Robert Browning said more blithely in Christian terms: "God's in his heaven and all's right with the world."

Although "my" Sophocles is quite different from this, first let us ask: What would young people today get out of this conventional interpretation of *Edipus Rex?* It might teach them salutary lessons about the sin of pride, the need of humility, the wisdom of resignation, the "utter insignificance" of man (Bowra's words), and other such lessons of conventional piety, which are no doubt pertinent in an impious age. But the more thoughtful ones would surely raise objections. It simply isn't so that all is as it ought to be. Whether there be gods or no, there is certainly no clear justice on earth, no reason to believe that men always deserve their fate. King Edipus of course had his faults, sprung from his fierce pride, but it was not right that he should suffer the terrible fate prophecied by the oracles—at that a fate he had done his best to escape by fleeing his native land. Why should he not be skeptical of a "divine governance" that had arbitrarily decreed such a fate even before he was born? And I should agree that if this is all that Sophocles has to say to us about the terms of man's life, young people might as well close the book on him.

Granted that we cannot be certain of his intentions, "my" Sophocles is at least much more relevant.[1] While he never questioned the existence or the power of the gods, he did question their justice. *Edipus Rex* above all evokes a sense of painful mystery. It is a mystery that all religious faith testifies to, since there would be no need of *faith* if all were clearly as it ought to be, and it remains when man is considered on wholly naturalistic grounds as an animal who in his evolution somehow developed consciousness, the powers of the human spirit: the tragic paradoxes of a creature who suffers because he is *not* utterly insignificant, a mere worm, but is conscious of the human condition, the wonders and the terrors of life. He is demonstrating his peculiar significance even when he speaks of the nothingness of life, declares that all is vanity. Hence we need not take seriously the gods and the oracles in *Edipus Rex,* any more than we do the witches in *Macbeth* or the ghost in *Hamlet;* the tragedy remains meaningful in humanistic terms as a powerfully dramatic expression of the common irony of man's fate, raising the unanswerable but inescapable questions about the meaning of his life. And to me Sophocles is clearly a spokesman of the distinctive humanism of Greek culture that entered our cultural heritage. He respected the gods in some Greek fashion (we even hear that he once entertained a new god, Asclepius, in his own home until a public shrine could be prepared for the visitor), but he respected as much the human spirit, above all the heroic spirit, which—as in Homer—could maintain its own dignity in the face of the sometimes awful power of the gods. The pride of King Edipus—what conventional scholars have seized on as his "tragic flaw"—brought on his tragedy in an entirely honorable sense, for he fiercely insisted on learning at any cost the truth about his identity, and the more fiercely as it became ever clearer that the truth was appalling. God forbid that contemporaries reduce his tragedy to an "identity crisis," but at least young people may respond with more feeling than their fathers did to his cry "I will know who I am!"

So considered, at any rate, the timeless themes of *Edipus Rex* become more apparent. Forget the nameless gods, or take the oracles only as dramatic conventions, and the tragic ironies of the drama remain as compelling as ever, probably more moving to us than they were to the

---

1. Here I am repeating the gist of my argument in *The Spirit of Tragedy,* where I considered at some length all his extant plays. I shall not go into a further complication I noted, that his plays are not all of a piece, but so varied that one cannot speak easily of "Sophoclean tragedy."

ancient Greeks. Strange as is the fate of Edipus, we still respond to
the sense of inevitability, a kind of inexorable logic that may govern
the fate of men. This has been complicated by our awareness of the
social causes of tragedy, the knowledge that men are products and
often victims of their environment, yet character—however formed—
has something to do with their fate; in the same environment some
may weakly succumb, others may struggle and assert themselves, perhaps to go down, perhaps to succeed. Hence we often feel, as we say,
that men may seem "fated" for defeat or disaster—by their weakness,
their ambition, their pride, or even their idealism. And usually too by
their blindness, of which King Edipus is a supremely ironic example.
By blinding himself at the end he illustrated a homelier expression: he
"had it coming to him."

Another possible approach to the drama is through the perennial
themes of myth and ritual, which anthropology and psychology have
helped to make a major interest in contemporary thought, and young
people are being drawn to. King Edipus is the ritual scapegoat, one of
the variants of the god-king—known all over the ancient world—who
suffers and dies to purify his people or assure their welfare. Thebes has
been suffering from a terrible plague and blight, presumably because
of some offense against piety, and he takes it upon himself to remove
the cause of the defilement, which the oracle tells him is that Thebes is
harboring the murderer of its former king. The apparent irony of his
discovery that he himself is the defiling thing is accordingly fitting, because essential to his role as ritual scapegoat. To the uninitiated modern
reader this approach may seem ultra-literary; at the tragic end of the
play, who is consoled by the thought that the citizenry of Thebes will
now be happier? For that matter, Sophocles makes no mention at all
of their good fortune; his Chorus says only "Call no man fortunate that
is not dead." But whether or not the ancient ritual pattern entered his
conscious intentions, it may help to explain the hold that *Edipus Rex*
still has on our imagination. The ritual scapegoat and the dying god
survive beneath later manifestations that we respond to, such as the
Christ, who suffered crucifixion in order to redeem mankind. We have
grown more aware of strange undercurrents in the depths of the mind,
symbols and images recurring in ancient myths and rituals that appear
in our dreams too, or what Jung called archetypal images and patterns.
Students might be interested in correspondences between the legend of
King Edipus and that of many other mythical heroes, including Moses,
Siegfried, and King Arthur.

Finally, however, I would stress most the essential values of the tragic spirit as I conceive it. The key to it is a seemingly strange but unquestionable fact, the *pleasure* that mature readers get from tragedy, even though it is a representation of painful experience. It is not a pure pleasure, to be sure, and is far from delight. It is naturally a complex experience, with various components that will differ in individual readers or spectators. It involves purely formal satisfactions, as of expectations fulfilled, the artistic "rightness" of the tragic ending, or a beautiful expression of sadness, which we may all enjoy in simple songs; it affords as well the satisfaction of realism, recognition of truths about man's life, and then of heightened consciousness, experience enriched; it may involve something like what Aristotle called catharsis, a purging of the emotions of pity and terror (though I would question the value of purging us of pity); and all generalization about it needs to be qualified by a recognition of the plain differences between Aeschylus, Sophocles, and Euripides, between all of them and Shakespeare, and between what critics and philosophers have read into them. But to me the most inspiring common element in the pleasure afforded by the greater tragedies—the reason why at the end we do not feel simple anguish, terror, or despair, but feel lifted, moved by a sense of awe, perhaps of sublimity—is their affirmation of human values, rooted in the dignity of man, that give the tragic heroes a dark splendor. The hero may be or do evil, like Macbeth, but he is not mean or simply vile, never utterly insignificant, always in some sense superior to his fate. Commonly he comes to accept the hard terms of his destiny, as Edipus and Hamlet did, but if he does not we may still appreciate his stature and force, his courage in suffering, his capacity for feeling deeply and greatly, asserting his own spirit, and maintaining his dignity in failure or death. He *must* suffer intensely, go through the worst, in order to make possible a full appreciation of his superiority over his fate.

To repeat, such language may sound phoney in our age, which in lieu of great tragic heroes commonly creates such pitiful creatures as little Willy the salesman, and now anti-heroes. It is often said that modern man is simply incapable of writing high tragedy, in anything like a grand style. Modern science has reduced the stature of man, made both him and his little planet insignificant in a soulless universe. As studied by behaviorists and many social scientists, he has little dignity, much less nobility. He is a creature of reflexes and complexes, a mechanical role-player, an alienated mass-man—anything but a human being freely choosing and carrying out high purposes of his own. He has suffered as well from the ambiguities of the American spirit, which in one aspect is given to complacence and a naive optimism, in another to the mean assumption that economic motives are primary. The American way of life scarcely produces either tragic heroes or a public capable of appreciating them. And there remain the national failures lacking in tragic dignity, including the positive indignity of the cheap talk about "our brave boys" in Vietnam, who have actually displayed far less heroism than the outnumbered, vastly outpowered Vietcong. Simple realism might lead honest young people to conclude that the great tragedies of the past are for us merely literary performances, possible sources of esthetic pleasure, but irrelevant to the conditions of our life, not to say alien to the spirit of Broadway, Hollywood, and the national networks.

Yet the values of high tragedy are by no means dead, nor utterly alien to the American spirit. Our democracy grew up on a belief in the dignity and worth of man, even of common men, which has often been given noble expression by our greater leaders and writers. It has characteristically been a somewhat naive faith, bolstered by too easy an optimism; it has too often been betrayed throughout our history, most obviously by the denial of the dignity of black people; it can therefore be exasperating when it is mouthed by sanctimonious politicians or demagogues; yet it remains a living belief, a constant source of inspiration. As for the spirit of the great tragic heroes, it was of course never representative of any society, the thought and feeling of the masses of ordinary people, who looked rather to their gods; but something like it too remains alive in common experience. Many ordinary people learn through bitter experience to accept the hard terms of man's life, and meet their death with fortitude and dignity. Every day one may read in the papers examples of unpretentious heroism, people rising to emergencies, sometimes risking their lives to save others. Also typically American is the legendary saying of the American sergeant of World War I as he led his men over the top: "Come on, you sons of bitches, d'you want to live forever?"—a legend more credible because he did not say "Come on, my fellow-Americans"; and anyway the sons kept going over even though they did want to live forever. The grand style is not for us ordinary mortals; but surely we have all known people who were not merely pitiful or contemptible, and whose story deserves to be told with compassion, respect, or even reverence.

As plainly the national scene is marked by not only strutting, self-seeking politicians but men of stature, force, and dignity. We have always had men who unselfishly devoted their lives to unpopular causes, carried on gallantly through repeated defeats, maintained their faith to a sometimes bitter end, as Norman Thomas did through the increasing afflictions of old age—except that in his indomitable spirit he did not think of himself as a tragic figure. But we have had our tragic heroes too. One was Abraham Lincoln, a magnanimous man of sorrows who in his martyrdom became the most popular of the national heroes. Another was John F. Kennedy, who was transformed into something of a mythical figure by the shock of his assassination, but whose fate had more than the obvious tragic quality: he had had a fatalistic sense that something of the kind might be in store for him—as his brother Robert would too. Still another was Martin Luther King. By their deaths all alike brought out the best as well as the worst in our land of violence.

For ardent young people I would still not prescribe an intensive education in the tragic spirit. They perhaps have more need of the comic spirit, in the philosophical ironic sense: "Oh Lord, what fools these mortals be!"—and then some sense that they too are mortals, and can be foolish. But take the frailties of these proud mortals seriously, view them with compassion as well as irony, or in a sombre spirit, and one is on his way to tragedy. Although the old saying has it that life is a comedy to one who thinks, a tragedy to one who feels, the great tragedies are of course compact of both thought and feeling, and I would repeat that they remain relevant for all thoughtful students today. A tragic sense of life could make more effective the living idealism in America, strengthen the cause of human dignity that has always demanded battling against odds, entailed the likelihood of frustration, never with assurance of complete or final victory. Or since the aroused youth want to be realistic, and may believe too easily that they are, they might heed a tragic wisdom stated by Thomas Hardy: "If way to the Better there be, it exacts a full look at the Worst."[2]

About the relevance of Shakespeare I have no doubt whatever. His plays remain a staple in the English curriculum, required reading for all students of literature, and quite properly so. No doubt insensitive students may be bored by him, more may think he is overrated, still more may complain of pedantic teaching of him, and all may safely

2. For their sake I should perhaps note that a few writers have been attacking the indignity of death and its tyranny, starting a kind of revolution against death, in the belief that even within our lifetime man can and will put an end to it, and make immortality the next phase of evolution. "We want the right to live forever," proclaims F.M. Esfandiary. I know of no reputable scientist, however, who endorses this hope or this right; and in any case death is not the ultimate tragedy. Often enough the painful thing is that people don't die, but have to live with some dreadful knowledge, as King Edipus did. As for the human race, already threatened by a population explosion, one might shudder at the thought of what would happen to it if people did begin living forever.

ignore the bulk of the vast literature about him; but I hear of no wide-spread resentment of him as a staple requirement, no serious question of his reputation as the greatest of English poets and the most universal in the range of his interests. His tragedies, above all *Hamlet,* have stood up magnificently under the test of time in spite of all the crude conventions of the Elizabethan theatre. Hamlet still speaks most eloquently to and for all thoughtful men as he broods over the conditions of man's life, himself embodies most fully the tragic ambiguities, incongruities, and paradoxes of the nature of man. Certainly he means far more to us than he did to his Elizabethan audience, who were likely to see little but a prince carrying out tardily but melodramatically a duty of bloody revenge. And though Shakespeare obviously put much more in him than this—more of himself—he could never have dreamed of the wealth of diverse meaning that scholars and critics are still busy reading into or out of his drama. We now have a choice of dozens of Hamlets, each usually offered with the assurance that the critic has "plucked out the heart" of his mystery, but at least illuminating some of the many facets of an endlessly fascinating character. No literary masterpiece is less "fixed" in its meaning, and none, I think, is more likely to remain richly meaningful as long as our civilization endures, or retains any devotion to basic human values.

With modern tragedy the issues are much more complicated.[3] In drama it began with Ibsen as realistic bourgeois tragedy, written in prose, obviously lacking the grandeur of Greek and Shakespearean tragedy. It of course had to be different; given modern knowledge and the very different conditions of life in our world, no honest writer could write like Sophocles or Shakespeare. It also grew much more varied than the tragedy of the past, more difficult to categorize; only the roughest generalizations will apply at once to Hauptmann, Strindberg, Chekhov, O'Neill, Eliot, Anouilh, Sartre, Arthur Miller, Hockhuth, and others whose drama has more or less tragic quality. Chekhov, my favorite among the moderns, may illustrate the complications. His realistic studies of futility, shot through with a kind of comic irony, lacking heroes or heroic action, having little dramatic action of any kind, do not correspond to any of the familiar definitions of tragedy;

3. I am neglecting to consider the neo-classical tragedy of Corneille and Racine for a possibly parochial reason. Although the French still revere them, they never became popular in the Anglo-American world, and in my experience few students are at all stirred by them. I myself find little tragic quality in the drama of Corneille, somewhat more in Racine, but still with no brooding sense of the mystery of the human condition, the tragic paradoxes that tormented Pascal —a much profounder writer of the period.

yet I find no modern plays more moving than his, more haunting, in part because of his magical artistry, but ultimately because he was the most humane of writers, with the rarest blend of irony, compassion, and reverence for life. No modern writer has in his practice more fully supported the simple credo in the Port Huron Statement of the Students for a Democratic Society: "We regard *men* as infinitely precious." Hence he brings up the question I raised in my study of modern tragedy, which for my present purposes remains the most important question: In the necessarily new terms imposed by our knowledge and experience, can it affirm equivalent values and afford an equivalent pleasure? The answer will depend in part on one's temperament and philosophical predisposition, not merely fine esthetic taste. But to me the answer is that it can, and that the best of it does.

This seems to me as clear in modern tragic fiction, beginning with Thomas Hardy and Joseph Conrad, in which a stark pessimism has been more pronounced than in drama, or than in ancient tragedy too. As a challenging example, I propose to consider at some length Conrad, who in my youth became my favorite novelist, and specifically *Nostromo,* to my mind his greatest novel. In a chapter on him written more than a generation ago, a decade after his death, I remarked that he had apparently already become a "classic" in that he was more admired than read, seldom referred to outside the classroom. Now his reputation as a major novelist appears to be solidly established; he has been getting ample attention in literary criticism and textbook editions. But now *Nostromo* may seem not at all modern to students, still more of a classic in the dreary sense, since it dates from 1904, before the World Wars.

In rereading the novel with this question in mind, I was pleased to find that I was again thrilled by it and still consider it a magnificent expression of the tragic spirit. I also realized that a major political theme, which to me had seemed incidental, has acquired much more relevance. Otherwise, however, I found reason to doubt that most students today would share my enthusiasm for the novel, and reason for not blaming them. My love of Conrad is temperamental; I would never maintain that my favorite novelist is the greatest, in a class with Shakespeare, nor that *Nostromo* belongs with the world's masterpieces. What follows therefore amounts to self-indulgence. My excuse for it is my belief that we nevertheless do have here a notable expression of the tragic spirit in our time, one that most directly raises the fundamental questions about the human condition, and that students might find more profoundly relevant than the negations in much contemporary

literature because it affirms positive human values despite an unflinch-
ing pessimism. Not to mention the work of an artist who could achieve
superbly the task he set himself, of before all making readers *see*.

3 / Interlude: Joseph Conrad's Nostromo

SET IN A CENTRAL AMERICAN COUNTRY called Costaguana, the main action of *Nostromo* centers about a revolution. This is only the latest of a
series of revolutions in a land of sordid, routine corruption and intrigue,
affairs suggesting to a European on-looker "a puerile and bloodthirsty
game of murder and rapine played with terrible earnestness by depraved children." The revolutionaries are not at all like the types familiar in Europe, Marxist or anarchist.[4] They are representative only of
Latin America, with its too many so-called revolutions that before the
era of Castro changed nothing because they were inspired chiefly by
greed or lust for power, repressive forces that still keep most of the
continent under the rule of military dictators. But there remains a
theme of wider, more enduring interest. Law and order are restored
in Costaguana through the power of the fabulously rich San Tomé
silver mine, owned and managed by an Englishman, supported by a
powerful American industrialist in the background—the "material interests" that dominate the country. In the guise of colonialism such interests would later provoke the revolt of the whole non-Western world,
but everywhere deeply affect the destiny of mankind.

Western imperialism had provided a theme in an earlier work by
Conrad, *Heart of Darkness*. Set in the Belgian Congo, this portrays
the callousness of the exploitation of the natives in many unforgettably
vivid images. But Conrad was more interested in another consequence
of imperialism that Americans might now take to heart—its sinister
effects on the Europeans. Some Americans have come to realize that
while Vietnam has suffered grievously from devastation and the death
of a million of its people, America has suffered more profoundly from

---

4. These provided the subject matter of two other of Conrad's novels, *Under
Western Eyes* and *The Secret Agent*. He treated them with little compassionate
understanding, since he was by temperament an aristocrat, averse to ideology.
His objections to their typically narrow, dogmatic, or fanatical mentality have
been vindicated by the Russian Revolution and its aftermath, but do not spring
from insights likely to impress students of politics today.

its barbarous war: the bitter, often violent internal dissension, the inhuman tactics to which our military have become inured, the common
atrocities committed by our "brave boys" in their contempt for the
"gooks," and withal not only the dishonesty of our national leaders but
the more dangerous self-deception, which has blunted the moral sense
of both the leaders and the "patriots" who support them. In *Heart of
Darkness* the protagonist is "Mistah Kurtz," a lonely agent in a jungle
outpost for the collection of the ivory so precious to Europeans, whom
the narrator Marlow finds on a feverish deathbed. An emissary of
"progress," Kurtz is a successful collector who fancies himself as one
bearing the white man's burden; he has been working on a report for
the International Society for the Suppression of Savage Customs in
which he eloquently expresses exalted sentiments about the "practically
unbounded" power for good that white men could assert. But the report breaks off abruptly: "Exterminate all the brutes!" Around his hut
are posts capped by skulls of some of the brutes he had exterminated.
Marlow also mentions discreetly—perhaps too discreetly for contemporary tastes—"unspeakable rites" Kurtz had participated in, the gratification of "monstrous passions." Corrupted by his power, he had
succumbed to the savagery he had exploited. The "heart of darkness"
was not just Africa—it was in Western man.

At the very end, however, Kurtz summoned up enough strength
and honesty to throw off his self-deception, pass judgment on his career.
His last words were a whisper: "The horror! The horror!" One may
wonder whether the military and political leaders implicated in the
horrors of our war in Vietnam will ever manage to be as honest with
themselves. Still, their self-deception sprang from more real devotion to
a cause. Call it American imperialism, it is nevertheless not inspired by
mere greed or lust for power. It is more akin to the kind of imperialism Conrad portrayed in *Nostromo,* a subtle, ambiguous force that
"could set in motion mighty machines" and also awaken in human
breasts "an unbounded devotion to the task."

Charles Gould, the English owner of the San Tomé mine, is a wholly
dedicated man who best illustrates the ambiguity. A good man at
heart, not at all avaricious, he is self-deceived by his need of idealizing
his aims and actions but essentially is quite sincere. So far from exploiting his miners, he provides them with a much more decent, secure life
than they had known. For in a land with a long tradition of corruption and misrule his mine is the one force that can provide law, order,
stability, good faith. "Any one can declaim about these things," he tells
his gentle wife, "but I pin my faith in material interests. Only let the

material interests once get a firm footing, and they are bound to impose the conditions on which alone they can continue to exist. That's how your money-making is justified here in the face of lawlessness and disorder." Before the revolution Gould had proved himself by using his wealth and influence to help replace a brutal dictatorship by a constitutional regime, under a colorless but decent, moderate president. When the usual sordid kind of revolutionaries overthrew this regime, with an eye to the wealth of the San Tomé mine, he again did most to put them down by standing firm, supporting the decent elements in his province, resolving to blow up his mine if need be rather than permit the outlaws to lay hands on it. His loyal miners marched on the provincial capital to rescue their Señor Administrador. We leave the land enjoying order and security again under a constitutional government with better prospects.

Holroyd, the American millionaire who stands behind Gould, is a much more bumptious dedicated type whose materialism is grosser, but still inspired by an idealism of sorts. Because of the immense silver and iron interests he heads the San Tomé mine is for him only a hobby, incidental to a much grander dream. Through him Conrad spoke prophetically of America's imperial destiny, at the expense of Great Britain among others. Some day, Holroyd tells Gould on his one visit to Costaguana, we Americans will of course step into the country—but there's no hurry:

> Time itself has got to wait on the greatest country in the whole of God's Universe. We shall be giving the word for everything: industry, trade, law, journalism, art, politics, and religion, from Cape Horn clear over to Smith's Sound, and beyond, too, if anything worth taking hold of turns up at the North Pole. And then we shall have the leisure to take in hand the outlying islands and continents of the earth. We shall run the world's business whether the world likes it or not. The world can't help it—and neither can we, I guess.

Today, more than half a century later, it appears that we couldn't help expanding all over the world. Although we are not running the world or its business, we have been imperialistic enough in defense of our national interests to force the question that did not occur to Holroyd: Are we fit to run it? Specifically, what does he himself have to offer beyond the development or the exploitation of its mineral resources? The last we hear of him is that he has been sending Protestant missionaries to Costaguana, betraying his lack of understanding and respect for the piety of its inhabitants—the characteristic disrespect of Americans for native cultures. But the basic question is forced more insistently by Charles Gould, who is on the scene from beginning to end. What does he have to offer Costaguana beyond his faith in material interests? Now that the law and order these interests need have been restored, what about community? Social justice? Human rights? Any ideal ends?

Although no democrat, Conrad pronounced a harsh verdict on capitalism or economic imperialism just because he was a true conservative of the old school. His spokesman is Dr. Monygham, a sardonic man who is devoted to Charles Gould's loyal wife Emilia and for her sake risks his life during the revolution to protect Gould's interests. "There is no peace and no rest in the development of material interests," he tells her afterward. "They have their law, and their justice. But it is founded on expediency, and is inhuman; it is without the continuity and the force that can be found only in a moral principle." He remarks that the miners would no longer march on the town to save their Señor Administrador; they are now beginning to feel the oppression of material interests battening on the wealth got from their toil. Emilia Gould then has a sombre vision of the San Tomé mine looming over the whole land: "feared, hated, wealthy; more soulless than any tyrant, more pitiless and autocratic than the worst Government; ready to crush innumerable lives in the expansion of its greatness." Now we may add that Castro won his enduring popularity by overthrowing the sovereignty of American material interests in Cuba, and that Latin Americans not only remain fearful of our imperialism but are complaining bitterly of American aid, because under its stipulated terms American business interests have profited much more from it than they have.

Mrs. Gould adds that her husband saw nothing of the evil, never would see it. So we are brought to Conrad's main interest, the effects of a devotion to material interests on his protagonists. For Charles Gould the San Tomé mine is the ruling passion of his life. "Incorrigible" in his devotion to it, he has become obsessed by it to the exclusion of all other interests, blind to all that he had sacrificed to it in simple humanity—and beginning with his domestic life. The chief victim of his passion is his devoted wife. "He was perfect, perfect," she reflects mournfully; "but she would never have him to herself"—never for even a short hour altogether to herself, in their old Spanish colonial house she loved. A small, dainty, still lovely woman who radiated gentleness and sweetness, and throughout her life in Costaguana had devoted herself to helping all those around her, she is left at the end "all alone in the Treasure House of the World," resembling "a good fairy, weary with a long career of well doing, touched by the withering suspicion of the uselessness of her labours, the powerlessness of her magic." Formally faithful to her, Charles Gould cannot see this either. The only one who senses her sorrow is Dr. Monygham. A lonely, embittered man who cannot respect himself because under torture by a dictator years past he had broken down and betrayed his cause, he had found in his silent devotion to Emilia Gould his one consolation and pleasure, and for this reason had spoken to her so harshly about material interests, knowing that she had been sacrificed to them—and that they had made powerless his own devotion.

Another victim is Gian' Battista, an obscure "man of the people" come from Italy, who became famous as Nostromo. He rose to fame as "the magnificent Capataz de Cargadores," whose prowess, daring, and fidelity to his reputation as the incorruptible "nostre uomo" made him the one man the Europeans turned to in all emergencies. As the victorious revolutionists approach the town, he is accordingly entrusted with what he regards as the most "desperate undertaking" of his life —sailing away at night in a lighter loaded with the silver of the mine. Although he manages to bury the silver on a barren island in the harbor after the lighter is run down in the darkness by a steamer, and then performs another typically daring feat, he returns to find that a companion on the lighter has disappeared, apparently drowned, and that the Europeans seem content to think that the silver he risked his life for was at the bottom of the sea—all they wanted was to keep it out of the hands of the revolutionists. Feeling betrayed, he keeps to himself the secret of the buried treasure. And he is cursed by it, no less when he begins gradually to enrich himself with it. He is a lost soul, the more bewildered and embittered because the mainspring of his career had been an immense vanity, "that finest form of egoism which can take on the aspect of every virtue," and which now made him feel that "the genuineness of all his qualities was destroyed." Finally he is killed by the treasure, shot by mistake one night when he comes stealthily to dig up some ingots of silver.

The mistake was made by old Giorgio, the "Garibaldino," keeper of a lighthouse on the barren island, who looked upon Nostromo as a son. He has some political significance as an austere republican who had fought with Garibaldi, fired by the ideal of liberty, and who is still devoted to the memory of his hero, but in the somber knowledge that he had fought in a lost cause. Scornful of the "rabble" who flock to the rapacious revolutionaries in Costaguana, he keeps entirely aloof from the political action, as from the material interests; in this land his simple type is antiquated, irrelevant. And no less ineffectual is a frail old aristocrat, Don José Avellanos, a dedicated patriot and idealist who had proved himself by long enduring bestial treatment as a prisoner of the last dictator, who now talks with an old-fashioned, somewhat tedious fervor about his hopes for Costaguana under a constitutional regime, and who cannot see that the material interests that support it are basically indifferent to his lofty principles and liberal ideals. Carried off on a stretcher when the revolutionists are marching on the town and its rabble is rising to greet them, he dies in flight, all his hopes shattered.

But his tragedy brings up the major concerns of Conrad, the pessimistic themes that run through all his novels. While he had little interest in political problems if only because he had no faith in political solutions, he had none either in religious or philosophical solutions for the "irremediable joylessness of human condition." The futility of the political life of Costaguana is only the background for a drama of frustration and futility that involves all the major characters, excepting the hollow success of Charles Gould. Another example is Martin Decoud, a blasé Paris boulevardier who in an ironic spirit enlists as a journalist in the struggle against the revolutionists, a patriotic cause in which he cannot believe, out of love for Antonia Avellanos, the high-minded daughter of Don José. The companion of Nostromo on the desperate venture to save the silver of the mine, he is left alone on the barren island, and after several days of sleepless solitude, in the company only of a mind that had "recognized no other virtue than intelligence," he rows out to sea to drown himself: "A victim of the disillusioned weariness which is the retribution meted out to intellectual audacity, the brilliant Don Martin Decoud, weighted by the bars of San Tomé silver, disappeared without a trace, swallowed up in the immense indifference of things." This cosmic indifference—an insistent theme in Conrad—envelopes as well Nostromo, by contrast with Decoud a masterful man of action, hence a "victim of the disenchanted vanity which is the reward of audacious action." Both illustrate all that Marlow could make out about the meaning of man's life in *Heart of Darkness,* "a mysterious arrangement of merciless logic for a futile purpose." Conrad lavishly embroiders the mystery with such adjectives as unfathomable, inscrutable, inexorable, and sinister.

Even more insistent is the theme of loneliness, the "tremendous fact of our isolation, of the indestructible loneliness that surrounds, envelopes, clothes every human soul from the cradle to the grave, and, perhaps, beyond." The old soul of the heroic Garibaldino dwells alone with its memories, "tender and violent, terrible and dreary."

Antonia Avellanos, who alone had shared the exaltation and the despair of her father, is then left alone to mourn the death of her lover too. Emilia Gould, lovable because of her sympathetic understanding of others, is herself the most pitiable victim, "wealthy beyond great dreams of wealth, considered, loved, respected, honored, and as solitary as any human being had ever been, perhaps, on this earth." Dr. Monygham, for many years a solitary himself, is alone in his mournful knowledge of her sorrow, which he is too considerate ever to intrude on her. Martin Decoud, always given to ironic detachment, dies of solitude on a deserted island, in a tense silence in which he comes to doubt the reality of his own existence. Nostromo bears alone his guilty secret, the knowledge that he has lost his integrity.

Now, students might reasonably be repelled by this vision of life. In attacking the "fettering dogmas" of most credos, Conrad himself once wrote that what is "so hopelessly barren in declared pessimism is just its arrogance," and surely he can seem arrogant in too many of his asides. The human condition is not in fact irremediably joyless, any more than futility is the universal fate. As for the "tremendous fact" of our loneliness, students know something of this from their own experience, perhaps need a more poignant sense of the truism that we all do suffer and die alone; yet they may rightly complain that Conrad insists too much. They also know that normally people are not in fact simply isolated, but share their joys and their sorrows with others; community too is a basic fact of man's life. There is little of such sharing in *Nostromo*, that chiefly by the frustrated good fairy Emilia Gould, and little of ordinary experience in general. The main characters chat now and then, but rarely if ever laugh. And though Conrad's neglect of the simplicities of common experience may be justified by his artistic purposes, one may feel that he is blind to them in his remorseless insistence on his tragic themes.

To students his world may seem alien for other reasons. In their popular phrase, they may find it hard to "relate to" the characters in *Nostromo*, and perhaps hardest of all to Nostromo himself, a "man of the people" quite unlike any they have known or heard about. The experience of the Garibaldino, Dr. Monygham, Don José Avellanos, Martin Decoud, and others is as remote from their experience. The scenes of Conrad's fiction are typically remote from civilized society, the dramas as typically strange or a-typical; he liked to isolate his characters amid elemental realities, thrust them into crises in which they could rely only on their own resources of character. Even the familiar "material interests" in *Nostromo* are far removed in time and space from these interests as they appear in our technological society, and impinge on the lives of students. And Conrad is least modern in another respect now important. Love enters his novel, but not sex: his treatment of sex is as delicate, and by contemporary standards as un-realistic, as that of Victorian novelists. Ardently in love with Antonia Avellanos, the sophisticated Martin Decoud never even kisses her. His author was quite innocent of Freud, or at least no more interested in him than he was in Marx or any other of the gods of the modern world.

Yet we may of course be critical of the visions of life offered by all writers. All are personal and partial, including that of the most nearly universal Shakespeare. Conrad's was at least not shallow, eccentric, or morbidly romantic. Rendered with a fidelity at once passionate and pitiless, it was far from irrelevant too. His detachment from current social problems, the distinctive interests of our age, enabled him to deal more directly with the enduring, essential themes of man's life. More to my immediate point, his vision embraced the possibilities of the human spirit that can evoke the exalted pleasure of tragedy. *Nostromo*, the most complete statement of his pessimism, is also the most grandly moving of his novels, in its sweep and stir a monumental expression of the tragic spirit. Or if students are not stirred by it, at least no mature reader should find it merely depressing, or its upshot simple despair.

Let Conrad speak for himself, first of all about a soulless universe. "I have come to suspect," he wrote in *A Personal Record*, "that the aim of creation cannot be ethical at all. I would fondly believe that its object is purely spectacular: a spectacle for awe, love, adoration, or hate, if you like, but in this view—and in this view alone—never for despair!" The marvelous, he noted elsewhere, fascinated him more than the "mere supernatural." About the human actors in this spec-tacle he wrote, "The history of man on this earth since the beginning of ages may be resumed in one phrase of infinite poignancy: They were born, they suffered, they died. . . . Yet it is a great tale!" *Nostromo* in particular is a great tale because in its sweep it most fully realized Conrad's conception of the enduring appeal of the artist through the changing wisdom of the generations—including, let us add, our own most knowing, and perhaps most foolish generation:

> He speaks to our capacity for delight and wonder, to the sense of mystery surrounding our lives: to our sense of pity, and beauty, and pain: to the latent feeling of fellowship with all creation—and to the subtle but in-vincible conviction of solidarity that knits together the loneliness of

innumerable hearts to the solidarity in dreams, in joy, in sorrow, in aspirations, in illusions, in hope, in fear, which binds men to each other,
which binds together all humanity—the dead to the living and the living
to the unborn.

This is not the kind of ideal solidarity that Walt Whitman exalted in
his hymns to democracy—the brotherhood of man, embracing above all
the common people. Conrad was too ironical and aloof to dream of
universal brotherhood, too much of an aristocrat to be deeply concerned
about the common people. Young radicals, I assume, will not be drawn
to him, nor many black students either. Yet he is pointing to a kind
of solidarity that has become more meaningful now that our earth is a
little space-ship, all mankind is in the same boat. Feelings of such
solidarity, which run pretty shallow in affluent America, have grown
stronger among the youth, and might be deepened by the sense Conrad
conveys of a fellowship through the ages in a common fate, no less
in loneliness, and a common mystery enveloping our lives, no less
when God is made their author. Even a religious sense, which is not
strong or deep in America either but toward which many of the young
are groping, might be more vital today if it were allied with a tragic
sense of life.

Most obviously, however, the poignant history of man through the
ages remains a great tale only because of the dignity of man. Of this
there is no question in *Nostromo*. Except for the sordid revolutionists,
the important characters maintain their dignity in the face of the
"immense indifference" and the common fate of frustration. All are
real persons, by no means mere products of their environment, nor
specimens of maladjustment, guinea pigs for analysis. Each is in his
different way somewhat larger than ordinary life size because he is
more purely himself, more consistently loyal to his own values. The
many lesser figures around them, all vividly portrayed, who fill out the
large canvas of the novel are likewise distinct individuals, illustrating
the manifold possibilities of the human spirit. For such reasons too the
world of Conrad may seem remote from familiar experience in a
standardized, regimented society, full of mass-men; yet the manifold
possibilities are of course still real and fascinating. Although young
people seeking to find or to be themselves will find no models in
Nostromo, they might cherish the experience of being transported out
of themselves and their too familiar little world.

Martin Decoud, the one important character whose dignity may be
questioned, illustrates an ambiguity at the heart of Conrad's vision
of life from which they might also draw a possible wisdom. He is like

other intellectuals who occasionally stray into Conrad's exotic or barbarous scenes, including Marlow, his alter-ego, who narrates a number
of his tales. All are ironic, detached, skeptical, melancholy—variants
on the intellectual in Conrad himself. "Only in the conduct of our
action," he writes in *Nostromo*, "can we find the sense of mastery
over the Fates." It is a flattering illusion, he adds, as Nostromo will
discover. Wisdom will recognize it as an illusion—yet also as a necessary, saving one because of the values of action in realizing our humanity, and the dangers of detachment, which can become inhuman.
Decoud's detachment came down to a "barren indifferentism posing as
intellectual superiority"; it was not merely skeptical but cynical; and so
he died from solitude, and from "want of faith in himself and others."
Heyst, an intellectual who is the hero of Conrad's *Victory*, sums up the
lesson most explicitly in his last words: "Woe to the man whose heart
has not learned while young to hope, to love—and to put its trust in
life!"

In short, we cannot actually trust life, and as we live we must.
Wisdom must recognize the complexities, ambiguities, ironies, but
also the simplicities—which today are perhaps harder to keep a steady
eye on than ever before. "Those who read me," Conrad wrote, "know
my conviction that the world, the temporal world, that is, rests on a
very few simple ideas, so simple that they must be as old as the hills.
It rests notably, among others, on the idea of Fidelity." In *Nostromo*
unwavering fidelity was a main source of the dignity of the Garibaldino, Don José and Antonia Avellanos, Emilia Gould, Dr. Monygham.
"Where did it get them?" skeptical students might ask; and the immediate answer has to be that it can never assure happiness or success,
any more than any other virtue can. Of many a fighter in lost causes
it might be said that fidelity was the soul of him, and the ruin of
him, the death of him. Then one may add that without fidelity there
can be no lofty pride, no genuine self-respect, only the gratifications
of vanity or self-deception. One may regret that, like honor, it is not
a popular word in America today; in its stead we have such words
as patriotism, too often of a vulgar kind, and in practice an unthinking
conformity to conventional virtues, with only lip service to ideals requiring any personal sacrifice. The youth too might ponder more the
simple idea of fidelity, since they enjoy an uncommon freedom due to
a slack permissiveness, in a society they are rebelling against because
of the hollowness of its avowed ideals.

Then they might brood over the tragedy of Nostromo: a simple
man who won fame by his fidelity in all emergencies, who after he was

led by wounded vanity to keep the fatal secret of the buried treasure retained all his personal prestige in the community, but who had lost his self-respect, destroyed the meaning of his whole career. And yet retained too something of splendor to the bitter end. I take leave to review the concluding scenes of *Nostromo*, in which all the ironic, tragic themes of Conrad are summed up dramatically.

As a man of the people, Nostromo, now captain of a schooner, had returned to them in his disillusionment, helping those in need with a lavish, careless generosity. He even attended meetings of anarchists, presided over by an "indigent, sickly, somewhat hunchbacked little photographer, with a white face and a magnanimous soul dyed crimson by a bloodthirsty hate of all capitalists, oppressors of the two hemispheres"; but the Captain remained silent during his harangues, frowning, his thoughts elsewhere. He had no real interest in politics, no more faith in it than Conrad. What solace he knew was in his love for one of the two daughters of the old Garibaldino, but this brought him more trouble. Everybody, including herself, assumed that he would marry the elder daughter Linda, an intense, passionate, uncompromising girl, "true daughter of the austere republican," whose blazing love for him was always apparent; only it gave him no promise of solace or peace. He had turned instead to her sister Giselle—fair, soft, indolent, submissive, yet under her placid appearance fond of excitement, yearning for rescue from the loneliness of the lighthouse on the barren island. Unfortunately, rumors had come from town that she was being courted at night by a man whom old Giorgio violently disliked. Lying in wait for him with his rifle, to protect the reputation of his daughter, he fatally wounds Nostromo, stealing across the open to dig up more of his buried treasure for the sake of the fair Giselle. Proud that he has shot "the thief of his honor," he will never know that it was the man he esteemed as his son. Only smiling when Linda tells him he has shot Gian' Battista—"women had strange fancies"—he calls for his Bible, approves when she leaves for her duty of tending the light, long sits immobile before he tries to make out the small print with glasses Emilia Gould had made him a present of, frowns slightly, and sways gently forward until his leonine head rests on the pages. "Growing slowly cold, the Garibaldino lay alone, rugged, undecayed, like an old oak uprooted by a treacherous gust of wind."

On his deathbed in a hospital, Nostromo assures Mrs. Gould that Giselle is innocent and tells her of his bitterness over his betrayal by the men who had been so casual about his most desperate undertaking. He also tells her of his guilt, the silver that had killed him;

but she refuses to let him tell her where the accursed treasure is—the silver that she hates too. She reports to Dr. Monygham that he has told her nothing, a statement he does not believe but in his devotion accepts, "like an inexplicable fatality affirming the victory of Nostromo's genius over his own." Nostromo also asserts himself by refusing all aid from the doctor. The last we see of him he is attended only by the bloodthirsty photographer, hater of capitalists, perched on a high stool, "shock-headed, wildly hairy, like a hunchbacked monkey," who inquires whether the doctor is really a dangerous enemy of the people:

> In the dimly lit room Nostromo rolled his head slowly on the pillow and opened his eyes, directing at the weird figure perched by his bedside a glance of enigmatic and profound inquiry. Then his head rolled back, his eyelids fell, and the Capataz de Cargadores died without a word or moan after an hour of immobility, broken by short shudders testifying to the most atrocious suffering.

Dr. Monygham then witnesses still another inexplicable fatality when Mrs. Gould, having consoled the sobbing, childlike Giselle, despatches him to take care of old Giorgio and Linda. Approaching the lighthouse, he calls to Linda from below, and upon her immediate inquiry, tells her that Nostromo is dead. Her response, as she too is left frustrate and alone, concludes the novel:

> Linda's black figure detached itself upright in the light of the lantern with her arms raised above her head as though she were going to throw herself over.
> "It is I who loved you," she whispered, with a face as set and white as marble in the moonlight. "I! Only I! She will forget thee, killed miserably for her pretty face. I cannot understand. I cannot understand. But I shall never forget thee. Never!"
> She stood silent and still, collecting her strength to throw all her fidelity, her pain, bewilderment, and despair into one great cry.
> "Never! Gian' Battista!"
> Dr. Monygham, pulling round in the police-galley, heard the name pass over his head. It was another of Nostromo's triumphs, the greatest, the most enviable, the most sinister of all. In that true cry of undying passion that seemed to ring aloud from Punta Mala to Azuera and away to the bright line of the horizon, overhung by a big white cloud shining like a mass of solid silver, the genius of the magnificent Capataz de Cargadores dominated the dark gulf containing his conquests of treasure and love.

To young people skeptical about undying passions, I suppose this ending may seem romantic. Others, bred on Hemingway, may complain that it is overwritten—and Conrad was never sparing with adjectives. Nevertheless I still find it unforgettable. In the echoes of Linda's cry I hear: "A great tale!"

4 / A Note on Contemporary Literature

ABOUT THE JUNGLE GROWTH of contemporary literature I shall add only a brief note, since I cannot pretend to be a close student of it. He who runs may read the commonplaces about the dearth of tragedy, of heroes, of affirmations of faith, much less of any qualities of splendor or grandeur. Most conspicuous are such qualities as violence, sensationalism, exhibitionism, hedonism, sadism, cynicism, the cult of "anti-life." In drama the vogue is a species of grotesque tragic comedy under various names, but with a common emphasis on the futility of the characters who pass for protagonists, the banality of their talk, the purposelessness of their lives. Although there is much faddishness in all this, there is enough seriousness to warrant concern over the plain symptoms of decadence or malaise. Contemporary literature is the last word in the tradition of estrangement or alienation from modern society as a "wasteland." Young people seeking personal identity, community, and a meaningful way of life may be excited by its revelations of the hollowness of contemporary life, or its negations, but otherwise are unlikely to find much positive inspiration.[5]

Yet this literature is not purely nihilistic. As Albert Camus observed, all art is an affirmation, first of all of the values of art itself, but then on behalf of something more. The negations of serious writers today suggest a disgust with contemporary life, a revolt against a dehumanized society lacking any clear sense of continuity, direction, and pur-

5. For me a clear example is the popular film *Easy Rider*. Its shocking ending, the pointless murder of its "heroes" by Southern rednecks, brings out the violence too common in America, but may obscure the pointlessness of their own lives. When the two carefree drug-pushers reach their destination, a whorehouse in New Orleans, and one says happily "We made it!", the other answers soberly no, "We blew it"; but what was "it"? They had not been seeking community, love, social justice, any significant goal—only fun on an open road that led nowhere. I wondered whether the many young people who were enthusiastic about the film realized that the easy riders had no meaningful destination, little more personal dignity than the rednecks who shot them down in cold blood.

pose, which seldom explicitly asserts positive values, but at least implies them. Few if any of these writers are saying that man's life has always and everywhere been futile, meaningless, hopeless: they are saying in effect that it need not be as empty as it has become. There remain what I consider legitimate complaints about their criticism of life, complaints that deserve the last word on behalf of human dignity, in a society that is not simply a wasteland. "A man becomes the image of the thing he hates," A.E. observed; so this literature can be as dehumanized as the society it caricatures. But first let us question the conclusions too often drawn from it, that tragedy is gone for good, together with the hero and the heroic ideal, and that negation is the wave of the literary future. And let us begin with the neglected simplicities.

There are of course still audiences for Sophocles, Shakespeare, Chekhov, O'Neill, and other old-timers, and also for some contemporaries who are not at all cynical or sensational. Arthur Miller, for example, has said that for him tragedy was "the only form there was." That he has focused it on social and political problems is only natural for a modern writer, a restriction that need not be fatal to the values of tragedy. The chief question he raises centers on little Willy, the hero of his most popular *Death of a Salesman.* In meeting the common charge that Willy lacked the stature and force of a tragic hero, Miller wrote that he considered the play "heroic," the drama of "a very brave spirit who cannot settle for half but must pursue his dream of himself to the end." I saw in it no such courage or heroism, little of the tragic significance that Miller strained to give it, only the pathos of a man of easy, shabby good nature who had sacrificed what little mind or soul of his own he had to his passion to be popular. At most it was the pathos of Everyman in the sense described by John Mason Brown: "what he would like to be, what he is, what he is not, and yet what he must live and die with." Still, Willy's story was surely worth telling, and the main point here is that Miller treated him with compassion, tried to endow him with dignity in his failure. I see no reason why honesty must oblige contemporaries to eschew the theme of human dignity. Similarly in films, where the vogue appears to be Bonnies and Clydes, easy riders, midnight cowboys, and such, it is still possible to produce *A Shop on Main Street*, a tragedy of ordinary people caught up in the horrors of our age, yet not just shocking, but deeply moving, heartrending in its simple humanity.

Of the much more varied work being done in the novel, one trend is exemplified by *The Erasers* of Alain Robbe-Grillet, exponent of the "new novel": interesting experiments in technique and style, but raising some question about how interesting the characters are, how significant their fate, or whether readers give a damn about what happens to them (as I didn't in this novel). More pertinent for my purposes here is J.D. Salinger, who in the 'fifties and early 'sixties was the most popular novelist among young people, his *The Catcher in the Rye* something like a bible for many. It heralded if not instigated the revolt of the youth by its compassionate treatment of a confused adolescent, alienated by the hypocrisy of his elders, repelled by all he considered "phoney" in the world around him, and devoted to the simple ideal of fidelity or integrity. Closer to pathos than to tragedy just because its narrator was so young, it could nevertheless stir something of terror as well as pity because he was an embryonic Hamlet, conscious that there was something rotten in the state of America. It made, I think, a wholesome guide for teenagers seeking identity and integrity, something to be true to. Since then Salinger has had little more to tell them as they matured, and for some years has been virtually silent. Today, I understand, he is considered old-hat by the latest generation, and I suppose those who grew up in the 'fifties and early 'sixties may not be grateful enough for what they owe him because they have outgrown him. If so, I wonder whether the youth today are finding better guides.

Among other writers who I suppose excite few of them, and may now appear to represent something like the old guard, is Saul Bellow. As one of the more distinguished writers of the day, who is nevertheless widely read, he is another reminder that contemporary literature is much more than a reflection of a wasteland. He sounds the fashionable themes through such characters as Herzog, studies in frustration and futility; yet these "heroes" are not anti-heroes either, for they struggle to maintain their dignity, refuse to blame all their woes on their society or their age, refuse to succumb to the seductions of either self-pity or simple negation. And Bellow himself has warned writers and critics against prevailing conventions, the uncritical acceptance of the tradition that they are necessarily estranged from a mass society that is just a wasteland and a horror. He has appealed to writers to think for themselves, look at the common world with their own eyes, and then to combat whatever evils they see:

> The artist, along with everyone else, must fight for his life, for his freedom. This is not to advise the novelist to rush immediately into the political sphere. But to begin with he must begin to use his intelligence, long unused. If he is to reject politics, he must understand what he is rejecting. He must begin to think, and to think not merely of his own

narrower interests and needs, but of the common world he has for so long failed to see. If he thinks his alienation has much significance, he is wrong. It is nine-tenths cant. If he thinks his rebellion significant, he is wrong again because the world is far more revolutionary in being simply what it is. In their attempts to imitate power, *Realpolitik,* by violence or vehemence, writers simply make themselves foolish. The "romantic criminal" or desperado cannot get within miles of the significant human truth. It is with this truth that the writer must be concerned.

Bellow might have cited the authority of William Faulkner, no prettifier of the contemporary scene, who in his Nobel Prize speech of acceptance spoke of "old universal truths lacking which any story is ephemeral and doomed—love and honor and pity and pride and compassion and sacrifice."

In this view I consider, lastly, Samuel Beckett's tragicomedy *Waiting for Godot.* It is of course a strikingly original play, by a distinguished writer who has unquestionably thought for himself and looked at the world with his own eyes; and it might be called the last word in anti-tragedy. "Nothing to be done," the play begins, with the two anti-heroes in a setting consisting only of a country road and a lone tree. In this unchanged setting they in fact do nothing but wait for Godot, a somebody whose name suggests God but about whom we hear nothing, and who never shows up. When one of them remarks that he had a dream, the other instantly says, "Don't tell me!" Presently the dreamer says, "Don't let's do anything. It's safer." Naturally they go on talking (the play must go on), or as one says, "blathering about nothing in particular," adding "That's been going on now for half a century." The one semblance of action in the play is the entrance of a callous master with a witless slave, suggesting the leaders of our world; the master appropriately goes blind. But this has no effect on the two nobodies who remain on the scene. As the curtain falls on each act the talk goes: "Well, shall we go?" "Yes, let's go." *They do not move.* They won't move, can't move, because they have nowhere to go.

Now, in this non-drama—a Happening in which nothing happens— one can make out elements of human dignity. The two non-protagonists express themselves with some dignity—flashes of humor, even of poignance, and an underlying honesty in recognizing their futility. There is always the dignity of their creator, an artist facing up unflinchingly, without whine or whimper, to his vision of the viewlessness and absurdity of modern life. And he permits his characters one eloquent outburst that expresses their latent humanity:

Let us not waste our time in idle discourse! Let us do something, while we have the chance! It is not every day that we are needed. Not indeed that we personally are needed. Others would meet the case equally well, if not better. To all mankind they were addressed, thóse cries for help still ringing in our ears! But at this place, at this moment of time, all mankind is us, whether we like it or not. Let us make the most of it, before it is too late! Let us represent worthily for once the foul brood to which a cruel fate consigned us! What do you say?

When the other says nothing, the speaker goes on to say something more on their behalf:

It is true that when with folded arms we weigh the pros and cons we are no less a credit to our species. . . . But that is not the question. What are we doing here, *that* is the question. And we are blessed in this, that we happen to know the answer. Yes, in this immense confusion one thing alone is clear. We are waiting for Godot to come—. (After a pause) We have kept our appointment and that's an end to that. We are not saints, but we have kept our appointment. How many people can boast as much?

But then the other answers "Billions" and the dialogue reverts to normal: "You think so?" "I don't know." "You may be right."

So the rest of us have a right to say that except for this outburst this pair do not really represent "mankind," even twentieth-century man. We remain indebted to Beckett for a striking play, perhaps the most memorable expression of a contemporary mood, which may endure because it also expresses "timeless" truths about the human condition, an aspect of futility that has struck men ever since they became self-conscious. "Vanity of vanities, sayeth the Preacher, all is vanity." But then we may add that these timeless truths are half-truths—all is not vanity. Although the visions of the great tragic poets are also partial, they include much more than this, more of the sense of human dignity that we must hang on to if there is to be any hope for us, any belief that we are worth saving. Among the qualities I miss in our tragicomedies is the cry echoing through the pessimistic fiction of Joseph Conrad: A great spectacle! A great tale! Few of us can hope for such greatness in our own life-story; but I still think our writers would not be untrue to our experience if they focused their drama or fiction on characters capable of feeling intensely, deeply, greatly. They might even brood over the simplicity remarked by Bertrand Russell: "When intellectuals question if life be worth living while gardeners feel no doubt of it, it looks as if intellectuals had still something to learn from gardeners, for so long as life seems worth living, worth living it is."

VII

DEMOCRACY IN AMERICA:

SOME RECONSIDERATIONS

1 / Alexis de Tocqueville

ONCE WHEN I assigned a report on de Tocqueville's *Democracy in America* I was startled by a furious attack on him by a very bright, radical student, all for revolution, who denounced him as an utter ignoramus and fool. Then a probable reason for the young man's rage occurred to me—one of the most original, prophetic chapters in a brilliant study. From Plato to Edmund Burke, political philosophers had maintained that democracy led naturally to revolution, civil war, anarchy. De Tocqueville, born during the French Revolution, forecast on the contrary that revolutions would become more rare in America. His reasons included some tributes to its democracy, such as the popular consensus on its principles, the faith of the people in their government, and the absence of the usual poverty-stricken masses, but chiefly they were unflattering. He dwelt in particular on the enervation, complacence, and conformism of a people devoted to business, private property, and material well-being, which would make them fearful of revolutions, or indeed of any bold efforts at social change. "I dread, and I confess it," he concluded, "lest they should at last so entirely give way to a cowardly love of present enjoyment as to lose sight of the interests of their future selves and those of their descendants and prefer to glide along the easy current of life rather than to make, when it is necessary, a strong and sudden effort to a higher purpose." In short, he foresaw precisely what the young radical was up against, the reasons why his hopes of a popular revolution were vain. In this respect de Tocqueville was a far better prophet than Karl Marx. And he might sober all of us, at a time of crisis when the American people appear to be in no mood for a strong effort to any high purpose.

Democracy in America is one political classic that I would recommend without reservation to all students, conservative, liberal, or radical. The first philosophical study of modern democracy, published in two volumes in 1835 and 1840, it not only remains basically as relevant today as in its own day but has become more so in the last generation, for de Tocqueville was looking to the future and we can now appreciate his insights more than his contemporaries could. John Stuart Mill hailed it as "the beginning of a new era in the scientific study of politics," but it was scientific only in de Tocqueville's efforts at an impartial, empirical analysis; he employed none of the methods that have become fashionable since the study of government was rechristened "political science." And so much the better, since as a positivistic "science" it has ceased to be philosophical and in America has produced no classics. In the same rough but important sense de Tocqueville may be regarded as a pioneer in social science, for he studied not only American government but American society and culture as a whole, without which its politics cannot be fully understood—another elementary truth that in practice has been forgotten by most political scientists. His study of American democracy is both more comprehensive and more penetrating than any contemporary studies I know of.

His main thesis, highly original in its day, has become a commonplace. He seized on the principle of equality as the essential principle of democracy; he perceived that so far from being virtually synonymous with liberty it was in important respects a menace to it; he worried over the tyranny of the majority, in both political and social life; and as a passionate lover of liberty, first and last, he dreaded the possibility that democracy might end as a new kind of despotism. But this points immediately to one of his most admirable qualities, a fair-mindedness rare in European observers at the time. An aristocrat by temperament and taste as well as by rank, he naturally found much in raw, boastful, uncouth America not to his liking. Nevertheless he made earnest efforts to be fair to it for a particular reason of historical importance. America was the first major experiment in democracy, which he foresaw was the wave of the future in Europe too; like it or not, there was no going back to the aristocratic society that had been the rule in Europe since its beginnings; and it was therefore all-important to understand this new kind of society so as to make the best of it. While he saw much to dread in its natural tendencies, he saw much good in America too, and insisted that dread was no reason for despair. He was an apparent determinist in that he believed that the spread of democracy was irresistible, inevitable; yet he flatly rejected the doctrine of historical determinism that Marx would build on, insisting that what men made of democracy was up to them, and that so long as they preserved their freedom they could hope to make the best of it.

This seeming inconsistency points to another reason for the abiding relevance of de Tocqueville, but one that has led to common simplifications of his views. He has been the darling of many conservatives, past and present, who can find much in his criticism of democracy to support their views. Because of his passion for liberty and his willingness to accept fundamental change, I should call him rather a liberal of the stamp of John Stuart Mill, who greatly admired his work. But chiefly I would stress his ambivalent attitudes. While they might involve some inconsistency, at best they sprang from a recognition of actual complexity and ambiguity that appears in all his major criticisms of America. Thus he by no means simply attacked the principle of equality, any more than he attempted to explain everything by it. As a Christian he recognized that it was after all a Christian principle, and a matter of justice. More to the immediate point, he praised it because it promoted self-respect and an independent spirit, naturally gave men "a taste for free institutions," and so provided the means for combatting its menace to freedom. In this view the conclusion of his book was quite consistent: "The nations of our time cannot prevent the conditions of men from becoming equal, but it depends upon themselves whether the principle of equality is to lead them to servitude or freedom, to knowledge or barbarism, to prosperity or wretchedness."

Now, this sentence should give us pause for a different reason. The conditions of men today are of course still far from equal, in either the Western democracies or the Communist countries. While the principle of equality has spread as de Tocqueville predicted, in such conditions as universal suffrage, there remains pronounced social and economic inequality everywhere, and no apparent danger at all of the "extreme equality" he feared. We must question too whether Americans ever had such a passion for equality as he attributed to them—a passion he described as "ardent, insatiable, incessant, invincible." The sentiment of equality has indeed been stronger in America than in most European countries, with their venerable aristocratic tradition, as indicated plainly in our informal manners and customs ("Call me Joe"); but it has been countered by other natural tendencies. He himself recognized that Americans never extended it to economic status, because of their devotion to business and the acquisition of property, and today one can hardly speak of an overriding passion for equality in a land of status-seekers, celebrity-worshippers, devotees of expertise, and all kinds of climbers. Just because his study is so rich in insights, we need to be clearly aware of his basic limitations.

In general, de Tocqueville had a thesis—an explicit thesis that he stated most insistently, that naturally influenced his observations, and that might dictate his findings in advance. He generalized too freely, in the common manner of French intellectuals devoted to lucidity and logic, and so tended to overlook the obvious diversities in America, regional, social, and cultural, including the different meanings of "democracy." While he had advantages as a foreigner, who could see things that Americans overlooked because they took them for granted, he as naturally lacked the advantage of an intimate, inside understanding—a handicap that was more marked because he wrote with an eye on Europe and its different problems, immediate and potential. Despite the chorus of praise that greeted his book in both Europe and America, critics noted that he mentioned no names at all—this in the age of Andrew Jackson—and that although he was an acute observer, he offered surprisingly little concrete evidence to back up his often sweeping generalizations.

More specifically, a tendency to overstate his thesis led him to make some observations that were simply not true. "The sovereignty of the majority is absolute in America," he declared. In fact it never was, and never would be. On the one hand, a Bill of Rights explicitly limited majority rule, specifying constitutional rights that were beyond its powers to deny. De Tocqueville offered little evidence of the tyranny of the majority in political life. On the other hand, he slighted the power of minorities—the kind of tyranny that had prevailed throughout most of history, and that to a modified, disguised extent would remain an obvious problem in America to this day. Even in the age of Jackson, which assured the nominal political equality of the common people, the wealthy class, or aristocrats of property interests, plainly had disproportionate power, which was due to be greatly increased with the rise of a ruling business class. De Tocqueville's neglect of the actual inequalities in America perhaps explains why he paid little attention to corruption, the venality of democratic politicians who then as always were serving minority interests.

Most obviously, however, many of his observations have been antiquated by profound changes that he could hardly anticipate—the transformation of a relatively simple, primarily agricultural, rural society into an immense industrial, urban society, the greatest power on earth. While this gives his study some added value as perspective, a means to a more vivid realization of how much that seems natural to us was unknown or alien to him, we have to discount and supplement him all along the line, with constant reference to bigness. One example is big business, the great corporations that produce most of the goods once produced by small business. This led to glaring economic inequality and complicated the genius he noted in Americans for forming private associations; in business these associations have great political power and contribute to the many pressure groups that make it absurd to speak of the absolute sovereignty of the majority. Similarly with the related growth of big government. He warned prophetically against the dangers of centralized administration, which would enervate democracy by diminishing the resources of local spirit, but he did not foresee the immense growth of bureaucracy, or its necessity in our kind of society. Again the growth of big cities invalidated much of his praise of local self-government, in which he thought of towns; its virtues would not be conspicuous in municipal government in America, which became notorious as the worst in the world. And so with all the big organizations, now including multiversities, that serve the needs of a technological society, but raise the invariable problems of bureaucracy, too often obscure the needs of *people.*

Yet these radical changes, through and through the society, make more astonishing how much of de Tocqueville's comment on American democracy is still valid, or has even grown more relevant.[1] One example was a prophetic Marx-like chapter on "How an Aristocracy May Be Created by Manufactures." This aristocracy would be unlike all others before it, he predicted, and on the whole "one of the harshest

---

1. Least rewarding is the first volume of *Democracy in America,* in which he concentrates on government; here he gives much information designed for European readers, with comment on institutions that was not always valid in his own day and has grown less so since. For students and general readers much richer is the second volume, a comprehensive study of American society and culture in which he speculates much more on future possibilities; it is on this volume that I am drawing in what follows. Since I am not attempting here to review all the many subjects he considered, I might add that in his prediction that revolutions would become more rare he made a significant exception, which would account for the Civil War. If ever there were a great revolution in America, he said, it would be because of not equality but inequality—the condition of the black people.

that ever existed"—not because manufacturers were more brutal than
the noblemen of the past, but because they merely bought human labor,
there was no "real association" between workman and master, the
workman was "debased" by his work, and the master was bound by
neither law nor custom to come to his relief. Hence Southerners would
later argue that at least they took care of their slaves when these were
sick, crippled, or old, whereas in the North factory workers were simply
discarded like old shoes. De Tocqueville concluded that friends of
democracy should keep their eyes anxiously fixed on the manufacturing aristocracy, "for if ever a permanent inequality of conditions and
aristocracy again penetrate into the world, it may be predicted that this
is the gate by which they will enter." So, of course, it turned out. But
with a reservation: after a century of bitter industrial strife workers
won a measure of security and relief, and manufacturers began cultivating "human relations." And herein is a particular reason for reading de
Tocqueville today. That so many of his observations are still incisive
despite the radical transformation of the country indicates that he got
down to the heart of American democracy, something like the essence
of this new kind of society; but when he needs to be qualified, we
may ask why and then get more insight into the changes that have
occurred. Among other things, the improved condition of workers
indicates that democratic ideals have been a real force, not the bourgeois
sham that Karl Marx saw in them.

De Tocqueville's comments on American culture as a whole reveal
immediately his fair-mindedness. When he wrote, before the dawn of
the American Renaissance, it was still a pretty raw, meager culture,
which Britishers typically sneered at. ("Who ever reads an American
book?") He needed no exceptional powers of insight to recognize
that because of the practical spirit of Americans and their absorption
in business they were not disposed to cultivate pure science, literature,
and the fine arts. But he recognized too that democracy provided a
huge potential audience for these higher interests, in that it provided
both opportunity and incentive for people to improve their minds and
therewith their fortunes; so he expected that Americans would cultivate
them after their own fashion, with "their peculiar qualifications and
deficiencies." Although he naturally could not foresee the big industries
that would manufacture mass culture, the desire for self-improvement
would indeed animate millions of Americans, today especially the
earnest middle-brows—types that aristocratic intellectuals may be too
supercilious about. And in particular he did foresee some distinctive
qualities of American culture.

Thus he noted that Americans were naturally addicted to practical rather than theoretical science—as in fact they would be until this generation. Every student has heard of Thomas Edison, for example, but how many have ever heard of Josiah Willard Gibbs? Over the years I have known no more than a half a dozen students who had some idea that he was an important theoretical physicist—the only one America produced in the last century—and that his importance was first recognized in Europe, which produced all the great pioneers in science. And even today, when Americans have at last discovered that basic research may be practical too (since it gave us our atomic bomb), they might ponder de Tocqueville's comments. In noting that the democratic principle would enormously increase the number of men cultivating science, he remarked that to their minds "every new method that leads by a shorter road to wealth, every machine that spares labor, every instrument that diminishes the cost of production, every discovery that facilitates pleasures or augments them seems to be the grandest effort of the human intellect"—briefly, the basic mentality that led President Nixon to hail the week of the moon-landing as the greatest week in history since the Creation. Most pertinent is de Tocqueville's conclusion: "If those who are called upon to guide the nations of our time clearly discerned from afar off these new tendencies, which will soon be irresistible, they would understand that, possessing education and freedom, men living in democratic ages cannot fail to improve the industrial part of science, and that henceforth all the efforts of the constituted authorities ought to be directed to support the highest branches of learning and to foster the noble passion for science itself." The new tendencies did indeed prove irresistible; so it is another misfortune that the nation's leaders—including most of its educators—have yet to heed his counsel.

In the cultivation of the arts, especially the handicrafts, de Tocqueville noted a similar tendency in the habitual preference for the useful to the beautiful. This naturally led to emphasis on quick and cheap production, quantity rather than quality, and many shoddy wares. With the shoddiness came much showiness, "the hypocrisy of luxury," in a democracy where the wants of a multitude were beyond their means. Needless to say, mass production has magnified these tendencies, but de Tocqueville's chapter now makes depressing reading for a further reason. The wares he was describing have become antiques, prized for their honest craftsmanship; so we may become more aware of how the fine old craftsmanship tradition is disappearing, how many fewer honest craftsmen there now are, especially among garage mechanics and repairmen—the most prominent of the dwindling survivors of an age-old tradition whose skills are still needed. But then we may also appreciate more some compensations, such as the new art of industrial design, the wedding of utility and beauty in clean lines or functional form, the growing sophistication in the public taste, and in suburbia a self-conscious, if somewhat ostentatious, avoidance of showiness. Given the immense growth in culture since de Tocqueville wrote, with its sprawling confusion and contradiction, all the dominant tendencies he spotted would call out various reactions. And he himself added that the works of culture are not merely the products of "society," but the works of individuals.

Thus with literature, for which in his day Americans still largely depended on England.[2] He predicted that Americans would in time create their own literature, and that it would be characteristically democratic; writers would be relatively indifferent to form, style, propriety, decorum, elegance—the qualities naturally prized by aristocratic societies (especially the *ancien régime* in France). This would in fact be a conspicuous tendency in American writers down to our day. But beginning with Edgar Allan Poe there would also be an opposed tradition of fine or pure art, coming down through Henry James, who in our day would be extravagantly admired. Most suggestive, however, are de Tocqueville's remarks about the sources of poetry in a nation that as yet had no poets. "Nothing conceivable is so petty, so insipid, so crowded with paltry interests—in one word, so anti-poetic—as the life of a man in the United States," he wrote, an observation that is even truer today when paltry interests have been multiplied. "In democratic countries," moreover, "each citizen is habitually engaged in the contemplation of a very puny object: namely, himself." If he ever raised his eyes, however, he beheld the magnificent images of Democracy—the conquest of a continent, the grandeur of America, the People, Mankind. Hence de Tocqueville did not fear that the poetry of America would be insipid, but thought rather that it would be "forever losing itself in the clouds." In short, he pictured to the life the Walt Whitman to come, and after him the Carl Sandburg of *The People, Yes.* Today he may therefore stir a sobering reflection: no poet of note is celebrating American democracy. Allen

2. Here one may be depressed by his remark that there was hardly a pioneer's cabin that did not contain a few volumes of Shakespeare. Some years ago a survey revealed that in about a quarter of American homes there were no books at all. Today I suppose many of these may have at least a few paperbacks, besides comic books, but I doubt that most American homes have volumes of Shakespeare.

Ginsburg, the most popular poet among the youth, characteristically used the popular idiom in his poem "America" to express a more common sentiment about his native land: "Go fuck yourself with your atom bomb."

On another branch of culture de Tocqueville passed a more sweeping judgment: "I think that in no country in the civilized world is less attention paid to philosophy than in the United States." While observing that it had "no philosophical school" of its own, he did not anticipate either that it would develop one, as it finally did under William James and John Dewey—a typically pragmatic, democratic philosophy. Even so, much of what he had to say still holds. Although philosophy is clearly a fundamental subject, it is not taught in the schools, as it commonly is in the secondary schools of Europe, and the great majority of college students never take a course in it either. What is taught in the schools is a consensus on broad generalities, especially popular in America because they spare any effort at hard thought. As de Tocqueville observed of the citizen in democracy, "His ideas are all either extremely minute and clear or extremely general and vague; what lies between is a void." Otherwise he noted the ambiguous consequences of the principle of equality. On the one hand, it led men to form their own opinions, distrust or resent intellectual authority, and take to "untried thoughts"; on the other hand, it led them to pick up ready-made opinions and accept the authority of the multitude like themselves, "prohibiting them from thinking at all." He dwelt chiefly on the latter tendency to unthinking conformity, the tyranny of public opinion. In his first volume he had said that he knew of no other country "where there was so little independence of mind and real freedom of discussion." Today, when there is so much talk about the pressures to conformity, he might remind us that they are due not merely to a mass society, the growth of suburbia, and other fashionable themes for scorn or alarm, but to the paradox of democracy itself, which politically proclaims the ideal of freedom and socially breeds attitudes that threaten it.

More controversial is de Tocqueville's argument for the necessity of dogmatic religion, apart from his own belief in the truth of Christianity. He maintained that for various reasons democracy had more need of it than any other kind of society. It gave men fixed ideas about God and man, with a principle of authority they were too inclined to distrust; it induced a respect for forms, the value of which they as naturally tended to ignore; it combatted the selfish kind of individualism bred by the principle of equality, the idea of every man for himself;

and above all it could temper the passion for material well-being, which seemed to him "the prominent and indelible feature of democratic times." Today we may add that it might also help to dispel the common feelings of aimlessness and hollowness from which even devotees of the American way of life may suffer. Those of us who have learned from history, and from our Fundamentalists, to distrust *dogmatic* religion might still agree that for most people some kind of religious belief is necessary as a steadying influence, and that ideally it can still be a vital inspiration. Conservatives who welcome de Tocqueville's stress on the necessity of religion might consider his statement that "a good Christian was a liberal who was unaware of his liberal commitment."

At any rate, what he has to say on the subject is still to the point. Unlike many conservatives today, he did not press the argument that American democracy was founded squarely on Christianity, if only because he was more aware that historically this had supported every kind of government, including despotism. (I do not recall whether he ever noted a significant omission in the American Constitution: its authors never mention God.) In particular he kept his eye on the realities of popular religion in America, which fell far short of achieving his ideal objectives. "Everybody there adopts great numbers of theories, on philosophy, morals, and politics, without inquiry, upon public trust; and if we examine it very closely, it will be perceived that religion holds sway there much less as a doctrine of revelation than as a commonly received opinion." As such, it still makes most Americans hostile to "free-thinkers," who rarely get on the air waves; but otherwise, as de Tocqueville observed, "no one undertakes either to attack or to defend" Christianity. And he also observed that the American clergy were not spiritual educators or leaders. They too went along with public opinion, which therefore supported and protected them— just as churchmen remain popular today because most of them demand no real sacrifice of the American way of life. The many men who express alarm over the decay of religion and therefore morality in America might learn from de Tocqueville that our supposedly God-fearing ancestors, in an age when according to the books Christianity was a more vital influence, were in this respect little different from Americans today.

By his report they were certainly as materialistic. On the historical record their passion for material well-being was by no means so "natural" as Americans consider it, but it was a natural consequence of the principle of equality, in a land where common people enjoyed more opportunity than they did in Europe; and I would stress more than de Tocqueville did the ideal aspect of such opportunity, the qualities that led Santayana to describe Americans as "idealists working on matter." Still, most of them don't need to be told this. Much more pertinent are the consequences he dwelt on: the restlessness and discontent amid what then passed for abundance, because of which vastly increased abundance would never make Americans a joyous people; the at once excited and monotonous aspect of a society in which "men and things are always changing" but "all these changes are alike," leading to increasing uniformity; a remarkable number of ambitious men, but very little lofty ambition; an apparent pride that masked a lack of genuine self-respect, since the same man who cannot endure inequality "has so contemptible an opinion of himself that he thinks he is born only to indulge in vulgar pleasures"; and always the slavery to this passion, which de Tocqueville described as "the mother of tyranny." It undermined another of his arguments for religion. "Most religions are only general, simple, and practical means of teaching men the doctrine of the immortality of the soul," which in his view was "the greatest benefit which a democratic people derives from its belief." In his day a literal belief in immortality was presumably more common than it is today (even though on polls most Americans say they still hold to it, and have at least some vague notions about a hereafter), but already it was evidently not a vital influence on a people so intent on acquiring material goods in this life. I suppose its chief benefit was its age-old one, as a consolation to the many poor.

In related democratic tendencies de Tocqueville stressed more the ambiguous effects. Thus with the new word "individualism," which made one of its earliest appearances in his work and signified an attitude he thought was of democratic origin. He deplored it as something more insidious, once more, than the simple selfishness to which men have always been prone: a mature, calm policy, springing "from erroneous judgment more than from depraved feelings" or "blind instinct," which tended to separate men from their fellows, weaken the ties that held traditional societies together. Today we can see more clearly the havoc it wrought in human relations with the growth of the "manufacturing aristocracy," blessed by the new gospel of free private enterprise. But he also recognized that Americans combatted the effects of individualism because of other consequences of democracy, especially free institutions. These induced more public spirit than was common in Europe; he was struck by how often Americans made "great and real sacrifices to the public welfare." Unlike aristocrats in Europe, the wealthier Americans took pains "not to stand aloof from the people." And ordinary Americans who felt like equals were disposed to cooperate with one another, as they did among other ways by their peculiarly insistent habit of forming private associations. Now that individualism has lost much of its old meaning in a massive industrial society, in which ordinary Americans are likely to feel equal chiefly in impotence, not at all "apt to imagine that their whole destiny is in their own hands," as de Tocqueville saw them, the whole picture is much more confused; but because of all the fashionable stereotypes about it we may forget that it is complicated still more by the kind of conflicting tendencies he noted. Impersonal as all its bureaucracies seem, such a society requires an extraordinary degree of cooperative effort, it has created thousands of new occupations, people have to carry on relations with many different kinds of other people at work and in their local communities, and they may combat their feelings of impotence by managing to maintain decent, friendly relations.

In another display of rare fair-mindedness, de Tocqueville pointed out how Americans combatted individualism by "the principle of self-interest rightly understood." They habitually talked of the utility of virtue, not of its beauty or of virtue as its own reward. As an aristocrat, he was keenly aware of the ignoble aspect of such an ethic, indicated by proverbial sayings like "Honesty is the best policy," i.e., it *pays* to be good. He remarked that Americans stressed even the utility of religion—a vulgar habit that has lately become more conspicuous as we constantly hear that it pays to believe, it makes you feel better. Yet he claimed no more virtue for aristocratic ages, in which the talk was always of its beauties. In Europe, where the principle of interest was less openly avowed, it was much grosser, and selfishness as much less enlightened. Americans not only maintained that virtue is useful but "prove it every day." He concluded philosophically:

> The principle of self-interest rightly understood is not a lofty one, but it is clear and sure. It does not aim at mighty objects, but attains without exertion all those at which it aims. As it lies within the reach of all capacities, everyone can without difficulty learn and retain it. By its admirable conformity to human weaknesses it easily obtains great dominion. . . .
>
> If the principle of self-interest rightly understood were to sway the whole moral world, extraordinary virtues would doubtless be more rare; but I think that gross depravity would then also be less common. The principle . . . perhaps prevents men from rising far above the level of

1 • *Alexis de Tocqueville*

mankind, but a great number of other men, who were falling far below it, are caught and restrained by it. Observe some few individuals, they are lowered by it; survey mankind, they are raised.

Today we may wonder: Do Americans really believe that virtue is useful? Conventionally they still talk as if they do, but in so commercialized a society, in which so much dishonesty is respectable, they often say too that it pays to be smart, or in practice to cheat. Their saying "Business is business" does not imply that honesty is the best policy. Then one may add hopefully that they may be deceiving themselves, as de Tocqueville thought. "They are more anxious to do honor to their philosophy than to themselves," for like people everywhere they sometimes "give way to those disinterested and spontaneous impulses that are natural to man." In any case, the main point is that if people are going to operate on the principle of self-interest rightly understood, it is all-important that they have an enlightened idea of their interest—not merely a smart one. In his account of the slavish materialism and conformism of Americans, their lack of self-respect, de Tocqueville was saying essentially that they did not rightly understand their personal interest. Hence he stressed the particular need of education, which was his own primary purpose in his study of American democracy:

> The first of the duties that are at this time imposed upon those who direct our affairs is to educate democracy; to reawaken, if possible, its religious beliefs; to purify its morals; to mold its actions; to substitute a knowledge of statecraft for its inexperience, and an awareness of its true interest for its blind instincts; to adapt its government to time and place, and to modify it according to man and to conditions.

This points to the remarkable concluding chapters of his study, in which he dwells on his fears of the future, acute insights into possibilities that by now have to a considerable extent been realized. In government he feared especially the drift toward increasingly centralized administration, or concentration of power, which was already under way in Europe. In America he anticipated it for much the same reasons he predicted that revolutions would become rare: engrossed in their private interests and pleasures, trustful of a government they considered *theirs,* people would be pleased to turn over to it the irksome responsibilities of public life. Here a more obvious reason for the growth of big government was the industrial transformation of the country, but this too he anticipated because at the time industry in Europe was more advanced; it required more services by the govern-

ment, such as roads, canals, and harbors, and in his belief the "manufacturing classes" also required more regulation and superintendence
than other classes.[3] For whatever reason, the effects would be the
same: increasing dependence on the government, the enervation of
the public, the weakening of individual independence, and increasing
uniformity, which central government is naturally fond of. Democratic
nations were prepared to resist tendencies to anarchy that might result
from an independent spirit, but were still unaware of the tendencies
that conduct men "by a longer, more secret, but more certain road to
servitude." And America in particular now illustrates a danger that
was much less apparent in the age of Andrew Jackson:

> It would seem as if the rulers of our time sought only to use men in
> order to make things great; I wish that they would try a little more to
> make great men; that they would set less value on the work and more
> upon the workman; that they would never forget that a nation cannot
> long remain strong when every man belonging to it is individually
> weak. . . .

Above all, de Tocqueville was haunted by the spectre of despotism,
the menace of a new kind of oppression that had never existed before.
For one thing, democracy and industrialism were giving rulers a
power, over the minds of men too, such as no absolute monarch of
the past ever did or could exercise—a power that would be demonstrated in our century by the dictators of totalitarian countries. The
public in a democracy was no less novel:

> The first thing that strikes the observation is an innumerable multi-
> tude of men, all equal and alike, incessantly endeavoring to procure the
> petty and paltry pleasures with which they glut their lives. Each of them,
> living apart, is as a stranger to the fate of all the rest; his children and
> his private friends constitute to him the whole of mankind. As for the
> rest of his fellow citizens, he is close to them, but does not see them; he
> touches them, but he does not feel them; he exists only in himself and

3. In a footnote he pointed to a basic inconsistency that would become most
apparent in American businessmen, as they demanded and got at once more
economic freedom and more government assistance than Europeans: "Such
persons will admit, as a general principle, that the public authority ought not to
interfere in private concerns; but, by an exception to that rule, eace of them craves
its assistance in the particular concern on which he is engaged and seeks to draw
upon the influence of the government for his own benefit, although he would
restrict it on all other occasions." For the rest of the century businessmen would
be lavishly supported by tariffs, subsidies, franchises, etc., but would resist any
government interference with their treatment of their workers or anything like
comparable assistance to them.

for himself alone; and if his kindred still remain to him, he may be said at any rate to have lost his country.

Given their trust in their government, the old words "despotism" and "tyranny" would no longer apply to the new menace; de Tocqueville confessed that he could think of no precise name for it. But what he described was in effect a benevolent despotism, an absolute power that would be "regular, provident, and mild." Its rule might be embodied by men like good old Ike, the Great White Father of his day; only in exercising the authority of a kindly parent its object would not be to prepare men for manhood, but "to keep them in perpetual childhood" by taking care of all their wants. Now that modern technology is providing for them far more abundantly than de Tocqueville dreamed, his question becomes more pertinent: "What remains, but to spare them all the care of thinking and all the trouble of living?" In short, he was the first important thinker to anticipate something like Aldous Huxley's Brave New World.

So it is now time to pause again and reconsider his prophecies. When totalitarianism appeared in our century, it did not appear in the established democracies, amid a multitude of men "all equal and alike." It took hold rather in Russia, Italy, and Germany, countries lacking a strong democratic tradition, and though it soon won much mass support, it was installed by tyrannical minorities. In America de Tocqueville overlooked the old tradition that the best government was the least government, and that any increase in its powers was a menace to the people's freedom. While Americans necessarily grew more dependent on it in an industrial society, in which the great majority were no longer self-employed or self-sufficient, they continued to be suspicious of it, often resentful or fearful of its increasing powers, specifically of all those bureaucrats in Washington. As usual, the tendencies he feared are complicated by different tendencies. And today by other reasons for fear that he could not anticipate, such as the power of the Pentagon. If for the long run Brave New World remains a real possibility, immediately there is much more reason to worry over the trend to a police state, the threats to constitutional rights in crime bills authorized by the current Administration.

Yet as an ardent lover of freedom de Tocqueville anticipated such dangers too, which might be heightened by the fears of a majority. "No private rights are so unimportant that they can be surrendered with impunity to the caprices of a government," especially because "the very notion of this kind of right constantly tends among us to be impaired and lost"; so to violate them is not merely to do an injustice to the individual, but "deeply to corrupt the manners of the nation." He felt more strongly about all such matters because of his conviction that freedom alone could arrest the democratic tendencies to oppression and servitude. Hence he recognized too the bulwarks of freedom, such as a free press and the judicial power to protect private interests; the latter he considered "peculiarly adapted" to our needs "at a time when the eye and finger of government are constantly intruding into the minutest details of human actions"—a statement that was not strictly true in the age of Jackson, but has grown all too true. And because of his belief in the power of freedom, his prophecies were never predictions of inevitable outcomes, with any of the Marxist pretense to "scientific" certainty. He merely pointed out dangers that he considered formidable but not insurmountable.

In the concluding pages of *Democracy in America* de Tocqueville is at his most admirable. He recognizes that the revolution taking place was still encumbered by ancient customs and institutions, how much of which would remain "none can say." He pays tribute again to the principle of equality whose consequences he has been worrying over all along: "its justice constitutes its greatness and its beauty," the more so because Christians may naturally believe that most pleasing to their Creator is "not the singular prosperity of the few, but the greater well-being of all." On humane grounds he pays tribute as well to the real goods that have come with democracy—tribute that today may even seem extravagant. ("If there are few instances of exalted heroism or of virtues of the highest, brightest, and purest temper, men's habits are regular, violence is rare, and cruelty almost unknown.") As one who had been accustomed to observe only the great men and great achievements of the aristocratic past, not the multitudes of poor men, he remarks that no man can affirm absolutely that the new state of society is better than the old, but he warns against the tendency to judge it simply by the standards of the old—a caution that still needs to be heeded by the many critics today who tend to idealize or sentimentalize the past. Our object should be "not to retain the peculiar advantages which the inequality of conditions bestows upon mankind, but to secure the new benefits which equality may supply." Having deliberately chosen to emphasize the "mighty dangers" that the friends of democracy seemed unaware of, he emphatically repeats that the dangers can be avoided, the evils at least alleviated. While granting that mankind can never be entirely free, nor nations completely their own masters, he insists that within these reasonable limits the future will be what we make it. Young people today can find more stirring statements of the basic challenge confronting them, but I doubt that they can find a fairer one.

2 / The Education of Henry Adams

EVEN THOUGH IT IS FIRMLY ESTABLISHED by now as one of the minor "classics" of American literature, *The Education of Henry Adams* is perhaps the most immediately relevant of them. To be sure, Adams came out of early America, which he remarked was closer to the year 1 than to 1900, and he completed his book before World War I, the great divide in modern history, which marked the end of an era that to the youth today may seem almost as remote as the year 1. Yet the *Education* is a first-hand survey, by a first-rate mind, of the revolutionary era that he lived through, and that he foresaw was producing the kind of world the youth would have to live in. In trying to make sense of this history he dwelt on basic themes, such as power, that have grown more pertinent in the history we are making. Through him students may get perspectives on the essential questions who they are, where they are, and how we all got this way. And when told that so grim, often difficult a book as this became a best-seller when it was published in 1918, they may get some idea of what a shock World War I was to thoughtful Westerners, or how prophetic was the remark of Sir Edward Grey on its eve: "The lamps are going out all over Europe; we shall not see them lit again in our lifetime." Unlike Eleanor Roosevelt, of whom it was said that she preferred to light a candle instead of cursing the darkness, Adams was given to cursing it; but as a historian, here directly concerned with education, he at least threw light on the darkness. "From cradle to grave," he wrote, "this problem of running order through chaos, direction through space, discipline through freedom, unity through multiplicity, has always been, and must always be, the task of education, as it is the moral of religion, philosophy, science, art, politics, and economy." To this task, which today is more difficult and more urgent than ever, Henry Adams devoted a lifetime.

Even so I should say at once that over the years I taught the *Education* few students were excited by it. Many found it often stimulating, but on the whole pretty heavy going; some were chiefly depressed by it, for understandable reasons. It is a cold book, often lit by flashes of wit and irony, but rarely warmed by genial humor. The personality of the author that comes through is unattractive. Adams was a snob, very fond of high society, with some disposition to anti-Semitism. Never having got his hands dirty, he would never stoop or let his mind get dirtied either in the world of affairs where he would have liked to exercise power; so he contented himself by insisting that power was poison, a friend in power was a friend lost. And despite his obsession with the theme of failure, including his personal failure, he was not really modest, humble, or as candid as he appears in such confessions as that he "had risked nothing and never played for high stakes." As intellectual autobiography, the *Education* is a work of art, carefully composed, brilliantly composed, but always with an eye to effects more than to the exact truth of his experience. The effects were designed immediately for his circle of friends, among whom he distributed privately printed copies in 1906, but not without regard to a public he affected indifference to. He wrote an "Editor's Preface" that was dutifully appended and signed by his friend Henry Cabot Lodge when the book was officially published after his death. Briefly, he was posing for posterity.

Such disagreeable personal qualities bring up the reasons why it is necessary to discount his record of the history he lived through. Alfred Kazin has said that Adams was one of "the ruling myth-makers of American history," whose *Education* "has become the great fable of the period." I doubt that this fable has in fact been widely accepted, at least in our time, and certainly not in the history taught in our schools or recorded in most college texts either; but in any case it is to some extent untrustworthy because of his bitterness and crankiness. Thus with his insistence on the theme of failure. By ordinary standards his career was of course a brilliant one: he was accepted in the highest circles as a man of the world, author of many books, one of the most eminent historians of his day. The immediate trouble was that he was an Adams, scion of a remarkable family, whose great-grandfather John Adams had signed the Declaration of Independence, whose grandfather John Quincy Adams had been another President of the United States, and whose father Charles Francis Adams had served as Ambassador to Great Britain during the critical period of the Civil War; whereas after the war Henry found that the new America heralded by the corrupt Grant administration, under the rule of a Republican Party that produced few statesmen as it faithfully served the interests of business, had no use for him in public life, which he had thought was his natural habitat. And for similar reasons he insisted too much on the failure of America. The Adamses had been aristocrats in public life, who took for granted that they should always be leaders, never servants of public opinion; Henry was even more aristocratic in his contempt for the masses and his remoteness from the common life; and he could not appreciate the epical quality in the conquest of a continent, the ideal quality in the new opportunities for common men, for whom the "progress" he despised or despaired of was quite real.

Hence he suffers by comparison with de Tocqueville, a fellow-aristocrat who was as critical of the naive popular faith in progress.[4] The Frenchman not only was much more fair-minded than Henry Adams managed to be in his *Education* (though in his histories he did much better), but in particular offered a more salutary, responsible kind of education. While he looked to the future with as much dread as Adams, or indeed more because he felt more deeply about it, he was as much more earnest in his efforts to enlighten the public, so that the dangers might be averted. Adams, more aloof, was not actually so resigned as he appears in some of his ironical or cynical comments, but he made no such effort to arouse his readers. His object, he wrote in his Preface, was "to fit young men, in universities, or elsewhere, to be men of the world, equipped for any emergency"—presumably equipped to understand what we now call crises, but not clearly to do anything about them. The chief reason, I suppose, why he leaves so many students cold is that he offers them little or no hope, no faith in the power of freedom and high resolve.

Still, in the last year or so I have known more students who were fascinated by the *Education,* finding it a revelation; and though I would not make it required reading, I would recommend it to the

4. It is pleasant to recall de Tocqueville's ironic comment on the city of Washington: "The Americans have traced out the circuit of an immense city on the site which they intend to make their capital, but which up to the present time is hardly more densely peopled than Pontoise, though, according to them, it will one day contain a million inhabitants. They have already rooted up trees for ten miles around lest they should interfere with the future citizens of this imaginary metropolis. They have erected a magnificent palace for Congress in the center of the city and have given it the pompous name of the Capitol." Today we may say God bless 'em—they were right about their imaginary metropolis, the historical joke was on de Tocqueville. And we may be more grateful for their foresight because Washington is one of the very few cities in America whose growth was planned, making possible a spaciousness it still retains.

thoughtful. With the advantage of wide acquaintance among the famous men of his time, both at home and abroad, Adams had an exceptionally keen mind, rare powers of acute and original observation. He had as well the virtues of his defects, a cool detachment and ironic sense. Always he brought his experience as a trained historian to his task of trying to understand the history modern man was making, and where it was taking us. His dogged efforts to understand have a heroic aspect when, as an elderly gentleman, he sits down before the dynamo, studies this symbol of his age, and remarks, "Only the young have time to linger in the rear." Add his literary gifts, and the young may find hundreds of memorable observations. Even his pessimism may be salutary, again on the grounds that if they wish to remain hopeful they had better take a hard look at the worst. Or at that only a foreshadowing of the worst. His concluding chapter begins with his sailing up New York bay in 1904, finding the approach to the city more striking than ever, "unlike anything man had ever seen—and like nothing he had ever much cared to see." Then he noted the anger and alarm of the citizens over the failure to bring under control the "new forces" of the day:

> Prosperity never before imagined, power never yet wielded by man, speed never reached by anything but a meteor, had made the world irritable, nervous, querulous, unreasonable and afraid. . . . Every municipal election shrieked chaos. . . . The two-thousand-years failure of Christianity roared upward from Broadway, and no Constantine the Great was in sight.

Today all this rings still truer; so let us imagine what Henry Adams would now make of congested, polluted, bankrupt New York, especially because he had permitted himself a faint note of hope at the end of the *Education*. Some day, he remarked, say 1938, his centenary, his spirit might be allowed to return, and might "find a world that sensitive and timid natures could regard without a shudder."

Of more immediate interest to students, however, is the formal education of Henry Adams. A graduate of the class of 1858 of Harvard College, he found it a "mild and liberal school" that offered chiefly social rather than intellectual advantages, and turned out men who were "self-possessed" but possessed of little solid education. That he never heard mentioned the names of Karl Marx and Auguste Comte, the most influential thinkers of the day, was but one illustration of his complaint that Harvard prepared him for life in the eighteenth century. Today students might accordingly think somewhat better of their universities, which at least offer an education more suited to the conditions of life in our own century. But they might ask themselves to what extent it is achieving the basic objectives stated by Adams, such as "running order through chaos," training the mind to respond with "vigor and economy," and equipping it to meet any emergency. Specifically, they might consider another of his basic complaints, that Harvard failed to give him the tools he needed for further self-education—foreign languages and the universal language of mathematics. The great majority of college graduates still lack a mastery of either of these tools, and students complain rather of the elementary requirements they have to meet, which in foreign languages generally amount to only a superficial reading knowledge of one language. Since most of them are not going to be scholars, they may say that they have no real need of these tools; but those who are interested in the humanities might reflect on the possibility that mastery of a foreign language would be highly desirable (as educated Europeans take for granted), and those who want to come to grips with the problems of a technological society would surely find useful a knowledge of the language of mathematics. For all critical students the judgments of Adams are at least worth thinking about.[5]

To come to his specific concerns as a historian, we need not take too seriously the "dynamic theory of history" presented in the concluding chapters of the *Education,* inasmuch as he himself was not satisfied with it; yet it raises important questions that are generally given too little attention. "You may be sure," Adams had said in a presidential address to the American Historical Association in 1894, "that four out of five serious students of history who are living today have, in the course of their work, felt that they stood on the brink of a great generalization that would reduce all history under a law as clear as the laws which govern the material world." His brother Brooks Adams had gone over the brink in his *Law of Civilization and Decay.* Today I suppose few

5. Those who are demanding relevance, with an eye to immediate problems, might also ponder the testimony of Robert Paul Wolff, an avowed radical, in *The Ideal of the University.* Trained as a philosopher, he reports that he did not venture into social studies until after he received his doctorate, but that in his subsequent efforts at social criticism he has found most useful studies, such as mathematical logic and the philosophy of Kant, that during his education seemed least relevant to politics or society. Although he does not pretend to know the answers about technical disciplines, which prolong the training of ardent, impatient students, he observes that the most stimulating social critics generally have mastered some one discipline, and he suggests that "a course in theoretical economics will do more to prepare a student for a socially relevant life than a course on poverty."

historians any longer dream of such comprehensive laws, for good reasons, but also for reasons not altogether to their credit. While most realize that no such law could be conclusively demonstrated, they avoid brinkmanship most obviously because they confine themselves to specialized studies and would not venture to stick their neck out except in their own "field." They are not given to philosophical views of the history of mankind, which lead naturally to a consideration of the "great generalizations" that bolder men have proposed.

At any rate, I have myself ventured one cheer for the big bad generalizations, for example of Voltaire, Hegel, Marx, Buckle, Spengler, and Toynbee. To all of them the plain objection is that they oversimplify and distort man's history; none has stood up as an adequate interpretation of it. Nevertheless all have thrown light on it. They raised new questions, opened up new dimensions, afforded new insights. They have grown more relevant because we are now more interested in global history, which demands more philosophical views. Simply in pointing out the objections to them we are forced to consider fundamental questions, and may hope for a more adequate understanding of man's history. They would be worth considering if only because they have had considerable influence on thought, much of it still surviving in contemporary thought, and therefore I assume some influence on the history modern man has made. On all counts, it should go without saying that no student of history or society today can afford to be ignorant of Karl Marx in particular.

As for Henry Adams, his efforts at great generalizations were more tentative and restricted, generally less impressive; yet they bore fruit. He sought clues in science, which he also tried to keep up with to the end of his working life. His study of Darwin's theory of evolution led only to skepticism for his purposes; he soon gave up any effort to apply it to history, much less to draw from it a theory of progress such as other thinkers saw in it. What he saw about him was chiefly "the survival of the cheapest." In America especially the administration of President Ulysses Grant—a Neanderthal type who "should have been extinct for ages," yet was a successor to George Washington—alone "made evolution ludicrous"; and if this argument is hardly scientific, it may at least serve as a reminder that there has scarcely been a progress in American statesmanship from the Founding Fathers to our present leaders. The "dynamic theory of history" that Adams finally ventured then illustrated a still common fallacy, the effort to apply the principles of physics to human affairs. Historians use freely such terms as energy, force, and movement, but in history these are metaphors and of course have different meanings than they have in physics; the energy is immeasurable, the forces are immaterial, the movements are not motions in space. Adams was led, however, to his hopes of plotting the course of Western history from the unity of the Middle Ages, symbolized by the Virgin, to the multiplicity of the modern world, symbolized by the Dynamo; and though these hopes would not be realized either, they inspired some illuminating speculation.

They call for consideration of his *Mont-Saint-Michel and Chartres*, to which the *Education* was a sequel. It is a much warmer book, often tender, even sentimental in its tribute to the Virgin, "Notre Dame," the most popular object of worship in the Middle Ages, whom Henry Adams loved even though (alas) he could not believe in her. Students should be warned that he much exaggerated the unity of the Middle Ages, and that adoration of the Virgin had little apparent influence on medieval behavior, which was commonly much ruder and more violent than the behavior of Americans today. But since few of them believe in her either, they should know that she was nevertheless a real power in an age when Notre Dame was the name of dozens of Gothic cathedrals, and did not suggest chiefly a football team. It was an immaterial, incalculable kind of power that "practical" Americans are apt to underrate when not to ignore, but that justifies the comment of Adams: "All the steam in the world could not, like the Virgin, build Chartres." Nominally Christian Americans should know too that Chartres was a small town, with only a minute fraction of the wealth of even a small American city, and that in our terms it devoted the equivalent of many millions of dollars to building its glorious cathedral —an enterprise unthinkable in an all-American city today, despite all the money bearing the inscription "In God we trust."

As for the multiplicity of our age, there is no question. Science had advanced far enough by 1900 to multiply uncertainties, while it presented nothing like a unified view of nature, man, or society. Adams had glimmers of the "knowledge explosion" to come. As a young man he had speculated that some day, because of the power of science, the human race might "commit suicide by blowing up the world." Now he made out "a law of acceleration" that obviously applies to the growth of modern technology, a related source of multiplicity. He estimated that the power at man's disposal was doubling every decade, a rate that led him to conjecture that it would reach a terrific climax in about fifty years—just about the time, indeed, when the atomic bomb was dropped.

Meanwhile what troubled him was that the acceleration seemed auto-matic, in effect uncontrolled. It was precisely the problem we face today, when the pace has been speeded up much more by the vast sums spent on research and development, and the elaborate appearances of plan-ning and control only accentuate the failure to control our terrific power for humane, civilized, or simply sane purposes. Adams also thought that within a generation this whole movement "would require a new social mind"—something we have barely begun to develop.

He was too cautious, or timid, to commit himself to a theory of historical determinism. (In his presidential address he had warned historians that if they ever did succeed in demonstrating the certainty of some great law, they would surely get into trouble with their society, for the church, the state, and property interests would never welcome a scientific law that conflicted with their interests.) Such a theory would have been inconsistent anyway with one of the main themes of the *Education*, that statesmen like the early Adamses who guided public opinion had been replaced by vulgar politicians who catered to it, and that men of intellect and culture were no longer in command. His ap-parent faith in such men, however, extended to few but his intimate friends, and was offset by his stress on the immense waste of mind throughout history. The history of his time as he recorded it clearly had deterministic implications, which were accentuated by another major theme that remains pertinent today. This was the theme of blindness —the blindness of the men in power, who had no understanding of the history they were making.

Adams told how appalled he had been by the confusion, blunder, and stupidity at the outbreak of the Civil War, for which nobody was prepared. After the war he had joined the great majority of Americans who elected General Grant to the Presidency, for much the same reason that Americans would turn to General Eisenhower, believing that the good soldier was "above politics"; so he was shocked when he soon realized that as a "pre-intellectual, archaic" type Grant was in effect below politics. As President his avowed policy was a policy of drift. Except for the active service of business interests, this would remain pretty much the policy of the political leaders of the nation, and the service itself was unenlightened, lacking any purpose beyond the ac-quisition of wealth and power. The real leaders—the makers of Amer-ica—were its business leaders. They were men of great energy but no sense of direction except a blind faith in material progress: "men who are socially as remote as heathen gods, alone worth knowing, but never known, and who could tell nothing of political value if one skinned them alive."[6] As Adams saw it, they did not really worship money, for "they had lost the sense of worship." The point was rather that "the American wasted money more recklessly than any one ever did before; he spent more to less purpose than any extravagant court aristocracy; he had no sense of relative values, and knew not what to do with his money when he got it, except use it to make more, or throw it away."

And so with the American mentality in general. The worst thing about the pursuit of money, once damned by Christians as avarice, was that it deflected Americans from all other pursuits. It set the standard of success, both personal and national. Everywhere there was great energy, not merely a faith in progress but a will to progress, only to no clear or lofty end, with no civilized idea of what constituted personal or national success. It was blinder because the American mind "shunned, distrusted, disliked, the dangerous attraction of ideals, and stood alone in history for its ignorance of the past." It was pathetic too because the ordinary American thought of himself as an energetic, ingenious fellow, "always awake and trying to get ahead," and so could not even understand that he was bored. Among the vivid vignettes offered by Adams is this of the American in Europe: "Bored, patient, helpless; pathetically dependent on his wife and daughters; indulgent to excess; mostly a modest, decent, excellent, valuable citizen; the American was to be met at every railway station in Europe, carefully explaining to every listener that the happiest day of his life would be the day he should land on the pier at New York."

Now, this whole critique of America is as usual too supercilious. Henry Adams himself can be charged with blindness to a real idealism to which even the cheap pretenses of idealism are a tribute; American leaders can proclaim their distrust of "mere theory," but never of the ideal theories on which the nation was founded. Or take him at his word, he may make us more aware of some heartening developments. Now that America has become a world leader, it has at least more

6. His brother Charles Francis Adams had entered business, an alternative to a political career that Henry had rejected, and by American standards was a success, becoming president of the great Union Pacific railroad; but he then quit in disgust, reporting that his business associates were not at all worth knowing: "I have known, and known tolerably well, a good many 'successful' men—'big' financially—men famous during the last half-century; and a less interesting crowd I do not care to encounter. Not one that I have ever known would I care to meet again, either in this world or the next; nor is one of them associated in my mind with the idea of humor, thought, or refinement. A set of mere money-getters and traders, they were essentially unattractive and uninteresting. . . . They were a coarse, realistic, bargaining crowd."

understanding of the history it has been making, and is no longer moving quite so blindly into the future. Its political leaders cannot possibly adopt a policy of drift, as they did as late as Harding and Coolidge; for all his limitations, President Eisenhower was a distinct improvement over Grant. Business leaders have been growing somewhat more enlightened and may have something of political value to tell, especially because many are doing business all over the world; it is chiefly small businessmen who remain economic and political illiterates. As travelers, ordinary Americans are now much more eager, less provincial. In general, the public remains slow to learn and never learns enough, but it has learned more than the youth realize. They may not know, for example, that before World War II "internationalism" was a smear word, associated with words like Red.

Yet most of Adams's critique of American democracy remains basically valid. He may convey a more vivid sense of the long tradition of irresponsible politics just because he came out of the aristocratic tradition of the Adamses, and did not regard the rule of politicians as normal. Among the many observations that are still relevant was a discovery that horrified him as a young man, that "the grossest satires on the American Senator and politician never failed to excite the laughter and applause of every audience," which joined in pouring contempt on their own representatives: "Society laughed a vacant, meaningless derision over its own failure." Because of his roots in colonial America he may likewise convey a vivid sense of the change he noticed in his youth in mercantile Boston, the rising sovereignty of business interests and business values, which most Americans would also regard as natural and normal; in their ignorance of the past they remain unaware that in no previous civilization had businessmen been the ruling class. Otherwise he may, like de Tocqueville, make young people realize that much in America today that is viewed with alarm is an old story, not another sign that a great people has become confused, corrupted, or demoralized. Thus he remarks that he was most puzzled by the disappearance of religion, which in his youth had already ceased to be a real influence. Americans have long managed, once more, to prosper after their fashion without fearing or serving God any more than they do today.

There remain the insights of Adams into a future that has become our recent past or our present. He wondered about the vast potential force of Russia, then like most of the world still inert: "Her movement might be the true movement of the future, against the hasty and unsure acceleration of America." He thought too that the future probably belonged to socialism, though he did not welcome the prospect. But most prophetic were his fears of the accelerating growth of power, the prospects of virtually unlimited power—and power of which man would be the servant. In an era of complacence over material progress, he stands out as one of the few far-sighted men who saw that the progress might lead to catastrophe. In his comments on his experience in the 1870's as a professor at Harvard, which he chose to regard as another failure (though he won a reputation as a brilliant teacher), he concluded that he had done his students more harm than good, and that the greatest good he could have done them would have been to hold his tongue. "They needed much faith then; they were likely to need more if they lived long." A student once asked me how, if so brilliant a man as Henry Adams failed in his lifelong effort to understand the history of our time, could ordinary students ever hope to understand it? There can be no assured answer, of course, except by doctrinaires. Still, students have the advantage of acquaintance with the efforts of Adams, which were by no means a simple failure. Many other writers have contributed to a much keener, fuller awareness of the conditions of our life than students had a century ago. In this awareness the youth have more need of faith, since there is so much more reason for fear. But in it lie also the reasons for hope.

3 / The Pragmatism of William James

"HAST ANY PHILOSOPHY IN THEE, SHEPHERD?" As a young man William James wrote that Touchstone's question "will never cease to be one of the tests of a well-born nature." What do the young men of today think about it? In their schooling they probably learned to trot out compositions on their "philosophy of life," ragbags of hand-me-down sentiments. As sophisticated college students they are more critical, wary of platitude, thoughtful enough to have roughly philosophical interests, while some may take a course or so in the philosophy department. Yet in practice most of them clearly do not agree with a more downright statement of James, made while he was engaged in scientific studies, that if colleges are to provide more than special technical training, philosophy is "the most important of all college studies." They have not been equipped to think hard about the basic problems of thought—the problems of man and his relations with the universe, of the criteria of "truth," of the grounds of value-judgments, of good and evil, or more broadly of the good life. They may not realize the importance for their own living purposes of the pragmatic aim of philosophy as stated by Santayana (a student of James at Harvard), "to unite a trustworthy conception of the conditions under which man lives with an adequate conception of his interests." As always they have an excuse in all the specialized courses they have to take, the fragmentation of thought and knowledge, the separation of major interests, and in formal philosophy the dominance of such technical disciplines as linguistic analysis. Nevertheless it seems to me that no subject is more important than philosophy in this broad, pragmatic sense, since it requires a proper appreciation of both the sciences and the humanities, with a clear conception of the limitations of both. And for students today I still know of no better introduction to it than the thought of William James, who in my youth became my favorite philosopher.

One reason I was drawn to him was the rich, warm humanity that led Whitehead to call him the "adorable" philosopher, and that still makes him delightful reading. His thought was also congenial because I had absorbed something of it before I read him, through his pervasive influence as a distinctively American philosopher on the climate of opinion in which I grew up.[7] Today I do not know how well acquainted students are with him, but suspect that relatively few have read him. (I have been startled by bright students of literature who had never even heard of him.) In some respects his thought is clearly dated because he spoke for the last generation before the World Wars (he died in 1910), and was not so prophetic as Henry Adams. Essentially, however, I think his philosophy has grown more relevant because of the extraordinary growth of science and technology since his day, and

7. Here a more appropriate subject for reconsideration might be the philosophy of John Dewey, who developed the pragmatism of James into a more systematic, comprehensive "instrumentalism," had much more to say about social and political problems, and had a wider and more direct influence, especially on education. While I still respect Dewey, who as a mentor of my generation has in recent years been much criticized, often I think unfairly, I chose James instead because he is much more readable and took an easier look at life. I bogged down in efforts to reread some of Dewey for reasons that are likely to make him heavier going for students; much of his once stimulating thought is now familiar. Ideas in James no less familiar may seem much fresher because of his concreteness, warmth, liveliness, and humor. Among his works that students might find both pleasurable and profitable are *The Will to Believe*, *The Varieties of Religious Experience*, *Pragmatism*, and collections of his letters. An introduction I found most useful was Ralph Barton Perry's two-volume *The Life and Thought of William James*, now available in an abridged paperback edition.

more lately because of the student revolt. While he always kept a pragmatic eye on the conditions under which man lives, he was especially concerned with an adequate conception of man's interests, the human values that even then were threatened by a society given to "herding and branding, licensing and degree-giving, authorizing and appointing, and in general regulating and administering by system the lives of human beings."

The originality of James in his day, and still the basic source of his possible appeal to the youth, lay in his rejection of the classical traditions of philosophy, the closed systems, the pretensions to certainty or finality, the monisms of idealism or materialism, the absolutism, eternalism, necessitarianism, and other products of a despotic abstract rationality that disparaged or denied the claims of immediate, concrete experience, made only concepts of universals really honorable, and generally offered an inadequate conception of either the external world or human interests. He found ample room—more than most philosophers still do—for immediacy, particularity and variety, individuality and spontaneity, chance and novelty, in what he called a "pluralistic universe," an open or a "wild world," which was still a *uni*verse because everything in it was somehow related, but was "more like a federal republic than like an empire or a kingdom." He made philosophy more relevant and more useful by stressing its limitations, including the inability of philosophers to agree on just what is "rational"; as he saw it, the utmost of rationality was "the feeling of sufficiency for the present moment." While he denied men the comforting illusions of certainty, stability, and security, he compensated by offering them "real possibilities" of things that might but need not be, a measure of freedom to make for the better through experiment and adventure, as Americans were pleased to think they had done in their New World. His underlying American optimism was more bracing because it was clear-eyed, or in his own words, never "tender-minded." Students should know that his philosophy was literally a "philosophy of life," a hard-won means to mental health, which he won to after painful experience in his youth, when a prolonged period of morbid depression had brought him to the brink of suicide. Upon his recovery he wrote that his belief *"can't* be optimistic," but that he would posit "the real, the good," life that could be built by "doing and suffering and creating."

More specifically, James built his philosophy on his "pragmatic rule" for determining the meaning or the truth of a concept. Every concept should be tested by the question: "What sensible difference to anybody will its truth make?" In other words, "What is the truth's cash value in experiential terms?" Once the pragmatist asks this question, he sees the answer:

> *True ideas are those that we can assimilate, validate, corroborate, and verify. False ideas are those that we cannot.* That is the practical difference it makes to us to have true ideas; that therefore is the meaning of truth, for it is all that truth is known as.

As for the "essential truth" dear to most philosophers, "the truth with no one thinking it," it is not more but less real than the verified article: "Pragmatist truth contains the whole of intellectualist truth and a hundred other things in addition." To his critics James replied, "We offer them the full quart-pot, and they cry for the empty quart-capacity." On this epistemological foundation, he added, thinkers could go on to develop different ideas about the constitution of the external realities pragmatism must assume. Hence he has been called a "meta-physical democrat."

Now, in his hospitality to all kinds of potentialities, his eagerness to hang on to every possible good, James was not at all a systematic philosopher, or ever distinguished for logical rigor and precision. His pragmatism is obviously liable to easy abuse. He himself confessed that his vocabulary was unfortunate in its stress on "practical" consequences, "what works," the "cash value" of truth, and other such loose terms that appealed to Americans typically impatient of logic, suspicious of theory, and eager for quick returns. As dubious was another statement he put in italics: "*The true,* to put it very briefly, *is only the expedient in the way of our thinking, just as the right is only the expedient in the way of our behaving.*" Although he added that he of course meant expedient "in the long run and on the whole," too many readers might be pleased by the idea that truth and right are "only" matters of expediency. In any case, this brings up the crucial difficulty with the pragmatic test of "truths" by their consequences. Not only are the most important beliefs that men live by strictly unverifiable, but it is impossible to determine their consequences with assurance, demonstrate positively what *is* most expedient in the long run and on the whole. James himself may be charged with assimilating too readily beliefs he found congenial. On the concept of God, for example, he said that "God means that you can dismiss certain kinds of fear"; but even as a youthful admirer I noted that God also means that you may be hounded by other kinds of fear, and only God—or the Devil—can know all that belief in him has meant throughout history, or may mean from now on.

Yet James conceived pragmatism as a discipline, by no means an invitation to wishful thinking, solipsism, or any notion that truth and right are whatever one chooses to believe they are. As initially a trained scientist, he took for granted a respect for the "irreducible and stubborn facts," and the constant need of checking all beliefs against the available evidence. His pragmatism was an expression of the scientific spirit in that it rejected all the absolute, universal, immutable, eternal truths accepted merely on traditional authority. It can therefore still serve as a discipline for both conservatives and doctrinaire Marxists, and for all students at least as a helpful guide. No systematist or rigorous logician myself, and perhaps too inclined to stress more the limitations than the usefulness of such types, I may also agree too readily with James that in questions of human significance and worth—the all-important questions—"conclusions can never be precise"; but anyway students can readily get plenty of training in system and precision, or the illusion thereof. For their living purposes James may serve them better because his readiness to adventure and his hospitality to new possibilities were always coupled with firm convictions about human values, the sources of significance and worth. He demonstrated the very important possibility of maintaining such convictions together with an unblinking acceptance of instability, insecurity, and uncertainty—the conditions of man's life that have never been plainer than they are today. Specifically, I propose to consider the relevance of his views on two basic interests, science and religion.

What he had to say about science remains essentially valid even though he wrote before the revolution in modern physics had made its impact. For him the value of science lay in its method rather than its specific content or any "fixed belief." Today students might still heed his expressions of gratitude for our "literally boundless debt" to it, above all to the patient, scrupulous, disinterested scientific spirit and its rare kind of intellectual honesty. They might contemplate too "the miracle of miracles," that beneath the immense variety of shifting appearances there is an order that lends itself to both our scientific and our artistic purposes. From his own experience James appreciated the esthetic values of science, for as a young man he had devoted a year to the study of painting, and when he turned to science he realized that naturalists at work might feel just like artists. He himself made an important pioneering contribution in his *Principles of Psychology* (1890), a once popular book that is still highly readable. Characteristically he built no system and left no school, but he ranged so widely and reported so sensitively the concrete realities of mental life that he anticipated most of the schools to come, including some elementary realities that specialists had to rediscover. (Among them was the "self," which an authority on personality writes had "perished as a psychological entity" by 1900; he thought that its revival was among the most noteworthy of recent tendencies.) It was also characteristic of his hospitality and generosity of spirit that as a dying man he heard Freud lecture and told him: "The future of psychology belongs to your work."

Chiefly, however, James dwelt on the limitations of science. While properly considered it stood for no fixed belief, in fact most scientists did identify it with such a belief, specifically with a monistic, positivistic, mechanistic, deterministic scheme of thought that excluded other ways of looking at life—poetic, ethical, religious—as merely personal, emotional, fanciful, or essentially irrational when taken seriously. This tendency remains strong, especially in the behavioral sciences that have proliferated so fantastically since James wrote, despite the revolution in physics that should have discredited it. Many men who are proud of their science today might anticipate the fate he predicted for the science of his day, that it would become old-fashioned because of "its omissions of fact, its ignorance of whole ranges and orders of complexity in the phenomena to be explained"; for they continue to ignore or dismiss phenomena that do not fit into their conveniently simplified schemes, intellectual labor-saving devices that may result in too little hard thought, in particular about fundamentals.

Both as psychologist and as philosopher James emphasized that man was distinguished from other animals primarily by the "the fantastic and unnecessary character of his wants, physical, moral, esthetic, and intellectual." "Prune his extravagance, sober him, and you undo him." Accordingly he emphasized the particular danger in psychology of dismissing the "wild facts" that threaten the accepted system—and that today many young people share his interest in. He noted the apparent anomaly in the debate between "the mystics and the scientifics," that while the latter had the better of it in their theories, the mystics "have usually proved to be right about the *facts*." Thus the facts about what had been called "animal magnetism" were dismissed contemptuously—until they were made respectable by a theory of "hypnotic suggestion." Similarly "stigmatizations, invulnerabilities, instantaneous cures, inspired discourses, and demoniacal possessions" were all regarded as mere superstitions until they were given the new name of "cases of hystero-epilepsy." After James, Freud would have a hard time attaining respectability in both psychological and medical circles, and today the old debate is raging over the claims of extrasensory perception. I myself still tend to be skeptical about such claims, especially because the ageless gullibility of the human race is still conspicuous in a supposedly scientific age, and all manner of plain superstitions (as about the number thirteen) still thrive; and I shall later return to this problem when considering the "counter culture" of the youth. But meanwhile I should emphasize that the mind unquestionably does have mysterious powers, no less mysterious when they are linked with the commonplace knowledge that people can have hallucinations, which means that somehow they can vividly see things that aren't there. This power may take the form of creative imagination, a very important subject to which "scientific" psychologists have given little attention.

At any rate, James's interest in these matters was both cause and effect of his interest in the varieties of religious experience, and more broadly in the claims of religion. Since I have so far had little to say about the relevance of religion, which throughout history was taken for granted, I am pausing to consider more closely his pragmatic arguments for the validity of religious experience, specifically for his own belief in God. "God is dead," it is now often said, echoing Nietzsche, and quite possibly the God of traditional Christianity is dying. But certainly religion more broadly defined is far from dead, innumerable people still have what they believe is religious experience, and many students have been growing more interested in religious possibilities, for good reasons. When Margaret Fuller exclaimed flamboyantly "I accept the universe!" Carlyle commented, "By gad she'd better"; yet she of course had a real choice—many people do not accept it. Religion has always been the major means of bringing people into harmonious or at least tolerable relations with the universe. Today spiritual leaders in all the higher religions have grown more concerned about demonstrating the relevance of their faith in the modern world, sometimes in international conferences out of which emerge their common aspirations to love and justice, as in their versions of the Golden Rule, and their common assumption that in a fast changing world man's nature too can be changed for the better. In Christianity a specific example is the recent movement toward a "theology of hope," which involves a religious restatement of the idea of progress and even some notion that God himself may be on the make.

James started from the premise that we can neither prove nor disprove the existence of God, but that the decision whether or not to believe in him was a live, momentous, *forced* option, and that whatever one's choice, one necessarily ran risks of being either duped or deprived. Agnostics (and I am speaking as one) may forget that their suspended judgment is nevertheless a positive stand, a commitment to do without whatever good may be afforded by a belief in God. James proceeded to argue that when the available evidence did not make it possible for reason to decide positively, we had a right to consult our "passional nature," or in popular terms, the reasons of the "heart." He offered a modern version of the famous wager of Pascal, who had also said that reason could prove nothing about this all-important question, but that we should bet on God because we had everything to gain and nothing to lose. He differed in that Pascal, a devout and otherwise orthodox Catholic, insisted on the absolute necessity of belief, on the grounds that without God man could know no happiness, no real good. James, knowing that unbelievers could be virtuous and contented enough, argued only for the *right* to believe, and promised only "a certain vital good." His God, moreover, was not the omni-God of orthodox Christianity, but a finite, limited power whose nature he did not pretend to know, and that he was content to describe as a "superhuman consciousness," a "wider self from which saving experiences flow in," an "ideal tendency in things," or a "larger power" that was friendly to man and his ideals.[8] Although he did not pretend to know either what limited the divine power, or where all the unideal tendencies in things came from, he was at least not troubled by the problem of evil that has tormented Christians as it did Job—the unanswerable question why an all-powerful, all-knowing, all-good God should have created a world so full of pain, misery, and evil. And always James presented his faith as an hypothesis, adding that our faiths do harm when they put on "rationalistic and authoritative pretensions."

Now, I myself remain skeptical. Never having felt a strong inclination to believe, still less a real need of belief, I incline to distrust his appeal to our passional nature, which for lack of circumstantial evidence can justify all kinds of belief (incidentally including disbelief). I might say, for example, that my nature demands a belief in Cupid, I can't be happy without Cupid, and since nobody can prove he doesn't exist, I'm going to hang on to Cupid; but if so, I should certainly be com-

8. Since the idea of a limited God may seem strange to those brought up in the Christian tradition, I should add that it is an ancient idea that can be found in Plato, who identified God with only the Good in the universe, and that it is quite common among modern religious thinkers. For that matter, as James pointed out, ordinary believers in practice identify him only with the good. When they come down with a streptococcus infection, they do not say, "Ah, they too are God's creatures, sent for my own good." If they think of God at all, they just wish to hell that he had left out the streptococci.

mitted to an institution. The point of this extreme case is that a belief in God is not a simple heads-or-tails, fifty-fifty option. To me the probabilities of a divine power seem much less strong than they did to James, for in the natural world with its law of tooth and claw I see little evidence of an ideal tendency apart from man, and his ideals he arrived at late in his evolution. As a student of history, I am also very much aware that Christianity, like Judaism and Islam, insisted on its "rationalistic and authoritative pretensions," as the Roman Catholic Church in particular still does, to my mind without rational justification; yet I also wonder. Can the mass of simple believers ever accept their faith as only an hypothesis? Do they not require the feeling of absolute certainty that the Church in its wisdom offers them?

Still, the authoritative pretensions of Christianity, come down from a pre-scientific age, are no longer valid for an increasing number of educated people, for whom much traditional teaching has become simply irrelevant. One may doubt that even most ordinary Americans have a sustaining conviction of religious certainty, much less an inspiring one; while few would say in so many words that their faith was a mere hypothesis, many have such vague ideas about God ("There must be something") and a hereafter as to suggest the schoolboy's definition cited by James: "Faith is when you believe something that you know ain't true." At any rate, James was not talking to them. As he said, there is no scientific or any other method for steering safely between the dangers of believing too little and too much, and he recognized that most people, now as always, tended to believe too much, and much too easily. He was addressing an educated audience, often an academic one, that in its fear of being duped was tending to believe too little, thinking it was simply wrong to believe anything on insufficient evidence. To them he freely admitted that in committing themselves to a belief in the supernatural or superhuman they might be wrong, but he added: Why not run the risk? As we all had to do with our living beliefs?

Since I think thoughtful students have no crying need of my agnosticism, and few are any longer offensively dogmatic or intolerant in such religious belief as they have, I am disposed to give James the last word here. To my mind there is no question at all of the *right* to believe, at least as he qualifies it. There is little question either of the positive value of belief, again if it is of his own humane, tolerant, civilized kind—free from the bigotry, fears, and hatreds inspired by the historic claim of Christianity that its God was the only true God, all

other religions were false, and by its preposterous dogma that God demanded first of all correct belief in him, even though Christians were
never able to agree what this was. James knew the value of faith from
his own painful experience as a young man, for his period of morbid
depression had involved religious doubt and despondency—torments
that are less common among students today, but that they may understand from their common enough feeling of the meaninglessness of
life. Although he could not give life a positive heavenly meaning, he
could be hopeful because his belief in a larger power concerned about
man and friendly to his ideals gave some assurance that man's loftiest
ideals would not perish with him. This may be more meaningful if one
considers the alternative, the scientific account of the end of man's
world as summed up starkly in a passage from Arthur Balfour cited
by James:

> The energies of our system will decay, the glory of the sun will be
> dimmed, and the earth, tideless and inert, will no longer tolerate the
> race which has for a moment disturbed its solitude. Man will go down
> into the pit, and all his thoughts will perish. The uneasy consciousness
> which in this obscure corner has for a brief space broken the contented
> silence of the universe, will be at rest. Matter will know itself no
> longer. 'Imperishable monuments' and 'immortal deeds,' death itself, and
> love stronger than death, will be as if they had never been. Nor will
> anything that is, be better or worse for all that the labor, genius, devotion,
> and suffering of man have striven through countless ages to effect.

As James recognized, however, the critical question is not the psychological value but the rational grounds of belief, the reasons why an
honest, thoughtful, enlightened man might legitimately believe. These
centered in the mysterious powers of mind—powers that in time psychologists may explain satisfactorily on naturalistic grounds (though as
yet they have not to my knowledge done a convincing job), but at
best are not to be explained *away*. Thus a "wider self" from which
saving experiences may come is a fact of mental life. It is one of the
various selves studied by James that complicate the question of one's
"real" self, or the problem of self-realization, but also enrich what it
means to be a human being. It points to forms of consciousness other
than the familiar waking state, such as a subconscious, the springs of
imagination and inspiration, states of trance, ecstatic states, the varieties
of religious experience, and a kind of superconsciousness. Of the latter
the supreme example is the mystical experience. Again I should add
that this is no proof of the existence of God, since mystics describe it

as ineffable but go on to interpret it volubly in different ways, depending on their culture. (When Pascal had a mystical experience, he believed he was communing with the God of Abraham, Jacob, and Moses.) But we have the testimony of many admirable men, in all the higher religions, that it is an extraordinarily rich experience, which can make a world of difference in a man's life. Hinduism, based on the belief that all men are capable in their best moments of communion with the World Soul, has by spiritual disciplines like yoga enabled countless men to attain such states of consciousness, means to a peace of mind rare in the West. And all of us, including rationalists, may know something like the mystical experience, feelings of transcendence of our little selves, through communion with nature, the enjoyment of art, or any experience that induces awe. Add that man's consciousness is the product of evolution, by natural processes, there remains something like an "ideal tendency" in a process that has culminated in the extraordinary powers of the human spirit.

So I would end with a tribute to the rare spirit of William James. In my present context I would remark in particular that he was a distinctively American philosopher not only as a pragmatist, always hopeful of making for the better, but as a good democrat. He liked to quote the remark of an unlearned carpenter he knew, that at bottom "there is very little difference between one man and another, but what little there is, is *very important*." James could accordingly do full justice to our common humanity, the courage, patience, and kindliness of ordinary people, "virtue with horny hands and dirty skin," and to the need of charity in our judgments, the ideal of live and let live. At the same time, he fully respected the values of culture and refinement, and especially of individuality, the importance of great men, which "scientific" thinkers were tending to minimize. In all questions of human significance and worth, in which the answer can never be precise, he said it is "always a matter of more or less, a balance struck by sympathy, insight, and good will." This balance he himself maintained in the subjects of general interest he took up, from education, the individual and society, and the American scene to the first and last questions of life and death. And always he combined an uncommonly full appreciation of the rich possibilities of the human spirit with a full awareness of the inescapable hazards, the realities of evil, the extravagant follies due to man's fantastically superfluous wants—and yet the necessity of some extravagance. In his spirit thoughtful students might venture to adopt a risky motto he suggested in passing: "Without too much you cannot have enough, of anything."

4 / Herbert Croly:
The Promise of American Life

PUBLISHED IN 1909, when I was a small boy, Herbert Croly's book remained unknown to me in my youth and many years thereafter; only lately did I at last read it. Then I realized, however, that it contributed to the education of my generation at least indirectly. A student of William James at Harvard, Croly applied the pragmatic test to the national creed, insisting that this "must be constantly modified in order to define new experiences and renewed in order to meet unforeseen emergencies." His radical critique of American democracy much impressed many young men who were to be influential, including Walter Lippmann, Edmund Wilson, and others I read. It led to the founding of the *New Republic,* on which Croly served as chief editor until 1928, and which before then was among my favorite journals. But what belatedly attracted me to his book was its title: *The Promise of American Life.* It came out of the national tradition—in his view our main tradition—that America was a land of ideal promise. The effort to realize the ideal under conditions unknown to the Founding Fathers was reflected in the title of his magazine, the *New Republic.* It would appear too in the New Freedom of Woodrow Wilson, the New Deal of Franklin D. Roosevelt, the New Frontier of John F. Kennedy, even among conservatives as the "new conservatism." And how many serious thinkers today are hailing the "promise" of American life? How many are confident that it still does have an ideal promise? How many ardent, dissident students, who as inheritors of the future most need to believe that it does?

Today Croly's book makes melancholy reading.[9] Although he did not set up as a prophet, and his main thesis was that radical changes would be needed in order to realize the promise, an underlying optimism appears in such phrases as "will inevitably tend," American

9. It is available in a paperback edition in the American Heritage Series, with an excellent introduction by John William Ward. Students can get enough out of it, I think, by reading this introduction and the opening and concluding chapters; for it is pretty wordy and repetitious, and neither Croly's long historical diagnosis nor his detailed prescriptions are as stimulating as they were in his day.

leaders "will find," and the people are "bound" to realize or to demand intelligent consideration of something or other; and so far things have not turned out as he thought they must. America has yet to face up to the basic challenge he set, in a distant pre-war age when he was already talking about an "existing crisis."

Yet by the same token his book remains essentially relevant. He emphasized the need of not only economic and political but social and above all moral reform. He dwelt on the responsibilities imposed by the ideal promise—the need of standards of excellence, disciplined behavior, self-denial, and in particular a clear national purpose beyond the material well-being that was the goal of most Americans. On the latter he quoted H. G. Wells: "When one talks to an American of his national purpose, he seems a little at a loss; if one speaks of his national destiny, he responds with alacrity." Specifically, Croly attacked the traditional "mixture of optimism, fatalism, and conservatism" that encouraged a belief that the future would take care of itself, or that the manifest national destiny would be realized without sacrifice of the undisciplined individualism and national irresponsibility sanctioned by conventional Americanism. Except for the current sense of frustration, this complacent mixture remains basically the "philosophy," such as it is, of the nation's leaders today and of the middle America they appeal to. The popular assumption that our chief enemy is Communism makes more meaningful what Croly wrote long ago:

> We do not have to cross the Atlantic in order to hunt for the enemies of American national independence and fulfillment. They sit at our political fireside and toast their feet on its coals. They poison American patriotic feeling until it becomes, not a leaven, but a kind of national gelatine. They enshrine this American democratic ideal in a temple of canting words which serves merely as a cover for a religion of personal profit. American moral and intellectual emancipation can be achieved only by a victory over the ideas, the conditions, and the standards which make Americanism tantamount to collective irresponsibility and to the moral and intellectual subordination of the individual to a commonplace popular average.

Now, I would immediately add some reservations about Croly's emphasis on the crying need of a national purpose. Fascist and Communist nations have not only proclaimed such a purpose but stirred up a fervor for it in many of their people, and sacrificed their rights to it. In America it may appear in the assumption of a national mission to defend whatever we call the cause of freedom all over the world, however imperialistic it looks to others. While I think Americans need more purpose in the sense of devotion to our avowed ideals of freedom, equality, and justice, and to the public rather than merely private interests, I would still defend the right of people to lead their own lives, not to feel that their primary duties are as citizens, or still less that their primary allegiance is to the nation. Although Croly had in mind the public welfare rather than national aggrandizement, he did maintain that positive freedom was not merely freedom from arbitrary constraints, but freedom to do good for one's country. He was still a believer in the modern religion of nationalism that exalted above all allegiance to the nation-state, which he declared was "the only possible foundation for a better social structure." He went so far as to say that "like all sacred causes," the American idea "must be propagated by the Word and by that right arm of the Word, which is the Sword."

Then we must remember that he wrote before the World Wars, never dreamed of a Pentagon, and naturally had no more idea that the Sword would be replaced by the Bomb. Similarly with other ideas that may seem surprising because Croly was a staunch democrat, the philosopher of the Progressive movement of his day. He much preferred Alexander Hamilton to Thomas Jefferson, despite Hamilton's bias against democracy, because he had a clearer conception of a national interest that could and should be promoted by government. He attacked Jacksonian democracy in particular, if for what now seem obvious reasons: although it achieved political democracy for the common people, it set them no standards of excellence and encouraged an unbridled, mindless individualism that would frustrate its vague ideals of social democracy. On the other hand he was lenient in his judgment of the ruthless industrialists who built up America, in part because as robber barons "their moral or immoral standards" were shared by the great majority of Americans, but especially because they provided the country with economic organization, which called for more than "mere energy" and fatalistic optimism. It set up standards by its demands for specialized training, expert skills, and coordinated effort, and thereby "imposed discipline upon the individual." Croly remained highly critical of the standards of his industrial society in other respects, which I shall return to shortly; but first it must be said that he had a limited insight into modern technology, and however understandably, failed to anticipate the problems it would create for American democracy.

Thus he insisted that the boundless future Americans had long assumed would automatically be better in their land of opportunity now had to be "planned and constructed," else the promise of their life would cease to be. Today the necessity of planning is accepted even by most conservatives, for whom it was long a horrid word suggesting what Communists did; both government and business are engaged in extensive, systematic planning; but it is primarily for limited technical purposes. So far from fulfilling any ideal promise, it may chiefly distract men from such notions, focus attention on merely administrative problems. More specifically, Croly put his faith in "efficient national organization," words that recur throughout his book. Organization has become even more clearly indispensable, and it has worked miracles such as he never dreamed of, for instance in the space program; but it too has created problems that have grown much more obvious since his day. The word "bureaucracy" does not appear in his Index; he had little inkling of the immense expansion and confusion of government, the multiplication of federal agencies, and the problem of keeping them under effective democratic control. Similarly he saw in organization a means whereby the individual could fulfill himself through specialized training and discipline; whereas we now see all the "organization men," the little interchangeable cogs in the system, the punch holes in cards, or at best a technical "meritocracy" that does not breed fully developed individuals. And so with his stress on efficiency. This has long since become the accepted national ideal—but again for narrow technical or bureaucratic purposes, at the expense of human values that for him constituted the ideal promise of American life. Apart from the extravagant inefficiency in American practice, it only forces the question whether or to what extent the good life can be planned and organized.

To give one more pertinent example of Croly's technological innocence, he deplored the interest of workers chiefly in getting higher wages, not in doing better work. While agreeing that many were underpaid, he maintained that the ultimate end was "the complete emancipation of the individual," which depended on "his complete disinterestedness"; so "he must become interested exclusively in the excellence of his work," and he could "never become disinterestedly interested in his work as long as heavy responsibilities and high achievements are supposed to be rewarded by increased pay." More than half a century earlier Karl Marx (who also does not appear in Croly's Index) had pointed out that machine-tending in factories forced workers to confine themselves to trivial, repetitive, mechanical operations that made it impossible for them to take pride in their work, fulfill themselves in it, or enjoy any feelings of excellence. So of course it still does on assembly lines, where workers complain that they have no chance to do as good work as they are capable of, or in Marx's terms, feel "alienated" from their work. I see no way of solving this problem in an industrial society, providing all workers with man-sized jobs, much less of realizing Croly's utopian ideal of "complete disinterestedness."

But all this is to say that what makes *The Promise of American Life* still relevant is not so much the answers he gives as the questions he raises. The essential condition of this promise as he saw it was "an improving popular economic condition, guaranteed by democratic political institutions, and resulting in moral and social amelioration," or as we might now say, in an improved quality of American life. The "new conditions" that were threatening it centered in the increasing concentration of wealth and financial power, with attendant privileges but without public responsibility, which was more undemocratic because it tended "to erect political abuses and social inequalities into a system." At the same time, it was the product of American democracy, specifically of the rampant individualism blessed by tradition; again Croly blamed not so much the irresponsible men who wielded the "money power" as an irresponsible public that shared their values, supported attitudes that tended to make Americans "disgracefully ignorant, politically corrupt, commercially unscrupulous, socially snobbish, vulgarly boastful, and morally coarse." Hence he argued that the reforms advocated by most other Progressives would not suffice, amounting only to "a species of higher conservatism"; it was necessary to go to the roots of the problem, the conventional Americanism that had connived at the rule of money. Although no socialist, he proposed such radical measures as a redistribution of wealth by imposing confiscatory taxation, setting a maximum allowable income, and guaranteeing every citizen "a certain minimum of economic power and responsibility." But fundamentally more radical was his whole conception of the true promise of American life, the standards it set, the responsibilities it imposed, the changes it demanded in popular attitudes and beliefs—all of which, he realized, would seem "fantastic and obnoxious to the great majority of Americans."

What, then, would a disciple of Croly think of America today? Regarding his essential conditions for realizing its promise, progress has clearly been made toward "an improving popular economic condition." Democratic political institutions have produced a graduated income tax, unemployment relief, social security, "welfare capitalism," lately efforts at a guaranteed minimum income. They have failed, however, to prevent continued political abuses of concentrated economic power and privilege, flagrant inequities in the distribution of the nation's wealth, and the growth of new social evils, notably pollution. In general, they

have helped to create a mixed economy, with combinations of government and private enterprise and much more government activity, which
is quite different from that known to Croly. At best, it represents efforts
at a democratically regulated and controlled economy, with approaches
to the "more highly socialized democracy" he thought necessary. At
worst, it has fortified privilege and created such new problems as a
military-industrial complex that he could not anticipate. On economic
and political issues, at any rate, I think he has little helpful to say to us,
for the soundest of his suggestions are no longer novel.[10]

More pertinent is his principal concern, "moral and social amelioration." To Croly democracy meant not merely majority rule, a form of
political organization, but primarily a "formative purpose," which he
defined as "the use of democratic organization for the joint benefit of
individual distinction and social improvement." In maintaining that
this alone made it superior to other forms of political organization,
which might be more efficient, he also asserted that it was a moral purpose, the superiority of democracy rested on "an authoritative and comprehensive moral idea," and it could therefore "claim the allegiance of
mankind on rational moral grounds." Throughout his book the word
"moral" constantly recurs, to an extent quite unfashionable in contemporary political thought, perhaps oppressive to our sophisticated youth,
but I think wholesome as a corrective to the usual shallow realism. At
the end he cited Santayana's conclusion about democracy:

> For such excellence to grow general mankind must be notably trans-
> formed. If a noble and civilized democracy is to subsist, the common
> citizen must be something of a saint and something of a hero. We see,
> therefore, how justly flattering and profound, and at the same time how
> ominous, was Montesquieu's saying that the principle of democracy is
> virtue.

10. The most radical of his proposals by current standards, the setting of a
maximum allowable income, may recall a bit of forgotten history he did not
live to brood over. During World War II President Roosevelt proposed that
for the duration incomes be limited to $25,000 a year, or what in buying power
then amounted to about $100,000 today. This got nowhere because it was at
once denounced as outrageous by Congressmen and conservatives all over the
land; among other things they argued patriotically that it would destroy the
incentives of businessmen on whom the country depended for war production.
In their moral indignation these champions of free private enterprise overlooked a
plain implication of their protests. Whereas millions of soldiers were expected to
risk their lives for their country on very small pay, it appeared that comfortable
businessmen at home were so swinish that they could not be expected to do
their patriotic best unless they retained an opportunity to make a lot of money.
Needless to add, no such outrageous proposals were made during the Cold
War and the hot wars in Korea and Vietnam.

Emphatically agreeing that its principle is indeed virtue, Croly added that in view of the state of America in his day, the saying might seem more ominous than flattering. Today students might ask: Has it grown more or less ominous? Or if the virtue of our ancestors has been exaggerated, and Americans have never been distinguished for saintliness, would they deny that virtue is at least among the primary requisites for the success of democracy? The realization of any ideal promise?

In expounding the democratic purpose to promote "individual distinction," Croly again attacked what for him was always the main enemy, the national gospel of individualism. He dwelt on the now familiar complaints about a purely economic individualism that distinguished Americans only by the energy and success with which they pursued the common purpose of making money, deprived individuality of "all serious moral and intellectual meaning," and in effect stifled it, made for "individual bondage." Because Americans neglected standards of excellence, they had "no popularly accepted ideals which are anything but an embarrassment to the aspiring individual." This is precisely what many students feel today. Croly's own ideals have grown more questionable, however, because of his stress on the "technical excellence" of the individual's work promoted by organization, and in particular his subordination of the individual to the national purpose, the primary obligation of serving one's country. While he took for granted that the democratic purpose included the maintenance of individual liberty and equal rights, he subordinated them too to patriotic duty; he complained that "the principle of equal rights encourages mutual suspicion and disloyalty." Any Negro today might ask: Why shouldn't it? Otherwise there is plain reason for the growing concern with the rights of the individual against the government, regarded as moral rights grounded on human dignity, and likewise for the concern with full personal development rather than technical proficiency.

Nevertheless many of Croly's scattered remarks imply a broader view of his goal of "individual emancipation and growth," which makes it easier to discount or supplement his specific proposals. Thus one need not agree that a man's highest loyalty is to the nation to accept his basic idea that the individual can fully realize himself only in and through community (as John Dewey too would emphasize), and only through loyalty to something greater than himself. Then students concerned with the rights of the individual might ask: Is there not still need of more stress on his duties too? Similarly with Croly's views on education, in which he typically called for a system of national education to realize the national purpose. His insistence on standards of excellence need not be confined to technical excellence in organization men. His basic idea that individual distinction achieved by superior performance in work "is not only the foundation of all genuine individuality, but is usually of the utmost social value" can be applied to all creative work, as in art; the changes in American values he called for included more respect for esthetic values. He also declared that the consummate expression of democratic moral values was "the religion of human brotherhood," an ideal well beyond either mere teamwork in organization or patriotism. And his major concern, both individual and social improvement, took him to the roots of the problem—human nature and its perfectibility.

As he noted, American tradition included a faith that democracy made for better men. Usually it appeared as a naive faith, inspiring the efforts of Americans to improve themselves or "uplift" their fellows with little or no attention to social and political institutions. Even so Croly committed himself to it: "Democracy must stand or fall on a platform of possible human perfectibility." To me this seems a necessary commitment for all democrats who wish to believe that American life still does have an ideal promise. If so, they must face the "practical questions" he raised: "How can the improvement best be brought about? and, How much may it amount to?" Then he got into the difficulties that beset all of us who do not bank on a faith in revolution.

Thus he remarked the "credulity" of socialists who expected to transform human nature "by merely institutional and legal changes"; yet he obviously believed that democratic institutions made a real difference, and counted on improvements in them to bring about "moral and social amelioration." At the outset he observed that although the average American was no more intelligent, wise, or virtuous than the average European, he was likely to be more energetic, hopeful, awake, alive, and so more susceptible to ideas of "promise" and efforts at improvement; yet the invariable trouble remained that this greater vitality was devoted to an irresponsible individualism that negated the ideal promise. Now both the strength and the weakness of the American economic and social system consisted in that it was based on "the realities of contemporary human nature." Croly accordingly argued that the system could be successfully attacked only by a body of opinion based "on a more salient individual and social interest and a more intense and vital method of life"—what he attempted to offer, and what today rebellious students are either seeking or asserting. Meanwhile he believed that the main hope lay in education, which could improve men much more surely than could any tinkering with laws and institutions, but this brought him up against another basic ambiguity: the traditional naive faith of Americans in education coupled with a distrust of the counsel of highly educated men, who had less influence than they had in any European country. This was more troublesome for Croly because he also staked his hopes on "constructive individualism," appealing to men of proved distinction to raise standards of excellence by consciously setting acceptable examples, ideally of "heroism and saintliness" but at least of integrity and good work, and by trying to address the people in an acceptable interesting manner, make the good thing look good to them.

All this would of course take time. Croly had no idea how much improvement could be expected in people, or how long it would take. Radicals may say that he offered no real program—he was merely exhorting Americans to seek excellence, and then to "uplift" their fellows in the traditional manner that on the public record has failed. Liberals may point to his inescapable dilemma as a sincere democrat. An elitest who made much of discipline, at times suggested some hankering to impose it on the majority whose interests differed from the true national interest, he nevertheless remained loyal to democratic political institutions and processes, and so could only exhort as he faced the old problem of reconciling standards of excellence with democratic ideals and popular institutions or interests. He retained too the essential democratic faith in the sufficient good sense and good will of the people, the grounds for hopes of educating them. At this point he placed the responsibility on their leaders, or his elite:

> They cannot be expected to be any better than they are, until they have been sufficiently shown the way; and they cannot be blamed for being as bad as they are, until it is proved that they have deliberately rejected better leadership. No such proof has ever been offered.

I should say that on the historic record there is much dismaying evidence of their rejection of better leadership, especially when it sought moral and intellectual improvement, but that there is at least no clear proof that they are incapable of responding to it, since they generally did respond to their greater Presidents. It is something that their most beloved national hero is Abraham Lincoln, who for Croly was the ideal symbol of the promise of American life.

Inasmuch as Croly's "constructive individualism" also called for more criticism, "a comparatively neglected art among Americans," I was reminded of Pascal's dictum that thought makes the whole dignity of man, and that the endeavor to think well is the basic morality. From this Carl Becker concluded: "The chief virtue of democracy, and in the long run the sole reason for cherishing it, is that with all its defects it still provides the most favorable conditions for the maintenance of that dignity and the practice of that morality." Now that students are given to much more criticism than they were in Croly's day (or my own), but not always to hard efforts to think well, they might consider his comparable dictum:

> For the time being the freedom which Americans need is the freedom of thought. The energy they need is the energy of thought. The moral unity they need cannot be obtained without intensity and integrity of thought.

5 / *Walter Lippmann*

To judge by the public record, Walter Lippmann has been the most influential political thinker in modern America. Writing steadily for more than half a century, he has published many books and articles, reached a much larger audience through editorials and newspaper columns, and altogether offered the public more than ten million words.[11] At least one must hope that his influence has been wider and deeper than may appear offhand in the state of America today. For he has never been merely a journalist commenting on topical matters, but always essentially a political philosopher. As early as *A Preface to Politics* (1913) he began earning wide respect by his concern with basic issues, specifically the challenges to democracy in a revolutionary era. Although he has no doubt often been harried by his duties as a newspaperman, and many of his thousands of editorials and columns are naturally perishable, on the whole he profited from his career in journalism in ways that students especially may appreciate. Without writing down to his audience, he wrote naturally an idiomatic English free from technical jargon. As naturally his daily concerns gave him an intimate acquaintance with political affairs, kept his thought pragmatic, and made it easier for him not to lose himself in cloudy abstractions, the dead language in which too much political theory is couched. At the

11. This rough estimate was made by Clinton Rossiter and James Lare, editors of *The Essential Lippmann*, a large anthology of his writings down to 1962 (Vintage Books). Although I have read several of his books and many of his columns, I am drawing largely on this anthology in my review of his thought.

same time, they kept him more philosophical than the practitioners of political "science." He had much broader interests than they, much more concern with human values, and therefore as much more to say to students. Knowing of no political thinker of our time who has been more consistently relevant, to both immediate and abiding problems, I am pleased to endorse Reinhold Niebuhr's tribute to him as "one of the great educators preparing a young and powerful nation to assume responsibilities commensurate with its power and to exercise them without too much self-righteousness."

Needless to add, a man who has written so many millions of words over so many years has fallen into inconsistencies or contradicted himself. Now and then he has disappointed his admirers by stands he took on specific issues, as he disappointed me when he supported General Eisenhower against Adlai Stevenson in 1952. Although Lippmann is essentially a liberal, or a supporter of what he has been pleased to call "liberal" democracy, there is a conservative in him too. But for the most part his apparent inconsistencies are not basic contradictions. He simply changed his mind on some matters, and was candid about it. He resisted what he himself remarked was the almost irresistible impulse for commentators to say: "That's my story and I stick to it." ("In private intercourse," he added, "anyone who sticks to his story regardless is set down by his friends as slightly batty. In public life he passes for a very strong fellow.") His changing opinions also indicated a capacity for growth not too common in American writers. Above all, they point to the reasons why Lippmann may be ranked with the greater educators of our time. While never complacent, he did not change his mind on matters of principle, remaining firmly committed to the values of liberal democracy. He shifted chiefly in his applications of these principles to a changing society, the age of perpetual crisis he lived through—crises much graver than were anticipated by his early associate Herbert Croly.

A particular reason for his shifts was his judgment about what the country most needed at a given moment. Thus he supported General Eisenhower in 1952 in the belief that only he could unify and quiet the country at a time when it was torn by fierce dissension, weary of the war in Korea. While the good simple soldier would keep sounding off on the need of "dynamic conservatism," spiritual crusades, etc., Lippmann wrote that "this country and the Western world had had all the dynamism, all the innovation, all the crusading that human nature can take." In 1960, however, after eight years of the rhetoric and the torpor of the Eisenhower administration, he wrote that "the country is waiting for another innovator," and expressed his confidence that the new generation would respond to the challenge; "it is not the nation which is old, but only its leaders." This was the challenge proclaimed by John F. Kennedy, and after his death reaffirmed by Lyndon Johnson's crusade for the Great Society, until it was ended by his war in Vietnam. Then in 1968 Richard Nixon exploited the national weariness with dynamism, innovation, and crusading, promising to unify and quiet the country again. And what about today? I do not know what Lippmann's views are at the moment, since I have not kept up with all his articles; but it does not matter. It is enough that in reading him, and incidentally getting insights into the history of our time, students may find themselves asking repeatedly—as I did in rereading him—what about today? Old man Nixon? What is it that a country again torn by fierce dissension most needs at this moment?

But the chief reason for Lippmann's shifts, or possible inconsistencies, has been a basically optimistic faith complicated by a strong sense both of difficulty and of urgency. In 1940 (before Pearl Harbor), he gave a reunion speech to his Harvard class of 1910 in which he dwelt on a theme that he has often returned to: Americans had been persistently taking "the easy way in all things." The victories of Hitler had been made possible by "the lazy, self-indulgent materialism, the amiable, lackadaisical, footless, confused complacency of the free nations of the world." Over the years always critical of the American people, he has had many harsh things to say about them, amplifying possible reasons for despairing of their democracy. Still, he never despaired. He concluded his reunion speech characteristically: "We shall turn from the soft vices in which a civilization decays, we shall return to the stern virtues by which a civilization is made . . . because finally we begin to see that the hard way is the only enduring way." So again one may ask: What about today? Do Americans really see this? Although Lippmann's optimism can be bracing because it is sprung from no easy faith, today it can seem excessive, sometimes sprung from illusion. (Students may read wryly what he wrote in 1945 after the end of the World War: "Never before have the young men of any American generation had spread out before them such a prospect of a long peace. . . . There was never a better time than this to be an American and to be young.") In any case, his diagnosis of problems always remains pertinent. When he concludes, as he often did, that something or other "will be" done, skeptics may translate it into "ought to be" or "still needs to be" done.

More questionable, however, are some of Lippmann's more conservative judgments, for in these he has tended to be more dogmatic. As a pragmatist and a warm admirer of William James (whom he knew when a student at Harvard), he indeed learned early that "the acids of modernity" had corroded the traditional faiths and sanctions; so he remarked that the moralist could no longer command but only persuade, and that his duty was "not to exhort men to be good but to elucidate what the good is." Even so the conservative in him became most apparent in his efforts to discharge this duty.

Thus he has tended to idealize the past, "the virtuous habits" on which the nation was founded, the "majestic story" of its past. In particular students are unlikely to feel either edified or enlightened by what he has said about religion and education. He came to accept the popular conservative doctrine that Christianity provided the foundations of our democracy, and concluded that our inherited liberties almost certainly could not survive the abandonment of "the great central religious tradition of Western civilization." He even asserted that the Bill of Rights "does not come from the people," but "comes from the nature of things" —presumably as ordained by the God whom its authors neglected to mention, and who had himself neglected for eighteen centuries to make clear to his worshippers that they were entitled to such rights. In education Lippmann deplored the neglect of both the religious and the classical heritage of the West, without going into the problems of relevance today. He attacked the "progressive education" of a generation ago, whose excesses were actually confined to relatively few schools, while the great majority carried on the traditional routines that have bored youngsters to this day. In the Eisenhower era, when there was growing alarm over the spread of vice and crime among the youth, the "new vogue of sadism," and other signs of a degeneracy that somehow (page Spiro Agnew) had set in under the administration of a good Republican President, Lippmann proposed increasing both parental responsibility and the disciplinary power of the schools—a power that was hardly weak at the time, and that is still usually exercised in an unenlightened, authoritarian spirit. As for the parents, he expressed a typical confidence that the complacency, self-indulgence, and breakdown of purpose in the 'fifties would be overcome in the 'sixties. How he felt about the student revolt I do not know (and I should add that he may have changed his mind about the views I have cited here); but anyway it was the presumably miseducated youth—not their conservative elders—who rebelled against the complacency and purposelessness.

The more ardent youth will not relish either Lippmann's conservative views about the duties of scholars. He stressed their need of detachment from immediate issues, for the sake of disinterestedness. Their province was theory, not political practice; the past, not the present; and the future only in that they prepared theory for it. In the New Deal era he declared that professors had a particular obligation not to get involved in political parties or movements, above all not to become office holders or political advisers to office holders; those who got into government turned out to be bad politicians or ceased to be scholars. Just because of the crisis the scholar could do no greater work for his nation "than to detach himself from its pre-occupations, refusing to let himself be absorbed by distractions about which, as a scholar, he can do almost nothing." Today, when the single crisis of the Great Depression may seem a slight affair in contrast to the whole set of crises we face, many of us feel rather differently (as maybe Lippmann now does too). For just this reason, however, I think students might give more thought to the possible virtues of detachment, the real need of some disinterestedness. They might consider too Lippmann's dictum that "the true scholar is always radical"—a statement that clearly does not hold true of most scholars today, but may apply to the more philosophical ones. As for professors in government, those of us who oppose the war in Vietnam are not happy about some President Kennedy brought in. Lippmann anticipated Maurice Merleau-Ponty's comment on Sartre, who remained a staunch Communist even though he was quite aware of the brutality of Stalinism: "There has been a political mania among philosophers which has not produced good politics or good philosophy. . . . Instead of combining their virtues, philosophy and politics exchanged their vices; practice became tricky and thought superstitious."

Most controversial was a fundamental belief Lippmann arrived at that endeared him to the "new conservatives" of the 'fifties, but drew the criticism of many liberals. This was his belief in a "higher law" above man, a version of the doctrine of "natural law" that came down from ancient Greece and Rome, which he called "the public philosophy," identified with "the Western tradition of civility," and defended as a universal truth. Natural law is obviously vulnerable to pragmatic or empirical criticism, especially when he implied that it is not man-made, but somehow embedded in "the nature of things." One has only to consider the immense diversity of man-made laws, and then ask what is the authority of these supposedly natural laws when men are unable to agree upon them? Or on the will of God either—presumably their author? The "public philosophy" appears to be a misnomer when Lippmann himself declared that it has not been the reigning philosophy, cannot be popular with the public, and the great problem today is to communicate it to the modern democracies. The doctine of natural law is more plainly vulnerable because it has had profoundly ambiguous consequences, as men interpreted it to suit their different purposes. Conservatives have used it to sanctify property rights, more broadly to defend the *status quo* or whatever seems to them "natural." Liberals have derived from it the doctrine of natural rights, the "inalienable" rights that Jefferson grounded on "the law of nature and nature's God." Among other things, Lippmann himself used it to deny the absolute rights of property and to defend freedom of speech. And it did not help when he added that natural laws are "the laws of a rational order of human society—in the sense that all men, when they are sincerely and lucidly rational, will regard them as self-evident." In the Western tradition of civility, I would not care to question the sincerity or lucidity of critics of his doctrine, or to declare that even the truths dearest to me are "self-evident."

Yet I think there is more to be said on behalf of the doctrine of natural law, which dissident students in particular need to consider. In their indignation over social injustice, they are implicitly appealing to some "higher" principle of justice, above the law as it stands. So I think we all must when we attack the actual laws of a society, especially if we believe in "human rights"—another name for "natural" rights. Although in their talk the youth may echo the sophisticated skepticism of our time, say that all is relative, there are no absolute standards of right and wrong, principles are only cultural prejudices or rationalizations of special interests, and so on, I doubt that they actually think this way when they grow concerned about principles of freedom, equality, justice, or simple humanity. At least they might think hard about the questions raised by Lippmann: "Is there a body of positive principles and precepts which a good citizen cannot deny or ignore?" He came to believe that there was, especially because of his experience of how hard it was to make democracy work in a self-indulgent society devoted to "the easy way"; so he appealed to what he called universal, fundamental truths about rights and duties, "the eternal values of truth, justice, and righteousness." We may question whether such verities are strictly universal or eternal, disagree about the specific commands of any higher laws, yet believe that there are positive principles and sovereign values grounded, not in the laws of nature and its unknown God, but in the demonstrable nature of man as a social, potentially rational being. Or let us say simply that we must hope the youth do not regard Lincoln's Gettysburg Address as just empty rhetoric.

Lippmann's "public philosophy" is more meaningful as a response to the concern he had expressed in a Phi Beta Kappa oration in 1935. "We are unable," he said, "to transmit from our generation to the next a credible and coherent tradition," one in which "the young men can find direction and meaning for their lives." What he said about these young men—now become an older generation—applies more clearly to the student revolt of our time:

> This new generation, to whom we can offer skill rather than wisdom and specialized knowledge without philosophy, is cheated and feels it is cheated if we do not know how to offer it a part in some great enterprise. For these men are young and they are not yet tired and they do not yet prefer comfort and security above all other things. They have courage unspoiled by the commitments of maturity and they have not lived until they have known a duty that transcends personal ambition. They must believe that they are needed. They must enter into an idea that will inform and transfigure their private worlds.

What lay ahead for Lippmann's audience was World War II, the threat of which most Americans refused to face as it approached. He complained repeatedly of President Roosevelt's habit of cleverly manipulating the people, cajoling or soothing them, treating them like children, failing to tell them plainly the hard truth—a failing all too common in democratic politicians, especially in times of crisis.[12] Hence Lippmann paid warmer tribute to the greatness of Winston Churchill as a war leader, apparently "the only statesman in the world who really believes that the people can and should be enabled to understand the war," and from whom, incidentally, the American people first learned the meaning of what happened at Pearl Harbor. Now I suppose our students cannot realize how thrilling his old-fashioned oratory was at a time when Britain stood alone before the triumphant might of Hitler, and how the British responded when he made them no easy promises, offering them only "blood, sweat, toil, and tears," with the compensa-

12. Oldsters may feel wistful over his tribute to Al Smith, an exception who offered the people "honest goods." Many of us were excited by the refreshing candor of Smith's campaign speeches in 1928 when he ran against Herbert Hoover, the apostle of Republican prosperity, who was still calling the indecent farce of Prohibition a "noble experiment." Now that we may appreciate his speeches more because they were not the slick products of ghost-writers, I am unhappy in the thought that most students today have barely heard of him, if at all.

tion, in Lippmann's words, of an "habitual vision of greatness." Yet he might make more meaningful the idea of eternal verities. "In the supreme moments of history," Lippmann wrote during the war, "terms like duty, truth, justice, and mercy—which in our torpid hours are tired words—become the measure of decision." He added that Americans, unhappily, were acting as if they had forgotten them. Once more we may ask: What about today? For the nation's leaders these terms are clearly not the measure of decision, but how much do they mean to Americans at large? To the youth?

Of the many specific problems of American democracy that Lippmann took up—too many for me to consider here—a major one was public opinion, which he was among the first political thinkers to study closely and realistically. (Among his mentors was Freud.) As early as the 'twenties he was saying that the public, which in the accepted theory of popular government determined the course of events, was a "mere phantom." By now sophisticated students distrust the traditional talk about popular sovereignty, the will of the people, and the majority that always rules, and they take for granted the notorious limitations of voters, but they are still likely to give the traditional answers: we have only to educate the people, make them better informed, get them more interested in the issues, maybe get them to read the right newspapers. They illustrate Lippmann's remark that we do not yet have "a body of intellectual and moral habits, customs, and attitudes to fit the realities of modern popular government." He flatly insisted that while popular education was indispensable, it was necessarily insufficient; the public would never be well informed and intelligently interested in all that concerned it. Although he deplored the tastes the press catered to, it was obviously unreasonable to expect the "sovereign citizen" to have an adequate understanding of the multifarious problems of modern society, or to take an active interest in all of them. In 1925 he stated the stark political reality still obscured by popular assumptions:

> We must assume that the members of a public will not anticipate a problem much before its crisis has become obvious, nor stay with the problem long after its crisis is past. They will not know the antecedent events, will not have seen the issue as it developed, will not have thought out or willed a program, and will not be able to predict the consequences of acting on that program. We must assume as a theoretically fixed premise of popular government that normally men as members of a public will not be well informed, continuously interested, nonpartisan, creative, or executive. We must assume that a public is inexpert in its

curiosity, intermittent, that it discerns only gross distinctions, is slow to be aroused and quickly diverted; that, since it acts by aligning itself, it personalizes whatever it considers, and is interested only when events have been melodramatized as a conflict.

The public will arrive in the middle of the third act and will leave before the last curtain, having stayed just long enough perhaps to decide who is the hero and who the villain of the piece. . . .

What, then, do we do about it? So far as I know, Lippmann never gave a clear or consistent answer, for what seems to me a sufficient reason: this side of utopia, there is no clear solution. In effect he banked as we all must on efforts to educate the public, a task to which he has devoted his long life as both journalist and political philosopher. In these efforts he himself learned a good deal, but chiefly about the difficulties of the problem. Long before David Riesman he was writing about the lonely crowd as he contemplated the huge city masses, "masses without roots," "crowds without convictions," who were "the spiritual proletariat of the modern age." In these masses the individual became anonymous, faceless, lacking personal autonomy, seeking refuge among his fellows, but remaining a prey to suspicion and fear. "He trusts nobody and nothing, not even himself. . . . He sees only confusion in himself and conspiracies in other men." One might add that today he may appear to be more confident, even aggressive, when politicians tell him that he represents middle America, but as a voter he has not become either more trusting or more trustworthy. Early in his career Lippmann was commenting on the apathy of the "phantom public," indicated by the decline in the proportion who bothered to vote, which political scientists have now taken to analyzing through surveys or polls. He observed that the voter lacking time, interest, or understanding of the problems of the day would not have a better public opinion because he was exhorted to express his opinion more often, but would "simply be more bewildered, more bored, and more ready to follow along."

Further difficulties were developments in Lippmann's lifetime that students now take as a matter of course, and so may not realize are new forms of corruption of the democratic process. One was the rise of the publicity expert, who by "scientific" methods sells ideas or images to the public. Some time after him came the ghost-writer, another means of creating a "synthetic public man." (Once upon a time, children, the leaders of America wrote their own speeches.) Now that the systematic manipulation of public opinion has become routine, Americans appear to be growing aware of its phoniness, but without realizing what a gross indignity it is, or how cynical an insult to them. Lippmann stated the simple truth by old-fashioned standards: "To act as if the people had to be manipulated is to deny the very virtues on which rests the hope of democracy." With the rise of television he expressed the now familiar complaints about how this "mighty instrument of education" had become in fact "the creature, the servant, and indeed the prostitute of merchandising," another form of manipulation. There is only to add that the TV merchandising methods that helped to sell Eisenhower to the public in his campaigns have become more brazen.

On the growth of modern technology in general and its whole impact on American democracy, Lippmann was not a major prophet, any more than were most of the thinkers of his generation. From his early writings we get on this score chiefly perspectives on a bygone America that had only faint premonitions, if any, of what lay in store for it, and that may now give a more vivid sense of lost opportunities. Thus before World War I he thought he saw "an unmistakable tendency to put men at the center of politics instead of machinery and things," and also "evidence to prove that we are turning . . . to the creation of finer environments." In the New Deal era he thought that in order to preserve freedom and provide individual security, the government should and would discourage the concentration of business, and deprive big business of "corporate privileges and other forms of legal and economic advantage which make it bigger than on economic grounds it needs to be." He was also confident that better understanding would make it easier to live with our machine technology, for its intrinsic ideals were making obsolete "the old distinction between public and private interest." Likewise he was confident that in the days ahead corporation executives would be held up to a new moral standard, would put their public responsibility ahead of money-making, and no man would ever be allowed again to make as much money as John D. Rockefeller had. He anticipated a future in which "to make a fortune will be considered as improper for the head of a big business as for the President of the United States." Since I still make out not the faintest intimations of such a future, in a land that today sports billionaires without social conscience to speak of, I would add only that on the side Lyndon Johnson and Richard Nixon too made fortunes, with the help of their political connections, in ways that I assume were quite legal and proper by American standards.

Yet Lippmann kept alert to the changes taking place, and his comments on them still have more than historical interest. Before World War I he also wrote: "Modern industry was created by the profiteer, and here it is, the great fact of our lives, blackening our cities, fed with the lives of children, a tyrant over men and women, turning out enormous stocks of produce, good, bad, and horrible." Even many liberals today might consider his conclusion radical: "Private commercialism is an antiquated, feeble, mean, and unimaginative way of dealing with the possibilities of modern industry." He liked big government no more than big business, foreseeing before the Russian Revolution that socialism had the seeds of a "great bureaucratic tyranny," but he attacked the conservative doctrine that the increasing activity of the government and interference with business were "creeping socialism," *ipso facto* undemocratic. At the outset of his career he stated the difficult position that liberals still have to defend:

> It is perfectly true that that government is best which governs least. It is equally true that that government is best which provides most. The first truth belongs to the eighteenth century; the second to the twentieth. Neither of them can be neglected in our attitude toward the state. Without the Jeffersonian distrust of the police we might easily grow into an impertinent and tyrannous collectivism; without a vivid sense of the possibilities of the state we abandon the supreme instrument of civilization. The two theories need to be held together, yet clearly distinguished.

In the New Deal era Lippmann proceeded to draw up "the agenda of liberalism" in terms of "the logic of the social readjustment required by the industrial revolution." Its method was that which the country was in fact adopting, but which lacked a magniloquent name or philosophy; he called it "free collectivism." It was collectivistic in that the state was recognizing its responsibility for maintaining a healthy economy and in various ways doing more to promote the public welfare, while refusing any longer to identify liberty with "absence of purpose in government." To the many who feared that we could not meet all our public needs without sacrificing freedom and individualism, he answered that we had to meet them in order to preserve real freedom and the values of individualism and self-reliance: "We must not put upon the individual person burdens that are greater than he can by self-reliance carry." While the old conservative slogans still obscure the fact that basically this has become the accepted national policy, he might be depressed by some statements in his early writings about the proper business of a statesman, which among other things was "to provide finer opportunities for the expression of human impulses—to surround children, youth, and age with homes and schools, cities and countryside that shall be stocked with interest and the chance for generous activity."

Much other unfinished business includes the challenge he laid down in
1935:

> We must answer the question that young men put to us. We must
> tell them that they will have to manage the social order. We must call
> them to the study, not warn them away from it, of how to achieve the
> healthy balance of the well-ordered commonwealth. We must call them
> to the task of preserving the integrity of our civilization as against pro-
> letarianism and plutocracy and the fatal diseases of concentrated power
> and concentrated wealth. We must call them to the defense of freedom,
> now imperiled throughout the world, by showing them not only its value
> but the method of its defense. We must dedicate them by rededicating
> ourselves to the promise of American life which is that men can govern a
> state in order to enlarge and to preserve the rights of men.

For the rest, Lippmann always had a finger on the pulse of a changing government. As early as the 'twenties he worried over the increasing power of the Presidency, the decline in the power and prestige of
Congress. At the same time, he recognized the complication raised
by the habitual irresponsibility of Congress, in its service of local interests and pressure groups. In times of crisis "only strong national
leadership by the President" could keep Congress responsible and representative; though this too was complicated in the American system of
government because the President served as not only chief magistrate
but leader of his party. With the enormous expansion of government,
he worried too over the loss of effective control of the bureaucracy, including the Pentagon. Ten years ago he noted an alarming development that has yet to alarm most Americans: "The talkativeness of
American military men, most of them reading speeches written by professional speech writers who are paid by the government, is an international scandal." But chiefly I would emphasize his acute awareness
from the outset of the basic problems of the modern world: in statesmanship the gap, wider than ever before, "between what we know and
what we need to know"; the difficulty of following the method of
reason when "we are unsettled to the very roots of our being," and
there are "no precedents to guide us, no wisdom that wasn't made for
a simpler age"; the need not only of better government but of a humanistic democratic culture, the work of educators and publicists,
scientists and artists; both the need and the difficulty of retaining firm
principles when the traditional faiths corroded by "the acids of modernity" cannot be restored by any effort to turn our backs on the advance
of science, the spread of rationalism, and the other secular conditions
of modernity; and always the recognition that "the war for liberty

never ends," its values have constantly to be defended against threats both old and new.

At the end I would therefore reconsider the basically optimistic faith that Lippmann retained in the face of these difficulties, throughout a period of perpetual crisis. One of its tokens was his defense of our two political parties, alike inglorious in their habit of compromising when not betraying the national principles they profess in keynote orations. He cited Herbert Croly to the effect that they were virtually indestructible because they were low-grade organisms, which had neither a brain nor a heart; like worms, they could keep on wiggling if cut in half and somehow grow together again. Nevertheless he argued that our unprincipled parties achieved the result that the authors of the Constitution had hoped to achieve by having no political parties; they subdued "partisan fury and factionalism" by compromising enough to embrace a medley of liberals and conservatives, stay close to something like a national consensus. Hence it was better that they fought over relatively superficial issues instead of basic differences in principle, which might split the nation. Lippmann ventured the belief that "the best elections are those which are not momentous." Today, when the issues are clearly momentous, I am not disposed to applaud such elections, any more than I did the campaign between Nixon and Humphrey. I do not rejoice either in the prevalent tendency of both parties to move toward the center, where moderation is too seldom backed by vigor, not to mention high principle or firm purpose. If, as Lippmann remarked, our system has kept us muddling *through*, I doubt that we can any longer afford so much muddling.

Yet I would not really care to see the parties split sharply over American imperialism, the war in Indochina, civil rights, the black ghettoes, and other issues that agitate students, and might make partisan politics still uglier and more dangerous. It would not be well if the center failed to hold or fell apart. Because I welcome the more radical tendencies of students, short of those who want to start a revolution or a guerrilla war, I think they may need to be reminded of some historical truths that supported Lippmann's faith. As he remarked, democracies with party systems have outlived all other forms of government in the modern world. Having lived through world wars, he could appreciate more than the youth the seeming anomaly that these complex modern societies, "where the old loyalties are most completely dissolved, where authority has so little prestige, where moral codes are held in such small esteem," have nevertheless proved more impervious to the strains of war and revolution than have more traditional countries, which have taken to the various forms of totalitarianism and dictatorship. As for America, he observed that there are countries where government is more efficient, honest, and truly representative, but that "there has as yet been no other country in the history of the world where so many people, so diverse in their origins and in their interests, have on so vast a territory governed themselves so long and preserved their freedom." To my mind no political thinker of our time has contributed more to the maintenance of this achievement, and hopes of prolonging it, than has Walter Lippmann.

VIII

THE PORTENTS OF

THE COUNTER CULTURE

1 / The Springs of the Counter Culture

T HE AIM OF A UNIVERSITY, said Woodrow Wilson early in our century, should be to make young gentlemen as unlike their fathers as possible. Despite its antique flavor, his statement might still serve as a manifesto. The universities are no more dedicated to this aim than they ever were; while turning out proportionately more professionals, with more expertise than the fathers, these are mostly prepared to serve the interests of the fathers. It is again the student rebels who in effect are proclaiming such an aim. While they scarcely aspire to be young gentlemen (and how they would have shocked Wilson by their dress, speech, and behavior!) they certainly do not want to be like most adults. They have different ideas about not only education and politics but race, class, sex, art, religion, and culture in general. Thereby they have to some extent been educating the more liberal of their fathers, but antagonizing the great majority. Except for the division between blacks and whites, it is the deepest of the divisions that split the nation.

Now, the conflict of the generations is of course another old story. The fathers should remember all the alarm over the younger generation after World War I, in the era of the flapper. The youth might be told that student revolts and youth movements have been common in Europe, flower children were wandering around Germany making music even before World War I; and it might do them good to study these movements, which like as not led to fascism.¹ Yet the story in America today is again by no means merely the latest chapter in an old story. It is significantly new in the extent of the alienation of the rebels, the depth of their anger against the sins of the fathers, the outspokenness that has made "bullshit" the most popular word on the campus, the pervasiveness and strength of "un-American" tendencies—altogether, the various forms of dissent that justify Theodore Roszak's study of it as a "counter culture." It is highly relevant because it represents immediately a kind of crisis of affluence, or revolt against the "consumer paradise," but more profoundly a revolt against a technological society, animated by a concern for neglected human values, a quest for self-realization through freedom, love, joy, and communion. Unlike most counter-revolutions of the past, it is not an effort to return to an idealized past but is seeking to develop new styles of life. Meanwhile it is helping to combat the common fallacy that modern technology is neutral, something that "we" too often abuse but could use for wholly good purposes. Obviously we could make far better use of it, and cannot simply blame it for the follies and evils men have always been prone to, but as obviously our technology has developed its own system of values, imposed a whole way of life that might be called an ideology. It is so formidable because we cannot do with it just what we please.

Although Roszak is critical of the counter culture, he sees in it something like "the saving vision our endangered civilization requires," or even our only hope: the dissenting young people not only merit but "desperately require" our consideration as the matrix of the radical discontent and innovation that alone can save us. I should say at once that I am more critical of it than he, and in particular less confident of its promise of "a new heaven and a new earth," a splendor that will wholly discredit the claims of technical expertise. We are again dealing with a minority of the young people, which is significant because it has been attracting an increasing number of thoughtful students, but which leaves cold when not hostile the majority, who still aspire to a good professional berth or conventional status. Always the dissenters have to contend with not only the powers that be but public hostility. Because I think most of them are basically reasonable I am troubled by the growing suspicion that what lies in store for the youth movement is not so much the common fate of petering out, like all the fashions of the past, as a radical disillusionment of its more ardent spirits. Then

1. A good text is a Commentary Report on "Student Revolts" by Walter Laqueur, published by *Commentary Magazine* (1969).

they might settle down to the ways of the fathers, as many young radicals did in the past; or their idealism might sour into cynicism, denying them the satisfactions of complacence; or it might lead them to join the many drop-outs from society; or they might settle for various modes of extremism, conclude that nothing but violence will work. In any event our society would be the worse for their failure.

Sympathetic observers have noted, like Roszak, a tragic aspect of the revolt of the youth. Often they have to pay a heavy price for their bold dissent, most obviously in their resistance to the draft. Despite their common appearance of feeling very superior, they may suffer as well from feelings of insecurity and anxiety, for their sense of discontinuity may leave them no firm ground to stand on, no coherence in their experience except immediate relevance, and their revolt may force them to live beyond their emotional means. All who are resolutely saying No to their elders, resisting the demands for conformity required by professional success, and themselves demanding that our society practice the ideals it preaches are assuming responsibilities for which they are not prepared by age and experience. Although the dissenters seem to me by no means so immature as their critics say, nor the whole youth movement a mere "children's crusade," they are not and cannot be expected to be thoroughly mature, or simply to know enough yet to create an adequate counter culture. They might even feel oppressed—not just gratified—when they are told that they represent the only hope for our society. I repeat George Wald's comment: "What we are up against is a generation that is by no means sure it has a future." The ardent Students for a Democratic Society said as much in the course of their Port Huron Statement of 1962: "We may be the last generation in the experiment with living."[2]

And so, like it or not, they need us—those of their elders, that is, who sympathize with their basic aims. Most plainly they need our support in some of their causes, such as their opposition to the war in Indochina. But they also need the aid of our critical judgment in efforts to distinguish what is valid, significant, and promising from what is extrava-

---

2. A graduate assistant told me of an especially disturbing example, her freshman composition class. These were ordinary or "average" students, since the better students were relieved of the requirement of taking an elementary course, and they were by no means radicals either. When she stimulated them to write freely by having them keep personal journals, they responded by often writing about their uncertainties and anxieties about the future—not so much their professional careers as the kind of world they would have to live in. During my many years of teaching I encountered no such widespread feeling among students, not even in the Great Depression.

gant, ephemeral, and unwholesome in the natural confusions of their dissenting culture. We have a responsibility, however embarrassing, to speak to as well as for the youth. Out of respect for them we need to express our judgments tactfully, but I think firmly too, maybe even to saying Bullshit! to some of the rant of Jerry Rubin and Abbie Hoffman. They cannot afford to be taken in by Abbie's clownish talk about "revolution for the hell of it," or his boast "Confusion is mightier than the sword!"

At any rate, I am here attempting a patient, dispassionate critical survey of the counter culture. First I should again confess that I am speaking from well behind the generation gap. While I feel on firm grounds when judging the political beliefs and activities of the youth, I do not when judging some of the popular culture that turns them on, perhaps too easily or modishly. When they say they want to "be with it," I may wonder what "it" means; and though I suspect they may not have a clear idea either (any more than the hero of the film *Easy Rider* appears to when he says at the climax "We blew it"), I know that I lack an intimate understanding or appreciation of their enthusiasms. As an example of my difficulties, amid possible extravagances, I cite the Beatles.

"Has anyone been able completely to ignore *Sgt. Pepper's Lonely Hearts Club Band?*" Richard Poirier began an article on "Learning from the Beatles." I had been able to do so until I read his piece. At first I had been repelled by them as they rose to fame under the influence of Elvis Presley, exploited their bushy hair, sent teenagers into the aisles screaming in hysteria, and began making millions. By now I recognize their genuine gaiety, light-hearted wit, love of song, affectionate satire of the sentimental songs of the past, and in general their rare blend of boyishness and sophistication. Charmingly the boys from Liverpool sang "A pretty nurse is selling poppies from a tray/ And tho' she feels as if she's in a play,/ She is anyway." I am troubled, however, by the frequent reminders of drugs or invitations to "trips" in their songs, and am still repelled by the vulgarity of some of their publicity (as when John Lennon had himself photographed in the nude with his wife, incidentally revealing himself as a most unprepossessing hairy male). In particular I do not see in them the "gestations of genius" that Poirier celebrates. "No one is ever in danger of reading too much into the lyrics of their songs," he writes, but to my mind he proceeds to illustrate the danger, which is common when intellectuals discover "genius" in popular culture. So he reads "the history of this century" into the *Sgt. Pepper* album. "Nothing less is being claimed by these songs than that the Beatles now exist not merely as a phenomenon of entertainment but as a force of historical consequence." Well, I doubt it (apart from the fact that they have since broken up); but maybe so, as I hear that they have been the biggest success in the history of show business. I am willing to let readers judge for themselves how much truth there is in the large claims Poirier makes.

Similarly with rock music in general. While in its early days I found it fearfully monotonous, much inferior to the old-time jazz I loved in my youth, as it developed and broadened I began to understand why young people got a comparable pleasure from it, and to appreciate especially the feelings of communion it stirs in them. But it raises another problem. Sophisticated students complain of the corruption of their culture by business interests rushing in to exploit it, opportunists springing up with flashy imitations. The problem is, how does one tell the "real" thing? Enthusiasts naturally have difficulty putting it into words; lovers of the old-time jazz know that one must feel the difference. As one who knows too little about rock music and contemporary jazz, I should merely remark that here is another difficulty besetting young people seeking self-realization through a culture of their own. In a highly commercialized society, quick to exploit fads and to counterfeit spontaneity, they will constantly have to distinguish the phoney from the genuine expression of their thought and feeling.

But now to get down to the basic problems of the counter culture that require no special initiation. In the spirit of Jacques Ellul, who insists that modern technology has become wholly autonomous and completely dominates our culture, Theodore Roszak rejects the demand for "a balanced view of science and technology," which he says amounts to "something like a con game which the technocracy plays with the general public," to buttress its rule. The notion of balance "implies the existence of well-defined values which can be brought to bear to distinguish a desirable from an undesirable achievement," whereas "the supposition that such values exist in our culture is misleading in the extreme." Nevertheless I am persisting in an effort to take a balanced view. There plainly are such values in our culture, to which the dissenting youth themselves are appealing. They did not originate these values either, but picked them up from our cultural tradition; countless critics have been asserting them ever since the rise of industrialism. So are many scientists today (as Roszak might find out by reading the *Bulletin of the Atomic Scientists*). Criticism of our "progress" is so widespread, indeed, that it becomes necessary to state the obvious: out of science and technology have come many real goods, achievements that we all find desirable. No more than the rest of us are the dissenting youth scorning all the products of modern technology, for among many other things they owe to it their motorcycles or cars, contraceptive pills, electric guitars, rock festivals, and other elements of their counter culture. The many who are not earning their own living may need to be reminded of their obvious indebtedness because their old man pays the bills.

I would also qualify Roszak's statement that the more discerning of the youth see that "building the good society is not primarily a social, but a psychic task." It is true that the dissenters are less prone to ideology than to what is now called privatism. They might invoke the perennial wisdom of prophets who appealed to the hearts of men, sought primarily moral or spiritual rather than social or political reform. Such conservatives as Joseph Wood Krutch have asked whether our civilization might not be better "if more people had thought less about how to improve society and more about how to improve themselves." Still, preachers in the West have been working on the hearts of men for two thousand years, preaching different gospels, but alike without making most people notably more virtuous or spiritual; on the record social and political reformers have been somewhat more effective, at least in the eyes of those who cherish democratic principles. For Roszak's "not-but" I would as usual substitute the statement that building the good society is both a social and a psychic task; and I would not assign definite priorities. As for the rebellious youth taken as a whole, they see it both ways. Many seem interested primarily in the psyche or the self they are trying to express and fulfill, and so have made much of Eros and psychedelic experience. Many others are attacking the Establishment or the System, seeking to improve their society. But while all are in their different ways rebelling against accepted ways that inhibit their personal development, they are alike seeking community, or development as social beings.

Hence Roszak makes out a principle of unity underlying an apparent opposition within the dissenting culture: on the one hand the beats, hippies, and other bohemian drop-outs; on the other hand the activists of the New Left. What unites them he calls "personalism." He finds an "extraordinary" measure of it in New Left activism since its beginnings, as expressed in the Port Huron Statement of the SDS:

> We are aware that to avoid platitudes we must analyze the concrete conditions of social order. But to direct such an analysis we must use the guideposts of basic principles. Our own social values involve conceptions of human beings, human relationships, and social systems.

We regard men as infinitely precious and possessed of unfulfilled capacities for reason, freedom, and love. . . . We oppose the depersonalization that reduces human beings to the status of things. If anything, the brutalities of the twentieth century teach that means and ends are intimately related, that vague appeals to 'posterity' cannot justify the mutilations of the present. . . .

Loneliness, estrangement, isolation describe the vast distance between man and man today. These dominant tendencies cannot be overcome by better personnel management, nor by improved gadgets, but only when a love of man overcomes the idolatrous worship of things by man.

This statement, which I consider admirable, may seem less "extraordinary" to those who recognize that there are fairly "well-defined values" in our cultural tradition. Any good humanist or liberal can accept it, as I suppose hippies would too. The questions arise over the means to the ideal end of realizing men's "unfulfilled capacities for reason, freedom, and love."

Then the differences between the two camps become more marked. The way of the hippies could at best set an example of freedom and love, but it hardly offers hope of improving our society, even before it became corrupted by publicity and attracted mostly teenagers who were simply self-indulgent, like many of their elders in suburbia. The yippies who have tried to bridge the two camps have only confused the issues; although Abbie Hoffman's showmanship can be amusing and infectious, as a sort of mini-radicalism, it seems to me basically irresponsible. But the radicals on the New Left, who are wholly serious, raise more difficult issues. Many could be said to suffer from a kind of Edipus complex: they must first of all kill their fathers—the liberals. I shall accordingly return to them at the end in a reconsideration of the liberal credo. Meanwhile I am attempting a "balanced" survey of their role in the counter culture.

2 / *The New Left*

WHILE MANY PANICKY CONSERVATIVES are still obsessed by the notion that the young radical movement is Communist-led or Communist-inspired, its novelty has become a commonplace in serious thought. There are of course some Communists in the movement, others who echo the old revolutionary slogans about the "workers," but few who look to the Soviet Union for either leadership or inspiration. Rebellious American students differ from European ones most obviously in that they draw much less on a radical or revolutionary tradition, if only because such a tradition has never been so strong here as in Europe. Mostly offspring of the prosperous middle class, they do not fit into the orthodox Marxist scheme because it is they—not the workers—who are the chief enemies of the bourgeois in America. For the same reason those who dream of an alliance with the workers look absent-minded, since they are appealing to the least revolutionary proletariat in the world. In their calls for "participatory democracy" and "more power to the people" they likewise tend to forget that most of the American people are dead set against them. By "the people" they mean in effect young people like themselves.

As activists, they might do better, indeed, if they had behind them the discipline of a radical tradition, or even an ideology. As it is, they have no clear, consistent program. They are positive enough about what they are against, but much less so about their goals, beyond generalities about justice, freedom, and brotherhood. Unable to agree about specific means either, they are likely to split, as the SDS recently did, and are exposed to the seductions of anarchism or nihilism. Yet they have also profited by not having a definite ideology, or blueprints for utopia. They are less prone to revolutionary clichés than their European counterparts, and generally more realistic, flexible, and resourceful. If they often talk loosely about the Establishment, they at least have an eye on the various power establishments—military, economic, political, academic—that have been working together closely enough to justify their protests. They are not so clear as Roszak suggests, I think, in their recognition of "technocracy" as the main enemy, but most recognize that it is not simply that old ogre "capitalism." Since America is the most advanced technological society, they have been able to see more clearly than European students the limitations and the abuses of professional expertise, the tendencies to dehumanization and depersonalization, the reign of things and thinginess, and other such affronts to human dignity. And their revolt is more admirable because except for the draft they had no such serious personal grievances as rebels have had in Europe, but rather had far better financial or professional prospects—better too than American students ever had in the past (including the generation in my own tame youth). As an unregenerate old liberal I remain critical of them, especially of tendencies that do not foster "reason, freedom, and love"; but first I am pleased to state the case for them.

The most thorough, systematic statement of this case that I know of is Charles Hampden-Turner's *Radical Man*. A social scientist, he is unlike most of his fellows in that he is very much concerned with human values and value-judgments, specifically with man's capacities for "psycho-social development," which are neglected when man is studied as a product of his class, occupation, role, status, culture, etc. In studying these capacities he sets up such scales as sensitivity of perception, concern for personal identity, competence in acting for oneself or assuming leadership, willingness to commit oneself and take risks, tolerance or ability to "bridge the distance to others," self-confirming and self-transcending capacities, and readiness to admit complexity. On these scales conservatives generally rank low.[3] He sees the essence of conservatism as not so much a fear of change—its champions welcome technological change—as a limited capacity for psycho-social development, a set of attitudes and beliefs that hamper or warp this development. He cites Silvan Tomkins on the basic difference between radical and conservative man:

> Is man the measure, an end in himself, an active thinking, desiring, loving force in nature? Or must man realize himself, attain his full stature only through a struggle toward, participation in, conformity to, a norm, a measure, an ideal essence basically independent of man?

Technological thinking, governed by "objective" norms and the needs of the system, accordingly tends by its nature to be conservative, while Republicans lose their fear of government when it serves the needs of technology rather than of people.

By these standards Soviet Communism is conservative. Likewise members of the "Old Left" rank low on Hampden-Turner's scales, together with extreme Rightists and religious Fundamentalists; they tend to be as narrow, rigid, dogmatic, and authoritarian as the stereotyped radical. The New Left, however, ranks consistently high. Our young radicals are generally not only bright and gifted but by no means so unbalanced as they are reputed to be. In our author's words, "Student

3. Hampden-Turner's book includes many tables that the general reader is likely to skim or skip, and can afford to. Although he perhaps puts too much trust in measurements, the important point is that he has thoroughly documented his conclusions by the findings of psychologists and other social scientists. Lest readers be scared off by this reference to his technical apparatus, I should add that his book is very readable, uncommonly lively and witty. Restive students majoring in the social sciences might enjoy especially his introductory chapter, a devastating critique of these sciences, the accepted premises and methodologies that drastically limit their human relevance—except for the purposes of conservative man.

leftists are more independent *and* more intimate, more liable to rebel *and* to participate in egalitarian relationships, more sensitive to beauty *and* more aroused by cruelty and ugliness, more impulsive *and* more intellectually efficient, more flexible in the suspension of their basic premises *and* more fiercely committed to those ethical principles that have survived a thousand suspensions to be constantly rediscovered and reaffirmed." More highly developed than conservative students, they are naturally more concerned over their further development as persons, more aroused by the threats to it that do not bother the docile vocationalists on the campus, the potential organization men in business and government. And their activism itself is a mode of personal development. Even professors who deplore their tactics might grant that it is a more stimulating, mature mode than the conventional "activities" on the campus—football games, rahrah gatherings, fraternities, proms, etc.—by which students are supposed to become well-rounded or smooth, and in which the leftists take little interest.

Their indifference to such "normal" interests has strengthened the popular impression that they are not good democratic Americans. They are of course un-American by conservative standards (not to mention all the patriots who are now aggressively wearing or flaunting American flags). They are not much interested either in the forms of democracy as taught in the schools, and may have too little respect for democratic processes, forget that they themselves in effect constitute an elite. Yet they typically consider themselves good democrats, and for good reasons. They have behind them the tradition of Jefferson and Lincoln in regarding democracy as not merely a matter of political forms and structures, checks and balances, but a way of realizing ideals of freedom, equality, and justice. However questionable their own ways, they are clearly more devoted to these ideals than are most conservative students, who have learned them by rote but appear little concerned, if aware at all, about how far America has fallen short of them in practice. I assume the leftists would also approve of Hampden-Turner's approach to democracy as first and foremost "a developed state of mind and a climate of relationships between citizens"—a climate that nurtures self-realization and self-expression. Here too they have behind them old American tradition, the fond belief that democracy makes for better men—free, independent, and self-reliant. Together, their activism and their idealism should not have seemed strange in a land that once fought a revolution to make good a Declaration of Independence, and then wrote a Bill of Rights.

At least they certainly made the student leftists effective, giving them an influence out of all proportion to their numbers, which might remind us that radical changes have always been initiated by small minorities. On the national scene the conspicuous example remains their early demonstrations against the war in Vietnam, which helped to make it unpopular among millions of young people, eventually safer for politicians to oppose it. However unfavorable, the increasing publicity they got testified to the stir they were causing. On the campus they aroused students, faculty, and even administrations, specifically by their protests against such unseemly activities as the secret research universities were doing for the military, but more significantly by spreading the realization that the universities badly needed stirring up. At Berkeley Nathan Glazer, who was highly critical of the Free Speech Movement that inaugurated the student revolt, later noted that "a great wave of energy has been released here," and that it had produced "prodigies of work—in organization, in research, in writing"; professors were startled to discover how much potential energy in students had been untapped by the normal academic routines. At Columbia the Cox Commission likewise reported that the crisis there had been "a creative source of renewal." Out of all this came various specific reforms, but again more significantly a change in the whole atmosphere of the university, above all in the attitudes of the large and still growing number of moderate students who have been aroused by the radicals, and sometimes have even elected one as president of their student government (as they have in my own conservative university). By now the spectrum from radical to liberal is filled by so many shades of shifting opinion that it has become hard to identify clearly a "New Left." But the many students who sympathize with its basic aims, no less because they would not call themselves radicals, also tend to be more highly developed than conservative students.

The successes of the activists complicate the issues raised by their often lawless tactics, such as their seizure of buildings. Since I am all for civil, reasonable discussion of differences, I should first grant that they had some good excuses for their insistence on "confrontations." "Come, let us reason together," we say; but then let us be honest and admit that reasonable appeals may not get very far with the powers that be, and that maintaining civility may be less important than combatting injustice. (Jesus himself was not very civil when he drove the money-changers out of the temple.) At Columbia, for instance, the SDS did at first petition peacefully, but to no effect—the administration ignored them. President Grayson Kirk summed up its authoritarian attitude in brushing off a group of students who confronted him: "You're only transitory birds, and therefore should have no voice." Only when the students seized some buildings did they succeed in making their voice heard, then chiefly by the faculty, and only after they had been bloodied by the police Kirk called in did a new administration try seriously to reason with them together. Likewise other universities began to listen to their legally powerless students only when they demonstrated their power to disrupt academic routines. Now that administrations have grown more conciliatory there is less excuse for confrontations, but students still have enough legitimate grievances to be impatient with mere petitions. They may appeal to the authority of Graham Wallas, who long ago wrote that "in order to make men think, one must begin by making them feel."

Similarly in Washington President Nixon made a point of ignoring the big peace demonstrations, announcing that he would not be influenced by them in the slightest, or in other words that he would simply ignore the opinions of all these ardent young Americans. Not until four students were martyred at Kent State did he begin to listen to them, or rather to make a pathetic effort to get them to listen to him, later to tell them that there really wasn't a generation gap. As understandable therefore is the impatience of many with normal democratic processes, which are always slow and uncertain. Indignant over Lyndon Johnson's war in Vietnam, students helped to get rid of him by their enthusiastic efforts on behalf of Senator Gene McCarthy; but their reward was the disgraceful Democratic National Convention in Chicago, where many activists were clubbed by Mayor Daley's uniformed thugs—to the approval of most Americans. Then democratic processes gave them a sorry choice between Richard Nixon and Hubert Humphrey. With Nixon's victory, they faced the prospect of four or even eight years of a President who manifestly had no sympathy with them or their ideals, depended for his support on a "great silent majority" that was more plainly hostile to them. His most trusted adviser was John Mitchell, to whose way of thinking student activists were on the forefront of the "liberal Communists." When Spiro Agnew swung into action he had worse words for them, including "paranoiacs," and worked busily (to loud applause from the silent majority) to fulfill the prophecy of Norman Mailer: "There is a shit-storm coming." Granted that this is not the whole truth about the Nixon administration, we should remember that many of the more radical students have a desperate sense of the urgency of our problems, and that all of them have reason for anxiety as a generation by no means sure it has a future.[4]

President Nixon brought all these issues to a head when he announced the invasion of Cambodia. Immediately students all over the land began gathering in spontaneous demonstrations, which involved some violence—the hurling of rocks, smashing of windows, burning of buildings—but also resistance to efforts by the SDS to take over the leadership. The spontaneity emphasized how intensely the students felt, how outraged moderate, non-violent ones were too by Nixon's extension of the war and the sanctimonious manner in which he justified it. There followed the Kent State affair, with polls that revealed that most Americans blamed the students, not the National Guardsmen who shot them down (a verdict that would later be officially confirmed by a grand jury, under the supervision of a special prosecutor who in an interview said the Guardsmen "should have shot all the troublemakers"). For young people the usual national chorus that went up about the need of maintaining Law and Order only made it plainer that there is no sanctity about the law as it is administered in America, or about an order that maintains flagrant social injustice. Even so most of the indignant students set to work by democratic processes, sending delegations to Washington to interview Congressmen, organizing campaigns to support peace candidates. By these campaigns they succeeded chiefly in arousing more public hostility; so again one may wonder. What will become of these ardent students if their efforts to work through democratic processes are frustrated? Their anxieties confirmed? Their emotional resources drained away?

Meanwhile the developments among the more radical students have not been heartening. They bring up the reasons for deploring their lawless tactics, beginning with a basic one suggested in the Port Huron Statement: "means and ends are intimately related." Violent means are not likely to promote ideal ends of "reason, freedom, and love," any more than they did in the Soviet Union. They are more likely to breed more violence, as they have of late. What I have been saying about the young radicals so far applies chiefly to the early years of the New Left. Today it calls for considerable qualification.

Among the difficulties in surveying the student revolt is the rapid

4. Repelled as many of us are by Nixon's mentor John Mitchell, let us try to imagine the anger and disgust of student leftists who read his complacent pronouncement on the state of America: "We have today in this nation more equality in the law, more honesty in politics, more ethics in science, more people employed and less people hungry, and more religious dedication to the problems of society than at any other period in our history."

change that makes it necessary to keep an eye on dates. Whether a statement was made in 1962, 1966, or 1970 may make a considerable difference. Thus in 1966 Tom Hayden of the SDS, who was largely responsible for the Port Huron Statement of 1962, still wrote soberly of the difficulty of "finding a basis for radical work when there is very little hope for positive change within a lifetime," as "little belief in utopia," and radicalism was "unable to bank fully on history or morality"— problems that were wearing down the strength of many of its young disciples; so its "realism and sanity" could be grounded "in nothing more than the ability to face whatever comes." Meanwhile he depended on an "organized left" to work in and with various American communities and build a "great popular base." Today (1971) the left is disorganized, farther from anything like such a base, and he himself appears to have lost his "realism and sanity." The SDS have split, after a bitter ideological struggle in a convention in which the ideal of participatory democracy went by the boards; on Hampden-Turner's scales, the convention displayed little tolerance or "ability to bridge the distance to others." A Weatherman faction took to open violence, endorsing when not inspiring the growing addiction to smashing, burning, and bombing. However understandable the violence in view of the frustrations of the youth, and the kind of therapeutic value it has for them, it is not only an ugly but a stupid mode of self-indulgence, irresponsible in its heedlessness of consequences. It can only hurt the ideal causes that have attracted so many reasonable students, for it intensifies the public hostility to them too, incites violent repression, and makes more conceivable a police state than the revolution these radicals presumably dream of.

A related development has been the rise of anti-intellectualism. The early leaders of the New Left were uncommonly well-read, but many of their recent converts will have none of such bookishness. While they have become more like hippies in their dress and their addiction to drugs, some just want action and are out to smash the university too. They accentuate a dangerous tendency that has run all through the radical movement, which has too readily exploited the vulnerability of universities to its disruptive tactics, the hesitancy of many administrators to call in the police. For the radical students of course need the university, and not merely for their own education; lacking popular or workers' support, they have no other base. For all its faults, it remains the most liberal institution in America, the one that permits the freest and fullest inquiry and criticism, and is therefore the best for their own purposes of agitation. Without it they could get nowhere.

That all such extremism has been incited by idealism is no reason for condoning it. Rather it recalls the fate of youth movements in Europe, especially Germany. These were all idealistic too, and necessarily so: there could be no real "movement" among young people without idealism (as the Young Republicans in America testify—their stodgy conservatism has enlisted no such fervor as have the radicals). German students were still idealistic when they flocked to the banner of Hitler before he came into power. If some were seeking selfish ends, just as some of our radicals have a lust for power, most were filled with patriotic fervor, willing to take risks and make sacrifices. Those of us who lived through the Hitler era remember that in the universities they also staged confrontations, threatened or abused defenders of academic freedom, and in general behaved like storm troopers. Our young radicals, who have no such memories, freely call public officials "fascists" but feel outraged when they are compared with Nazi students. Their avowed goals are quite different, to be sure; yet their tactics have been comparable, even to their habit of indiscriminately calling all policemen "pigs," which recalls the Nazi word for Jews—*Schwein-hunde.* Those of us who sympathized with them could do so more easily because there was no prospect whatever of their getting into power, running either the universities or the country. Today the factions within the SDS that would make us shudder at such a prospect are not at all surprising, but a natural consequence of tendencies that marked the New Left from the outset.

Though the radicals had little recourse but to stay in the universities, in a society that had little use for them, or in Bruno Bettelheim's words has made youth "obsolete," few showed gratitude for the privileges they enjoyed there. Those who idolized Castro, Mao, or Ho Chi Minh conveniently forgot that under their authoritarian regimes they would not enjoy the right to basic dissent, the very considerable measure of freedom the universities granted them. Many more forgot as well the responsibilities of academic freedom, its necessary conditions of civil, reasonable discourse with a respect for the rights of others. In their common insistence on "non-negotiable" demands, their habits of howling down speakers and disrupting lectures, and their assertion of their "right" to disrupt academic processes (recently reaffirmed by the New University Conference), they denied the rights of other students, not to mention of professors. Similarly in strikes or boycotts of classes they have forcibly debarred other students from entering buildings. And all such intolerance has been encouraged by their popular intellectual guru, Herbert Marcuse. He has told them that freedom in

America is essentially a bourgeois sham, they have a right to "progressive" restraints on the freedom of people hostile to their cause, they are also entitled to the "violence of defense," the strong anarchist element in their revolt is a "very progressive force"—and no less because he also declared there was no possibility of revolution in America.[5]

My own experience with radical students leads me to believe that Hampden-Turner's profile of them (which went to press in 1969) is somewhat idealized. They are certainly brighter than the average student, more sensitive, articulate, independent, and courageous in their commitments and willingness to take risks; but in action they have not been distinguished by ability to bridge distance to others (including their liberal elders, whom they have treated much as doctrinaire Communists used to treat democratic socialists). Their proclivities to intolerance, arrogance, and self-righteousness are spread all over the record. In particular I doubt the readiness of most of them to admit and face complexity, for again more conspicuous on the record are their tendencies to oversimplify, reduce to blacks and whites. "Everything is really very clear, distinct," wrote the very bright president of the local SDS on a report for me a few years ago on the state of America. Specifically, the "real meaning" of the war in Vietnam was "really very simple"—it was the needs of American capitalism. And so on, in a confused semi-utopianism that has also been characteristic of the New Left: dreams of a society without repression, exploitation, or militarism, in which people will be "really free"—dreams becoming to ardent, idealistic youth, but much like those of the Old Left, only vaguer about means since the revolutionary slogans about the triumph and dictatorship of the proletariat have been discredited by the example of the Soviet Union. The new slogans—participatory democracy, more power to the people, giving the government back to the people—would in

5. I should confess that I am not much impressed by Marcuse as a social philosopher. He has made Marx more relevant by dwelling on the humanism of his early manuscripts (which he himself chose to put aside), distinguishing between Soviet Communism and "true" socialism, attacking the technology that Marx assumed would be simply beneficial when not run by capitalists, and supplementing him with a doctored-up Freudianism that brought Eros in, made room for the necessary "psychic" revolution that young people also aspire to; but while all this may make some kind of revolution seem desirable, it does not constitute a clear guide for any kind. I am dismissing Marcuse briefly because I doubt that he has deeply influenced the thought of young radicals. My impression is that they honor him as a venerable radical critic of our society and a sympathizer, but not as a prophet. He himself has said that he thought very few students had really read him.

"real" life mean at best majority rule; and the brute fact remains that the majority want nothing like what the young radicals want.

"The American people must demand the right of a revolution," wrote my SDS student. What's more, "The people must make their own revolution." He went on to say that this must come about "somehow," it might not happen in his own lifetime, as an American he could only hope—revealing again the anxieties of a generation that cannot be sure it has a future, and so cannot believe as wholeheartedly in its utopian dreams as the Old Left could. Meanwhile the radicals have yet to come to grips with the complication they know well enough in both their calmer and their more bitter moments, the intense public hostility to them. As fervent young people they cannot be expected to have a steady vision of complexity, but the point remains that in this respect they are not mature. In identifying "the people" with young people like themselves, they are introducing another version of the American cult of youth—a cult that has always obscured the values of maturity, and that too often leads them to talk as if they had a monopoly on virtue.

All this I say in sympathy, not in scorn or anger—or anger only at the minority of extremists who jeopardize the whole cause of the dissenting youth. Then I should add a note of sympathy, such as radicals seldom express, for the many Americans who are angry at them, especially the lower middle class. They resent the elitism of the rebellious students, the common scorn of their own conventional virtues as hard-working, law-abiding, patriotic Americans. As naturally the more affluent resent the attacks on the whole American way of life. It is a hard truth the students are telling them, one they cannot bear; for if taken literally it means that they have been simply wasting their lives. Still, the feeling of all these people is often ugly. And the racism of most of these supposedly decent Americans brings up still another complication for the young radicals—the revolt of the Negroes.

Given their concern for social justice, the radicals naturally sympathize with the blacks, as do the great majority of aroused students. In seeking an alliance with the black rebels, who have turned against the Jews, the SDS went so far as to endorse a resolution condemning the "aggression" of Israel against the Arabs, whose Nasser had obviously provoked the disastrous war in 1967. It was an uneasy alliance, however, and short-lived. While they have common enemies, many of the black rebels prefer to fight their own battle in their own way. And if they are too suspicious of any collaboration with Whitey, their interests are in any case not identical. Unlike rebellious white students, they do have serious personal grievances, and are seeking immediately the rights and privileges these take for granted in their own lives.

In their understandable bitterness, black rebels are more likely to be fanatical, or at least to talk wildly on occasion. If "total liberty for black people" should be refused, Eldridge Cleaver has written, the Black Panthers were determined to bring about the "total destruction of America"—a cause in which most white radicals would presumably be unwilling to participate. But they might feel more troubled because Cleaver is of course not at all representative of the black people. While in the national elections of 1968 the radicals typically concentrated their fire on pathetic Hubert Humphrey (like the Communists of yore), ignoring the more dangerous candidacy of Richard Nixon, more than ninety percent of black voters voted for Humphrey. The great majority of Negroes plainly aspire to no more than the status of the white middle class, with all the perquisites of consumerism. Even most of the black rebels might be content if their people were given an equal opportunity to enter the "consumer paradise" despised by white radicals. Meanwhile they are naturally much less concerned about "technocracy," which is not the source of the prejudice they have to battle.

With, however, a significant exception—education. Efforts to enroll more black students in universities, give them more nearly an equal opportunity for a higher education, run into the obvious difficulty that most of them are ill-prepared because they had to attend inferior schools in their ghettoes. They rank lower in I.Q. tests too, and though by now educators and some white parents have begun to realize that these do not test simply native intelligence, but abilities influenced by schooling and culture, they are still highly regarded as measures of something or other that qualifies youngsters for higher education. The bitter controversy over Arthur Jensen's contention, derived from such measures, that there are significant innate differences between blacks and whites in ability to learn has obscured an important issue. Possibly there are significant differences in cognitive styles—whether due to heredity or to culture—that make it harder for blacks to acquire the abilities demanded by our technological society; but possibly they have other abilities that might be valued more by critics of this society. They appear to have, for example, more natural talent for expressing themselves in music and dancing, and their dialect—criticized by schoolmarms because it is not "good English"—is more expressive than the language of suburban white youngsters. At any rate, one complaint of the dissenting youth in the universities is that in putting a premium on the ra-

tionally cognitive—the kind of knowledge and proficiency that i
on examinations—they slight the emotional, affective, imaginativ
creative capacities. Hence we are brought back to the issues ‹
counter culture as a whole.

3 / *The Revolt Against Rationalism*

THE MOST FUNDAMENTAL ISSUE raised by the dissenting culture, though
it may not be clearly perceived or conceived by many of the dissenters, is
the revolt against science and technology: science, that is, regarded as
the sole arbiter of truth, the last court of appeals; technology as the
arbiter of efficiency, rationality, and realism in the world of practical
affairs; and both enshrined in the temple of Knowledge, Reason, and
Progress. The revolt is obviously welcome to those concerned about the
human values represented by the arts and humanities, or simply about
the basic human needs that have been neglected when not disparaged
in the worship of our twin-god. As obviously the revolt is dangerous because it may degenerate into a simple revolt against reason; an assertion
of the claims of the non-rational may end as a celebration of the positively irrational. Theodore Roszak recognizes the dangers but emphasizes chiefly the values of the revolt in his attack on "the myth of
objective consciousness." I am again more critical than he because I do
not regard this as a mere myth, and as an older man perhaps remember
more vividly how we suffered from the intuitions, visions, and myths of
Hitler. So again I am attempting a balanced survey of what I agree is
a significant movement, in particular because it is by no means confined
to the young. On this subject they might learn considerable from
people over the unspeakable age of thirty.

We begin with the old dichotomy of reason vs. emotion, the head vs.
the heart. It has generated a great deal of unprofitable debate because the
terms are of course not at all precise, head and heart alike have legitimate claims, one man's emotional need is another man's irrationality,
reason itself may become a passion for truth, and so on. Confusions
may deepen when one tries to apply the terms concretely in judgments
of behavior. Of Richard Nixon, for instance, one may ask: Is he too
coldly rational and calculating? Is he appealing to too easy, sloppy
emotion by his rhetoric? Or may not both his head and his heart be in
this corny rhetoric? In any case, it is plain that neither head nor heart

assures responsible, ethical behavior. Accordingly I still like to describe my own ideal as not rationalism but "reasonableness," which leaves room for the claims of both reason and emotion and has ethical implications; but this still leaves open the question of just what is reasonable. Only an unreasonable man will insist on drawing hard-and-fast lines.

Yet we of course have to go on trying to judge and to draw lines. It is at least possible to make out some extremes—an inhuman or even "mad rationality" (in Lewis Mumford's words) in too many manifestations of our technology, but also heedless, irresponsible, even mad excesses in the counter culture. It also seems to me easy enough to make out some positive values in both; so it is simple reasonableness that calls for an effort at balance. And since science and technology are the dominant forces in our society, hardly in need of defense and sure to continue making progress by their own standards, I begin by considering the legitimacy of the revolt against them.

In my own experience students seldom directly attack "science," if only because they would have a hard time defining it. What they resent implicitly is the mystique of science, or more specifically the positivism it has fostered: the assumption that it is the only way of really "knowing," it alone can speak with authority about the "real" world, unverifiable statements are meaningless or at best merely subjective, and so forth. Except for the hunches or imaginative leaps of scientists that produce verifiable theory, this leaves no room for the powers of intuition, fantasy, and vision, private illumination or the inner light, mystical experience, and other such possibilities of mental life in which students have grown much more interested. While science has so conspicuously promoted the main accepted function of the university, the accumulation and transmission of knowledge, it cannot answer the question that most concerns them, what is most *important* to know. Especially in the social and behavioral sciences, they are rebelling against the too common pretense that scientists do know the answer, which too often turns out to have little relevance to their interest in personal development. Thus behaviorists may point out proudly the difference between the statements "This person is shedding tears" and "This person is feeling sad": the former refers to observable behavior, a proper subject for scientific study; the latter is inference, referring to something that cannot be strictly observed. It is an important epistemological distinction (and a behaviorist has told me happily that the word "emotion" was on its way out in his science, to join in limbo such unmentionable words as "thought," "imagination," and the "human mind"). As persons, students are nevertheless more interested in sadness, which they know damned well is very real.

Chiefly, however, their revolt has been concentrated on modern technology. The familiar reasons include the power of the Pentagon, the subordination of the individual to the requirements of organization or bureaucracy, the processing of persons by computers, the manipulation of people, the growth of consumerism, the pollution of the environment—in general, the obvious reasons why no thoughtful student can join in the popular celebration of our wealth and power, or regard our wondrous technology as the main source of America's greatness. Perhaps less conscious, but still implicit in the protests of students, are the underlying reasons suggested by Hampden-Turner in his chapter on "The Crypto-Conservatism of Technological Thinking," the mentality of its high priests. Wedded to technology, they have an emotional attachment to it, but pass for pure rationalists or realists. Thus they commonly dismiss fears of our Frankenstein's monsters as "over-emotional" or "purely personal"—presumably a womanish kind of feeling. As the last word in this kind of realism, or what Erich Fromm has called a "low grade chronic schizophrenia," we have Herman Kahn very coolly "thinking about the unthinkable," the possibilities and the consequences of a thermonuclear war—no doubt a necessary effort in view of our preposterous situation today, but intimating no revulsion against the "mad rationality" that got us into this situation.

To me almost as frightening is the attitude of Robert Strausz-Hupé (a devout conservative) on the fundamental problem of controlling our terrific technology, directing it to more sensible, civilized ends. "It would seem," he wrote, "that there are no practical ways to *guide* the further development of technology." Since it has been a spontaneous growth and as a whole tends to be integrated, selective efforts to guide it would be "counter-productive," creating problems and dangers just as grave as we now face. In the words of Hampden-Turner, this means that we who created this technology *"are not fit to guide it."* So indeed it may turn out—given the kind of men in control of it (who are fond of such jargon as "counter-productive"). Citing Emmanuel Mesthene, who stresses that technology is a prime creator of opportunities and new freedoms, Hampden-Turner comments that students of engineering ought then to benefit most richly from these opportunities and freedoms; whereas surveys have shown that these students are in fact more narrow-minded, parochial, materialistic, authoritarian, anti-intellectual, and unimaginative than the average. In college they grow more conservative, less concerned about *people*.

It would therefore seem that hopes for the guidance of our technology must rest on the more highly developed dissenting students, with their live concern for human values. According to Theodore Roszak, these students "are invading the technocracy's citadels of academic learning and bidding fair to take them over." I very much doubt, however, that they will take over the citadels, and doubt too that they are prepared for the task of helping to guide our technology. While all but a few want our electricity and running water, automobiles and telephones, and countless other things we depend on in daily life, I have heard little discussion of how they propose to keep all these things running. Sometimes the word is that business too should be turned over to "the people," but what people? If the dissenters ever do succeed in having their way, whatever that is, they will surely need the aid of all kinds of technically skilled people, including engineers. Meanwhile they could do with a better understanding of both science and technology, and perhaps more appreciation of their elementary values.

Having already considered the uses of science, I should merely repeat that its values are not merely practical or logical but esthetic, imaginative, moral, and humanistic. If we need more heart and will in dealing with our social and political problems, we could do with more genuine scientific spirit too, more disinterestedness and less biased or wishful thinking. As for technology, we cannot afford to regard it as simply the enemy, even apart from the many goods it produces that almost all of us are glad to have. Aldous Huxley, no idolater of it, paid elementary tribute to the advances in it as "fruits of genius and persistent hard work, of logic, imagination and self-denial—in a word, of moral and intellectual virtues for which one can feel nothing but admiration." Or in another word, of a discipline that many students could do with more of. For the rest, there is doubtless far too much faith in techniques, but they are obviously indispensable and by no means necessarily soul-killing, any more than farming is. Neither is organization fatal to individual initiative and integrity, nor the individual simply at the mercy of the institutions serving his needs; even bureaucratic routines can not only smooth operations but release energy and imagination for dealing with other than routine problems. Anyway, all but the few anarchists among student rebels know that organization too is indispensable, immediately for purposes of effective agitation, ultimately for all efforts to manage a society that technology has made so massive, complex, and interdependent. And so on, through all the simplicities that are too often forgotten or slurred over by critics of our technological society.

Since I gather that Roszak's book bids fair to become a bible for the dissenting culture, I should add my hope that students are reading him with more discrimination than he displays in his attacks on science and technology, or the alleged "myth" of objectivity. Thus he writes that "nothing less is required than the subversion of the scientific world view," and its replacement by a "new culture" in which the arbiters of the good, the true, and the beautiful become "the non-intellective capacities of the personality." Actually there is no possibility of overthrowing the scientific world view, but no need of it either; enough to recognize that it is hypothetical, partial, and inadequate for our living purposes, and to keep it under constant criticism—as the more philosophical scientists themselves do. At the same time, the "non-intellective capacities" are also inadequate for civilized living. They can never serve as arbiters of the true, the reliable knowledge we cannot do without; we must rely on science too in the necessary objective efforts to distinguish between real and unreal, fact and fiction, truth and falsity. Intellect, informed by knowledge, must enter our judgments of the good as well, and even of the beautiful, once we go beyond simple song to sophisticated works of art. Roszak seems pleased to emphasize that "in dealing with the reality our non-intellective powers grasp, *there are no experts"*—the curse of the technological society; but presently he finds such an expert in the shaman, the tribal magician who was "the culture hero *par excellence"*—not only artist, poet, dramatist, dancer, but "his people's healer, moral counsellor, diviner, and cosmologer." While he allows that we must distinguish between good and bad magic, this gives him no trouble. Like the artist, the shaman is a good magician because he tries to make available the full power of his non-intellective experience; the technical expert is a bad magician because he uses his monopoly of esoteric knowledge to befuddle or cow people.

Inasmuch as this kind of sophisticated primitivism appears to be popular with many dissenting students (who may not know that historically it is far from being novel), I think it necessary to make such elementary remarks as that Roszak of course had to make considerable use of his intellect in his argument, or even that he will go to a doctor—not a shaman—when he gets sick. But at least he recognizes that an exaltation of the non-intellective can lead to a dangerous irrationality. He grants that Hitler was echoing D. H.

Lawrence when he commanded his followers: "Think with your blood!" He is troubled by some manifestations on the "fringes" of the counter culture, such as intrusive "elements of pornographic grotesquery and blood-curdling sadomasochism." As an example he cites a rave review by an underground newspaper of an acid-rock group called The Doors: "Their style is early cunnilingual with overtones of the Massacre of the Innocents. An electrified sex slaughter. A musical blood-bath. . . ." Such manifestations can be written off as youthful extravagances, confined to the lunatic fringes to be found on almost all movements, and as yet I see no reason to believe that they indicate the direction in which the main body of the dissenting youth is likely to move. But they are related to other tendencies, closer to the heart of the counter culture, that are more worrisome, above all the addiction to psychedelic experience through drugs.

Now, the whole problem of the popularity of drugs among the youth—perhaps the most novel development in their culture, and certainly the most publicized—has been distorted by the popular hysteria over marijuana. Although we cannot be certain yet of its long-range effects, all thoughtful people should know by now that the evidence indicates it is no more habit-forming than tobacco, and unquestionably much less dangerous than alcohol, in a country that has up to eight million alcoholics. The hostility to it is especially irrational because Americans are by far the most drugged people on earth, consuming annually hundreds of tons of tranquillizers, sleeping pills, pep pills—pills for every problem.[6] As for LSD, there is some evidence that it can be dangerous, but it may be more frightening because so little is known as yet about its physiological effects. Meanwhile the problem is confused by the popular fallacy that drugs have uniform, invariable effects, whereas they plainly affect different people in different

6. How marijuana acquired the evil reputation that has justified the atrocious legal penalties for its use—not simply its sale, as with alcohol under Prohibition—is not altogether clear, but some good American reasons for it are fairly apparent. One was racism: it was at first smoked chiefly in the black ghettoes. Another was the sensational exploitation of it by the news media when white suburban youngsters took to it. Still another was the opposition of the liquor industry, which recognized a dangerous competitor. This might have reminded people that ever since the dawn of history, when beer appeared, the human race has employed artificial means of stimulation or relaxation, but as it was, conservatives have made it a prime symbol of what's wrong with our long-haired dissenting youth. They do not entertain the horrid thought that if marijuana is as dangerous as they think, its growing popularity—among older people too—would be a damning indictment of our society, any more than they ponder the question why the American way of life has made so many millions of affluent people, especially housewives, dependent on drugs of all kinds.

ways (just as drinking may make people gayer or more morose). Some young people have had bad trips, with painful or even disastrous aftermaths; others have reported wonderful experiences, including feelings of universal harmony such as ordinary life in America rarely affords. And these latter might appeal to the authority of wholly reputable thinkers. William James experimented with narcotics as one means of access to valuable forms of consciousness other than our normal waking "rational" consciousness. In *Doors of Perception* Aldous Huxley reported on his more systematic psychedelic experiments.

As Roszak points out, however (and on this matter he is highly critical of the counter culture), their attitude toward such psychic adventures was quite different from that of the young. They were mature, disciplined thinkers seriously exploring other modes of consciousness, possible approaches to the "perennial wisdom" of the mystics. Too many if not most of the young people are seeking only kicks, the temporary pleasure or excitement of a trip. As one kick leads to another, under the pressure of the peers, teenagers have taken to sniffling airplane glue, "blowing" their minds. And the youngsters only accentuate the basic reasons for misgivings about the whole drug culture. While it may relieve the tensions and frustrations of American life, provide valuable experiences of harmony, or more broadly promote the quest of community, it also promotes the cult of immediacy, the preoccupation with the here and now. This too may be valuable as an antidote to the excessive preoccupation with the future induced by the many years the youth now have to spend preparing for it in education, but it is not clearly a means to growth or full personal development. Again the question is what the habitual trippers bring back from their trips, whether they are thereby growing more mature, responsible, equipped to deal intelligently with a future they will sooner or later have to make a living in. Even the feelings of harmony may lead to an indifference to questions of right and wrong, suggest a return to the infantile Id. Most plainly, the drug culture is now promoting a hedonism that is not too different from the self-indulgence in suburbia or the consumer's paradise.

Such hedonism tends to make the youth set-ups for the manipulators of a commercialized society, the providers of new brands of opium for the masses. Underground journals glamorize the narcotics business by advertisements of all kinds of psychedelic paraphernalia, "head equipment" for the hipsters. The ads recall the uglier commercialization of psychedelia by the drug-pushers, who by now have built up a flourishing racket. In this view the trippers look like good old American types—suckers. They do not look spontaneous, joyous, or really happy. And to me they look no more spiritual when they appeal to the mystique of Timothy Leary, the early prophet and high priest of LSD.

As an academic pioneer in psychedelic research, he might recall William James and Aldous Huxley by his League for Spiritual Discovery, based on his claim that LSD was a sacramental means to genuinely religious experience. "In the beginning was the Turn-On," began the bible he published after he claimed exemption from narcotic laws in the name of religious freedom. He made his cult more attractive by promising free sexuality with abundant orgasm. (In an interview with *Playboy* he said, "In a carefully prepared, loving LSD session, a woman will inevitably have several hundred orgasms.") Although at first his pitch as a prophet was "turn on, tune in, and drop out," he later appealed to young radicals too by offering them the "politics of ecstasy," assuring them that the key to the psychedelic movement was "individual freedom," and that by becoming "ecstatic saints" they would become a social force.[7] The unsaintly may therefore wonder: Is Leary a mere poseur, a charlatan, or a sincerely deluded man? Most likely, I assume, he is something of each. But I have given his religion a paragraph chiefly because beneath its novel appearances it is typically American: an easy, guaranteed way to spiritual bliss, requiring neither spiritual effort nor spiritual discipline. So far from its being a "psychedelic revolution," it is another symptom of a slack society growing ever more dependent on drugs for peace of mind, or rather a temporary illusion of contentment.

Otherwise it is worth noting only because many of the young are engaged in a serious spiritual quest, in ways deserving much more respect. Since their limited experience makes them naturally liable to confusion or distraction by modish ways, I mention one other example that has surprised me more—the growing popularity of astrology. This form of magic is simply irrational. Astrology is a hoary superstition that in the ancient world had some connection with religious

7. Possibly his influence inspired a young graduate student at my university, a leftist who at the beginning of a public lecture by Clark Kerr exercised his freedom or his ecstasy by running up to the stage, gaily costumed, and throwing a pie at Kerr. Although it seemed to me an utterly irresponsible, indefensible action, which could not possibly do any good for whatever his cause was, I was informed that it was a "symbolic gesture," nice and absurd. When he was jailed, a couple hundred students, headed by a leader of the SDS, made a hero of him by marching to the jail, bailing him out, and carrying him out on their shoulders.

belief, but now has neither scientific nor religious foundation. Its popularity is not a form of dissent either, for over many years most American newspapers have had astrologers' columns to cater to the gullibility of millions of Americans. Today it is novel only in that it has been more efficiently commercialized with the help of computers: the suckers can call up the computer at any hour of the day or night, report the date of their birth, and learn instantly what the stars have to tell them. But so much for what I assume is only a passing fad among the youth. Now for the signs of a serious spiritual quest, more significant and more promising. To my mind the healthiest of them is the growing interest in Oriental religion, especially Zen Buddhism.

How much the youth are getting out of Zen it is hard to say. They have had the help of such dedicated, sophisticated popularizers as Alan Watts, but not the personal illumination that the Zen masters sought to communicate or evoke by a subtle, arduous discipline; I suppose that very few students have learned to live, or in our very different culture are even trying hard to live, in a way the masters would approve. How far can they get with its cardinal principle, "Those who know do not speak; those who speak do not know"? But at least it seems clear that they are getting a fuller awareness of "the non-intellective capacities of the personality" that Roszak makes too much of, but that are nevertheless real and important. Zen offers a wholesome transcendence of the positivistic world view because of its humor, compassion, gentleness, grace, and sense of beauty, and also because in spite of its stress on an ineffable kind of wisdom it by no means spurns intellect or reason, which perforce enters its efforts at communication. For the purposes of the young it merely asserts— quite reasonably—that intellect alone is never an adequate guide. It offers a serene answer to the perennial questions about the good life that science cannot answer. It is a better guide to the art of living so sadly neglected in our society. And that to almost all the youth it is not a whole way of life is just as well, for they may escape the selfish or callous kind of passivity that throughout history made the holy men of the East indifferent to political tyranny and social injustice, as to the wretched poverty of the masses.

Needless to add, Zen has been abused—as all gospels invariably are. Because of its unconcern with sex it became another excuse for free sexuality, a mode of self-indulgence rather than a discipline; Alan Watts complained that the early "Beat Zen," as of Jack Kerouac, was a "pretext for license . . . a simple rationalization." Similarly other

Oriental influences have been mixed. The spiritual help the Beatles sought from a swami was a temporary affair, of little apparent lasting consequence; more likely to last is their contribution to the popularity of Indian music. Of the Hinduism of Allen Ginsberg, the most popular guru in America, I doubt that it has gone deep. At least I am no more impressed by his visionary powers than by most of his chanting; though I may be prejudiced because I find too much self-conscious shagginess, cheap antic, and simple vulgarity in what his many youthful admirers see as an adorable informality, naturalness, and sincerity. (His lover opened a public performance at my university by reciting a poem he said he had composed with one hand while masturbating Allen with the other.) In general "mysticism" does not seem to me the right word for the popular cults of myth and ritual, mystery and magic. At best I see a healthy protest against the stifling climate of positivistic opinion, but always complicated by failure to discriminate between "good" and "bad" magic. The whole movement looks silly when *The East Village Other* rejoices in a "mystic revolution" because the thousands of anti-war activists who stormed the Pentagon in 1967 included "witches, warlocks, holymen, seers, prophets, mystics, saints, sorcerers, shamans, troubadours, minstrels, bards, roadmen, and madmen."

With the more serious-minded youth it is also hard to say to what extent they are seeking specifically religious experience, in what Henry Adams called "the aching consciousness of a religious void." Few appear to be seeking salvation in the traditional sense, conversion in the name of either God or World Soul, any supernatural Being. But since "religion" does not have a precise meaning nor necessarily imply a specific set of beliefs, it seems to me enough that they are open to broadly religious possibilities of a kind obscured by the traditional dogmatism of Christianity. The giddy talk of some about holy men, prophets, saints, shamans, etc. is more unfortunate because it too obscures the spiritual quality in the revolt and the quest of the earnest youth, the yearning for some kind of spiritual rebirth. At the same time, significant changes are also going on within Christianity. These were illustrated most attractively by a symposium *Commonweal* held in 1967 with six students from Catholic college backgrounds, representative of the New Left.

Agreed that they found most Catholic theology dull, sterile, or irrelevant, they had a low opinion of Pope Paul, considering him bigoted when not dishonest, and rejected the dogmatism of the Church. They were troubled by the question whether, despite their revolt against the Church and much of their education, they could still regard themselves as real Catholics, but they at least felt that they were religious. Like other students, they were developing their own kind of inner religious life, worshiping God in their own way. They also questioned to what extent they owed their very live social conscience to the Gospels or Christian tradition; one said he had got it "right out on the streets." But they were more attractive than many young radicals, perhaps because of Christian humility, perhaps their intimate acquaintance with the inhumanity of dogmatism. Several remarked that they tended to be too sure of themselves, needed more tolerance and patience—and patience too with the great majority of students who were understandably complacent about their professional future, still socially apathetic; for many of these were at least getting more and more interested in finding out who they were.

No doubt these students will go in different ways as they try to develop their own religious life. They may draw on some startling Protestant innovations that have attracted many young people, and some Catholic priests too. Joyous jazz and rock liturgies heralded a growing stress on festivity and literal celebration, fantasy and wonder. Harvey Cox, a theological leader in this development, both states and exemplifies its significance. Whereas his best seller *The Secular City* of some years ago expressed a cool rationalism suited to our culture, he has now published *The Feast of Fools,* in which he prescribes fantasy and festivity as an antidote to a too pragmatic, bureaucratic, "tight" culture that has made man "incapable of experiencing the nonrational dimensions of existence." The whole movement may be summed up as a union of the ecstatic and the sacred—or more strictly a reunion, a recovery of the Dionysiac element in ancient religion that was still apparent in the Middle Ages, but was later smothered by both Protestantism and Catholicism. Father Andrew Greeley, an authority in opinion research, has ventured a prophecy: "A decade of secularity ends with a very strong promise that the next decade will be a decade of the ecstatic and the sacred."

As usual, I doubt this promise, at least for society as a whole. However goatish, most Americans would have to change a great deal to become capable of this Dionysiac religion. Conceivably it could sweep the youth culture, but then it would raise the usual questions about genuineness and depth; meanwhile its manifestations are too often faddish or synthetic. Harvey Cox himself is uneasy because "so much of today's experimentation with the Dionysiac . . . tends to drift toward death and chaos for its own sake." And while he has become involved in radical politics too, Father Greeley worries about what will become of the religious quest for social relevance in the 'sixties, simplistic though this was: Will the "turning on" of the mystical and transcendent signal the "turning out" of the quest for relevance? On this score I am more hopeful because of the earnestness of so many of the youth, who presumably will give the answers; but what if they are frustrated in their efforts at social and political reform? Although they might then tune out through religion, it is hard to imagine their developing a deep sense of the sacred in America, or much capacity for pure ecstasy.

Except, perhaps, in communities of their own. These bring up another central theme of the counter culture.

4 / The Quest of Community

THE QUEST OF COMMUNITY that has become most apparent in the hippies has taken many other forms, such as the interest in sensitivity training, the emphasis on "relating to" other people, and on campus the very indifference to sports and fraternities—superficial or artificial kinds of human relationships that satisfy only conventional students and Peter Pan alumni. And here the youth can look to Paul Goodman, until recently their foremost champion. Well before the war in Vietnam he anticipated the student revolt in *Growing Up Absurd* (1959). In this he asked basic questions that the dissenting youth would pick up:

> Is it possible, *how* is it possible, to have more meaning and honor in work? to put wealth to some real use? to have a high standard of living of whose quality we are not ashamed? to get social justice for those who have been shamefully left out? to have a use of leisure that is not a dismaying waste of a hundred million adults?

Always his main concern has been the rich potentialities of human nature that have been stunted in a society lacking honor, lacking community, that makes it hard if not impossible for the youth really to grow up. So he called on them to make their own communities.

It is unfortunate that the most publicized of those who did so were the hippies. In their early days they were indeed carefree and loving enough in their psychedelic communities, with their slogan

"Make Love, Not War," to suggest comparison with the early Christians. They also suggested the best in primitive societies, which within their narrow range of choice or opportunity assured their members a full life, relatively free from alienation or neurosis, and enriched by feelings of kinship with nature; they evolved some engaging rituals, such as gathering on a hill to greet the midsummer sun by dancing, singing, making love, or doing whatever the spirit moved. They grew less spontaneous and engaging, however, as they gathered in crowds for rock festivals, with drug-pushers plying their trade. They soon had a harder time playing their role as flower children because of all the sensational publicity they got and the attendant commercialization, merchants exploiting their own brand of consumerism by mod clothing, trinkets, and all the other accessories of the self-conscious barefoot, unwashed life. Many of the youngsters attracted to their communities by their free sex and all the opportunities to turn on—more freedom, to repeat, than youngsters ever enjoyed in the past, anywhere—are hardly dedicated to any ideal role, and are unlikely to grow up very much in a culture that otherwise provides little but rock music. I have yet to hear of a hippie library or browsing room.

At best the hippie communities have a doubtful future. To my knowledge few if any are wholly self-supporting or have clear prospects of becoming so; to live like lilies in the field they depend on money got from parents or by panhandling. If they survive, by the continued indulgence of parents, it would presumably be chiefly as a subculture for dropouts. They could not be expected to set an ideal example for the great society or have a significant influence on it, any more than did the utopian communities in America in the past century. They only make one wonder, as about many other semi-hippie types too: What are they going to be like when they grow up? raise children? approach middle age?

Serious students who have organized temporary communities for summer vacations have run into practical difficulties. One reported that half the group wanted to wander off with their guitars and make music, while the rest went to town to pass out pamphlets or engage in some kind of political activity; but nobody wanted to collect the garbage. Those of us disposed to encourage such experiments (as I am) might remind the youth that the ideal of community may be threatened by the necessity of chores. (One ex-hippie girl told me bitterly that the answer was simple—the girls did the household chores.) Yet one may doubt that community is actually a serious problem for the dissenting youth. They can find plenty of kindred spirits, at least in the larger cities and universities, just because the counter culture is so widespread. If it proves to have lasting significance, it should make unnecessary the deliberate formation of separate communities, except for those who like Paul Goodman dream of self-sustaining rural communities, or for the relatively few who find intolerable the conventional compromises that people have always had to make in all societies. Meanwhile the university provides a kind of community that some young radicals, once more, fail to appreciate. Although it is no longer anything like the community of scholars that European universities once were, it does offer a shelter where young people of like interests can freely associate, without the compulsive togetherness of suburbia, as freely express their criticism of conventional society, and in general enjoy the privileges that antagonize the public. While demanding the right to participate more in university affairs, they have otherwise demanded for themselves chiefly the right to live more freely as they please, on or off campus.

As for the related movement for sexual liberation, or more community between men and women, I assume it is impossible to generalize with confidence about the infinitely varied love-lives of the young, or the extent to which their experience corresponds to their voluble talk; but one can make out some clear enough tendencies. The most conspicuous, as usual, have been the most questionable. In the eyes of those who still cherish privacy and intimacy, the movement has led to such obvious excesses as love-ins and fuck-ins, the Berkeley SDS slogan that "People who screw together, glue together," Jerry Rubin's call for an ideal society in which people will do it whenever and wherever they please, and so on, to Timothy Leary's promise of orgasms by the hundred. On the approaches to the hippie world there is much casual coming and going, in and out of transitory affairs. Whereas the early hippies set up an ideal of equality and comradeliness in which love would no longer be a "conquest," it now appears that males are regaining their dominance, rock stars attract a hippie harem of "groupies," and camp followers look on hippie chicks as easy lays, free of charge. And naturally even the most serious of the young people are likely to pay some price for the new freedoms, just because they are new, self-conscious, not yet easy and natural.

In their sophistication they are liable to worries over their sexual "performance," heightened by all the manuals on the art or the "techniques" of making love. No longer fearful of passion as a sinful thing, they may worry because they don't feel enough passion, or arouse enough in their partner. Or since sex has become a commonplace, no longer hushed up, perhaps even banal, they may fear passion as a possible commitment. "The Victorian person sought to have love without falling into sex," writes Rollo May, a psychiatrist; "the modern person seeks to have sex without falling in love." One may therefore wonder how much warmth there is in the relationships of the liberated young, how much tenderness. And though I feel fairly sure that there was no more tenderness in the Victorian era, even unabashed love may now stir some uneasiness. Interviews with unmarried couples living together (not merely shacking up on occasional weekends) indicate that most of them shy away from marriage because they fear it as a commitment; they think first of the problems it causes, not of its possible rewards. Add that they have some reason to be scared off, since sophistication encourages free and easy relations more than fidelity, it points to a significant element in sex and love that Rollo May observes is almost universally repressed in our culture—"the tragic, daimonic element." This appears in the most famous of our love stories, as of Abelard and Héloise, Tristan and Isolde, and Romeo and Juliet, but seldom in sophisticated talk or writing today. Although there would seem to be no crying need of it in a society racked by plenty of other problems, May concludes that an appreciation of it could help young people not only to avoid simplifying the subject of sex and love, but to love better. I like the idea of sending them back to school under Romeo and Juliet, to learn a deeper relevance.

On the whole, however, the movement toward more freedom and equality in sexual relations seems to me clearly healthy. Unquestionably it is healthier than all the "sophisticated" exploitation of sexiness exemplified by *Playboy*, in which bunnies serve as mindless sex objects for organization men—the business, in Roszak's words, "of inventing and flourishing treacherous parodies of freedom, joy, and fulfillment"; and a business, I would repeat, more corrupting than the pornography that our pharisaical national leaders express a horror of. In a historical perspective we may otherwise discount the common charge (by Rollo May among others) that sexual relations have grown more mechanical. Although we can never know how much warmth and tenderness there was in the love-lives of past societies, or in the courting of the young, the inferior status of women plainly tended to much mechanical intercourse, in which apart from procreation women served chiefly to gratify the momentary passions of the male. In Western civilization the novel tradition of romantic love hardly made Romeos and Juliets of most young people, whose marriage in the old countries was commonly arranged by parents for prudential reasons. In America, as in Victorian England, wives were not until modern times generally expected to enjoy intercourse thoroughly, any more than to know anything about its art until they got married. All in all, it remains impossible to summarize with confidence; but my impression is that there is likely to be more warmth and companionship in the sexual relations of the youth, even in affairs that are not lasting, than there was in the straitlaced past, including the many occasions when the laces were broken.[8]

Similarly with the startling change in their speech habits, the suddenness with which all the once tabooed four-letter words were freely used. At first they were flaunted too ostentatiously by militants attacking the Establishment, a "Dirty Speech Movement," and the habit can still be irritating to elders who are not at all shocked by it. By now, however, many of the youth use the words quite naturally and casually, no longer defiantly. While their propriety or their effectiveness may be questioned, especially by those who appreciated their earthy humor before they became clichés, I think that in this respect the young are succeeding in being themselves unaffectedly, realizing a kind of refreshing candor preferable to the formalities of the past that veiled so much hypocritical pretense. The interesting question is whether all such linguistic taboos—apparent relics of a primitive irrationality—are as passé or as socially needless as they are inclined to think, given the usefulness of "dirty" words as safety-valves for letting off excess emotion on occasion.

As for the art, lastly, that has come out of the counter culture, or been associated with it, my limited acquaintance with it has not steeled a resolve to explore it thoroughly. Most of it is plainly ephemeral, even deliberately so, in keeping with the cult of immediacy that reflects the uncertainty of the youth about the future, no doubt helps them to feel more at home in a world of flux, but hardly compels close study. Of pop art Roy Lichtenstein wrote that it has "very immediate and of-the-moment meanings which will vanish." Allan Kaprow, an improvisor

8. In *Optimism One*, where F.M. Esfandiary emphasizes that woman in the Old World was always essentially a passive means to a man's sexual gratification, he not only states the case for modern youth with complete assurance but concludes that marriage has become essentially "irrelevant" because of its exclusiveness. "How can marriage survive in a fluid open world in which people will not and cannot permanently commit themselves to anyone?" I doubt, however, that many of the more serious young people are considering it irrelevant, or that they find its commitments intolerable even though they no longer consider it necessarily permanent either. Their common desire to be more "involved" and "committed" extends to personal relationships too.

of Happenings, the quintessence of immediacy, declared in his *Manifestoes* that "the current blurring of boundaries dividing the arts, and dividing art and life," makes the old questions of standards of excellence "not only futile but naive." As a naive type, I was not much impressed even by Susan Sontag's portentous essay on "Camp," from which I gathered that among many other things this meant an effort "to dethrone the serious." Students have told me that to them "Camp" meant simply something that was so bad it was funny and so in a way good, but that the fashion was on its way out.

Short of an old-fashioned effort to uphold standards of excellence, I might remark that much of this art is not so fresh or original as youthful enthusiasts think. The possibly amusing mockeries of pop art recall Dada, two generations ago, but are less imaginative or personally expressive; it has already vanished from the art scene. Allen Ginsberg, whose "Howl" was hailed by the beats as a Declaration of Independence, appears to be solidly established as the leading poet even though he is a relative oldster, but however "natural" his outpourings, they can become pretty monotonous to real oldsters who have known free verse ever since their youth. Even popular song and dance are reminiscent. A devotee of rock 'n roll writes that it brought dances in which young people could express themselves much more freely and fully than people could in the fox-trot of the swing era, but the Charleston did much the same for the youth of my generation. Except for the young radicals and the stronger note of dissent, the counter culture as a whole is often reminiscent of the post-war mood of the 'twenties.

It is more novel, however, as a possible anticipation of the electronic culture that Marshall McLuhan tells us will replace the old print culture. "Nowadays," wrote John Cage to the *Village Voice,* "everything happens at once and our souls are conveniently electronic, omniattentive." This convenience might seem a discordant note in the revolt against a technological society, but in any case the youth are much dependent on modern technology for their modes of self-expression and communion—tape recorders, electric guitars and amplifiers, rock and roll dances with light shows, light and sound effects to go with Happenings, electronic strobes, assorted electronic and psychedelic gear. For serious art, John Cage emphasizes the indebtedness of music in particular; magnetic tape made possible not only high-fidelity recordings —one of the passions of the youth—but a new kind of free-ranging music. Knowing little of this abstract, nonmelodic music, and doubting that it has really doomed tonality for good, I find more promising the recent work in films, especially by contrast with the dreary staples of the big studios in Hollywood—an industry in the doldrums that possibly the youth may revive by restoring the possibilities of the moving picture as a serious art form.

On all counts it would seem that Marshall McLuhan ought to be one of the gods, even the supreme god, of the counter culture. His remorselessly repetitious insistence that "the medium is the message," not the "content," strikes me as another example of the common "not-but" fallacy, but I assume that the new media have unquestionably made a real difference, and that the youth are naturally more sensitive to them than are their bookish elders. The more radical among them presumably should be gratified by his assurance that the TV generation of students is bound to overthrow the Establishment, especially because the "real" activists haven't reached the scene of action yet—they are still in their early teens. The youth might also welcome his message that mini-skirts are only the first step toward "Instant-Sex." In my experience, however, few students are excited by McLuhan, and least of all the more radical ones. They do not share his enthusiasm for TV, which they typically regard as the "boob tube"; the students who remain faithful to it are typically conventional and passive. Certainly the dissenters are not so rhapsodical as he over the wondrous possibilities of computers as extensions of the central nervous system or the "whole man." Possibly he may emerge as the great prophet of the culture of the future; but meanwhile the most characteristic, energetic artistic expression of the counter culture still appears to be in popular song and music, the chief means to feelings of community.

"For the reality of what's happening today in America," wrote Ralph Gleason (in *The American Scholar*), "we must go to rock 'n roll, to popular music." In the words of Bob Dylan's song, "The Times They Are A-Changin'." Unlike jazz, rock and the new folk music are not a Negro but a white creation. With the Twist, the Frug, the Philly Dog, and whatever the latest dances are called, they express the Dionysiac element in the youth culture. "Believe in the magic, it will set you free," sings a group called the Lovin' Spoonful. Again this suggests apparent anomalies, discordant notes in the counter culture. Bob Dylan, who was among the first to sound the strong note of social criticism in the new music, also sings "There's no left wing and no right wing, only upwing and down wing." Technology provided the record-players, albums, transistor radios, and TV that produced the first generation in America brought up on music, hearing it day in and day out. The big record companies were quick to capitalize on it, making a flourishing business of its direct or implied criticism of a society devoted to technical rationality. They lend weight to Gleason's conclusion, which supports the contention of Richard Poirier that the Beatles are a "force of historical consequence." He quotes Plato on the importance of new styles of music: "The new style quietly insinuates itself into manners and customs and from there it issues a greater force . . . goes on to attack laws and constitutions, displaying the utmost impudence, until it ends by overthrowing everything, both in public and in private."

Again maybe so. At least this is pretty much what most Americans seem to fear in our dissenting youth. I remain inclined to doubt that the new music is making so much difference in their thought and feeling, and also to doubt that it promises "a new heaven and a new earth." (The best of it that I have heard is the rock opera "Jesus Christ Superstar," a very moving version of the tragedy of the human Jesus, essentially reverent, but with nothing of Dionysiac ecstasy or any promise of a new faith.) About the art of the counter culture as a whole, I cannot share the faith that Jonas Mekas wrested from shocked disillusionment in America, a period of desperation: "There is a renaissance, a spiritual renaissance coming upon us, and it's through artists that this new age is bringing to us its first voices and visions." Yet I would not conclude with this weary refrain. One cannot reasonably expect great art to come out of so youthful and still confused a culture, whose giddier manifestations get the most attention from the news media. For the long run more significant than the particular modes of innovation and dissent is the basic discontent with the values and the goals of American society that has stirred so many young people to seek more meaningful, satisfying ways of life, and so many more who still behave more or less conventionally to be increasingly critical of the accepted ways. The last word belongs, I think, to the healthy impulse behind the counter culture.

IX

AN OLD LIBERAL

TO THE YOUTH

1 / The Nature of Liberalism

THE SOUL-SEARCHING and breast-beating of many liberals today
have led to apparently contrary confessions. Some say that liberalism has been corrupted by its "success" as exemplified in the Kennedy and Johnson administrations, in particular by men who supported the war in Vietnam; others lament its "failure," as indicated by its apparent inability to offer bold leadership, an adequate program, or effective opposition to the conservative forces that dominate the country. In my opinion they alike tend to exaggerate, for its partial success in putting through social and political reforms has always been offset by its failure to win over the American electorate to a steady devotion to its basic principles. But my immediate point here is that on both counts liberalism is open to the charge of irrelevance—and that again it is the rebellious students who have pressed the charge most vigorously. Hence I am speaking again in a seemingly ambiguous role: as an uneasy liberal who throughout this book has acknowledged indebtedness to these students for forcing me to reconsider my life-long principles, admit more reservations, perhaps achieve more humility; but also as an unregenerate liberal who upon reconsideration essentially adheres to these principles, qualifying their application rather than their substance. My stance nevertheless seems to me basically consistent because liberalism as I conceive it necessarily entails some uneasiness, admissions of

uncertainty, and willingness to question successes and admit failures. Although I must think that I still have something to say to the youth, if only because as a university teacher I keep on talking, on this ground I can do so in good conscience.

Now to come to speaking terms, there are of course liberals and liberals. I freely confess to irritation when young radicals and black militants to whom "liberal" is just a dirty word lump me with people whose beliefs I do not share. As in general an attitude that welcomes change in the name of "improvement" or "reform," liberalism leaves open such questions as what change, how much change, and by what means, short of violent revolution. It embraces a broad spectrum, ranging from mildly liberal Republicans to socialists like Michael Harrington, "radicals" who remain liberal in their devotion to democratic processes and civil liberties.[1] Historically it has also embraced quite different policies, ranging from *laissez faire* in the early nineteenth century to a perhaps excessive faith in federal action today. Yet through the years liberalism has meant as well a broad agreement on some basic attitudes that are not too hard to define.

Adlai Stevenson, who remarked that no liberal could precisely define it without getting into an argument with another liberal, nevertheless ventured a definition that included not only a faith in the possibility of a better future, but the basic beliefs "that *people* are all that is important, and that *all* people are equally important." The faith in a better future has long ceased to distinguish liberals, since conservatives have been no less optimistic, in modern America if anything even more so; businessmen have been the most boastful about our material progress, the most confident that things would continue indefinitely to get bigger and better. The difference is that liberals have been more concerned about *people,* in particular the common people, and the democratic principle of equality. Conservatives have typically been devoted primarily to the interests of the upper classes: Edmund Burke and the American Federalists on the grounds of a principle of natural aristocracy that was more or less philosophical, even if it reflected their economic interests, and that in any case led them to oppose equal suffrage; the Republican Party over the last hundred years on more

---

1. I am not bothering to consider what Spiro Agnew called "radical liberals," by which he meant in effect chiefly Democrats opposed to the policies of the Nixon administration—campaign rhetoric that is significant only because it contributes nothing to a serious discussion of vital issues. Possibly the name-calling was heartfelt, like John Mitchell's "liberal Communists," but if so it throws light only on the mentality of these White House spokesmen, and is of more medical than philosophical interest.

purely economic grounds, the interests of the ruling business class, however rationalized, which led this privileged class to oppose every major social and political reform in this century. In time conservatives came to accept most of the reforms, but the battle for them was led chiefly by liberals, in the interests of the underprivileged. Like John Stuart Mill, they ceased defending wholly free private enterprise when they realized how workers, including women and children, were suffering from it.

This whole struggle against the abuses of privilege and power implied a faith in the people, meaning again the common people. It is a faith that in theory has long been habitually expressed by American conservatives too, or at least that few of them have dared to attack openly, but that has been asserted most explicitly by liberals ever since Jefferson, and affirmed most consistently in their political practice. It appears as well in their faith in freedom, their much more consistent defense of freedom of inquiry, criticism, and dissent. This is always a risky freedom, in the view of conservatives often too risky; they are prone to alarm over the danger of radical, subversive, un-American, or godless doctrines, which presumably may seduce or corrupt people, especially the youth. Liberals have been more willing to run the risks, trust to the sufficient good sense of the people. John Stuart Mill went further as one of the first thinkers to maintain that diversity of opinion, with the endless controversy and dissent it entailed, was not merely the price society had to pay for intellectual freedom, but a positive good, the necessary means to any possible improvement of society; it was essential to the pursuit of truth, which in social and political life came down to an endless collision of half-truths, for only by full, free discussion can the element of truth in unpopular doctrines be preserved, the element of truth in popular doctrines be kept alive as a reasoned belief instead of a prejudice or dead dogma. Likewise Mill laid down another cardinal principle of liberalism in his related insistence on the value of individual liberty, or personal freedom other than the economic freedom most prized by American conservatives.[2]

2. It is easy to point out, as Robert Wolff (among many others) has recently done in *The Poverty of Liberalism*, the vulnerability of the principle of utility, in terms of "the greatest happiness of the greatest number," on which Mill based his whole argument for liberty. We can never demonstrate empirically that the sum of human happiness has been or will be increased by allowing men freely to dissent from the majority, smoke and drink too much, make fools of themselves, or kill themselves. Wolff concludes that although Mill explicitly rejected the advantage of any appeal to abstract or "natural" rights, "an adequate defense of free speech will after all be forced to invoke some notion of

By now the historic liberal faith in man, reason, and progress may seem naive, as Mill himself does in his habitual reference to man's interests as a "rational being." Yet his apparent optimism was tempered by an element of skepticism that is also at the heart of liberalism. For one thing, liberals have not had the naive faith of conservatives in the superior wisdom, virtue, or integrity of the upper classes, or in early American terms of "men of property," later of successful businessmen. Their faith in man was accordingly tempered by a livelier awareness of the inveterate tendencies to abuse power and privilege, and the constant need of defending hard-won rights, in time against the possible tyranny of the majority too. More profoundly, their faith in reason was tempered by an awareness of the limitations of reason, an implicit admission of ultimate uncertainty in the first and last questions. Mill argued that society had no right to silence any opinion, even if it were held by but one man, because no man or no society can rightfully claim infallibility; and though liberals can of course be too sure of the rightness of their views, their insistence on the need of intellectual freedom and their opposition to authoritarianism imply an admission that there is no absolute right or wrong known to man. By contrast conservatives have typically appealed to the absolute truth of some body of principles. Formerly they did so in the name of God, to whom they may still pay lip service and occasionally the tribute of a reasoned argument for the necessity of religion; but now they appeal more vaguely to some kind of permanent order, norm, or standard of conduct that appears to be external to man, not of his own making, beyond his power to alter. However vague, or however inconsistent conservatives are in naming or defining it, it enables them to speak more confidently of a "true" morality or a "true" philosophy, to condemn "wrong" principles or suppress "wrong" opinions, and to defend authoritarian attitudes or policies (as in education) that support "sound" conservative views.

This brings up an essential quality of reasonableness that is to me an especially precious principle of liberalism. "To have doubted one's own first principles," wrote Justice Holmes, "is the mark of a civilized man." Harry Ashmore sees it specifically as the mark of the liberal: "Thinking, in his view, requires a degree of detachment, of self-doubt,

---

man's rights as a free and rational agent." I think, however, that Mill does smuggle in some such notion, even to the sanctity of the person, and in any case I am myself quite willing to defend personal freedom on this basis, or like most liberals to add that men are entitled to some rights simply by virtue of their humanity.

even of self-irony, all of which are conspicuous elements in the liberal style, and are conspicuously absent in that of the radical. The liberal's habit of skepticism, and his concession that his own human limitations embody the possibility of error, apply even in the most weighty considerations of life and death." Such humility and skepticism have not in fact been conspicuous or habitual in the style of many avowed liberals, nor would I claim for liberalism a monopoly on reasonableness; by Justice Holmes' standard there have surely been civilized conservatives too (though in America, I would add, not many in high office). But these qualities are at least natural, logical attributes of liberalism, and have been common enough in its style. They explain why liberals have been going in for more soul-searching and breast-beating than have either conservatives or radicals.

About conservatism I shall say little more at this point because in America for more than a century it has seldom been philosophical. Inasmuch as it evidently suits the mood of the country at present, it offers liberals a political challenge, but it hardly challenges them to reconsider their first principles, except perhaps their traditional faith in the "common people"—a phrase that in the affluent society has lost much of its traditional meaning, and in ordinary usage does not embrace such large underprivileged groups as Negroes, Puerto Ricans, and Mexican-Americans.[3] In recent years the real challenge to liberalism has come rather from radicals, mostly young. And this, I think, should give us pause.

Now, there are of course radicals and radicals too, beginning with the differences between the Old and the New Left. I have already remarked that it has grown more difficult to classify everybody in the broad spectrum between liberalism and radicalism; many men who once thought of themselves as radicals (such as Dwight MacDonald,

3. In the 'fifties the "new conservatism" did offer liberals a philosophical challenge by going back to Edmund Burke, John Adams, and other "fathers," but this movement already appears to have petered out. Those of its spokesmen who were most clearly "new," such as Clinton Rossiter and Peter Viereck, were embarrassed because they frankly acknowledged that the reigning conservatism, represented by the Republican Party, was radically different from the conservatism of Burke, and also because their own attitudes as good American democrats were often essentially liberal, as different from Burke's. Rossiter, for example, cited Ralph Barton Perry: "The extent to which a man may be considered a lover of liberty is . . . to be measured in terms of his passion for the liberty of others." Then he confessed that while conservatives in business never tired of protesting their love of liberty, "their passion for the liberty of others burns notoriously low." Today it burns no brighter in the leaders of the Republican Party, and still less in the breast of William F. Buckley, Jr., the liveliest champion of conservatism, but among the most heartless.

Irving Howe, Paul Goodman, and Robert Brustein) might now be called liberal radicals or radical liberals (always disregarding conservative politicians who use such terms as mere epithets). But again one may begin with some broad historical generalizations that distinguish the poles clearly enough. Like liberals, radicals have typically championed the underprivileged, upheld ideals of equality, and expressed a faith in the common people; many turned against Russian Communism because it denied political equality and freedom. They differ from liberals in that they call for more fundamental, far-reaching changes in the social and political system, beyond mere reform. They differ as well in that they have not habitually been content with peaceful, democratic means of achieving their goals; though many fewer now call for violent revolution, they are still more disposed to condone violence or strictly lawless tactics. Similarly they are more doctrinaire, or absolutist. They have made much less of the virtues of civility, tolerance, open-mindedness, or what I should call reasonableness. Today many are saying in effect, or even explicitly, that liberal attitudes and policies are unreasonable at a time of crisis, in a country dominated by conservative power establishments. For all their disagreements over means and ends, radicals are at least agreed that gradual, piecemeal reform will no longer do.

And so let us grant at once that they may be right. I have myself been echoing many thinkers who do not call themselves radicals, yet insist on the need of drastic changes in attitudes and policies, perhaps of a thorough reorganization of government and society, and so might recall the challenge of Trotsky. "The fundamental premise of a revolution," he wrote, "is that the existing social structure has become incapable of solving the urgent problems of development of the nation." Those of us who do not want a revolution might reasonably be asked: Just how do we propose to institute the drastic changes needed? In a society that is not clearly capable of solving problems much graver and more urgent than Trotsky conceived, and that is averse to any fundamental changes? Or let us consider Lewis Mumford, long the foremost American crusader against the idols of modern technology, "the myth of the machine" and "the Pentagon of Power" it has engendered. How does he propose to get rid of a system that he keeps insisting has created a world unfit for human beings to live in? About all he has to say, beyond the need of "something like a spontaneous religious conversion," is that for all of us who see through the monstrous myth, "the next move is ours: for the gates of the technocratic prison will open automatically, despite their rusty ancient hinges, as soon as we choose

to walk out." It sounds like an easy, agreeable substitute for revolution
—until we ask where we go when we walk out, and what happens to
the society we leave.

It is now time to ask a disagreeable question: *Why* should so many
ardent, idealistic young people be so contemptuous of liberals? So far
I have used chiefly "good" words to describe the essence of liberalism,
but there are of course unflattering ones too. Rebellious students have
some plain reasons for distrusting it.

2 / *The Failings of American Liberals*

IN GENERAL, liberalism is by its nature liable to obvious shortcomings,
or at best the defects of its virtues. Thus "reasonableness" may shade
into flabby compromise, the more readily because it is impossible to
draw a clear, fast line between them. It may also become too insistent
on the necessity of calm reason at all times, excessively distrustful of
passion, violent indignation, ardent impatience, or any "youthful" excess. On both counts liberals are always likely to be too content with
superficial or partial reform, comfortable accommodation to political
"reality," in the agreeable belief that moderate men who stay near the
middle of the road are necessarily wiser than extremists—a belief that
they might be reminded was not held by the men who signed the
Declaration of Independence, or for that matter by Jesus Christ. Many
today are of the type called "custodial liberals," who are quite willing
to accept the basic power establishments or the system so long as they
can preserve the appearances of being progressive by pushing a little
further the reforms put through by their bolder predecessors under the
New Deal. Their essentially complacent, non-rebellious, middle-aged
kind of liberalism has been too much at home in the "middle-class
ancien regime" in America. They may get angrier at young radicals
than at conservative defenders of a system that maintains injustice,
flourishes on hypocrisy, and gives plenty of reason for the anger of
the young.

More specifically, even the more rebellious liberals remain vulnerable
to the charge that they are not radical enough for the times because
of their historic faith in gradualism. This was akin to Edmund Burke's
conventional wisdom in his insistence that change must always be
slow and gradual—a wisdom of the ages that was no longer clearly

suited to his revolutionary age. Liberals were willing to go much faster and farther, but still on the comfortable assumption of basic stability and security, confidence in the future of their society. Now it may be said that they too are not prepared to go fast enough, especially for a generation that enjoys no such confidence; they need to consider whether gradualism may not be more dangerous today than militant insistence on drastic action. Certainly liberals as a whole were not on the forefront in the revolutionary 'sixties. Both in the universities and on the national scene they began to realize the possible need of drastic action only when they were stirred up by the young radicals and the black militants. The common charges of "the failure of liberalism" are documented chiefly by its record in this most revolutionary of decades in the nation's history.

As for the war in Vietnam, I do not think that liberals were primarily responsible for it. It was a natural consequence of American foreign policy throughout the Cold War, the official line that the Communists were bent on aggression everywhere and had to be stopped—a policy that was supported most vigorously by conservatives. Still, many liberals did support the war, were tardy in joining the revulsion against it, and then at first deplored it as only a tactical mistake, not a moral outrage; they regarded Bertrand Russell as a mere crank when he attacked American imperialism and supported the charge of war crimes against our leaders at the Stockholm Tribunal. One reason was that they had taken a hard anti-Communist line, chiefly because of their natural opposition to tyranny, but with those in government partly too because of sensitivity to Republican charges that they were "soft on Communism." In any case they were slow to realize what non-Communist radicals saw earlier—that as dangerous a menace to the cause of both peace and freedom might be the aggressiveness of the Pentagon.

On the domestic front another reason for their lag is that liberalism largely remains what it grew up as, a middle-class attitude. While championing the ideal of social justice, its reformers usually had a limited, second-hand knowledge of the underprivileged, and so were long content with New Deal reforms that benefited the middle class much more than the poor. It was not Adlai Stevenson but Michael Harrington, a socialist, who made liberals realize belatedly how many millions of poor people there were in affluent America, how hopeless most of them felt, how far they were from being treated as "equally important." They were as tardy in realizing too how humiliating was the common treatment of the poor on welfare rolls, and how hollow the fanfare of Lyndon Johnson about his "war" on poverty.

It is chiefly the black people, however, who have exposed the limitations of American liberals. From Thomas Jefferson on, most of them betrayed their lofty principles by their willingness to put up with the abomination of chattel slavery; the crusade to do away with the abomination was led by radical Abolitionists, no doubt with liberal support, but clouded by liberal dismay over their "extremism" or refusal to compromise. After the Civil War they again put up with the deliberate degradation of the Negroes in the South, and the discrimination against them in the North too. Doubtless they mostly deplored racial prejudice, sympathized with the Negroes, denounced lynchings, applauded the Supreme Court decision to desegregate the schools, later supported the struggle for civil rights; but the disagreeable fact remains that for a hundred years liberals had not led a vigorous, sustained movement to achieve both social and political equality for millions of victims of racism. Hence they were caught off-guard by the fury of the revolt in the black ghettoes, for they had little idea of how deep and bitter was the resentment of the whites. As moderate men of good will, many perhaps still find it impossible to admit there can be so much violent hatred in America, after all they think they have done, and to realize that some more liberal reforms may not be enough to contain the violence or assuage the hatred.

Now let me make it harder for all of us by reconsidering one of my favorite Americans of our time—Adlai Stevenson. To me he exemplified the best in our liberal tradition by his faith, his idealism, his warm humanity, his civility and reasonableness, his style. With his deep involvement and commitment he nevertheless maintained the habit of self-doubt and self-irony, as deep a humility. He was also engaged in the pursuit of relevance, the task of adapting the liberal democratic tradition he revered to the needs of a fast-changing society. So it would appear that he had much to say to the youth. In fact he did arouse much fervor among them in his presidential campaign against General Eisenhower in 1952, and again in 1960 at the Democratic National Convention, which with much less fervor nominated John F. Kennedy instead of him. By the time of his death in 1965, however, he was no longer their hero, and today he already seems to be almost forgotten. The chief reason may be simply that time passes so quickly these days, bringing so much change; to me too his death seems very long ago. Also the youth have no memories of what most of his admirers regard as his finest hour, his campaign in 1952—they were in their cradles then.

Nevertheless he had lost his hold on most of them before he died.

On the grievances of the blacks his heart was in the right place, as he proved by playing some part in liberal efforts at reform, but he incurred considerable hostility by what they considered his excessive moderation, his counsel of patience after all they had put up with for a hundred years; obviously he failed both to realize the fierceness of their resentment and to appreciate the sufficient reasons for it. He did not lead the way either in the growing moral indignation over Johnson's war in Vietnam. Though deeply troubled by it, he continued to support it, I assume in good faith, on the grounds that we had to contain Communist aggression, never could permit violence to have its own way; but he appeared to be wobbling to those who perceived more clearly the extent of our own aggression and violence. On the basic challenge of our time, the fabulous, fearful power of modern technology, he did see clearly the need of directing it to civilized ends; but again he did not speak out boldly and insistently about the flagrant abuses of this power by both government and business, or especially by the military-industrial complex. Granted that he was kept restrained as well as busy by his duties as Ambassador at the United Nations, the point remains that in his last years he no longer seemed the gallant leader he had once been. For all his admirable qualities, or perhaps just because of his efforts at sweet reasonableness, the times were apparently too much for him. To many young people he had become just another elder statesman, his kind of wisdom no longer relevant.

Even so it still seems to me basically as relevant as ever, for the long run our best hope, as I shall argue presently. Having acknowledged Stevenson's shortcomings, his possibly mistaken policies on specific issues, I am pleased to repeat my summary of his rare qualities: "a clear intelligence, informed by a sufficient awareness of complexity and difficulty, sobered by a tragic sense, but sweetened by a spirit of faith, hope, and charity." Then I wonder: How would Stevenson have responded to the student revolt? Presumably he would have been distressed by its excesses, perhaps angered. But I like to believe that it would have brought him to his liberal senses, as it did with many others. He was apt to see that all the talk about what's wrong with our youth was distracting attention from the much more serious question students were trying to force: What's wrong with America? He too was much concerned over this question, and like them recognized it as ultimately a moral challenge.[4] He would have seen what most

4. This he stated eloquently in the most sombre of his speeches, "Our Broken Mainspring," published in *Putting First Things First* (1960), but to my knowledge seldom quoted. Our mainspring—the traditional faith and purpose of a

conservatives still refuse to admit, that campus unrest had sprung from the moral failures of America, which were not just "pretenses for student violence." Hence he might have wondered why these students have grown so much more sensitive to the old evils of imperialism, racism, hypocrisy, poverty, and injustice than previous generations were —and than too many liberals have been.

Having remarked that the youth need us, I should now say that liberals need radicals too. In the West they have always been indebted to them for agitation starting movements that moderates would in time join; ever since the rise of democracy in particular history is strewn with once radical or revolutionary proposals—including some in the *Communist Manifesto*—that are now generally accepted. Today liberals need to listen to young radicals if only out of simple humanity, remembering their anxieties, but out of humility too, or gratitude for their agitation. Let us acknowledge again that it was members of the New Left, not liberals, who first went down South to work for the civil rights movement, which they also strengthened by providing martyrs, murdered by white racists; that they took the lead in dramatizing opposition to the war in Vietnam, risking jail by demonstrations; that their possibly wild talk about the big bad Establishment called attention to the services the universities were providing for the military and business establishments; and that in general they were on the front line in the major battles. And it is not enough to tell them that they offer no practicable solutions for the problems that disturb them—unless we come up with such solutions, and some assurance of making them good. Even their romantic, "impossible" dreams might remind us of George Bernard Shaw's remark: "I hear you say 'Why?' always 'Why?' . . . But I dream things that never were; and I say 'Why not?'" Given the plain absurdities in the state of America today, liberals perhaps need to ask more often, Why not? "If politics is the art of the possible," comments Charles Hampden-Turner, "it is only because enough radical men once dared advocate the impossible."

Then I for one am again embarrassed. While largely agreeing with the militant students on what's wrong with America, I cannot offer them any assurance that it will be set right, or that the whole set of

nation dedicated to ideal propositions, especially the cause of freedom—had obviously run down, in "the purposeless tyranny of a confused and aimless way of life"; so he raised the critical question: Was it broken, "broken beyond repair"? Needless to add, Stevenson was here saying something quite different from the exhortations of leaders who in defending our war in Indochina say that we must "never doubt our national mission."

crises confronting the nation will be satisfactorily resolved by democratic means. Neither can I ring out with the traditional faith in the American people that Adlai Stevenson reaffirmed to the end of his days, despite his defeats; while I do not despair of the people, I see no reason for confidence that they will rise to the urgent challenges, especially the moral challenge. Not many liberals are prone any longer to the shallow optimism with which they have been charged, partly because of the conservative mood of the country, more because of a fuller awareness of the complexity and the gravity of our problems today; but what I see as gains in wisdom are unlikely to impress or inspire the aroused young people.

Yet the youth will in any case have to answer a basic question: What are the alternatives to liberalism? Are there any that are more practicable? Broadly speaking, as we must at first, those who reject the liberal credo have a choice between conservatism and radicalism; so let us take another look at them.

3 / *A Preliminary Consideration of Alternatives*

FOR WHAT SEEM TO ME good reasons, relatively few of the most thoughtful students are turning to conservatism, in particular as represented by the Republican Party and Southern Democrats. It can no longer offer the illusion of stability and security that President Eisenhower once did, and that Nixon has obviously failed to create, even in the Middle America he appeals to—the America that the youth hardly look to as a citadel of democratic idealism. Otherwise I know of no spokesman for conservatism (including the bright William F. Buckley, Jr.) who is attracting a large following among them, offering either a philosophy or a program likely to appeal to them. For the aroused students, accordingly, the chief if not the only real alternative to liberalism is offered by the varieties of radicalism, which in fact did most to arouse them. With these the immediate difficulty is that they are getting harder to pin down since the New Left has splintered, and that no one faction provides a substantial nucleus or offers a clear promise of leadership; radicalism today is more diffuse and confused than ever before, lacking both an ideology and a political program such as Marxism once offered. But we might at least begin by considering its historic connection with revolution.

This is by no means a thing of the past even though doctrinaire Marxism, Russian Communism, and the Communist Party in America have lost caste. "Revolution" remains a magic word for the many rebels whose idols appear to be Mao, Ho Chi Minh, Castro, and Che Guevara. It is more appealing because many liberals too agree that a world so often barbarously irrational, so busy polluting itself and arming itself at a fantastically exorbitant cost while basic human needs are neglected, ought somehow to be revolutionized. Yet in America especially the hope of political revolution still looks like a strictly impossible dream. Always there remains the brute fact that the avowed revolutionaries have no mass support, no apparent prospect of winning such support. As Christopher Lasch has remarked gloomily of leftists, they seem to have a "particular flair" for failure; or one might add, possibly even an unconscious craving for it. Since they usually think of themselves as tough realists, it becomes necessary to repeat that they are naive romantics (as they might learn by reading Marx). The most that can be said for them in this respect is that, like the John Birchers, Minutemen, Christian Crusaders, and others on the extreme Right, they are perhaps having some success in creating a revolutionary situation, in particular by provoking violence. Then the objection is that whether consciously or no, they are exploiting legitimate grievances for their own purposes, sacrificing the interests of "the people" to which they presumably are devoted, just as doctrinaire Marxists in the past were too often willing to sacrifice the plainest interests of the workers for the sake of the Revolution.

Specifically, they raise again the issue of violence, the traditional means to revolution. Some radicals explicitly make a virtue of violence; others regard it as a necessary evil, in America the only possible means to revolution; while many of the less radical young who sympathize with the militants at least condone it. For that matter, almost all of us who are not pure pacifists condone it in particular circumstances, such as resistance to brutality or tyranny. The serious questions arise when a group deliberately resorts to violence as a continuous strategy. Here I shall not dwell on the immediate practical objection that it calls out the forces of reaction, which in America are much stronger. I am more concerned with the intellectual and moral issues that challenge liberals. Can we trust the judgment of a group that declares a right to use violent means? The answer is not necessarily No, in a land that won its independence by violence, but I think the experience of our time makes it most unlikely to be Yes. Such groups are typically outraged by it when it is employed by the police against them, or by other groups they consider reactionary. In effect they declare that they alone are the proper judges, never the society they are rebelling against or trying to revolutionize. And in view of their self-righteousness one may question not only their intellectual but their moral judgment— a judgment that has been more obviously fallible in the makers of revolutions in our century, such as the Bolsheviks in Russia and the Nazis in Germany. Despite their moral indignation, it is not clear that they are always morally superior to the police, whom they make indignant by constantly calling them pigs, or to the extremists on the Right, who are as ardent and sincere in their devotion to what they consider true Americanism.

Today the clearest example of the reasons for distrusting them is provided, unfortunately, by the Black Panthers. While as revolution-aries they have a natural appeal to white radicals, as apparent martyrs they have won the sympathy of many liberals too; on the campus Bobby Seale became a symbolic hero, with the help of Judge Hoffman. There is little question that the F.B.I. and the police have been out to smash them, and that they cannot count on impartial justice in the courts (not to mention the often brutal treatment of blacks in jails, as gruesomely detailed by George Jackson in his letters from Soledad prison). White men of good will are also troubled by the usual feelings of guilt: they condone the crimes of the oppressed because they belong to the class of the oppressors. Yet there is little question either that the Black Panthers provoked the violent treatment they complain of, immediately by either committing or inciting crimes. From the outset, as Bobby Seale has proudly set forth in *Seize the Time,* their leaders exalted violence, settled on "offing the pig" as a prime tactic. While they might have known that cop-killing was sure to arouse the hatred of the police, their moral case has been weakened by their rhetorical violence too. Understandable as is the hatred they are seething with, it has taken such other ugly forms as anti-Semitism and contempt for black moderates as well as white liberals. And if by any chance they did succeed in winning their revolution, or killing most of the pigs, what then? Seale mentions such goals as releasing all blacks from jail, exempting them all from military service, and arranging for them to determine their own destiny, presumably by setting up somewhere or somehow their own nation; but he has nothing to say about the nature of either this black society or the white society that would be left.[5] Meanwhile he heedlessly exploits the grievances of the blacks for the sake of a revolution that most of them either do not want or realize has no chance of success.

In short, the diverse radicals who take seriously the talk about revolution are untrustworthy alike as prophets, political leaders, and preachers or moralists. Those who do not take it seriously have a closer resemblance to what may be called radical liberals. They recall us to the fact that the great majority of aroused students are not radicals, but essentially liberals. And they recall me to the task of defending my conviction that for the long run—what the youth above all have to bank on, despite their natural anxiety and impatience—the liberal creed represents our best hope, even though it can offer no absolute truths, no guaranteed solutions, no promises of utopia; or rather just because it offers nothing of this—only a humane faith that we must hope is still reasonable.

4 / In Defense of the Liberal Creed

To BEGIN WITH, by any reasonable historical standard liberalism has by no means been a political "failure." Granted that it has never succeeded in fully establishing its principles, in either practice or accepted theory, neither has Christianity, Communism, or any ideal cause; throughout history "success" has always been relative and mixed. The partial reforms won by liberals have nevertheless been real reforms,

---

5. In some universities black students have demanded separate departments or institutes of black studies, with a purely black faculty and freedom to set their own standards. Apart from the practical objection that a degree awarded for such studies would have less value in our society, such separatism would be deplorable because blacks and whites can obviously learn from one another. White students can profit from studies of black culture, as many are eager to, and can also help black students to guard against the dangers of narrowness or cultural provincialism (as they might realize if Southern Baptists began demanding exclusive studies of Baptist culture by Baptist standards). Meanwhile all black scholars and writers are perforce indebted to Western culture, from which they have derived their ideals of freedom and equality, a clearer image of themselves, the means of asserting and realizing their human dignity, or in general the grounds of the revolution that some are now demanding. None of the African tribal societies from which the slaves of America came could have produced a Bobby Seale.)

solid gains. Thus the New Deal, which may be called on the whole an economic and political failure, succeeded in establishing such innovations as unemployment relief and social security. One measure of the success of liberalism that the young may not appreciate has been its education of conservatives, most of whom now accept reforms that their fathers bitterly fought in the days of Herbert Hoover, and more lately have come around to accepting medicare, which as "socialized medicine" was anathema only a decade ago. All along liberals have also done most to create a climate of opinion in which once radical or revolutionary proposals could be put into effect, as has happened in all the Western democracies. If they lagged behind radicals in the revolutionary 'sixties, they again provided the support necessary to make protests effective; and the youth may forget that it was a liberal Supreme Court that initially ordered the desegregation of the schools. Today there are still many fighting liberals, who belie the common assumption that we have all grown too tired or jaded, too oppressed by a suspicion of our obsolescence or irrelevance, to be at all effective.

Similarly with the cause of liberal democracy. Many leftists are pleased to say that America is not "really" democratic, "really" free, echoing the old Marxist dogma that its alleged freedom was a bourgeois sham. With most Americans one should no doubt emphasize chiefly the obvious shortcomings of their democracy, the violations of a Bill of Rights they are ignorant of—what I have been emphasizing throughout this book. Nevertheless their Constitution still includes a Bill of Rights, historically a most remarkable document, because of which such violations are in fact shortcomings—not just the rule. The youth cannot know how precious the cause of liberal democracy seemed in the time of Hitler and Stalin, to them only figures in textbooks, and how precarious a cause too, since there was much talk about totalitarianism as "the wave of the future." The youth may not realize either that it was liberals who led the fight for constitutional rights and liberties during the Red hysteria after World War I, and then in the dangerous days of Joe McCarthy, when they were little tots. Now that Spiro Agnew has made the dangers seem real again, they may forget that it was liberals he singled out for attack. Not fully aware of the depressing truth that constitutional liberties have always had to be defended in America, they may overlook the heartening truth that there has always been a defense, effective enough to preserve these liberties. So radicals may freely proclaim their dissent, loudly insist that America is not really free, even get fat fees for haranguing audiences at universities—and then express their scorn of mere liberals who defend their right to harangue. Let the youth consider the tribute of Ortega y Gasset:

> Liberalism—it is well to recall this today—is the supreme form of generosity; it is the right which the majority concedes to minorities and hence it is the noblest cry that has ever resounded in this planet. It announces the determination to share existence with the enemy; more than that, with an enemy which is weak. It was incredible that the human species should have arrived at so noble an attitude, so paradoxical, so refined, so acrobatic, so anti-natural. Hence it is not to be wondered at that this same humanity should soon appear anxious to get rid of it.

Of the traditional liberal values, none is more essential today to hopes of a decent society than freedom of inquiry, criticism, and peaceful dissent. As a form of freedom *from* constraint it has been described as "negative," but it is essential too for social justice and for self-realization, positive freedom *to* choose and carry out one's own purposes. Then it is fair to repeat that conservatives in America have not typically cherished this freedom. While Russian Communists have of course denied it, young admirers of Mao and Ho Chi Minh apparently need to be reminded that their regimes do not permit fundamental criticism or open dissent, and that in so far as Castro has permitted freer criticism his regime is rightly described as more "liberal."[6] For by its nature doctrinaire radicalism tends to be positively illiberal, on principle to reject the freedom that John Stuart Mill passionately defended as at once an ethical and a political principle. He maintained that men could fully realize both their humanity and their individuality only by making their own choices, whether right or wrong; and he defended the right to be wrong by rejecting all claims to infallibility. Like conservatives, radicals are more inclined to dictate choices or suppress "wrong" ones because they usually believe in the absolute rightness of their own judgment of error or evil. They have also been less devoted

---

6. Fidel Castro stood out most conspicuously as an exception in his extraordinary speech of July 1970, in which he not only dwelt at length on the grievous economic failures of the Cuban Revolution but blamed them chiefly on himself. One can hardly imagine an American President making such a speech, least of all today. Yet the failures might have been less grievous had he encouraged full, free discussion and criticism of his policies in the Cuban press, and given workers too some voice in decisions about goals and methods. And though he has been less repressive than other Marxist dictators, like them he has imposed a severe discipline—much more discipline than American students have to submit to. Cuba is no promised land for hippies and yippies in particular.

than Mill to the rights of the individual (saving persons like themselves) because less convinced that the good of society too would be promoted by variety of opinion. No revolutionary regime has permitted such variety and freedom to anything like the extent that radicals enjoy in America.

The fundamental freedom of inquiry, criticism, and peaceful dissent in turn requires what I consider the cardinal liberal virtues, notably tolerance and civility. With these I would link rationality, on which Mill put a premium, except that it has been confused by the technical rationality to which conservatives in both business and government are devoted; so again I prefer the term "reasonableness." Granted that it would be intolerably arrogant to claim for liberalism a monopoly on reasonableness, it has nevertheless typically upheld Mill's kind of critical rationality, trusted to broadly reasonable methods, sought as broadly reasonable goals short of utopia, and rejected the positively irrational, as in Hitler's scorn of reason. Today the issues are complicated by more than the urgency of our problems; anger, disgust, and sometimes even hatred seem to me reasonable responses to the worst failures of America or of the nation's leaders. Yet they are never sufficient responses, much less trustworthy guides to means of redeeming the failures. Although appeals to reason or reasonableness may no longer suffice either, at a time of bitter dissension, they are therefore all the more necessary. There can be no hope for America—or for any free society—if such appeals are scorned, or become as ineffectual as some radicals insist they are.

Nor if tolerance is no longer regarded as a virtue. While this too is by no means an exclusive possession of liberals, it raises questions that trouble them more because traditionally they erected it into a principle, recognizing that it was indispensable to the attainment and preservation of freedom of thought, speech, and press. On the one hand, conservatives are attacking tolerance as mere "permissiveness"—which indeed it may become; with many Americans it is a matter not of principle but of indifference, or lack of principle, just as many have become more tolerant of religious differences chiefly because religion is no longer a vital concern for them. On the other hand, radicals force an old question that is more troublesome for liberals: To what extent should we tolerate intolerance? The Ku Klux Klan, the American Nazis, the many organizations preaching racism, anti-Semitism, and other ugly prejudices? We may agree that they should not be permitted to terrorize people, or to use the mails to disseminate virulent hate literature; but what about the hate preaching of the Black Panthers?

The radicals who say that we should never tolerate the forces upholding social injustice? The old-line Communists who would not tolerate opposition if they got into power? Liberals cannot draw hard-and-fast lines in these matters, for the simple reason that there can never be "pure" tolerance.

Yet they can and do uphold the essential principle of tolerance, or of respect for the rights of those with whom one disagrees, more firmly than either conservatives or radicals. The "permissiveness" of most Americans does not extend to peace demonstrators, student rebels, long hairs, radicals, atheists—to toleration of any basic dissent from the American way of life. It is more like the permissiveness in which Spiro Agnew indulges in his slashing attacks on liberals, and his threats to the news media when they dare to be critical of the Nixon administration, exercise the rights of a free press. This kind of intolerance liberals have long been accustomed to; while deploring or despising it, and resisting it when it directly interferes with civil liberties, they accept it as the price we have to pay for democracy and its freedoms. Hence they do not call for the suppression of all Right-wing organizations, or censorship of the press that supports them (without arousing the ire of Agnew); we have to put up with them if we are to have a Left wing too. And though to my mind these represent a more serious danger to American democracy today, liberals may be more troubled by the common intolerance of radicals, whose indignation they share. Once more we cannot expect the indignant youth to be always sweetly reasonable. But we can expect them at least to recognize that a principle of tolerance is a prerequisite of a free, democratic society, not just a cowardly compromise with evil. The revolutionaries among them might consider more closely the dogmatic intolerance of Marx and Lenin, the seeds of the tyranny that flowered under Stalin.[7]

And so with the related virtue of civility. Nothing is more frighten-

7. In *The Poverty of Liberalism* Robert Paul Wolff offers an acute analysis of the shortcomings of theories of tolerance, or in particular of the "pluralism" with which it has come to be associated, which misrepresents the power struggle in America. Again, however, most liberals can accept his critique, and in fact try to combat the injustices resulting from the power of privileged groups. I would also note that Wolff never defends an alternative theory of intolerance, as a Communist would. His avowed radicalism itself looks rather impoverished when, in a concluding chapter, he proposes only a "new" social philosophy based on the values of community, which by an elaborate academic argument he demonstrates are real and important—something liberals generally take for granted. Throughout he makes it too easy to demonstrate the "poverty" of liberalism by equating it with *laissez faire* individualism, or at times even with value-free social science.

ing than the barbarism of our time: most conspicuous in modern war, as we have waged it in Vietnam, but also apparent in the violence at home, and more subtly and pervasively in the worship of power, the autonomy of technology, the reign of commercial interests, the vulgarity of mass culture—all the common menaces to human values, or sources of spiritual pollution. What is at stake in the current crises is ultimately the survival of the human race, but immediately the cause of civilization. It is the cause of human dignity implicit in the teaching of the higher religions. In American democracy it is more specifically concepts of human rights that were developed by Western civilization. It is also the possibility of civil discourse on which democracy depends—political debates in which differences of opinion are respected, do not end in violent dissension, and are not settled by force. On all counts the richest, most powerful nation on earth today is not ideally cast for the role of defender of civilization.

Now, again I would not maintain that liberals are necessarily more civil than conservatives. They may appear so today for adventitious temporal reasons: a President who made a name for himself as a campaigner by going for the jugular, a Vice-President whose fondness for alliterative epithet—the superficial appearance of "style"—accentuates his lack of civility, and the ugly campaign of 1970 in which the Republicans swamped television with spot commercials smearing liberal candidates. But such politicking made clearer the reasons why liberals tend to make more of the virtue of civility than do conservatives—their principle of tolerance, their more consistent concern for human dignity, and their more common willingness to question their first principles, admit doubt and uncertainty. The late E. M. Forster, the foremost literary liberal, beautifully exemplified the ideal when he gave "two cheers" for democracy, "one because it admits variety and two because it permits criticism," but added that two were quite enough: "Only Love, the Beloved Republic," deserved three.

As for radicals, there is no question on this score. Always granted that a passion for justice or hatred of injustice may be more admirable than the habit of civility it naturally tends to threaten, the fact remains that radicals past and present have not typically been addicted to this habit, any more than to the habit of tolerance. It has therefore been harder for them to do justice to liberals than for liberals to do justice to them. It has also been harder for them to be honest with themselves, especially about the possible measure of self-indulgence in the tactics they employ. The youth who have relieved themselves by shouting obscenities at Agnew and Nixon were not only hurting their cause by providing their enemies with more ammunition—they were disgusting many sympathizers too. They were another frightening example of the violence, both rhetorical and physical, that is menacing the civil dialogue without which democracy cannot survive.

On the campus I see almost no need of qualifying the liberal values. As by and large the most liberal, progressive institution in the country, the university has provided for much more freedom of inquiry, criticism, and dissent than we can expect in either government or business, and for this purpose it absolutely must cultivate the values of rationality, tolerance, and civility, a respect for the rights of both conservatives and radicals to express their opinions freely and fully. Indignant students who protest against the university's service of government and business forget that it has come under strong attack by conservatives too because of all the social criticism coming out of it, the radicals it harbors. However foolish Agnew's charge that campus unrest has been due solely to radical agitators and weak-kneed administrators, it is sufficient proof that the university has not been run simply in the interests of the Establishment. Nor can it be run just by and for radicals either—if it is to maintain its ideal of academic freedom, not become a servant of a revolutionary Establishment, as it has in the Soviets and China. Now that "elite" has become a bad word, I should add that neither can it be run simply in the interests of "the people," as these interests are conceived either by radicals or by most Americans; I am among the elitists who feel free to say a civil equivalent of "The public be damned" when it intrudes its anti-intellectual and illiberal proclivities. All in all, the university as it stands is full of faults, serious enough to warrant misgivings about its future; but if it goes down we are all lost—including those radical students who have been too pleased to disrupt it by defying the academic decencies, and to intensify a conflict with society in which it is a poor bet to win.

Meanwhile the country as a whole is in much worse shape, bad enough to warrant much more serious misgivings—and so to bring up the much more difficult questions for liberals. It is easy enough to defend their traditional values in the abstract, but what concrete program do they have to offer? While they might agree in opposing the devotion of conservatives to vested business interests, which too often mean economic power without clear public responsibility, they obviously disagree on specific policies and mostly offer nothing like a comprehensive program. Speaking for myself, I would approve more radical measures than most would to deal with the central problem of the uses and the distribution of the country's vast wealth: considerably more regulation of big business, with much more severe penalties for defiance of federal regulations; measures to provide something like industrial democracy by placing representatives of consumers and workers on boards of directors of corporations; heavier taxation of the wealthy, immediately by closing the notorious loopholes; much greater appropriations for education, health, housing, and other domestic programs, including a real war on pollution; and so on, into what in general would be called more "socialism." It accordingly points to another basic problem, even apart from the difficulty of getting Congress and the voters to approve such measures: at once the obvious need and the common curse of bureaucracy in all industrialized countries, under whatever form of government. I know of no way of assuring efficient, honest, just, and humane administration. I am uncertain too about other serious matters, in particular how to curb the drive to perpetual economic growth, or how much to discourage such growth, inasmuch as it still appears necessary if we are to provide enough jobs for a growing population, finance an adequate program to restore a decent environment, raise the standard of living of the blacks and the poor, and provide anything like the massive aid needed by all the poor peoples of the world.

Still, conservatives and radicals are no more agreed on programs for dealing with the crises of our time. On the face of it, none of us can offer a sure-fire solution. And so, at the end, I would point to the common ground occupied by all but mere "custodial" liberals and all but extreme radicals or revolutionaries, including most thoughtful students. We are alike concerned about the serious threats to ideals of freedom, justice, and human dignity, alike engaged in efforts to get at the roots of the problems, and alike critical of conservatives who substantially accept the economic, social, and political *status quo,* with its irrational priorities. The common ground was staked out in the Port Huron Statement of the Students for a Democratic Society in 1962: to my mind the most admirable manifesto issued by the youth of any country, now apparently unknown to most students, in effect repudiated by many survivors of the SDS, but therefore all the more worthy of reconsideration as an agenda for the youth.

"We are people of this generation," they began, "bred in at least modest comfort, housed now in universities, looking uncomfortably to the world we inherit." After a temperate statement of the reasons for their concern—reasons that have since become much plainer, to many more students—they summed up their agenda as a "search for truly democratic alternatives to the present." It had to be a search because the old slogans would no longer do: "Perhaps matured by the past, we have no sure formulas, no closed theories." Nevertheless they were firmly committed to the values of liberal democracy. They explicitly rejected violence as a means to social change for the soundest of humane reasons: "it requires generally the transformation of the target, be it a human being or a community of people, into a depersonalized object of hate"—the hate that today too often reduces the question what do you stand for to what do you hate. So far from scorning their elders, they declared that "a new left must include liberals and socialists, the former for their relevance, the latter for their sense of thoroughgoing reforms in the system." Knowing that they were a small minority, they had to seek liberal allies wherever they could find them.

By the same token they had no illusions about the American people. The vast majority of Americans believed in effect that the contemporary system was eternal, saw no real alternative to it, and were not merely apathetic but fearful of change, suspicious of "all crusades" (except, I might add, the "spiritual" crusades that President Eisenhower was fond of proclaiming—a harmless kind that called for no real effort or sacrifice). The students sensed, however, that beneath the apparent contentment of Americans with their prosperity were "deeply-felt anxieties about their role in the new world," and on these they banked their hopes. The anxieties might produce "a yearning to believe there *is* an alternative to the present, something *can* be done to change circumstances in the school, the workplaces, the bureaucracies, the government." Although so far they have produced rather a growing resentment, especially of the students, I suppose we must all bank on the possibility of such a yearning. Otherwise the students expressed an implicit faith in the American people by their call for participatory democracy. More broadly, they exressed a faith in man, specifically in human potentialities. Together with "unfulfilled capacities for reason, freedom, and love," people had "unrealized potential for self-cultivation, self-direction, self-understanding, and creativity." It was to this potential that they appealed—as again we all must.

Although they also recognized "the human potentiality for violence, unreason, and submisssion to authority," they will no doubt seem too idealistic to the "realists" who dominate not only government and business but the realm of the technical intelligentsia. They themselves recognized that idealism was out of fashion, together with dreams of utopia. "Doubt has replaced hopefulness," quite understandably in view of the horrors of Hitler's concentration camps and gas ovens, Stalin's tyranny, our own atomic bombs; though at that the horrors of our war in Vietnam had yet to come when they wrote. As a doubter who is not too hopeful, I should none the less insist that people do have unrealized potentials, that these can be realized only through idealism, and that like these students we must all oppose "a defeatism that is labeled realistic."

About the universities they had much to say, all to the point. They began with a temperate statement of the now familiar complaints about them, including their as yet unpublicized service of the arms race. As reasonable was their demand for what had yet to be popularized as relevance: "The questions we might want raised—what is really important? can we live in a different and better way? if we wanted to change society, how would we do it?—are not thought to be questions of a 'fruitful, empirical nature,' and thus are brushed aside." Yet they recognized that the university was indispensable, for their own purposes too. It was "a crucial institution in the formation of social attitudes," the "central institution for organizing, evaluating, and transmitting knowledge," and "the only mainstream institution that is open to participation by individuals of nearly any viewpoint." Although the main concern of the New Left was political action, it had to be "a left with real intellectual skills, committed to deliberativeness, honesty, reflection as working tools." The university was also the obvious place for them to begin recruiting the young people of their generation and discussing their differences with the liberals and socialists whose support they needed. Ideally it was "a community of controversy." This community would be disrupted by leftists who reduced civil controversy to confrontation or replaced it by violence, but it remains an ideal for all of us who regard social criticism as a major function of the university.

Other admirable goals proposed by the SDS bring back the obvious questions. "We would replace power rooted in possession, privilege, or circumstance by power and uniqueness rooted in love, reflectiveness, reason, and creativity." Similarly the economy should be based on the principle of participatory democracy, and of work that is "educative, not stultifying; creative, not mechanical; self-directed, not manipulated." The question is: *How* are such goals to be achieved? The students gave no answer, beyond generalities about stimulating a broad social movement inspired by this kind of vision. Having no answer myself, I might repeat that their dream too seems to me impossible, because of not only the realities of power in America but the nature of a technological society. Yet without vision or dream we are lost. Certainly no liberal should simply discourage such idealism in the youth, or leave them at the mercy of the "realists" who are bequeathing them so absurd a world. All their elders might well ponder the conclusion of the Port Huron Statement: "If we appear to seek the unattainable, as it has been said, then let it be known that we do so to avoid the unimaginable." I would also repeat that it is reasonable to supplement the question "How?" with the question "Why not?"

INDEX